THE INSTITUTIONALIZATION OF TORTURE BY THE BUSH ADMINISTRATION

THE INSTITUTIONALIZATION OF TORTURE BY THE BUSH ADMINISTRATION

Is Anyone Responsible?

M. Cherif Bassiouni

intersentia

Antwerp – Oxford – Portland

Distribution for the UK:
Hart Publishing Ltd.
16C Worcester Place
Oxford OX1 2JW
UK
Tel.: +44 1865 51 75 30
Email: mail@hartpub.co.uk

Distribution for the USA and Canada:
International Specialized Book Services
920 NE 58th Ave. Suite 300
Portland, OR 97213
USA
Tel.: +1 800 944 6190 (toll free)
Tel.: +1 503 287 3093
Email: info@isbs.com

Distribution for Austria:
Neuer Wissenschaftlicher Verlag
Argentinierstraße 42/6
1040 Wien
Austria
Tel.: +43 1 535 61 03 24
Email: office@nwv.at

Distribution for other countries:
Intersentia Publishers
Groenstraat 31
2640 Mortsel
Belgium
Tel.: +32 3 680 15 50
Email: mail@intersentia.be

The Institutionalization of Torture by the Bush Administration. Is Anyone Responsible?
M. Cherif Bassiouni

The photograph used on the cover of this book was taken by United States Army personnel in Abu Ghraib prison (Iraq). This picture was selected because it is a real – not staged – witness to the abhorrent practices the author wishes to denounce in this book.

ISBN 978-94-000-0005-6
D/2010/7849/87
NUR 828

DEDICATION

Between September 11, 2001 and April 1, 2010, it is believed that nearly 800 persons had been detained at Guantánamo Bay (official Department of Defense reports put the total at 660, while a variety of outside media and human rights organizations report a much higher population). As of February 2010, 189 remain. The 600 or so detainees who were released during that period of time were found not have committed any crime under international or U.S. law, and until 2006, they were even denied access to habeas corpus. In accordance with U.S. and international legal standards they were innocent persons held in violation of due process of law. Most were tortured or subjected to cruel, inhuman or degrading treatment or punishment in violation of international law, the U.S. constitution, and U.S. laws. Notwithstanding the knowledge that these 600 or so persons were innocent, they were kept between three and seven years before their release.

In Iraq, Afghanistan, in CIA "black sites" and in the prisons of surrogate states, an estimated 150,000 to 200,000 persons have been arbitrarily arrested and detained over a period of nine years, and many of them were tortured. These practices are still ongoing in Afghanistan. It is estimated that over 100 persons have died while in U.S. detention in Guantánamo, Afghanistan, and Iraq.

This experience is one of the worst blots on the history of this nation, and on its military and intelligence services. The honor of this great nation has been defiled by a few who subverted the rule of law under the guise of higher interests.

This is why this book is dedicated to the victims of torture and other forms of cruel, inhuman, and degrading treatment or punishment, who have suffered such treatment at the hands of U.S. public agents, surrogates, and private contractors since 2001, as well as their families. They should know that some of us in this nation care about what happened to them, seek justice for them by calling for the accountability of the perpetrators, and continue to believe in the rule of law, even after this abhorrent historical experience.

This by no means is intented to justify criminal acts committed by such persons. This is about us a a nation, not about others.

ACKNOWLEDGMENTS

ACKNOWLEDGMENTS

My appreciation goes to Kelly McCracken for her editorial and research assistance in late 2009 and early 2010, as well as to Dr. Katrina Sifferd, Ryan Carey, and Emily Martin Benson for their research assistance over the past three years. My appreciation also goes to Sarah Forbes Orwig, who read and contributed edits to a previous version of the text.

Appreciation also goes to the International Center for Transitional Justice, for permission to reprint a section from Carolyn Patty Blum, Lisa Magarrell, and Marieke Wierda, *Prosecuting Abuses of Detainees in U.S. Counter-Terrorism Operations* (2009). It appears as an appendix to chapter 2 herein.

ABOUT THE AUTHOR

M. Cherif Bassiouni is Distinguished Research Professor of Law Emeritus at DePaul University College of Law in Chicago, Illinois, and President Emeritus of the College's International Human Rights Law Institute (IHRLI). He is also president of the International Institute of Higher Studies in Criminal Sciences (ISISC) in Siracusa, Italy, and Honorary President of the International Association of Penal Law (AIDP) in Paris, France.

From 1977 to 1978, he was co-chair of the Committee of Experts which prepared the first draft of the 1984 Convention Against Torture. From 1992 to 1994, he was member, then chairman, of the Security Council's Commission to Investigate War Crimes in the Former Yugoslavia. He was an Independent Expert for the Commission on Human Rights on The Rights to Restitution, Compensation and Rehabilitation for Victims of Grave Violations of Human Rights and Fundamental Freedoms (1998–2000), and the United Nations Independent Expert on Human Rights in Afghanistan between 2004 and 2006. In the former Yugoslavia and in Afghanistan, Professor Bassiouni had first-hand experience in recording many cases of arbitrary arrest and detention of innocent persons, rape and torture.

FOREWORD

Dante once said that the hottest places in hell are reserved for those who,
in a time of great moral crisis, maintain their neutrality.
– John F. Kennedy[*]

All men make mistakes, but a good man yields when he knows his course
is wrong and he repairs the evil.
– Sophocles, *Antigone*

The United States of America has long struggled for the establishment of the rule of law throughout its history, as well as to be a model for other nations. Yet, between 2001 and 2009, the U.S. committed the same abhorrent practices of torture which it has consistently opposed when committed by other states. What is astonishing is that such practices were initiated at the highest level of government, became official policy, and were carried out by the U.S. military, CIA, and private contractors in territory under U.S. control (Guantánamo Bay, Iraq, and Afghanistan), in secret prisons abroad called "black sites," with the connivance of other governments under the euphemism of "extraordinary rendition."[1] The seven-year long program involved an estimated 150,000 to 200,000 persons, some 800 of whom were held in Guantánamo, and resulted in over 100 deaths.[2] All of this took place within a climate of general public indifference among Americans that coincided with an unexpectedly high percentage of public support.[3] Time and again, observers of tragic historic events

---

[*]   John F. Kennedy, Bonn, West Germany, at the signing of a charter establishing the German Peace Corps, June 24, 1963.

[1]   *See* THE TORTURE DEBATE IN AMERICA (Karen J. Greenberg ed., 2006). For a collection of the orders and directives, see THE TORTURE PAPERS: THE ROAD TO ABU GHRAIB (Karen J. Greenburg & Joshua L. Dratel eds., 2005) [hereinafter THE TORTURE PAPERS], and the many books and articles cited within this publication.

[2]   *See* Glenn Greenwald, *The Suppressed Fact: Deaths by U.S. Torture*, SALON.COM, Jun. 30, 2009, reporting on research undertaken by John Sifton of Human Rights Watch, published online as *The Bush Administration Homicides*, THEDAILYBEAST.COM, May 5, 2009. For a detailed report on deaths in custody by 2006, see Hina Shamsi, *Command's Responsibility: Detainee Deaths in U.S. Custody in Iraq and Afghanistan* (Human Rights First, Feb. 2006). On April 20, 2009, Gen. Barry McCaffrey, retired army general, was quoted on television on MSNBC as having said "We should never, as a policy, maltreat people under our control, detainees. We tortured people unmercifully. We probably murdered dozens of them during the course of that, both the armed forces and the C.I.A." *Id.*

[3]   *See Public Remains Divided Over Use of Torture* (Pew Research Center for the People & the Press, Apr. 23, 2009), showing that approximately 45 percent of Americans believe that

note that it is not so much the evildoing of a few that allows the worst atrocities to occur, as it is the indifference of the many.[4] The veneer of our legal civilization proved to be very thin.

In time, future generations of Americans, as well as non-Americans who have historically regarded the U.S. as a moral leader opening the pathway for human rights around the world, will wonder why these actions were allowed to occur, why the organized bar failed to oppose such crimes or investigate for possible ethical violations those lawyers who wrote memoranda justifying torture, why so many Americans supported torture, and why the Obama Administration has failed the principled test of investigating the crimes allegedly committed. Future generations will wonder why human and civil rights defenders did not demonstrate against these practices as they did in the past, and why major media organizations failed to determinedly pursue these stories as they did others of moral and ethical significance. They will ask, how did this happen in America? If and when this happens, the mere asking of these questions will mean that the nation's moral and ethical compass is once again pointing in the right direction.

At this point in time, however, America is at best ambivalent about torture, as evidenced by the fact that Vice President Dick Cheney unabashedly stated on television in February 2010 that he "was a big supporter of waterboarding... of 'enhanced interrogation' techniques."[5] If not a public admission of a potential crime, it was at least an admission against interest. That Cheney had no fear of legal consequences, and that such a public statement did not cause public consternation, is a sign of how acceptable torture has become in this country. In May 2010, Senator Joseph Lieberman urged the Senate to pass a law stripping a U.S. citizen of his citizenship for merely being a suspected terrorist.[6] Indeed, the veneer of our legal civilization is thin, and it may be getting thinner – the Constitution notwithstanding. History teaches us that abusive regimes always start on a slippery slope, with one erosion of the rule of law leading to another, and during that process, the general public accepts these erosions out of fear, indifference, or callousness. When that happens, the nation's moral compass no longer points to the right direction, and the right path is last.

Thomas Paine, a great American patriot of the founding period, wrote in 1777 "those who expect to reap the blessing of freedom must, like men, undergo the fatigue of supporting it."[7] By that he meant that they must also undergo the

---

torture is sometimes justified, and that approximately 20 percent believe that torture is often justified.

[4]   For an insightful and thoughtful contemporary analysis see MARK J. OSIEL, THE END OF RECIPROCITY: TERROR, TORTURE, AND THE LAW OF WAR (2009); Mark J. Osiel, *The Banality of Good: Aligning Incentives Against Mass Atrocity*, 105 COLUM. L. REV. 1751 (Oct. 2005).

[5]   Interview with Jonathan Karl, *This Week*, ABC News, Feb. 14, 2010.

[6]   *See* Charlie Savage & Carl Hulse, *Bill Targets Citizenship of Terrorists' Allies*, N.Y. TIMES, May 6, 2010, discussing the introduction of the Terrorist Expatriation Act in Congress.

[7]   Attributed to Thomas Paine, Sept. 12, 1777.

sacrifices necessary to uphold their values, which means that even in times of danger, a great nation does not step down from the high moral road. As to the dangers of indifference, Martin Niemoller, a Protestant minister who lived through the Nazi period, uttered this stirring statement in 1946: "First they came for the Communists, but I was not a Communist, so I said nothing. Then they came for the Social Democrats, but I was not a Social Democrat, so I did nothing. Then came the trade unionists, but I was not a trade unionist. And then they came for the Jews, but I was not a Jew, so I did little. Then when they came for me, there was no one left who could stand up for me."[8] Americans may see themselves in the same position as the Reverend Niemoller was at that time, namely: they came for the alleged terrorists, but not being terrorists, they did nothing. Worse, however, many Americans supported torture, either explicitly or implicitly, or stood by indifferently. The time of facing up to our country's wrongdoing is upon us, and we must live up to the test of truth.

When the practice of torture came to an end in January 2009, after Barack Obama became the 49th President of the United States, the few voices who urged criminal investigations and eventual prosecutions were drowned in deafening silence. Will it end that way? Perhaps, but how future events will unfold is unpredictable. A formal undertaking such as the Attorney General naming a special prosecutor, or a Committee of the Senate or the House initiating robust hearings, are possible options. Other accountability processes include bar associations' ethics investigations and civil litigation for damages. These options depend on the perseverance of those seeking justice, and so far the Obama Administration has vacillated between principle and politics, with the latter ostensibly prevailing.

From 1977 to 1978, I served as co-chair of the Committee of Experts which prepared the first draft of what became the Convention Against Torture and Other Cruel, Inhuman or Degrading Treatment or Punishment (CAT), along with the late Niall MacDermott.[9] That text, which I had the honor of drafting, was first submitted in 1978 to the Sub-Commission on the Prevention of Discrimination and Protection of Minorities, which in turn forwarded it to the Commission on Human Rights.[10] The text was then formally reintroduced by

---

[8]   The origins of this quote come from a speech Rev. Martin Niemoller gave to the representatives of the Confessing Church in Frankfurt Germany, Jan. 6, 1946. Niemoller expanded upon this quote in OF GUILT AND HOPE 13–16 (1947).

[9]   Convention Against Torture and Other Cruel, Inhuman or Degrading Treatment or Punishment, Dec. 10, 1984, 1465 U.N.T.S. 85 [hereinafter CAT]. For a detailed commentary on the convention, see J. HERMAN BURGERS & HANS DANELIUS, THE UNITED NATIONS CONVENTION AGAINST TORTURE (1988); JOSÉ LUIS DE LA CUESTA ARZAMENDI, EL DELITO DE TORTURA (1990); MANFRED NOWAK & ELIZABETH MCARTHUR, THE UNITED NATIONS CONVENTION AGAINST TORTURE: A COMMENTARY (2008).

[10]   *See* U.N. Economic & Social Council, Commission on Human Rights, 34th Sess., *Question of the Human Rights of All Persons Subjected to Any Form of Detention or Imprisonment and in Particular the Body of Principles for the Protection of All Persons Under Any Form of Detention*

Sweden, whose representative had served as a member of the aforementioned Committee of Experts, as did representatives from The Netherlands and Austria, whose governments were the initial supporters of a convention against torture, along with Sweden. Many of the provisions of the text that I prepared in 1977, including the definition of torture, were embodied in the 1984 CAT. Thus, when I read of the Bush Administration lawyers' perversion of the language and purpose of the CAT, I was shocked. The blatant distortion of the definition of torture in Article 1 of the CAT, as discussed in this book, could not in my mind have been anything but deliberate. Yet in February 2010, the Office of Professional Responsibility of the Department of Justice (DOJ) concluded that the two lawyers responsible for authoring the most egregious memoranda authorizing such "enhanced interrogation" techniques which amount to torture, namely John Yoo and Jay Bybee, were found simply to have acted with poor judgment, and not as having violated their ethical, professional responsibilities.[11]

During the work of the aforementioned Committee of Experts which convened at the International Institute for Higher Studies in Criminal Sciences (Siracusa, Italy) under the joint chairmanship of myself and MacDermott, a member of the Committee from one of the U.N. Permanent Five asked me privately one late evening what would I do – since I urged an absolute prohibition against all forms of infliction of physical harm – if I knew that a bomb was about to go off in a building with the potential of killing 10,000 persons. This hypothesis is called the "ticking bomb" situation.[12] Would I torture the person who knew

---

of Imprisonment, Written Statement submitted by the International Association of Penal Law, a non-governmental organization in category II consultative status, E/CN.4/NGO/213, 1 Feb. 1978 *and* 48 REVUE INTERNATIONALE DE DROIT PENAL (1978, No. 3–4). *See also* M. Cherif Bassiouni, *An Appraisal of Torture in International Law and Practice: The Need for an International Convention for the Prevention and Suppression of Torture, in* 48 REVUE INTERNATIONALE DE DROIT PÉNAL 23, 23–114 (1977).

[11] *See* Memorandum for the Attorney General, Memorandum of Decision Regarding the Objections to the Findings of Professional Misconduct in the Office of Professional Responsibility's Report of Investigation Into the Office of Legal Counsel's Memoranda Concerning Issues Relating to the CIA's Use of "Enhanced Interrogation Techniques" on Suspected Terrorists, Jan. 5, 2010. The author of the report, Associate Deputy Attorney General David Margolis, wrote that while he did not believe that the the written opinions of Yoo and Bybee rose to the level of "professional misconduct," his decision "should not be viewed as an endorsement of the legal work that underlies those memoranda." *Id.* at 2. *See also* Eric Lichtblau & Scott Shane, *Justice Department Report Finds John Yoo and Jay Bybee Not Guilty of Misconduct*, N.Y. TIMES, Feb. 19, 2010.

[12] For a discussion of the moral considerations in the "ticking bomb" scenario, see David Luban, *Liberalism, Torture, and the Ticking Bomb*, 91 VA. L. REV. 1425 (2005). For a proponent of the "ticking bom" scenario, see ALAN DERSHOWITZ, WHY TERRORISM WORKS (2002); Alan Dershowitz, *Is There a Torturous Road to Justice?*, L.A. TIMES, Nov. 8, 2001, at M4. Dershowitz represents the view whereby justification for torture is found in retribution for the acts of the perpetrator. This, of course, presupposes having certainty that the person tortured is the perpetrator of a particularly heinous crime which is likely to cause harm to a large number of persons. Dershowitz does not, however, address the implications of such a practice on the character of the society engaging in it, nor in the consequences that it would have on

where the bomb had been placed if it meant that many could be saved? I responded with a well-known American legal maxim that "hard facts make bad law." The facts in this hypothetical, I told him, should not be relied upon to make a law addressing a wide variety of factual patterns. Extremely rare possibilities or highly improbable ones should not guide the making of law. He pressed me for an answer, however, and I admitted to him that if I knew with reasonable certainty that this person could help in discovering the whereabouts of the bomb, and, thus, that I could save many lives, I would acquiesce to torture to obtain the information. I added that I would then write a full report and turn myself in to the authorities for having committed a crime.[13] With hope, I added, the judge would be lenient and take my motive into account, even though I had broken the law. The Bush Administration assumed neither moral nor legal responsibility, and in the end, it is hard to show what results may have been obtained for so many transgressions.

The scenario of the "ticking bomb" has rarely if ever been proven to have occurred, yet it is argued by some as the *ultima ratio* justification for torture.[14] Moreover, the proposition that torture prevents terrorism cannot be proven. On the contrary, torture engenders violence through alienation and revenge seeking. Torture is not only counter-productive, but also unreliable. Under it, people tend to say whatever is expected of them. The practices described in this book have proven that hard evidence is unlikely to be attained under torture, and that said evidence or information could be obtained from other sources. Furthermore, most of the tortured detainees in Guantánamo, Abu Ghraib, and other detention facilities in Iraq, Afghanistan, and in the CIA's "black sites" and surrogate countries involved in the "extraordinary rendition" program have been proven to have no connection to terrorism and have been released because they had been wrongly arrested.[15] The history of law and legal institutions has long proven

---

perpetrators of terrorism who could then find legitimacy in the acts of torture as a way of further perpetrating such crimes. A different view is taken by Judge Richard Posner, who considers that torture under some conditions may benefit from the defense of necessity, even though necessity in criminal law has never been a defense for the acts of another. Moreover, he departs from an objective definition of torture to make it a subjective one. He states that torture begins at "the point along a continuum at which the observers' queasiness turns to revulsion." Richard A. Posner, *Torture, Terrorism, and Interrogation, in* TORTURE: A COLLECTION 291 (Sanford Levinson ed., 2004). For a historical perspective, see JOHN H. LANGBEIN, TORTURE AND THE LAW OF PROOF (1977).

13   This position has also been represented in connection with civil disobedience and other forms of breaches of the law whereby the person who violates the law has to assume responsibility. For a further discussion see THE LAW OF DISSENT AND RIOTS (M. Cherif Bassiouni ed., 1971); HENRY DAVID THOREAU, CIVIL DISOBEDIENCE (1849).

14   *See supra* note 10.

15   Editorial, *Gitmo, Justice – and justice,* CHI. TRIB., May 14, 2007. Of the nearly 800 prisoners who have been detained at Guantánamo since 2002, 189 remain as of February 24, 2010. *See* Press Release, Attorney General, U.S. Dep't. of Justice, *U.S. Transfers Three Guantanamo Bay Detainees to Albania,* Feb. 24, 2010.

the error of accepting the Machiavellian principle that the ends justify the means.

The practice of torture has done much damage to the moral authority of the U.S.[16] Whatever the practical reasons for it are presumed to be, it is inherently a question of morality. Philosophers and moralists have historically argued against the practice of torture, which tyrannical rulers and regimes have used to preserve power. Torture is a crime, and it is also a transgression against a humanity created by God in the image of God. There is no way to rationalize this transgression against the physical integrity of fellow human beings.

President Obama's third, fourth, and fifth Executive Orders, issued on January 27, 2009, were to ensure lawful interrogations, set a one-year deadline to close the detention facility at Guantánamo Bay, and establish a Special Task Force on Detainee Disposition.[17] Torture at Guantánamo and in Iraq has ceased, and apparently the CIA has stopped its use of "black sites," although torture in Afghanistan continues at the hands of Afghan forces acting as surrogates for the U.S.[18]

It is estimated that over 100 people have died under torture between 2002 and 2008, and those who are responsible for their deaths must account for these crimes.[19] Similarly, those who tortured and wrongly detained the many innocent bystanders who were captured under erroneous assumptions must also be held accountable. An example is the case of Canadian Maher Arar, a software engineer who was erroneously suspected of being a terrorist by the Canadian police. Syrian-born Arar was unlawfully arrested and sent to Syria by the U.S., where he was imprisoned and tortured. A two-and-a-half year Canadian commission of inquiry exonerated Arar of all suspicion of terrorist activity and urged the Canadian government to pay him compensation. "They arrested me. They never

---

[16] *See* Committee Against Torture, *Consideration of Reports Submitted by State Parties under Article 19 of the Convention, Conclusions and Recommendations of the Committee against Torture: United States of America*, CAT/C/USA/CO2 (May 18, 2006) [hereinafter Committee Response]; *Colin Powell Says Guantánamo Should be Closed*, REUTERS, June 10, 2007.

[17] Exec. Order No. 13,491, Ensuring Lawful Interrogations, 74 Fed. Reg. 4893 (Jan. 27, 2009), which created a Special Interagency Task Force on Interrogation and Transfer Policies; Exec. Order No. 13,492, Review and Disposition of Individuals Detained at the Guantánamo Bay Naval Base and Closure of Detention Facilities, 74 Fed. Reg. 4,897 (Jan. 27, 2009); Exec. Order No. 13,493, Review of Detention Policy Operations, 74 Fed. Reg. 4901 (Jan. 27, 2009), which created a Special Interagency Task Force on Detainee Disposition to "identify lawful options for the disposition of individuals captured or apprehended in connection with armed conflicts and counterterrorism operations". The Task Force, comprised of officials from the DOD, the DOS, the DOJ, the Department of Homeland Security, as well as agencies such as the CIA and the FBI, completed its work in January 2010, and Attorney General Holder forwarded the recommendations to President Obama for his approval. As of February 2010, the report had not been publicly released. *See infra* Chapter 6, *A Review of the Obama Administration*.

[18] *See* Ian Austen, *Canadian General Acknowledges Risk to Afghan Detainees*, N.Y. TIMES, Dec. 9, 2009.

[19] *See supra* note 2.

told me what they had against me," Arar told a CBS news correspondent. "I was a disappeared person. My family did not know where I was."[20]

Another example is Khaled El-Masri, a German citizen, who was on vacation in Macedonia when local police took him off a bus and held him for three weeks. El-Masri was then sent to a U.S. prison in Afghanistan, where he was harshly interrogated by Americans through an interpreter for five months before being simply dumped on a deserted road in Albania.[21] As described in the case studies herein in Chapter 2, many of the 800 or so Guantánamo detainees were wrongly taken in for reasons yet to be disclosed, and kept for an unconscionable length of time ranging from two to eight years while being tortured. In fact, an analysis of U.S. government documents undertaken by Seton Hall University shows that only five percent of the detainees at Guantánamo were arrested by U.S. forces – the vast majority had been captured by Pakistani or Afghan Northern Alliance forces and handed over the U.S. government.[22] Some of the detainees were only released after signing an affidavit that they would never disclose what happened to them while in detention. Such was the case of a 73-year-old Guantánamo detainee who was released nearly three years after it had been immediately ascertained that he had been implicated by a fellow Pashto Afghan to whom he had loaned money, and who had earned a $5,000 reward for turning the man in (thus freeing himself of having to repay the loan). Another case is that of Shafiq Rasul, Asif Iqbal, Rhuhel Ahmed, and Jamal Al-Harith, all of whom were bought by the U.S. military in Afghanistan for a bounty.[23] Nothing is more telling than the contents of the CIA flyers which were distributed in the Pashto region, overlapping Afghanistan and Pakistan, which stated:

> Get wealth and power beyond your dreams… You can receive millions of dollars helping the anti-Taliban forces catch al-Qaida and Taliban murders. This is enough money to take care of your family, your village, your tribe for the rest of your life. Pay for livestock and doctors and school books and housing for all your people.[24]

It should not have taken too long for experienced intelligence officers who were interrogating those who were turned in for bounty money to realize that most of them were not threats to the U.S. However, even when such facts became known, the detainees were not released, and their torture or mistreatment did not stop. Detaining and torturing persons known to be innocent so as to cover up their unlawful apprehension rises to the level of the worst immoral acts of a degraded

---

[20]   *See Canadian Falsely Accused of Terrorism*, CBS NEWS, Sep. 19, 2006.

[21]   *See CIA Flying Suspects To Torture?* CBS NEWS, 60 MINUTES, Mar. 6, 2005.

[22]   *See* Mark Denbeaux & Joshua Denbeaux, *The Guantanamo Detainees: A Profile of 517 Detainees through Analysis of Department of Defense Data* (Seton Hall University School of Law, 2006), at 2.

[23]   *See* Chapter 2, section 2.4, *Selected Case Studies of "Enhanced Interrogation" Techniques.*

[24]   *See* Denbeaux & Denbeaux, *The Guantanamo Detainees, supra* note 21, at 15.

system. Despite all of this, torture was advocated by some as necessary because "the ends justify the means."[25] Surprisingly, as stated earlier, these views have not generated much negative reaction from the legal profession, despite the fact that the CAT, the Geneva Conventions, the U.S. Constitution, and the laws of the U.S. clearly prohibit such practices.[26]

Are the events of September 11, 2001 enough to reopen the question of whether the medieval practice of torture should be allowed? Is this event, tragic as it was, sufficient for our country to unilaterally turn back the clock to medieval times, a time when law was not about human rights protection and rule of law but about the imposition of power? The answer to these questions must be a resounding and unqualified *no*. As the United Nations Independent Expert on Human Rights in Afghanistan between 2004 and 2006, I have had first hand experience in observing how opportunistic circumstances led to the arbitrary arrest and detention of innocent persons, and how torture was rampant and out of control in that country.[27] I shudder at the thought that American military personnel may fall into the hands of violent militants who would torture them. Will their answer to pleas not to torture our detainees be that they are doing nothing more than what the U.S. has been doing? What would we say then? That they are barbarians and we are not?

Torture is an outrage on human decency, and has been criminalized under the Geneva Conventions, the CAT, and U.S. law. Its institutionalized practice undermined the integrity of the American legal process, and its depravity undermined our moral leadership in the world. It lent credibility to the violent acts of anti-American militants and made enemies of the tortured persons, as well as members of their families, thus generating more enemies likely to threaten the security of our country and our people. Lastly, torture is known not to produce reliable information, and certainly not after months, let alone years of incarceration. To morally denounce torture is not unpatriotic – it is the right thing to do.

There have been many in the military who opposed the practice of torture. Perhaps they remembered the words of the late General Douglas MacArthur

---

[25] *See supra* note 10.

[26] Geneva Convention for the Amelioration of the Condition of the Wounded and Sick in Armed Forces in the Field art. 3, Aug. 12, 1949, 6 U.S.T. 3114, 75 U.N.T.S. 31 [hereinafter Geneva I]; Geneva Convention for the Amelioration of the Condition of Wounded, Sick and Shipwrecked Members of Armed Forces at Sea art. 3, Aug. 12, 1949, 6 U.S.T. 3217, 75 U.N.T.S. 85 [hereinafter Geneva II]; Geneva Convention Relative to the Treatment of Prisoners of War art. 3, Aug. 12, 1949, 6 U.S.T. 3316, 75 U.N.T.S. 135 [hereinafter Geneva III]; Geneva Convention Relative to the Protection of Civilian Persons in Time of War, Aug. 12, 1949, art. 2, 6 U.S.T. 3516, 75 U.N.T.S. 287 [hereinafter Geneva IV]; CAT, *supra* note 7; 18 U.S.C. §2340 (2000).

[27] *See* Report of the Independent Expert on the Situation of Human Rights in Afghanistan, M. Cherif Bassiouni, to the General Assembly, U.N. Doc. A/59/370 (21 Sep. 2004); Report of the Independent Expert on the Situation of Human Rights in Afghanistan, M. Cherif Bassiouni, to the Commission on Human Rights, E/CN.4/2005/122 (11 Mar. 2005).

contained in his farewell speech to the corps of cadets at West Point, May 12, 1962, and understood their meaning:

> The code which those words perpetuate embraces the highest moral laws and will stand the test of any ethics or philosophies ever promulgated for the uplift of mankind. Its requirements are for the things that are right, and its restraints are from the things that are wrong.
>
> …
>
> Others will debate the controversial issues, national and international, which divide men's minds; but serene, calm, aloof, you stand as the Nation's war-guardian, as its lifeguard from the raging tides of international conflict, as its gladiator in the arena of battle. For a century and a half you have defended, guarded and protected its hallowed traditions of liberty and freedom, of right and justice.
>
> … These great national problems are not for your professional participation or military solution. Your guidepost stands out like a ten-fold beacon in the night: Duty, Honor, and Country.
>
> … The Long Gray Line has never failed us. Were you to do so, a million ghosts in olive drab, in brown khaki, in blue and gray, would rise from their white crosses thundering those magic words: Duty, Honor, Country. Duty requires remaining within the boundaries of the law. Honor requires doing the right thing as dictated by morality and ethics. And country is best served when we fulfill our respective duties with honor.[28]

Too many in the military have forgotten these words. Were they so strongly influenced by their commanders? Were they so eager to advance their careers? Or were they simply callous and with too little moral character to refuse to obey unlawful orders? As to those in the CIA, what ever happened to the engraving in its Langley headquarters, urging those in the service to "speak truth to power"? The nation needs to know why relatively few did so much harm to so many victims because a handful at the top made it happen.

Brigadier General Patrick Finnegan, Dean of the Academic Board at West Point, wrote in a letter to the Editor of *The New Yorker* magazine:

> Jane Mayer, in her review of Marc Thiessen's *Courting Disaster*, offers a fine dissection of that book's flaws. Torture is wrong under any circumstances. As General David H.

---

[28] General Douglas MacArthur, *Duty, Honor, Country*, Thayer Award Acceptance Address, West Point, NY (May 12, 1962). *See also* KAREN J. GREENBERG, THE LEAST WORST PLACE: GUANTANAMO'S FIRST 100 DAYS (2009), which tells the story through a group of career Marine officers who tried – and ultimately failed – to stymie the Pentagon's desire to implement harsh new policies in Guantánamo and bypass the Geneva Conventions.

Petraeus recently remarked (specifically referring to Abu Ghraib and to Guantanamo), such abusive techniques are "nonbiodegradable… The enemy continues to beat you with them like a stick." He's right – the pictures from Abu Ghraib and the publicity surrounding Guantanamo, waterboarding, and other "enhanced interrogation techniques" have created far more terrorists than most people understand. For a country that professes to stand for the rule of law and individual rights, we look like the worst kind of hypocrites. Consider a war we fought in the past against a brutal enemy that tortured and killed prisoners, executed civilians, and engaged in a number of atrocities. Several American leaders argued that the only way to prevail was to engage in the same kind of tactics, because that was the only thing that the enemy understood or respected (sound familiar)? But other leaders believed that it was not enough to win; they also had to do it in a way that was consistent with the values of their society and the principles of their cause. That conflict was the Revolutionary War, and the leaders included George Washington and John Adams. If we mean what we say – if we really believe that we're the good guys, and I hope we do – then this is the time to stand by those principles which our Founding Fathers professed and lived by. That's what, I hope, makes us the leaders of the free world.[29]

President Bush stated in the 2006 State of the Union Address that his Administration would "determine the character of our country."[30] If the policy and practices described throughout this book have become the character of this nation then it is a betrayal of this nation's character, and those responsible for it should be investigated and prosecuted if probable cause exists.

For the U.S. to have given up the high moral road of observing international and national law in the name of the "war on terrorism" was an egregious policy enabling torture, whose effects will be long felt by this country and abroad. To redeem itself, the U.S. must, therefore, take action to make amends and to hold accountable those who promoted a policy of torture and those who practiced it.

In the wise words of George Santayana, "Progress, far from consisting in change, depends on retentiveness. When change is absolute there remains no being to improve and no direction is set for possible improvement: and when experience is not retained, as among savages, infancy is perpetual. Those who cannot remember the past are condemned to repeat it."[31] We must fully understand our past failings in order to thoughtfully move beyond them in the future.

---

[29] Brigadier General Patrick Finnegan, *Letter to the Editor*, THE NEW YORKER, May 3, 2010, at 3.

[30] George W. Bush, Report on the State of the Union (Jan. 31, 2006). "In this decisive year, you and I will make choices that determine both the future and the character of our country. … Every step toward freedom in the world makes our country safer – so we will act boldly in freedom's cause. …We will renew the defining moral commitments of this land."

[31] GEORGE SANTAYANA, THE LIFE OF REASON (1905).

The Obama Administration must pursue a principled path toward the discovery of truth and the pursuit of justice. It cannot allow political considerations to stand in the way of what the Constitution and laws of the U.S. require, and what the imperatives of morality demand.

M. Cherif Bassiouni
Chicago, May 2010

CONTENTS

KEY ACTORS

Government Actors (in alphabetical order, and titles listed at the time of the events discussed in the book)

David Addington *(Legal Counsel, Chief of Staff for Vice President Cheney)*

Pasquale D'Amuro *(Assistant Director for Counterterrorism, Federal Bureau of Investigation)**

John Ashcroft *(Attorney General, 2001–05)*

Lieutenant Colonel Diane Beaver *(Guantánamo Staff Judge Advocate)*

John Bellinger III *(Legal Advisor to Secretary of State)**

Major General Scott C. Black *(Judge Advocate General, U.S. Army)**

Stephen Bradbury *(Principal Deputy Assistant Attorney General – OLC)*

John Brennan *(Interim Director of National Counterterrorism Center)*

George W. Bush *(President of the United States)*

Jay Bybee *(Assistant Attorney General, 2001–03)*

Richard Cheney *(Vice President of the United States)*

Michael Chertoff *(Secretary of Homeland Security)*

James Corney *(Deputy Attorney General, Acting Assistant Attorney)*

Judge Susan J. Crawford *(Convening Authority, Military Commissions at Guantánamo)**

Rear Admiral Jane Dalton *(Counsel to Joint Chiefs)**

Robert Delahunty *(Deputy Assistant Attorney General, Special Counsel, 2001–03)*

Major General Charles Dunlap, Jr. *(Deputy Judge Advocate General, U.S. Air Force)**

Major General Michael Dunlavey *(Commanding General, JTF GTMO)*

Douglas Feith *(Under Secretary of Defense for Policy)*

Timothy Flanigan *(Deputy Attorney General)*

Robert Gates *(Secretary of Defense, 2006-present)*

Jack Goldsmith *(Assistant Attorney General, Office of Legal Counsel, 2003–04)**

Alberto Gonzales *(White House Legal Counsel; Attorney General, 2005–07)*

Porter Goss *(Director, Central Intelligence Agency, 2004–05)*

Rear Admiral Don Guter *(Judge Advocate General)**

Stephen Hadley *(National Security Advisor, 2005–09)*

Michael Hayden *(Director, Central Intelligence Agency, 2005–09)*

William "Jim" Haynes II *(General Counsel, Department of Defense)*

Staff Sergeant Joseph Hickman *(Prison Guard, JTF 160 at Guantánamo)**

General James Hill *(U.S. Southern Command, including Guantánamo Base)*

Admiral John Hutson *(Retired Judge Advocate General)**

Brigadier General Janis Karpinski *(Commander of the Abu Ghraib Prison in Iraq)*

Senator Patrick Leahy *(Ranking Member, Judiciary Committee)**

Brigadier General Michael Lehnert, USMC *(Commanding General, JTF 160 at Guantánamo)**

Daniel Levin *(Acting Assistant Attorney General, OLC 2004–05)*

Colonel John Ley *(Army Legal Counsel)**

Lewis Libby *(Chief of Staff to the Vice President 2001–05)*

Rear Admiral Michael Lohr *(Judge Advocate General)**

Major General Geoffrey Miller *(Commander of Detention Facilities in Guantánamo and Iraq)*

Rear Admiral Bruce MacDonald *(Convening Authority, Military Commissions at Guantánamo)**

Alberto J. Mora *(General Counsel of the Navy)**

Robert Mueller *(Director, Federal Bureau of Investigation)**

Michael Mukasey *(Attorney General, 2007–09)*

Colonel Thomas Pappas *(Commander of Military Intelligence Brigade, Responsible for Interrogations at Abu Ghraib)*

Patrick Philbin *(Deputy Assistant Attorney General, OLC 2001–03 / National Security 2003–05)*

Colin Powell *(Secretary of State)**

Condoleezza Rice *(National Security Advisor 2001–05, Secretary of State 2005–09)*

John Rizzo *(General Counsel, Central Intelligence Agency)*

Donald Rumsfeld *(Secretary of Defense, 2001–06)*

Lieutenant General Ricardo Sanchez *(Commander of Allied Forces in Iraq)*

Ali Soufan *(Special Agent, Federal Bureau of Investigation)**

Colonel Manuel Supervielle *(Staff Judge Advocate, U.S. Southern Command)**

Colonel Donald Richburg *(Legal Counsel for Air Force)**

Lieutenant General Jack Rives *(Legal Adviser to the Secretary of the Air Force)**

William H. Taft IV *(Legal Advisor, Department of State)**

Major General Antonio Taguba *

George Tenet *(Director, Central Intelligence Agency, 2001–04)*

Captain D.D. Thompson *(Special Assistant to CNO for JCS Matters)**

Darrel. J. Vandeveld *(Resigned Prosecutor, Military Commissions at Guantánamo)**

Paul Wolfowitz *(Deputy Secretary of Defense, 2001–05)*

Carolyn Wood *(Head of Interrogation Unit, Bagram)*

John Yoo *(Deputy Assistant Attorney General, Office of Legal Counsel, 2001–03)*

* Denotes those who disagreed with Bush Administration policy, in whole or in part, as publicly disclosed.

The author disclaims any legal or personal characterization of those identified in this list and those mentioned in the book.

ABBREVIATIONS

A. TERMS OF REFERENCE

BAU	Behavioral Assessment Unit (FBI)
BSCT	Behavioral Consultation Team
CENTCOM	U.S. Central Command
CAT	Convention Against Torture and Other Cruel, Inhuman, or Degrading Treatment or Punishment
CIA	Central Intelligence Agency
CID	Criminal Investigation Division (FBI)
CITF	Criminal Investigation Task Force (DOD)
CJTF-7	Coalition Joint Task Force (Iraq)
CSRT	Combatant Status Review Trial
CRS	Congressional Research Service
DHS	Defense Human Intelligence Service (DOD)
DIA	Defense Intelligence Agency (DOD)
DOD	Department of Defense
DOJ	Department of Justice
DTA	Detainee Treatment Act
ECHR	European Commission on Human Rights
FBI	Federal Bureau of Investigation
HUMINT	Human Intelligence
ICC	International Criminal Court
ICCPR	International Covenant on Civil and Political Rights
ICE	Interrogation Control Element (DOD)
ICRC	International Committee of the Red Cross
ICTY	International Criminal Tribunal for Yugoslavia
ICTR	International Criminal Tribunal for Rwanda
JAG	Judge Advocate General
JITF-CT	Joint Intelligence Task Force for Combating Terrorism (DOD)
JTF	Joint Task Force
GTMO	Guantánamo
MEJA	Military Extraterritorial Jurisdiction Act of 2000, 18 U.S.C. §3261
MCA	Military Commissions Act
MLDU	Military Liaison Detainee Unit

NCIS	Naval Criminal Investigation Service
NSC	National Security Council
NSC/PC	National Security Council Principals Committee
OLC	Office of Legal Counsel (DOJ)
POW	Prisoner of War
RICO	Racketeer Influenced and Corrupt Organizations Act
SERE	Survive Evasion Resistance Escape program
SOUTHCOM	U.S. Southern Command
UCMJ	Uniform Code of Military Justice
UDHR	Universal Declaration of Human Rights
USC	United States Code
WCA	War Crimes Act

B. DOCUMENTS

FM 34–52	US Army Field Manual 34–52, United States (1992)
MCA	Military Commissions Act of 2006, 10 U.S.C. §948 (2006)
MCM	Manual For Courts-Martial, United States (2008)
Fay-Jones Report	AR 16–6 Investigation of Intelligence Activities at Abu Ghraib, LTG Anthony R. Jones, MG George F. Ray (2004)
Schmidt-Furlow Report	AR 15–6 Investigation of Detainee Abuse at Guantánamo Bay, Cuba Detention Facility. LTG Randall Schmidt, BG John Furlow (2005)
Schlesinger Report	Final Report of the Independent Panel to Review DOD Detention Operations. James Schlesinger (2004)
Taguba Report	AR 15–6 Investigation of the 800th Military Police Brigade MG Antonio Taguba (2004)
OIG Report	Review of the FBI's Involvement in and Observations of Detainee Interrogations in Guantánamo Bay, Afghanistan, and Iraq. Justice Dept. Office of Inspector General (2008)
Rumsfeld Memo	Memorandum from Donald Rumsfeld, Secretary of Defense to James T. Hill, Commander of the U.S. Southern Command, Counter-Resistance Techniques in the War on Terrorism (April 16, 2003)
JTF-GTMO Memo	Memorandum from William Haynes II to Donald Rumsfeld, Secretary of Defense, Counter-resistance Techniques (Nov. 27, 2002)

Bybee Memo	Memorandum from Jay S. Bybee, Assistant Attorney Gen., Office of Legal Counsel, U.S. Dep't of Justice, to Alberto R. Gonzales, Counsel to the President, Standards of Conduct for Interrogation under 18 U.S.C. §§2340–2340A (Aug. 1, 2002)
Bybee Memo II	Memorandum for John Rizzo, Acting General Counsel of the C.I.A., Interrogation of al-Qaeda Operative. (August 1, 2002)
Yoo Memo	Memorandum from Deputy Ass't Atty General John Yoo to William J. Haynes II, General Counsel of the Dep't of Defense, memorandum on Military Interrogation of Alien Unlawful combatants Held Outside the United States (March 14, 2003)
Bradbury Memo I	Memorandum for John Rizzo, Senior Deputy General Counsel, C.I.A., Application of 18 U.S.C. §§2340 to Certain Techniques That May Be Used in the Interrogation of a High Value al-Qaeda Detainee (May 10, 2005)
Bradbury Memo II	Memorandum for John Rizzo, Senior Deputy General Counsel, C.I.A., Application of 18 U.S.C. §§2340 to the Combined Use of Certain Techniques in the Interrogation of High Value al-Qaeda Detainees (May 10, 2005)
Bradbury Memo III	Memorandum for John Rizzo, Senior Deputy General Counsel, C.I.A., Application of United States Obligations Under Article 16 of the Convention Against Torture to Certain Techniques that May Be Used in the Interrogation of High Value al-Qaeda Detainees (May 30, 2005)

CHRONOLOGY OF EVENTS

September 11, 2001	Attacks on the World Trade Center in New York and the Pentagon. President Bush signs a secret Presidential Finding authorizing the CIA to create paramilitary teams to "hunt, capture, detain, or kill designated terrorists" anywhere in the world.
September 25, 2001	John Yoo Memo: advises that the President has "broad constitutional powers" when dealing with the military and terrorists.
October 7, 2001	Launch of Operation 'Enduring Freedom' in Afghanistan. The U.S. did not seek authorization from the United Nations Security Council for the invasion, but military action is predicated on 'self-defense'.
October 26, 2001	President Bush signs the PATRIOT Act into law, greatly expanding law enforcement and intelligence agencies' scope and authority, both domestically and internationally, in their activities in the "war on terror".
November 13, 2001	Issuance of Military Order on Detention, Treatment and Trial of Certain Non-Citizens in the War against Terrorism.
December 28, 2001	John Yoo and Patrick Philbin Memo counsels that Federal Courts lack the jurisdiction to hear habeas corpus petitions from prisoners held in Guantánamo Bay. This memo is used to justify the government's actions in Guantánamo.
December 2001	Camp Delta is established in Guantánamo Bay, Cuba.
January 9, 2002	John Yoo Memo: "Customary international law has no binding legal effect on either the President or the military because it is not Federal law, as recognized by the Constitution…"

January 16, 2002 — First arrival of 20 prisoners to camp X-Ray, Guantánamo Bay. Photos are circulated showing prisoners shackled and bound, in orange jump suits, with outdoor 8x8 foot cages for housing.

January 25, 2002 — Alberto Gonzales Memo on the Application of the Geneva Convention on Prisoners of War to Conflict with al-Qaeda and the Taliban: "In my judgment, this new paradigm renders obsolete Geneva's strict limitations on questioning of enemy prisoners and renders quaint some of its provisions."

January 26, 2002 — Colin Powell Memo: Not applying the Geneva Conventions will "reverse over a century of U.S. policy and practice..."

February 2, 2002 — William H. Taft IV Memo: Geneva Conventions should apply to the conflict in Afghanistan.

February 7, 2002 — President Bush reaffirms his order requiring that detainees be treated humanely, and – to the extent appropriate and consistent with military necessity – in a manner consistent with the principles of the Geneva Conventions.

March 2002 — Abu Zubaydah is captured and detained in CIA "black sites". Over the next year his interrogations become the central argument between several governmental agencies over which techniques were and were not permissible. The CIA eventually admits to having waterboarded Abu Zubaydah 83 times.

June 2002 — The U.S. ratifies the Optional Protocol to the Convention on the Rights of the Child on the Involvement of Children in Armed Conflicts, which obligates state parties to "take all feasible measures to ensure that persons within their jurisdiction recruited or used in hostilities contrary to [the] Protocol are demobilized or otherwise released from service. State Parties shall, when necessary, accord to these persons all appropriate assistance for their physical and psychological recovery and their social reintegration."

July 24, 2002	Chief of Psychological Services Memo (Subject: Psychological Effects of Resistance Training) sent to USAF Chief of Staff Baumgartner in response to his request for information. Memo states that a small minority of students in USAF resistance training (from which interrogation tactics were adopted) have adverse psychological responses; the overall percentage is less than 5%. Navy uses waterboarding in training but Air Force does not. Training studies show this method has 100% capitulation rate.
July 25, 2002	Baumgartner Memo (Subject: Exploitation) Response to a request to understand which interrogation techniques have proven useful against U.S. military trainees through the SERE (Survival, Evasion, Rescue and Escape) program. Lists statement summary of six attached documents, including a list of 'Exploitation Processes Used Against American Prisoners and Detainees'.
August 1, 2002	Jay S. Bybee Memo to Alberto Gonzales, on Standards of Conduct for Interrogation: "Physical pain amounting to torture must be equivalent in intensity to the pain accompanying serious physical injury such as organ failure, impairment of bodily function, or even death."
	The Bybee II Memo is completed, authorizing the CIA to use torture methods and indicates how the CIA may sidestep anti-torture laws in doing so.
September 2002	Haynes, Gonzales, and Addington visit Guantánamo to observe interrogations and meet with Maj. Gen. Michael E. Dunlavey, Commander of JTF-170 at Guantánamo and tasked with handling interrogation operations for the DOD. In this meeting the signal was sent that interrogators should "do whatever needs to be done" to get information.
	This same month, Maher Arar, a Canadian national, is detained and transferred by "extraordinary rendition" to Syria.

October 2, 2002	Meeting at Guantánamo concerning Counter Resistance Strategy. In attendance: COL Cummings, LTC Phifer, CDR Bridges, LTC Beaver, MAJ Burney, MAJ Leso, Dave Becker, John Fredman, 1LT Seek, and SPC Pimentel. Excerpts from notes:

1. "The DOJ has provided much guidance on this issue…The CIA is not held to the same rules as the military. [Whether a given technique is 'torture'] is basically subject to perception. If the detainee dies you're doing it wrong… Everything on the BSCT white paper is legal from a civilian standpoint." – John Fredman

2. "We will need documentation to protect us." – Diane Beaver

October 11, 2002	Phifer Memo lists the following interrogations procedures for detainees at GTMO:

Category I:
a) Yelling
b) Deception
c) Interrogator identity

Category II:
a) Stress positions
b) Falsified documents
c) Isolation
d) Non-standard interrogation environments
e) Deprivation of light or auditory stimuli
f) Hooding
g) 20 hour continuous interrogation
h) Removal of all comfort items
i) Switch from hot rations to MREs
j) Removal of clothing
k) Forced grooming
l) Use individual phobias.

Category III:
a) Convince detainee of the death or painful consequence imminent for he or his family
b) Exposure to cold or water

c) Wet towel

d) Use of non injurious physical contact

Included in the Phifer memo sent out for approval on October 11, 2002 is a legal analysis of the techniques by LTC Beaver in the Beaver Memo: "The detainees currently held at GTMO are not protected by the Geneva Conventions…although no international body of law directly applies, the more notable international treaties are listed below…" Interprets the CAT as only prohibiting "…committing those acts that would otherwise be prohibited under the U.S. Constitution Amendment prohibiting cruel and unusual punishment." States that some federal law and the UCMJ may still apply to those interrogating detainees. Sum of analysis: "The counter-resistance techniques proposed in the JTF-170-J2 memo are lawful because they do not violate the 8th Amendment of the Constitution or the federal torture statute…an international law analysis is not required for the current proposal because the Geneva Conventions do not apply…" LTC Beaver's recommendation: Category I methods are okay, but Category II and III methods should undergo a "legal, medical, behavioral science, and intelligence review prior to commencement."

Maj. Gen. Michael Dunlavey memo (Commander of U.S. Southern Command, Subject: Counter-Resistance Strategies.) Requests approval for techniques outlined in attached October 11, 2002 Phifer memo. Dunlavey states that he concurs with Phifer's legal analysis, and that based on analysis, the techniques listed in Beaver memo do not violate international or U.S. law. States that these techniques differ from those currently employed in the Global War on Terrorism…they will 'enhance efforts to extract additional information.' The approved Phifer memo and the Beaver legal analysis make up the JTF 170-J2 memo, later called the JTF-GTMO memo.

October 25, 2002

Gen. James T. Hill memo (Subject: Counter Resistance Techniques) forwards the contents of the JTF-GTMO memo to the Chairman of the Joint Chiefs of Staff. States that Category I and II techniques are legal and humane, and that it is "uncertain whether all the techniques in the third category are legal under U.S. law. …Although I am cognizant of the important policy ramifications of some of these proposed techniques, I firmly believe that we must quickly provide Joint Task Force 170 counter-resistance techniques to maximize the value of our intelligence collection mission."

October 28, 2002   Mark Fallon, Deputy Commander of the Criminal Investigation Task Force (CITF), sends an email to Sam McCahon, Major JA, Chief Legal Advisor to DOD Criminal Investigation Task Force, in response to receiving notes from this meeting. "This looks like the kinds of stuff Congressional hearings are made of. … Quotes from LTC Beaver regarding things that are not being reported give the appearance of impropriety. … Talk of 'wet towel treatment' which results in the lymphatic gland reacting as if you are suffocating, would, in my opinion, shock the conscience of any legal body. …Someone needs to be considering how history will look back at this."

November 4, 2002   Sam McCahon Memo (Memorandum for Commander, CITF, Subject: Assessment of JTF 170 Counter Resistance Strategies and the Potential Impact on CITF Mission and Intelligence.) Details the Dunlavey/Beaver memoranda to determine liability of personnel, indicating responsibility could be allocated via the 8th Amendment, the UCMJ, or 18 U.S.C. § 2340. Notes that "Both the utility and legality of applying certain techniques identified in the memo listed above are, in my opinion, questionable. Any policy decision to use the Tier III techniques, or any technique inconsistent with the analysis herein, will be contrary to my recommendation." Notes that the legal analysis attached to the JTF 170 memo focuses upon clearing the U.S. from civil liability, and indicates that inflicting pain or treating detainees in a degrading manner is permitted if it is meant to produce information (and not intended to be painful or degrading in itself). "The intended use of Tier III techniques, if detected, will establish new case law in this area, much to the detriment of the U.S.

foreign and domestic interests. I cannot advocate any action, interrogation or otherwise, that is predicated upon the principle that all is well if the ends justify the means and others are not aware of how we conduct our business."

A series of responses to the JTF-GTMO memo coming from the Army, Air Force, Navy, and Marines.

Army – Army Legal Counsel John Ley states the "Army interposes significant legal, policy, and practical concerns regarding most of Category II and all of Category III techniques proposed" and "… concurs in the recommendation for a comprehensive legal review of this proposal in its entirety by the DOD and DOJ." Legal concerns include:

1. President in Military Order 1 (November 13, 2001), and reaffirmed on February 2, 2002, stated that detainees would be treated humanely.
2. Techniques must be consistent with federal law and the UCMJ.
3. Category III techniques violate the President's Order, several UCMJ articles, and the Federal Torture Statute.

Also states that the plan does not "adequately lay out how these techniques will result in our forces gaining any useful information."

Air Force – Col. Donald Richburg recommends "an in-depth legal and policy assessment… prior to the proposed counter-resistance interrogation techniques." Legal concerns include:

1. Many proposed techniques, especially those under Category III, may not be legal. Some could be construed as torture, as defined by 18 U.S.C. § 2340.
2. Techniques could undermine the ability to prosecute interrogated persons.
3. Techniques may fail to meet requirements outlined in the military order to treat detainees humanely. (See Army concern above.)

	Navy – Cpt. D.D. Thompson, Special Assistant to CNO for JCS Matters, recommends "a more detailed interagency legal and policy review be conducted on proposed techniques. …Navy staff also recommend that the classification level of counter-resistance techniques be increased to Top Secret level."
November 23, 2002	Secretary Rumsfeld gives VOCO (Verbal Orders of Commanding Officer) to begin aggressive interrogation of Mohammed Al-Qahtani.
November 27, 2002	JTF GTMO Action Memorandum from William J Haynes, General Counsel to Secretary of Defense Donald Rumsfeld (Subject: Counter Resistance Techniques.) Summary of the Dunlavey/Beaver memo. States that the JTF GTMO Memo has been previously discussed with Deputy Secretary Feith and General Myers, and that all agree, "as a matter of policy, you authorize the Commander of US SOUTHCOM to employ his discretion, only Categories I and II and the fourth technique listed in Category III. …While all Category III techniques may be legally available, we believe, as a matter of policy, a blanket approval of Category III techniques is not warranted."
December 2, 2002	Secretary Rumsfeld approves the JTF-GTMO Memo, giving authority to interrogators at Guantánamo to use all Category II and one Category III techniques.
December 17, 2002	Timothy James Memo: (Special Agent in Charge, Criminal Investigation Task Force, Guantánamo) in response to the JTF-GTMO memo, states that "CITF-G objects to these aggressive interrogation techniques," and that "LEA agents only use rapport-based methods that not only yield results, but also are legally sound. [W]hen coercive techniques are used in closed environments, there is a real potential for mistreatment to occur. This holds true even for highly trained and disciplined interrogators…"
January 15, 2003	John F. Rankin (SERE Training Specialist) Memo to Christopher Ross, SERE Coordinator (Subject: After Action Report of the Joint Task Force Guantánamo Bay

(JTF-GTMO) Training Evolution.) Notes that on December 30, 2002 a contingent from SERE went to GTMO to train ICE staff on coercive techniques outlined in the JTF-GTMO memo, and something referred to as the Biderman Technique.

Secretary Rumsfeld Memo 1 to US SOUTHCOM Commander (Subject: Counter-Resistance Techniques in the War on Terrorism) outlines the following actions:

1. Establish a working group within the DOD to assess the legal, policy and operational issues relating to the interrogation of detainees
2. Address legal considerations raised by interrogations of detainees held
3. Address policy considerations with respect to choice of technique
4. Address recommendations for employment of particular techniques.

Secretary Rumsfeld Memo 2 to the US SOUTHCOM Commander and DOD General Counsel Haynes (Subject: Counter Resistance Techniques) rescinds actions outlined in December 2, 2002 memo giving authority to use all Category II techniques and one Category III. All requests for using these techniques must be justified on a case-by-case basis with requests forwarded to Rumsfeld. States that all interrogations should continue the humane treatment of detainees regardless of the type of interrogation used.

February 5, 2003
Secretary Colin Powell presents the case against Iraq to the U.N. Security Council in an effort to rally international support for military action against Iraq.

March 1, 2003
Khaled Sheikh Mohammed, the alleged architect of the 9/11 attacks, is captured in Pakistan and held in CIA "black sites" for the next three years. CIA documents reveal that Mohammed is waterboarded 183 times during his first month in detention.

March 14, 2003	The U.S. invades Iraq. From the outset, the U.S. states that the Geneva Conventions apply to the conflict in Iraq.

John Yoo Second Memo to Haynes (Subject: Military Interrogations of Alien Unlawful Combatants Held Outside of the United States) states that the Fifth and Eighth Amendments do not hold for alien enemy combatants held outside of the U.S.; that federal criminal laws do not apply for properly-authorized military interrogations of enemy combatants; that U.S. obligations under the CAT extend only to conduct that is "cruel and unusual" under the Eighth Amendment or which "shocks the conscience" under the Fifth and Fourteenth Amendments; that customary international law does impose obligations beyond the CAT and may be overridden by the President; and, finally, advises claims of "necessity or self-defense" as responses to possible criminal prosecution for interrogation techniques.

April 4, 2003 — Working Group Report on Detainee Interrogations in the Global War on Terrorism: Assessment of Legal, Historical, Policy, and Operational Considerations. Written in response to Secretary Rumsfeld's memorandum of January 15, 2003.

April 16, 2003 — Secretary Rumsfeld's Third Memo to the Commander, US SOUTHCOMM (Subject, Subject: Counter Resistance Techniques in the War on Terrorism) notes the completion of the Working Group Report. Approves the techniques lettered A-X in an attachment; techniques must be used in coordination with safeguards also laid out, and are limited to unlawful combatants at GTMO. Also states that actions should still be based on humane treatment and consistent with principles of the Geneva Conventions. States that techniques B (removal or giving of incentives – point of contention is related to religious items), I (Attacking/insulting detainee ego – states provisions of Geneva are not applicable to the interrogation of unlawful combatants, consideration should be given to view prior to application of technique), O (Mutt and Jeff, friendly and harsh interrogator), and X (Isolation – states some nations may view this, especially if greater than 30 days, as a POW violation of Geneva III) require his notification in advance. Other techniques of note: T (dietary manipulation), U (environmental manipulation), and V (sleep adjustment).

May 2003	Laid Saidi rendered by U.S. officials from Tanzania to Afghanistan.
October 7, 2003	A group of non-governmental organizations, including the American Civil Liberties Union, the Center for Constitutional Rights, Physicians for Human Rights, Veterans for Common Sense, and Veterans for Peace submit its first request under the Freedom of Information Act for records concerning the treatment, death, and rendition of detainees and other individuals in U.S. custody. Agencies included in the request include the DOD (including the Departments of the Army, Navy and Air Force, and the Defense Intelligence Agency), DOJ (including the FBI and the Office of Intelligence Policy and Review), DOS, and the CIA.
January 2004	Khaled El-Masri rendered by U.S. officials from Macedonia to Afghanistan.
February 2004	The International Committee of the Red Cross releases a comprehensive report of the recorded abuses of detainees in Iraq by Coalition Forces.
March 19, 2004	Jack Goldsmith Memo on the Permissibility of Relocating Certain "Protected Persons" from Occupied Iraq.
April 28, 2004	First set of photos detailing torture at Abu Ghraib appear in the U.S. media.
May 2004	The Taguba Report on treatment of prisoners at Abu Ghraib is made publicly available.
May 7, 2004	Secretary Rumsfeld and General Myers testify before the Senate Armed Services Committee regarding abuses of prisoners in Iraq.

June 29, 2004   The U.S. confirms that it is in conformance with domestic and international law regarding its torture policy.

August 24, 2004   The Final Report of the Independent Panel to Review DOD Detention Operations is released. The Panel, headed by former Defense Secretary James R. Schlesinger, found that Secretary Rumsfeld had contributed to confusion over permissible interrogation techniques in Iraq.

September 15, 2004   The U.S. District Court for the Southern District of New York orders the government to respond to the ACLU FOIA request for records. The first documents are released on December 7, 2004. [Note, as of April 2010, the government is continuing to release documents under the original FOIA request. The complete database of documents can be found online at www.aclu.org/accountability/.]

October 24, 2004   Contents of the Goldsmith Memo reported in the media.

November 30, 2004   The *New York Times* publishes extracts from the February ICRC report, stating the U.S. has used psychological, and sometimes physical, coercion "tantamount to torture" against Guantánamo prisoners.

January 2005   The Pentagon announces an internal investigation into allegations of prisoner abuse. A Council of Europe investigator concludes that 100 people were kidnapped by the CIA in Europe and rendered to other countries.

March 2, 2005   The Vice Admiral Albert T. Church Report on Detainee Interrogation and Incarceration is released. The panel examined 187 investigations of allegations of detainee abuse that had been completed as of September 30, 2004. Of those, 117 cases were unsubstantiated or did not constitute abuse, and of the 70 remaining completed cases of substantiated abuse, six were deaths, 26 were considered serious, and 38 were called minor abuse cases. Church declines to single out any specific persons to be held accountable, and human rights organizations call the report a "whitewash". Within a week of the Church report, officials from the Army and Navy admit that 26, not 6, detainee deaths merited charges of homicide.

May 5, 2005

Bradbury sends two memoranda to the C.I.A. asserting that SERE techniques, alone and in combination, may be legally used on detainees.

May 30, 2005

Bradbury sends a third memo addressing the applicability, or rather inapplicability, of the CAT. The memo also notes the scores of times waterboarding had been used on two detainees.

November 29, 2005

President Bush states: "The United States of America does not torture. And that's important for the people around the world to understand."

December 5, 2005

The *Washington Post* reports that the CIA's Inspector General is investigating what it calls "erroneous renditions".

December 30, 2005

The Detainee Treatment Act of 2005 is signed into law by President Bush. The Act bans cruel, inhuman or degrading treatment of detainees in U.S. custody, and prohibits U.S. military interrogators from using techniques not listed in the U.S. Army Field Manual on Intelligence Interrogation. However, Bush issues a signing statement declaring that he will view the interrogation limits within the context of his broader Executive powers to protect national security.

January 22, 2006

The Council of Europe issues a report condemning both the U.S. and European countries for the practice of "extraordinary rendition", referring to the practice as the "'outsourcing' of torture."

February 2006

A United Nations report denounces the abuse of U.S. prisoners as tantamount to torture, and says detainees should be either tried or freed without further delay.

May 2006

A United Nations Committee Against Torture report calls for the U.S. to stop use of "enhanced interrogation" techniques and the use of secret prisons, which it considers to amount to torture.

May 15, 2006	The DOD exhausts all legal appeals and publishes a list of names, ages, or estimated dates of birth of all detainees who had been in military custody at Guantánamo.
June 9, 2006	Yasser Al-Zahrani, Mani Al-Utaybi, and Salah Ahmed Al-Salami are found dead in their cells at Guantánamo under mysterious circumstances, and determined to have simultaneously committed suicide. In 2009, guards who were on duty that evening come forward with evidence that the men were murdered.
June 29, 2006	The U.S. Supreme Court holds in *Hamdan v. Rumsfeld* that the Third Geneva Convention applies to all detainees in the 'War on Terror'. The Court holds that the President lacked necessary Congressional authorization to establish the special military commissions, and found these commissions to be illegal under both military justice law and the Geneva Conventions.
July 11, 2006	The Bush Administration publicly expresses that detainees at Guantánamo and in U.S. military custody throughout the world are entitled to protections under the Geneva Conventions.
September 2006	Fourteen key terror suspects previously held in secret CIA prisons, including Khalid Sheikh Mohammed, are sent to Guantánamo.
September 9, 2006	President Bush publicly acknowledges the existence of the U.S. "extraordinary rendition" program.
October 17, 2006	President Bush signs the Military Commissions Act of 2006. Drafted in the wake of *Hamdan v. Rumsfeld*, the Act's stated purpose is "To authorize trial by military commission for violations of the law of war, and for other purposes."

November 2006	The DOD's Criminal Investigative Task Force reports that Mohamed Al-Qahtani, the alleged '20ᵗʰ Hijacker' of the 9/11 attacks and in U.S. custody since 2001, would likely be unprosecutable due to the extent of the abuses he endured during interrogations.

November 2006 — The DOD's Criminal Investigative Task Force reports that Mohamed Al-Qahtani, the alleged '20th Hijacker' of the 9/11 attacks and in U.S. custody since 2001, would likely be unprosecutable due to the extent of the abuses he endured during interrogations.

January 26, 2007 — A European Parliament report concludes that the CIA has conducted 1,245 flights, many of them to destinations where suspects could face torture, in violation of Article 3 of the CAT.

February 14, 2007 — The International Committee of the Red Cross issues a report on the treatment of fourteen "high value" detainees in custody of the CIA, detailing the use of several "enhanced interrogation" techniques, as well as the involvement of medical staff in interrogations.

March 29, 2007 — Secretary of Defense Robert Gates urges Congress to seek ways to close Guantánamo, arguing that military trials at the camp lacked credibility because they had been tainted by the reported harsh treatment of detainees.

May 20, 2007 — David Hicks, the first detainee to be tried and convicted in the military commissions of Guantánamo, is flown to Australia to serve out the remaining seven months of his sentence. He was released December 29, 2007, and continues to reside in Australia.

July 20, 2007 — President Bush signs an Executive Order prohibiting torture and cruel, inhuman, or degrading treatment or punishment, while leaving room for the CIA to continue to violate Common Article 3 of the Geneva Conventions. Violent acts are prohibited, but only those serious enough to be considered comparable to murder, torture, mutilation, and cruel or inhuman treatment, as defined by the Military Commissions Act of 2005.

December 7, 2007 — The *New York Times* reports that intelligence officials have said that of about 100 prisoners held to date in the CIA program, "enhanced interrogation" techniques were used on about 30, and that waterboarding was used on just three. The article also reveals for the first time the CIA's destruction of videotapes showing interrogations which employed waterboarding.

December 20, 2007 — The House Judiciary Committee holds hearings on the applicability of federal criminal laws to the interrogation of detainees.

February 13, 2008 — The U.S. Senate, in a 51 to 45 vote, approves a bill restricting the CIA to only those interrogation techniques explicitly authorized by the 2006 Army Field Manual. The legislation would bar the CIA from using waterboarding, sensory deprivation, or other coercive methods to break a prisoner who refuses to answer questions. President Bush vetoes the bill in March. In discussing his veto, Bush said, "The best source of information about terrorist attacks is the terrorist themselves. If we were to shut down this program and restrict the CIA to methods in the Field Manual, we could lose vital information from senior al-Qaeda terrorists, and that could cost American lives."

May 2008 — Charges against Mohamed Al-Qahtani at the Military Commission at Guantánamo are dropped.

May 20, 2008 — The DOJ's Office of the Inspector General issues its *Review of the FBI's Involvement in and Observations of Detainee Interrogations in Guantánamo Bay, Afghanistan, and Iraq.* The report documents internal dissent and confusion among Bush Administration agencies and officials with regard to interrogation policies, drawing particular concern with CIA practices.

July 2008 — The Senate Committee on Armed Services holds hearings on the treatment of 'war on terror' detainees in U.S. custody.

January 20, 2009 — Barack Hussein Obama is inaugurated as the 44th President of the United States.

January 22, 2009 — President Obama signs three Executive Orders closing the Guantánamo Bay detention center, ending the CIA's use of "black site" secret prisons, and requiring that all interrogations meet the requirements of the Geneva Conventions by following the non-coercive methods of the Army Field Manual.

March 2, 2009   The CIA acknowledges that 92 videotapes of interrogations were destroyed, including 12 which documented use of "enhanced interrogation" techniques.

April 16, 2009   President Obama states that "[w]e have been through a dark and painful chapter in our history. But at a time of great challenges and disturbing disunity, nothing will be gained by spending our time and energy laying blame for the past," indicating that no prosecutions would be undertaken for any of the illegal practices which took place during the Bush Administration's "war on terror".

May 13, 2009   The Obama Administration reverses an earlier commitment to release photos documenting acts of torture.

August 2009   Attorney General Eric Holder opens an investigation into CIA interrogation practices that went beyond the scope of permitted interrogation techniques.

November 4, 2009   Twenty-two CIA agents are convicted in absentia in Milan, Italy for violations of Italian and international law with regard to acts of torture as a result of the practice of "extraordinary rendition".

November 13, 2009   AG Holder announces the intention to move those scheduled to face trial before military commissions in Guantánamo to the jurisdiction of the Federal District Court for the Southern District of New York. The announcement causes a political firestorm surrounding the venue and process, which as of April 2010 has yet to be settled.

December 15, 2009   The Obama Administration announces a plan to purchase a state correctional facility in Thompson, Illinois and transfer the remaining detainees at Guantánamo to it. The purchase of the facility and transfer of detainees to U.S. soil continues to face substantial political opposition, and as of February 2010, 189 detainees remain at Guantánamo.

January 2010

Susan J. Crawford, Convening Authority over the Military Commissions at Guantánamo, admits in the *Washington Post* that Al-Qahtani could not be tried because his interrogations rose to the level of torture.

February 20, 2010

The DOJ's Office of Professional Responsibility issues its final report on allegations of professional misconduct by Yoo and Bybee, concluding that the legal opinions they produced were simply "poor judgment".

INTRODUCTION

> *Where is the world to save us from torture?*
> *Where is the world to save us from the fire and sadness?*
> *Where is the world to save the hunger strikers?*[*]
> – Adnan Al-Jallil Abdelrahman,
> Guantánamo Bay Detainee

> *Take my blood.*
> *Take my death shroud and*
> *The remnants of my body.*
> *Take photographs of my corpse at the grave, lonely.*

> *Send them to the world,*
> *To the judges and*
> *To the people of conscience,*
> *Send them to the principled men and the fair-minded.*

> *And, let them bear the guilt burden, before the world,*
> *Of this innocent soul.*
> *Let them bear the burden, before their children and before history,*
> *Of this wasted, sinless soul,*
> *Of this soul which has suffered at the hands of the "protectors of peace"*[**]
> – Jumah Al-Dossari
> Guantánamo Bay Detainee

The world's most egregious institutionalized human rights abuses since the beginning of the twentieth century have occurred at the hands of tyrannical regimes whose abuses of power occurred in a social context characterized by some popular support, and by the indifference and apathy of the many who could

---

[*] POEMS FROM GUANTÁNAMO: THE DETAINEES SPEAK (Marc Falkoff ed. 2007). Adnan is a Yemeni national who was captured by Pakistani forces in Afghanistan and handed over to the U.S. military for a $5,000 bounty. Adnan had been fleeing the conflict in Afghanistan after having traveled there for medical reasons. When asked at Guantánamo if he was a member of al-Qaeda, he became confused, thinking the interrogators meant if he was from Qaeda, a small village in Yemen. *See* Marc Falkoff, *This is To Whom it May Concern: A Guantánamo Narrative*, 1 DEPAUL J. SOCIAL JUSTICE 153 (2008).

[**] Jumah Al-Dossari, *Death Poem*. Al-Dossari is a 33-year old Bahraini national, father of a young daughter, who has been held at Guantánamo for over five years and in solitary confinement since 2003. According to the U.S. military, he has tried to kill himself twelve times.

have opposed them. History reveals that these regimes orchestrated the execution of abuses by compartmentalizing the roles of different governmental institutions and by manipulating the institutionalized systems of hierarchical control such as military, paramilitary, police and other public organizations. At the same time, these regimes conditioned public opinion by enhancing security threats, creating or heightening fear, and by objectifying or sub-humanizing those whom they identified as the real or perceived source of threats. The institutionalization of torture by the U.S. under the Bush Administration between 2001 and 2008, in violation of the Constitution and laws of the U.S., as well as in violation of international law, had some of these characteristics. The torture policy developed by the Bush Administration emerges clearly when the puzzle pieces are put together.[1] They include actions and influences emanating from the White House, the Department of Defense (DOD), and the Department of Justice (DOJ).

The Bush Administration developed a policy of institutionalized torture, euphemistically referred to as "enhanced interrogation," and by a practice called "extraordinary rendition." As more pieces of the puzzle are discovered, the emerging picture is more likely to be that of a hub-like conspiracy whereby the center radiates its influence out through the wheel's spokes. At the center of that wheel was Vice President Cheney and government lawyers whose influence and actions radiated the policy outward to DOJ through the Office of the General Counsel, DOD, and the White House's Office of Legal Counsel. The policy further continued to radiate outward via a legal trickle-down effect enhanced by military and civilian command influence.

As this book and others document, patterns of interrogation and rendition practice by different arms of the government reveal a policy designed to produce intelligence by means of information-gathering techniques which include torture. It started from the premise that the U.S. is not necessarily bound by international law, and even when it chooses to comply, international law could be redefined to suit the Administration's purposes. The scenario is reminiscent of Lewis Carroll's Alice in Wonderland in 1871: "'When I use a word,' Humpty Dumpty said, in a rather scornful tone, 'it means just what I chose it to mean – neither more nor less.' 'The question is,' said Alice, 'whether you can make words mean so many different things.'"[2] The answer to that question by the Bush Administration's legal experts is yes.

The Bush Administration redefined the prohibition against torture and other cruel and unusual treatment, and evaded the applicability of the Geneva Conventions and the CAT. When the Administration coined the benign sounding term, "enhanced interrogation" techniques in support of its attempt to wage a successful "war on terror," it echoed similar terminology coined by the

---

[1]   *See* Scott Horton, *State of Exception: Bush's War on the Rule of Law*, HARPER'S MAGAZINE (July 2007).

[2]   THE ANNOTATED ALICE: THE DEFINITIVE EDITION 213 (Martin Gardner ed., 2000).

Gestapo in 1937: *verschärfte Vernehmung* ("sharpened interrogation").[3] The same words, outlining the same formula, were used for the same purposes in two different contexts – a dictatorship and a democracy. If nothing else, this shows how simple it is to move from the latter to the former.

A close examination of what occurred reveals a policy concealed under different labels, and widespread and systematic practices that could not have been what some referred to as the work of "a few bad apples."[4] What happened in Guantánamo Bay, Afghanistan, Iraq, and as part of CIA "extraordinary rendition" practices and "black sites" (secret prisons located in different countries), is a pattern of illegal practices that clearly reflect a policy – one without which the practices could not have taken place, at least not with so many similarities, at so many levels, involving so many people, and at so many different times and places.

This book examines the policy of the Bush Administration on the adoption of techniques under the cover of an elastic definition of permissible physical and psychological harm during interrogation, which amounts to torture. Part of that governmental policy includes a pattern of cover-up, concealment, and obfuscation whose apparent design was to create a maze of legal memoranda, including Presidential Executive Orders concerning interrogation methods by the CIA and military. To its credit, the FBI did not partake in these practices, and many in the military opposed them as well.[5]

Despite the widespread compartmentalization of various memoranda, decisions, and authorizations, in particular by the Office of the President's Counsel in the White House, the Office of General Counsel of the DOJ, the Office of the Secretary of Defense, the Deputy Secretary of Defense, and the Under-Secretary of Defense for Policy, the combined actions reveal a coordinated effort between the White House, DOD, and DOJ. Each element of the policy, when combined with others, takes the shape of a conspiracy that violates the Uniform Code of Military Justice (UCMJ)[6] and a number of Title 18 crimes including murder, torture, assault, manslaughter, sexual abuse, obstruction of justice, as well as violations under the Racketeer Influenced and Corrupt Organizations

---

[3] *See* Andrew Sullivan, *How the Nazis Defended "Enhanced Interrogation"*, THE ATLANTIC (June 2007).

[4] *See* Carolyn Patty Blum, Lisa Magarrell, & Marieke Wierda, *Prosecuting Abuses of Detainees in U.S. Counter-terrorism Operations* (International Center for Transitional Justice, Nov. 2009), at 21–23.

[5] For a decription of the early days of Guantánamo which identified those who opposed it and those who expressed their perpelexities, see KAREN J. GREENBERG, THE LEAST WORST PLACE: GUANTANAMO'S FIRST 100 DAYS (2009).

[6] Uniform Code of Military Justice, 10 U.S.C. §§801–941 (2000). *See also* John Warner National Defense Authorization Act for Fiscal Year 2007, Pub. L. 109–364 (amending the UCMJ to include persons supporting the armed forces during a "declared war or a contingency operation").

(RICO) Act.[7] The Bush Administration's policy also resulted in the deprivation of the civil rights of U.S. citizens and others, which are protected under the Fourth, Fifth, Sixth, and Eighth Amendments.[8] Moreover, it should be noted that torture is an international crime under the law of armed conflict which makes it a war crime,[9] as well as under the CAT.[10] These international crimes are not subject to statutes of limitations,[11] and can be subject to prosecution by universal jurisdiction in other countries.[12] The U.S. has ratified these conventions and is bound by their obligations, even though some senior Bush Administration lawyers and others were quick to argue that international law is not necessarily binding on the U.S. if it went against its proclaimed sovereign interests.[13]

As it pursued its new policy, the Bush Administration developed a number of preventive responses in an attempt to avoid responsibility for potential charges relating to torture. These included amending the War Crimes Act of 1996 to limit the risk of criminal prosecution of political appointees, CIA officers, and former military personnel;[14] transferring blame onto other governments via "extraordinary rendition"; using secret CIA operated "black sites" in other countries to conceal torture and claim ignorance of it (leaving open the prospects of potentially blaming individual CIA officers); categorizing detainees as

---

[7]   Title 18 U.S.C. §§1111–1122, homicide, including manslaughter; §§2340, 2340A, torture; §§111–119, assault; §§2241–48, sexual abuse; §§1501–1521, obstruction of justice; §§1961–68, Racketeer Influenced and Corrupt Organizations.

[8]   U.S. Const. Amends. V, VI, and VIII.

[9]   *See* Geneva Convention II Aug. 12, 1949, 6 U.S.T. 3217, 75 U.N.T.S. 85; Geneva Convention III Aug. 12, 1949, 6 U.S.T. 3316, 75 U.N.T.S. 135; and Geneva Convention IV, Aug. 12, 1949, 6 U.S.T. 3516, 75 U.N.T.S. 287. *See* Yves Sandoz, *Penal Aspects of International Humanitarian Law, in* 1 International Criminal Law 293 (M. Cherif Bassiouni ed., 3d ed. 2008).

[10]   CAT, Dec. 10, 1984, 1465 U.N.T.S. 85. For a detailed commentary on the convention, see J. Herman Burgers & Hans Danelius, The United Nations Convention Against Torture (1988); José L. de la Cuesta Arzamendi, El Delito de Tortura (1990); Manfred Nowak & Elizabeth McArthur, The United Nations Convention against Torture: A Commentary (2008).

[11]   *See* Convention on the Non-Applicability of Statutory Limitations to War Crimes and Crimes Against Humanity, U.N. Doc. A/7218 (1968), *entered into force* Nov. 11, 1970. *See also* Christine Van den Wyngaert, *War Crimes, Genocide and Crimes Against Humanity – Are States Taking National Prosecutions Seriously?, in* 3 International Criminal Law 235 (M. Cherif Bassiouni ed., 3d ed. 2008).

[12]   *See infra* Chapter 4, section 4.6, *Criminal Responsibility for Acts Performed as Part of the "Extraordinary Rendition" Program. See also* Kai Ambos, *Prosecuting Guantánamo in Europe: Can and Shall the Masterminds of the "Torture Memos" be Held Criminally Responsible on the Basis of Universal Jurisdiction?*, 42 Case W. Res. J. Int'l L. 405 (2009). On universal jurisdiction generally, see M. Cherif Bassiouni, *The History of Universal Jurisdiction and Its Place in International Law, in* Universal Jurisdiction: National Courts and the Prosecution of Serious Crimes Under International Law (Stephen Macedo, ed. 2004).

[13]   *See* Jack Goldsmith, The Limits of International Law (2005); Eric A. Posner, *Do States Have a Moral Obligation to Obey International Law?*, 55 Stan. L. Rev. 1901 (2003).

[14]   The Military Commissions Act of 2006, Pub. L. 103–366 §6(b)(2006). *See* R. Jeffrey Smith, *War Crimes Act Changes Would Reduce Threat of Prosecution*, Wash. Post, Aug. 9 2006. For a discussion of the original legislation, see Mark S. Zaid, *The U.S. War Crimes Act of 1996, in* 3 International Criminal Law 407 (M. Cherif Bassiouni ed., 3d ed. 2008).

"unlawful enemy combatants"; and using private contractors in interrogations outside the U.S. These practices were designed to achieve what in political terms is called "plausible deniability" to avoid possible criminal charges that must be proven beyond a reasonable doubt. Senior officials were thus placed in a position of invoking "plausible deniability" as an argument to overcome the standard of proof in criminal cases. The same argument would probably not extend to lesser ranking persons, who would, for all practical purposes, take the fall for their superiors, both civilian and military. Cumulatively, these efforts can be seen as evidence that the Bush Administration was aware of its officials' legal vulnerabilities for unlawful action.

The Bush Administration tended to keep its policy and practices secret until it was forced to disclose them after certain practices became public knowledge. When President Bush authorized the establishment of Camp Delta at Guantánamo Bay, he concluded that the Geneva Conventions did not apply to "unlawful enemy combatants" seized in Afghanistan and elsewhere; approved the use of "enhanced interrogation" techniques; issued an Executive Order that bypassed Congress; and unilaterally established a new parallel system of justice to deal with "unlawful enemy combatants" through Military Commissions.[15] Once these actions and the various memoranda discussed below are put together, the Bush Administration's torture policy becomes clearer.

These measures, adopted towards the end of 2001 or soon thereafter, were supplemented by others, such as the interrogation regulations issued by Secretary of Defense Donald Rumsfeld and the procedures that he issued in connection with the Military Commissions at Guantánamo.[16] Subsequently, President Bush, Vice President Cheney, and Secretary Rumsfeld made several official statements about how U.S. interrogators needed to obtain results to spare the country from another attack like 9/11. These orders and statements created a top-down command influence which encouraged or condoned subordinates' actions who engaged in harsh interrogation techniques bordering on, and in some cases constituting, torture. These practices have been publicly reported, deplored, and denounced by inter-governmental organizations (IGOs) and non-governmental

---

[15] Military Order of Nov. 13, 2001, Detention, Treatment, and Trial of Certain Non-Citizens in the War Against Terrorism, 66 Fed. Reg. 57,833 (Nov. 16, 2001). *See also* Jordan J. Paust, *War and Enemy Status After 9/11: Attacks on the Laws of War*, 28 YALE J. INT'L L. 325 (2003); Steven W. Becker, *"Mirror, Mirror on the Wall…": Assessing the Aftermath of September 11th*, 37 VAL. U. L. REV. 563, 580–92 (2003), describing President Bush's Military Order in detail and arguing that it is *ultra vires* because it was issued without Congress first formally declaring war. The Order was patterned after a proclamation/military order by President Franklin D. Roosevelt in 1942 concerning the trial by a military commission of Nazi agents. *See however* Curtis A. Bradley, *The Military Commissions Act, Habeas Corpus, and the Geneva Conventions*, 101 AM. J. INT'L L. 322, 323–24 (April 2007), *discussing Ex parte* Quirin, 317 U.S. 1 (1942); Proclamation No. 2561, 7 Fed. Reg. 5101 (July 7, 1942).

[16] *See* Memorandum from Donald Rumsfeld, Secretary of Defense to James T. Hill, Commander of the U.S. Southern Command, Counter-Resistance Techniques in the War on Terrorism (Apr. 16, 2003).

organizations (NGOs) such as the United Nations (UN), the European Parliament, the International Committee of the Red Cross (ICRC), Human Rights Watch, Human Rights First, Amnesty International, and the American Civil Liberties Union (ACLU);[17] as well as by some of the military's Judge Advocates General and the U.S. Assistant Secretary of the Navy,[18] who opposed them as violating the Constitution, U.S. laws in Title 10 and Title 18 U.S. Code, international humanitarian law (IHL), and the CAT. These practices resulted in the estimated deaths of over 100 detainees in U.S. custody,[19] and possibly thousands of persons who may have been subjected to torture during interrogation at U.S.-controlled detention facilities and at foreign detention facilities operated by officials acting on behalf of the U.S.[20]

---

[17] *See e.g.,* U.N. High Commissioner for Human Rights, *Human Rights, Terrorism and Counter-terrorism* (Fact Sheet No. 32, July 2008); Council of Europe, Res. 1539 (2007); Committee Against Torture, *Consideration of Reports Submitted by State Parties under Article 19 of the Convention, Conclusions and Recommendations of the Committee against Torture: United States of America,* CAT/C/USA/CO2 (May 18, 2006) [hereinafter Committee Response]; ECOSOC, Committee on Human Rights, *Situation of Detainees at Guantánamo Bay,* U.N. Doc E/CN.4/2006/120 (Feb. 15, 2006) (prepared by Leila Zerrougui et al.); Hina Shamsi, *Command's Responsibility: Detainee Deaths in U.S. Custody in Iraq and Afghanistan* (Human Rights First, Feb. 2006); Council of Europe Parliamentary Assembly, Committee on Legal Affairs and Human Rights, *Alleged Secret Detentions in Council of Europe Member States* (Jan. 22, 2006); European Parliamentary Assembly, Report from the Commission on Legal Affairs & Human Rights, *Lawfulness of Detentions by the United States in Guantánamo Bay,* Doc. No. 10497 (2005); U.N. Comm. Against Torture, *Consideration of Reports Submitted by State Parties Under Article 19 of the Convention, Second Periodic Reports of States Parties Due in 1999,* U.N. Doc. CAT/C/48/Add.3 (June 29, 2005) [hereinafter *Article 19 Reports*]; International Committee of the Red Cross, *Report of the ICRC on the Treatment by the Coalition Forces of Prisoners of War and Other Protected Persons by the Geneva Convention in Iraq During Arrest, Internment, and Interrogation* (Feb. 2004).

[18] *See, e.g.,* Navy General Counsel Alberto Mora's prepared statement for the June 17, 2008 hearings on the treatment of detainees held by the Senate Committee on Armed Services, where he says "[O]ur Nation's policy decision to use so-called 'harsh' interrogation techniques during the War on Terror was a mistake of massive proportions. ...The net effect of this policy of cruelty has been to weaken our defenses, not to strengthen them, and has been greatly contrary to our national interest." Statement of Alberto J. Mora to the Senate Committee on Armed Services, Hearing on the Treatment of Detainees in U.S. Custody, June 17, 2008.

[19] Different numbers have apeared in various media sources. The uncertainty derives from the failure of the DOD to issue non-obfuscatory reports. *See* Glenn Greenwald, *The Suppressed Fact: Deaths by U.S. Torture,* SALON.COM, Jun. 30, 2009, reporting on research undertaken by John Sifton of Human Rights Watch, published online as *The Bush Administration Homicides,* THEDAILYBEAST.COM, May 5, 2009. For a detailed report on deaths in custody by 2006, see Shamsi, *Command's Responsibility, supra* note 17, at 103.

[20] FINAL REPORT OF THE INDEPENDENT PANEL TO REVIEW DOD DETENTION OPERATIONS (Aug. 2004). It was reported by the Independent Panel to Review Department of Defense Detention Operations in 2004 that at least 50,000 persons had been detained at Guantánamo and sites in Afghanistan and Iraq. The Independent Panel further reported Rumsfeld's "augmented techniques for Guantánamo migrated to Afghanistan and Iraq." *See also* JORDAN J. PAUST, BEYOND THE LAW: THE BUSH ADMINISTRATION'S UNLAWFUL RESPONSES IN THE "WAR" ON TERROR 17 (2007).

At first, media sources reported this torture with eyewitness accounts.[21] These reports were followed by military investigations resulting in published and unpublished reports, documents released under the Freedom of Information Act,[22] autopsy reports, information gathered from courts martial, officers' statements and reports, and finally, by the Senate Armed Services Committee inquiry into the treatment of U.S. detainees.[23] These sources offer some information on what may have taken place. However, to date, there have been no known prosecutions of officers or other high-ranking officials for torture.[24]

While the acts of torture were happening, the Bush Administration, pursuant to Article 19 of the CAT, submitted on June 29, 2005 a report to the Committee Against Torture, established by the CAT's Article 17. In that report, the U.S. expressed its total conformity with the provisions of the Convention.[25] It claimed, among other things, that:

> In fighting terrorism, the U.S. remains committed to respecting the rule of law, including the U.S. Constitution, federal statutes, and international treaty obligations, including the Torture Convention.[26]

---

[21] *See* Lila Rajiva, The Language of Empire: Abu Ghraib and the American Media 11–19, 35–54 (2005); Erik Saar & Viveca Novak, Inside the Wire: A Military Intelligence Soldier's Eyewitness Account of Life at Guantánamo (2005); Mark Danner, Torture and Truth: America, Abu Ghraib, and the War on Terror (2004); Seymour M. Hersh, Chain of Command: The Road from 9/11 to Abu Ghraib (2004).

[22] Over 100,000 pages of documents related to the Bush Administration's torture policy have been released through a FOIA litigation undertaken by the American Civil Liberties Union (ACLU). All of these documents are availabe online at www.aclu.org/accountability/released.html (last visited Feb. 16, 2010). Both the ACLU and the Center for Constitutional Rights in New York have done an admirable job of representing the victims of torture and pursuing those responsible for these criminal violations through the U.S. courts.

[23] *See* Report of the Committee on Armed Services, U.S. Senate, *Inquiry into the Treatment of Detainees in U.S. Custody* (Nov. 20, 2008); Department of Defense, Article 15–6 Investigation of CJSOTF-AP and 5th SF Group Detention Operations (Abu Ghraib) by BG Richard P. Formica, Investigating Officer, Nov. 8, 2004 (declassified June 7, 2006); Federal Bureau of Investigation, Guantánamo Bay Inquiry (a survey of 493 FBI personnel who were asked whether they observed aggressive mistreatment, interrogations or interview techniques), *available at* http://foia.fbi.gov/guantanamo/122106.htm (last visited January 25, 2010); Interview by Majorie Cohn with Brig. Gen. Janis Karpinski, truthout.org, Aug. 3, 2005; Army Inspector General, *Detainee Operations Inspections* (July 21, 2004); Maj. Gen. Geoffrey D. Miller, *Assessment of DOD Counter-terrorism Interrogation and Detention Operations in Iraq* (Sept. 2003); Anthony R. Jones & George R. Fay, *Investigation of Intelligence Activities at Abu Ghraib* (2004); Inspector Gen., U.S. Dep't of the Army, *Detainee Operations Inspection, The Mikolashek Report* (July 21, 2004); Antonio M. Taguba, Major Gen., U.S. Dep't of the Army, *Article 15–6 Investigation of the 800th Military Police Brigade* (2004); Donald J. Ryder, *Report on Detention and Corrections Operations in Iraq* (Nov. 2003); James R. Schlesinger, *U.S. Dep't of Defense, Final Report of the Independent Panel to Review DOD Detention Operations 80* (2004).

[24] *See* Carolyn Patty Blum, Lisa Magarell & Marieke Wierda, *Prosecuting Abuses of Detainees in U.S. Counter-terrorism Operations* (International Center for Transitional Justice, Nov. 2009), at 21–24.

[25] *Article 19 Reports, supra* note 17.

[26] *Id.* at para. 4.

The report continued:

> The President of the United States has made clear that the United States stands against and will not tolerate torture under any circumstances… [T]he President confirmed the continued importance of these protections and of U.S. obligations under the Torture Convention, stating:

> [T]he United States reaffirms its commitment to the worldwide elimination of torture… To help fulfill this commitment, the U.S. has joined 135 other nations in ratifying the Convention Against Torture and Other Cruel, Inhuman or Degrading Treatment or Punishment. America stands against and will not tolerate torture. We will investigate and prosecute all acts of torture and undertake to prevent other cruel and unusual punishment in all territory under our jurisdiction…[27]

The report went on to further emphasize that the U.S. affirmed its obligations under the CAT, as well as its applicability to U.S. Armed Forces in Afghanistan and Guantánamo Bay. It reiterated U.S. legal obligations under the Constitution and laws of the U.S., including the need to apply both the CAT and U.S. legislation extraterritorially, as well as investigating and prosecuting violations.[28]

The Committee Against Torture responded by recommending the closure of the Guantánamo Bay prison,[29] a move which former Secretary of State Colin Powell supported.[30] The closure of the Guantánamo Bay, Bagram, and Abu Ghraib prisons was recommended by many who also recommended an end to the CIA's "extraordinary rendition" program and the "black sites" operations.[31] The Bush Administration refused to follow these recommendations.

Clearly, the Bush Administration's CAT report cited above was either a deliberate attempt to mislead the Committee Against Torture (as well as its 135

---

[27] *Id.* at para. 5 (citing George W. Bush, Statement on the United Nations International Day in Support of Victims of Torture (June 26, 2004)).

[28] *Id.* at para. 19, 51.

[29] Committee Response, *supra* note 17, at 6, para. 22, 24, stating "The [United States] should rescind any interrogation technique, including methods involving sexual humiliation, 'waterboarding,' 'short shackling' and using dogs to induce fear, that constitutes torture or cruel, inhuman or degrading treatment or punishment, in all places of detention under its de facto effective control, in order to comply with… the Convention.".

[30] *Colin Powell says Guantánamo Should be Closed*, REUTERS, June 10, 2007. *See also* John R. Crook, *Contemporary Practice of the United States Relating to International Law* 101 AM. J. INT'L L. 487, 488 (April 2007), discussing the desire to close Guantánamo by Secretary Gates and Secretary Rice; Thom Shanker & David E. Sander, *New to Pentagon, Gates Argued for Closing Guantánamo Prison*, N.Y. TIMES, Mar. 23, 2007, at A1.

[31] *See infra* Chapter 4, *The Practice of "Extraordinary Rendition" and the Use of "Black Sites"*. As of January 2010, the detention center at the Bagram Air Base in Afghanistan remains open, with no indication of its closure from the Obama Administration. *See* Alissa J. Rubin & Sangar Rahimi, *Bagram Detainees Named by U.S.*, N.Y. TIMES, Jan. 17, 2010; Editorial, *A Bagram Reckoning*, N.Y. TIMES, Jan. 18, 2010.

member states), or else it represented a case of political schizophrenia in which one side of the Administration told the world that it was in conformity with its international obligations, while the other side acted in the opposite. In the same vein, President Bush consistently claimed that his Administration did not engage in torture. He was either misinformed or he was misrepresenting the facts.[32]

There are many questions we must now ask ourselves. How did the U.S. – a nation whose Constitution is designed to protect human rights and a leader in international human rights protection since World War II – come to institutionalize torture? How is it that our system of government, offering itself as a model for the rule of law, lost its ability to maintain checks and balances through Congress and the judiciary in effective oversight of abuses of law by the Executive branch? Why is it that Americans have remained so complacent against the commission of crimes under both U.S. and international law?[33] Why have state bar associations not taken disciplinary measures against their government-employed members for a breach of their ethical obligations?[34]

The answers are not very different than those given in similar situations by regimes that the U.S. in decades past considered violators of human rights, namely: Congress was timid, the judiciary was overly restrained, the public was indifferent, the bar associations were silent, the media was largely compliant, and many of those in power agreed with or condoned these policies, or simply looked the other way to preserve their careers.

The rule of law is the difference between barbarism and civilization. Nations which uphold the rule of law in times of crisis attain a higher standing among their counterparts, in contrast to mighty nations that rely on force as an expression of their national character. The American legal system benefited from the historic struggle of the English people for the supremacy of the rule of law over the absolute powers of the monarchy. That struggle for the rule of law and due process in England was brought to the U.S. by the settlers of the Colonies. After the Declaration of Independence in 1776 and the adoption of the Constitution in 1787, the American legal system strived for fairness and fundamental justice, which took over two hundred years to mature. The growth and development of this system was at times painful and arduous, as seen during

---

[32] *See* Richard Benedetto, *Bush Defends Interrogation Tactics: 'We do not torture'*, USA Today, Nov. 11, 2005.

[33] On the question of the state of American values in foreign affairs, see Jimmy Carter, Our Endangered Values: America's Moral Crisis (2005). *See also* M. Cherif Bassiouni, *Great Nations and Torture*, in The Torture Debate in America 256 (Karen J. Greenberg ed., 2006); Chalmers Johnson, The Sorrows of Empire: Militarism, Secrecy, and the End of the Republic (2004); David Harvey, The New Imperialism (2003).

[34] The American Bar Association has reported on torture and other abuses surrounding it, but has brought no sanctions or even investigations against any lawyer. *See* the American Bar Association Report to the House of Delegates (2004) and American Bar Association Recommendations (Adopted Aug. 13–14, 2007), *infra* Appendix 4.

the period of slavery and subsequently up to the 1900s, but it was irreversible until the Bush Administration.

The Bush Administration needed to insulate its torture policy from judicial scrutiny. This required curtailing access to justice by legislation suspending federal habeas corpus jurisdiction, thereby denying access to a determination of the legality of a person's arrest.[35] This had not occurred since the Civil War, when President Abraham Lincoln briefly suspended habeas corpus in 1863. Another tactic used by the Bush Administration was curtailing the right to counsel, even though this right is guaranteed by the Sixth Amendment and by international treaties subscribed to by the U.S.[36] Administrative measures against lawyers' ability to represent their clients at Guantánamo and elsewhere were unprecedented abridgments of the right to counsel, the worst this country has witnessed since its independence in 1776.[37] We seem to have forgotten an important historic legal moment from March 1770, when with quiet and sober dignity, John Adams defended British Captain Preston and other soldiers for what was called the Boston Massacre, where five colonists were killed and six injured when fired upon by a British unit facing American Patriots who opposed the Townshend Act taxing imports. Adams stood up for the principle that every accused is entitled to a fair trial. More significantly, a jury of the people of Boston acquitted Captain Preston and others, and all but two of the British men were found guilty of manslaughter. In his diary Adams states about this case: "[It] procured me Anxiety, and Obloquy enough. It was, however, on of the most gallant, generous, manly and disinterested Actions of my whole Life, and one of the best pieces of Service I ever rendered my Country."[38]

In one of his many articles about the Bush Administration's attacks upon the rule of law, attorney Scott Horton notes that curtailing the right to legal representation is a technique used by dictatorships and points to the deliberate manner in which Nazi Germany and the U.S.S.R. employed the technique to achieve the ends of their regimes.[39] For example, the ideas of German theorist Carl Schmitt, a conservative who longed for the restoration of the authoritarian style of Wilhelmine Germany, were used to exile prominent members of Weimar

---

[35] *See* the U.S. Military Commissions Act of 2006 [hereinafter MCA] Pub. L. 109–3666, 120 Stat. 2600. The U.S. Supreme Court has recently struck down the MCA to extent that it infringes upon a detainee's right to habeas corpus. *See* Boumediene v. Bush, 128 S. Ct. 2229 (2008).

[36] *See e.g.,* American Convention on Human Rights, *adopted* Nov. 22, 1969, 1144 U.N.T.S. 123.

[37] *See* Scott Horton, *State of Exception: Bush's War on the Rule of Law*, HARPER'S MAGAZINE (July 2007).

[38] *See* DAVID MCCULLOUGH, JOHN ADAMS (2001), at 68. The U.S. has stood up for fair trials at many times of crisis. *See* OREN GROSS & FIONNUALA NI AOLAIN, LAW IN TIMES OF CRISIS: EMERGENCY POWERS IN THEORY AND PRACTICE (2006). Justice Robert Jackson was one of the champions of the principle of the rule of law principle after World War II, arguing that it was not enough to achieve justice, but also that it is perceived that justice is being done. *See* John Q. Barrett, *The Nuremberg Roles of Justice Robert Jackson*, 512 WASH. U. GLOBE S. REV. 511 (2007).

[39] *Id.*

Germany's defense bar. "Schmitt was a convinced enemy of the liberal democratic principles embodied by the Weimar Constitution that was adopted after the close of World War I."[40] Horton sees a parallel between the theories of Schmitt that the Nazis put in effect and the Bush Administration's policy of "lawfare," meaning war against the lawyers. He also points out that the same policy was carried out during the Great Purge of the 1930s under Stalin, which was choreographed by Andrei Vishinsky.[41] The parallels between these practices and what was done under the Bush Administration are chilling.

In 1873, Émile Zola, a French journalist, published a book entitled *J'Accuse*. In it he decried the anti-Semitism that existed in the French Army and its prosecution and conviction of Major Alfred Dreyfus for the crime of treason which he did not commit. This case became the epitome of injustice, caused by a system which had lost its moral compass. The works of a few like Marjorie Cohn, David Cole, Barton Gellman, Karen Greenberg, Seymour Hersh, Scott Horton, Joseph Margulies, Jane Mayer, Barbara Olshansky, Jordan Paust, Philippe Sands and others, have in some ways become the American *J'accuse* of our time.[42] This book merely adds its contribution to the increasing denunciation of the abuses of our Constitution and laws and our international legal obligations which are described below.

The chapters that follow open with a discussion of international laws against torture and the historic association of the U.S. with those laws, as well as specific U.S. laws prohibiting torture and discusses possible theories of liability for actors in the Bush Administration. Because the so-called "enhanced interrogation" techniques were at the center of the policy and practices of torture, Chapter 2 identifies the specific interrogation techniques that were known to have been used in the Bush Administration's war on terror. The stories of several detainees are included in this chapter which underline just how inhuman these techniques were. Chapter 3 then outlines the torture-enabling policy under which the

---

[40] *Id.* at 80.

[41] *Id.* at 89, note 8.

[42] These writers have been diligent over the past several years in their reportage of these issues, and have published many books and articles. Their major works include: DAVID COLE, ENEMY ALIENS: DOUBLE STANDARDS AND CONSTITUTIONAL FREEDOMS IN THE WAR ON TERRORISM (2003); THE TORTURE PAPERS: THE ROAD TO ABU GHRAIB (Karen J. Greenburg & Joshua L. Dratel eds., 2005); THE TORTURE DEBATE IN AMERICA (Karen J. Greenberg ed., 2006); JOSEPH MARGULIES, GUANTÁNAMO AND THE ABUSE OF PRESIDENTIAL POWER (2006); JORDAN J. PAUST, BEYOND THE LAW: THE BUSH ADMINISTRATION'S UNLAWFUL RESPONSES IN THE "WAR" ON TERROR (2007); MARJORIE COHN, COWBOY REPUBLIC: SIX WAYS THE BUSH GANG HAS DEFIED THE LAW (2007); BARBARA OLSHANSKY, DEMOCRACY DETAINED: SECRET UNCONSTITUTIONAL PRACTICES IN THE U.S. WAR ON TERROR (2007); PHILIPPE SANDS, TORTURE TEAM: RUMSFELD'S MEMO AND THE BETRAYAL OF AMERICAN VALUES (2008); JANE MAYER, THE DARK SIDE: THE INSIDE STORY OF HOW THE WAR ON TERROR TURNED INTO A WAR ON AMERICAN IDEALS (2008); BARTON GELLMAN, ANGLER: THE CHENEY VICE PRESIDENCY (2008); THE ENEMY COMBATANT PAPERS: AMERICAN JUSTICE, THE COURTS, AND THE WAR ON TERROR (Karen J. Greenberg & Joshua Dratel eds., 2008).

"enhanced interrogation" techniques were allowed to happen. It is fairly obvious that the Bush Administration knew it was violating laws; this is one of the reasons why due process was curtailed, as this chapter demonstrates. Chapter 4 covers the practice of the CIA during the Bush Administration of "extraordinary rendition" and use of "black sites," and it includes an analysis of U.S. and international laws that were violated through this coordinated program of extradition. Chapter 5 reviews both the criminal and ethical responsibility of those who allowed the policy and practices of torture to occur. The complicity of Congress in its failure to challenge suspected torture practices is questioned, as well as the role of private contractors. Most importantly, however, after outlining the precedents established by post-World War II war crimes prosecutions, the chapter examines the ethical obligations of professionals – specifically medical and legal practitioners – and asks why the relevant professional associations failed to enforce their ethical codes when violations were evident. Lastly, Chapter 6 reviews the actions of the Obama Administration, and in which ways it has and has not worked to repair the dangerous and un-American policies of the Bush Administration

CHAPTER 1

THE PROHIBITION OF TORTURE UNDER INTERNATIONAL AND UNITED STATES LAW

*There have been, and are now, certain foreign nations with governments…
which convict individuals with testimony obtained by police
organizations possessed of an unrestrained power to seize persons
suspected of crimes against the state, hold them in secret custody,
and wring from them confessions by physical or mental torture.
So long as the Constitution remains the basic law of our Republic,
America will not have that kind of government.*[*]
– U.S. Supreme Court Justice Hugo Black, 1946

1.1. INTRODUCTION

For over half a century, the United States led the effort to prohibit torture under international law. It was the most active supporter in the drafting and adoption of the Universal Declaration of Human Rights (UDHR) in 1948, whose Article 5 contains a prohibition against "cruel, inhuman or degrading treatment or punishment."[1] The UDHR was subsequently recognized as part of customary international law.[2] The U.S. then led the efforts at the United Nations for the adoption in 1966 of the International Covenant on Civil and Political Rights (ICCPR), whose Article 7 contains the same prohibition as that included in Article 5 of the UDHR.[3] Finally, the U.S. was a strong supporter of the CAT, which was adopted by the United Nations in 1984.[4] During the period of time

---

[*] Ashcraft v. State of Tennessee, 327 U.S. 274 (1946).

[1] Universal Declaration of Human Rights, art. 5, G.A. Res. 217A, at 71, U.N. GAOR, 3d Sess., 1st plen. mtg., U.N. Doc. H/810 (Dec. 12, 1948).

[2] *See generally* David Weissbrodt & Connie de la Varga, International Human Rights Law: An Introduction (2007); Henry J. Steiner & Philip Alston, International Human Rights in Context (2007).

[3] International Covenant on Civil and Political Rights, art. 7, Dec. 19, 1966, 999 U.N.T.S. 171.

[4] CAT, Dec. 10, 1984, 1465 U.N.T.S. 85. For a detailed commentary on the convention, see J. Herman Burgers & Hans Danelius, The United Nations Convention Against Torture (1988); Manfred Nowak & Elizabeth McArthur, The United Nations

between the UDHR in 1948 and the CAT in 1984, the U.S. was at the forefront of international efforts to eliminate the practice of torture in countries whose governments resorted to it, and it consistently denounced such prohibited practices in the Congressionally-mandated Annual Country Reports on Human Rights Practices published by DOS.[5] The U.S. has amply demonstrated over years of practice its opposition to torture and other forms of cruel, inhuman and degrading treatment or punishment. The prohibition of this practice constitutes part of customary international law which is binding upon the U.S. Contrary to what Bush Administration ideologues argued, customary international law – and surely that part of it which has been led by the U.S. and evidenced by its consistent practice – is binding upon the U.S.[6]

Torture is not only proscribed by the CAT; it has long been prohibited under international humanitarian law (IHL), beginning with the 1899 Hague Convention on the Laws and Customs of War on Land[7] and the 1907 Hague Convention on the Laws and Customs of War on Land, which are still in effect to date.[8] Torture has also been a war crime under conventional IHL with its embodiment in the 1929 Geneva Convention Relating to the Prisoners of War,[9] and the Four Geneva Conventions of August 12, 1949,[10] which the U.S. has ratified.[11] The two 1977 Additional Protocols to the Geneva Conventions of

---

CONVENTION AGAINST TORTURE: A COMMENTARY (2008). *See also* JOSÉ L. DE LA CUESTA ARZAMENDI, EL DELITO DE TORTURA (1990). For an understanding of the history leading to the CAT, see *The Prevention and Suppression of Torture*, 48 REVUE INTERNATIONALE DE DROIT PÉNAL (1977). None of these sources were cited by any of the Bush Administration lawyers who opined on the CAT's definition of torture.

[5] The DOS' Bureau of Democracy, Human Rights, and Labor annually submits Country Reports on Human Rights to Congress in compliance with §§116(d) and 502B(b) of the Foreign Assistance Act of 1961 (FAA), as amended, and §504 of the Trade Act of 1974, as amended. They are available at www.state.gov/g/drl/rls/hrrpt/ (last visited Feb. 20, 2010).

[6] *See e.g.*, Jordan J. Paust, *Customary International Law and Human Rights Treates* are *Law of the United States*, 20 MICH. J. INT'L L. 301 (1999). *See also* MICHAEL P. SCHARF & PAUL R. WILLIAMS, SHAPING FOREIGN POLICY IN TIMES OF CRISIS: THE ROLE OF INTERNATIONAL LAW AND THE STATE DEPARTMENT LEGAL ADVISOR (2010), which reviews how important international law was to U.S. foreign policy from the Carter Administration through the Bush Administration, when its importance decidedly took a backseat.

[7] Convention with Respect to the Laws and Customs of War on Land art. 4, July 29, 1899, 32 Stat. 1803, *reprinted in* 1 AM. J. INT'L L. 129 (Supp. 1907).

[8] Convention Respecting the Laws and Customs of War on Land art. 4, Oct. 18, 1907, 36 Stat. 2277, *reprinted in* 2 AM. J. INT'L L. 90 (Supp. 1908) [hereinafter Hague Convention].

[9] Geneva Convention Relative to the Treatment of Prisoners of War art. 2, July 27, 1929 47 Stat. 2021, *reprinted in* 27 AM J. INT'L L. 63 (Supp. 1933).

[10] Geneva I, Aug. 12, 1949, 6 U.S.T. 3114, 75 U.N.T.S. 31; Geneva II, Aug. 12, 1949, 6 U.S.T. 3217, 75 U.N.T.S. 85; Geneva III, Aug. 12, 1949, 6 U.S.T. 3316, 75 U.N.T.S. 135; Geneva IV, Aug. 12, 1949, 6 U.S.T. 3516, 75 U.N.T.S. 287.

[11] Both the Geneva Conventions and the CAT are firmly grounded within the Nuremberg Principles, which were adopted by the UN General Assembly immediately upon the establishment of the United Nations. (G.A. Res. 95 (I), AT 188, U.N. DOC. A/61/00ADD.1 (Dec. 11, 1946)). These principles "...Eschew collective responsibility in favor of individual criminal responsibility; provide that no human being, even a head of state or other responsible

1949[12] have not been ratified by the U.S., parts of which are however recognized by the U.S. as reflecting customary international law.[13]

Furthermore, in December 2002, the U.S. ratified the Optional Protocol to the Convention on the Rights of the Child on the Involvement of Children in Armed Conflict, which obligates state parties to undertake the rehabilitation and special treatment of juveniles detained in the course of armed conflict.[14] The detention and treatment of juveniles at Guantánamo is yet another violation of U.S. obligations under international law.

Torture is an international crime under customary and conventional international law, and its prohibition applies in times of war and in times of peace. Only a cursory review of applicable international law follows as this is amply covered in many writings, including those cited throughout this book.

As discussed below, the U.S. ratified the CAT, with some attached "reservations, declarations, and understandings,"[15] and embodied part of the Convention's obligations in Title 18 U.S.C. §§2340, 2340A definition,[16] and the Torture Victim Protection Act, which provides for a civil remedy.[17] However, other CAT provisions have not yet been included in domestic legislation. As to the four Geneva Conventions of 1949, they were ratified in 1950, but no national implementing legislation has been adopted. The "grave breaches" provisions and

---

government official, is above the law with respect to the most serious crimes of concern to humanity as a whole, such as war crimes, crimes against humanity and the crime of aggressive war; and provide that reliance on internal law is no defense to a crime for which a leader may have responsibility under international law." Leila Nadya Sadat, *Extraordinary Rendition, Torture and Other Nightmares from the War on Terror*, 75 GEO. WASH. L. REV. 1200, 1207 (2007).

[12]   Protocol Additional to the Geneva Conventions of 12 August 1949, and Relating to the Protection of Victims of International Armed Conflicts, June 8, 1977, 1125 U.N.T.S. 3; Protocol Additional to the Geneva Convention of 12 August 1949, and Relating to the Protection of Victims of Non-International Armed Conflicts, June 8, 1977, 1125 U.N.T.S. 609.

[13]   George H. Aldrich, *Prospects for United States Ratification of Additional Protocol I to the 1949 Geneva Conventions*, 85 AM. J. INT'L. L. 1 (1991); David Wippman, *Introduction: Do New Wars Call for New Laws? in* NEW WARS, NEW LAWS? APPLYING THE LAW OF WAR IN 21ST CENTURY CONFLICTS 11 (David Wippman & Matthew Evangelista eds. 2005). Wippman notes that "Protocol I effectively enlarged the category of international armed conflicts by including within its coverage "armed conflicts which peoples are fighting against colonial domination and alien occupation and against racist regimes in the exercise of their right of self-determination" as well as more traditional inter-state conflicts." *Id.* at 16, note 34.

[14]   Optional Protocol to the Convention on the Rights of the Child on the Involvement of Children in Armed Conflicts, G.A. Res. 54/263, Annex I, 54 U.N. GAOR Supp. (No. 49) at 7, U.N. Doc. A/54/49 (2000), *entered into force* Feb. 12, 2002. It is interesting to note that while the U.S. has ratified the Optional Protocol, it has not yet acceded to the Convention on the Rights of the Child itself, which has 193 state parties. For a description of the treatment of juveniles at Guantánamo, see *infra* Chapter 2, section 2.5, *Interrogations of Juveniles*.

[15]   U.S. Reservations, Declarations, and Understandings, Convention Against Torture and Other Cruel, Inhuman or Degrading Treatment or Punishment, Cong. Rec. S17486–01 (daily ed., Oct. 27, 1990).

[16]   18 U.S.C. §2340, 2340A (2000).

[17]   Torture Victim Protection Act, 28 U.S.C. §1350 (2000).

others have been incorporated into the UCMJ and other legislation discussed below.[18] Independent of the above, the U.S. Constitution's Eighth Amendment prohibits "cruel and unusual punishment or treatment," and Title 18 U.S.C. §§2340, 2340A prohibits torture.

Since the entry into effect of the CAT and as a result of international monitoring (such as that of the U.N. Committee Against Torture established under the CAT) and national monitoring (undertaken by individual states such as the U.S.), states that engage in torture have become more secretive about their practices, thus making detection more difficult. In the case of the U.S., the institutionalization of torture during the Bush Administration was concealed through a series of legal memoranda authorizing "enhanced interrogation" techniques, a euphemism for torture. This policy and the ensuing practices, some of which have been publicly disclosed, are in violation of the following: the CAT, which the U.S. ratified;[19] the 1907 Hague Convention on the Laws and Customs of War on Land;[20] customary international humanitarian law first codified in the 1949 Geneva Conventions, which the U.S. ratified;[21] the UCMJ, which in its war crimes as well as other provisions prohibits torture by U.S. military personnel and those to whom the UCMJ applies;[22] Title 18 U.S.C. §§2340 and 2340(A), which incorporate the provisions of the CAT into U.S. criminal law;[23] the Torture Victim Protection Act, which provides for a civil remedy under the CAT;[24] and the Eighth Amendment to the U.S. Constitution, which prohibits the infliction of "cruel and unusual punishment."[25] Because these legal sources are all too well known and discussed in many texts, what follows is only a brief overview of these international and domestic sources of law.

---

[18]   In a D.C. Circuit Appeals decision, Hamdan v. Rumsfeld No. 04–5393 (D.C. Cir., July 15, 2005), the Court raised doubts about the applicability of the Conventions' provisions in the U.S. due to the absence of national legislation. The Court, however, erroneously ignored the embodiment of the Geneva Conventions in U.S. legislation and its application in U.S. practice.

[19]   *See* CAT, *supra* note 4.

[20]   Hague Convention, *supra* note 8.

[21]   Four Geneva Conventions, *supra* note 10.

[22]   Uniform Code of Military Justice (UCMJ), 10 U.S.C. §§801–941 (2000).

[23]   18 U.S.C. §2340 (2000).

[24]   Torture Victim Protection Act, *supra* note 16.

[25]   U.S. CONST. amend. VIII. For an enlightened commentary on the Bush Administration's double standards, see DAVID COLE, ENEMY ALIENS: DOUBLE STANDARDS AND CONSTITUTIONAL FREEDOMS IN THE WAR ON TERRORISM (2003). *See also* David E. Graham, *The Dual U.S. Standard for the Treatment and Interrogation of Detainees: Unlawful and Workable*, 48 WASHBURN L.J. 325, 352 (2009).

1.2. THE CONVENTION AGAINST TORTURE AND OTHER CRUEL, INHUMAN AND DEGRADING TREATMENT OR PUNISHMENT

Article 1 of the CAT defines torture as follows:

> [A]ny act by which severe pain or suffering, whether physical or mental, is intentionally inflicted on a person for such purposes as obtaining from him or a third person information or a confession, punishing him for an act he or a third person has committed or is suspected of having committed, or intimidating or coercing him or a third person, or for any reason based on discrimination of any kind, when such pain or suffering is inflicted by or at the instigation of or with the consent or acquiescence of a public official or other person acting in an official capacity. It does not include pain or suffering arising only from, inherent in or incidental to lawful sanctions.[26]

Article 16 contains a provision designed to ensure that anything that does not fall within this definition of torture but is essentially similar, is still prohibited as "other acts of cruel, inhuman, or degrading treatment or punishment":

> Each state party shall undertake to prevent in any territory under its jurisdiction other acts of cruel, inhuman or degrading treatment or punishment which do not amount to torture as defined in article 1, when such acts are committed by or at the instigation of or with the consent or acquiescence of a public official or other person acting in an official capacity.[27]

The prohibition against the infliction of any pain or suffering is intended to be absolute by the CAT, although the CAT requires that the pain and suffering must be "severe." The drafters of the CAT were not creating a loophole that could be exploited by potential torturers; rather, the term "severe" was added to distinguish non-abusive and not intentionally hurtful physical contacts of the common or ordinary sort that sometimes occur in securing physical control over a person taken into custody.[28] Situations involving use of force by law

---

[26] *See* CAT, *supra* note 4, at art. 1. Many of the issues involving severe pain and suffering (whether done by a public official or not and the manner in which it is done, etc.) have been addressed in the context of the European Convention on Human Rights and the American Convention on Human Rights, both of which prohibit torture, the European Convention for the Prevention of Torture and Inhuman or Degrading Treatment or Punishment, as well as in a number of cases decided by the European Court of Human Rights, the Inter-American Court of Human Rights, as well as in criminal and civil cases before U.S. Federal District Courts. *See* Gail H. Miller, Defining Torture (2005).

[27] CAT, *supra* note 4, at art. 16.

[28] On the history and application of the CAT, see Burgers & Danelius, The United Nations Convention Against Torture; Arzamendi, El Delito de Tortura; and Nowak & McArthur, The United Nations Convention against Torture, *supra* note 4. *See also* Daniel Derby, *The International Prohibition of Torture, in* 1 International Criminal Law:

enforcement officers in preventing crime or in self-defense permit the use of proportionate and reasonable force. In these cases, the physical harm imposed can be neither gratuitous, vindictive, nor for the purposes of extracting a confession or information.[29] This is how the U.S. Supreme Court has interpreted the Eighth Amendment with regard to "cruel and unusual treatment" and the Fifth Amendment with regard to "self-incrimination."[30]

Treaty obligations are binding upon state parties, but their enforceability depends upon domestic implementing legislation.[31] Article VI of the U.S. Constitution states that all treaties become part of the "Supreme Law of the Land," however, the Senate-approved version required the adoption of implementing legislation before provisions of the CAT could become domestically enforceable, namely, acts of torture committed abroad.[32] The

---

SOURCES, SUBJECTS, AND CONTENTS 621 (M. Cherif Bassiouni ed., 3d ed. 2008); Manfred Nowak, *What Practices Constitute Torture: U.S. and U.N. Standards*, 28 HUM. RTS. Q. 809 (2006); Winston Nagan & Lucie Atkins, *The International Law of Torture: From Universal Proscription to Effective Application and Enforcement*, 14 HARV. HUM. RTS. J. 87, 97 (2001).

[29] The issue arose first before the European Court of Human Rights in *The Republic of Ireland v. The United Kingdom*, as to whether the distinction between torture and inhumane or degrading treatment was based on the severity of the pain and suffering, as well as the type of treatment to which the detainee was subjected. Ireland v. United Kingdom, 25 Eur. Ct. H.R. (ser. A) (1978). Many cases have followed which resulted in the condemnation of state practice that violates Article III of the ECHR.

[30] U.S. CONST. amend. V; U.S. CONST. amend. VIII. For early cases, see Brown v. Mississippi, 297 U.S. 298 (1936), which held that a defendant's confession that is extracted by police violence cannot be entered as evidence and violates the due process clause, and Chambers v. Florida, 309 U.S. 227 (1940), where the court held that detaining suspects for a period of a week and subjecting them to questioning on a random basis, often alone in a room with up to ten police officers constituted coercion and violated the right to due process. *See also* Trop v. Dulles, 356 U.S. 86 (1958), where the court adopted the evolving standards of decency test to determine which punishments might be considered 'cruel and unusual' under the Eighth Amendment. The Court applies this standard not only to say what punishments are inherently cruel, but also to say what punishments that are not inherently cruel are nevertheless cruelly disproportionate to the offense in question.

[31] *Id.*

[32] *See* U.S. Reservations, Declarations, and Understandings, *supra* note 15, at Declaration 1. 18 U.S.C. §2340A(a)(2000) (originally enacted as Act of Apr. 30, 1994, §506(a), 108 Stat. 382, 463). *See* Michael John Garcia, CRS Report RL32438, *UN Convention Against Torture (CAT): Overview and Application to Interrogation Techniques* (Congressional Research Service, Library of Congress, Jan. 25, 2006):

> The U.S. ratified CAT, subject to certain declarations, reservations, and understandings, including that the Convention was not self-executing and therefore required domestic implementing legislation to be enforced by U.S. courts. In order to ensure compliance with CAT obligations to criminalize all acts of torture, the U.S. enacted sections 2340 and 2340A of the U.S. Criminal Code, which prohibit torture occurring *outside* the U.S. The applicability and scope of these statutes was the subject of widely-reported memorandums by the Department of Defense and Department of Justice in 2002. In late 2004, the Department of Justice released a memorandum superseding its earlier memo and modifying some of its conclusions.
>
> *Id.* at introduction.

"Torture Convention Implementation Act," contained in 18 U.S.C. §§2340 and 2340(A), became law in 2003.

1.2.1. INTERPRETING THE CAT

The U.S. signed the CAT on April 18, 1988 and ratified it on October 21, 1994, subject to several reservations, understandings, and declarations made by the Senate in its "Advice and Consent" constitutional role, which alter or cancel out some legal aspects of the treaty.[33] In its Reservations, the U.S. Senate limited the definition of torture to acts of "cruel, inhuman or degrading treatment or punishment" to the extent that such acts are "prohibited by the Fifth, Eighth and/or Fourteenth Amendments to the Constitution."[34] Torture was restricted to acts "committed by a person acting under the color of law *specifically intended* to inflict *severe* physical or mental pain or suffering… upon another person within his custody or physical control" (emphasis added).[35] Furthermore, the Senate declaration states that:

> mental pain and suffering refers to prolonged mental pain caused by or resulting from (1) severe physical pain or suffering; (2) administration or application, or threatened administration or application, of mind-altering substances or other procedures calculated to disrupt profoundly the senses or the personality; (3) the threat of imminent death; or (4) the threat that another person will imminently be subjected to death, severe physical pain or mind-altering substances or other procedures calculated to disrupt profoundly the senses or personality.[36]

The understanding adds a specific intent element to the definition of the crime which the Convention's Article 1 did not require. That specific intent is to inflict severe physical or mental pain or suffering, however, the U.S. understanding limits the scope of severe mental pain or suffering to those acts which result in prolonged mental harm caused by one of four enumerated acts. Article 1(1) of the CAT does not make such distinctions as to mental harm or suffering by referring only to severe pain or suffering, whether physical or mental.

Reservation II also limited torture to acts occurring within the "offender's custody or physical control."[37] The CAT's original text prohibits countries from delivering an individual to a foreign country if "there are substantial grounds he

---

[33] U.S. Reservations, Declarations, and Understandings, *supra* note 15. *See also* Jamie Mayerfield, *Playing by Our Own Rules: How U.S. Marginalization of International Human Rights Law Led to Torture*, 20 HARV. HUM. RTS. J. 89 (2007).

[34] *Id.* at Reservation (1).

[35] *Id.* at Understanding (1)(a).

[36] S. Exec. Rep. No. 101–30, at 36 (1990).

[37] U.S. Reservations, Declarations, and Understandings, *supra* note 15, at Understanding (1)(b).

would be in danger of being subjected to torture."[38] The text approved by the U.S. Senate limits this restriction to situations where it "is more likely than not that he would be tortured."[39] With respect to "extraordinary renditions," it is claimed that certain "diplomatic assurances" may absolve the U.S. of responsibility for the torture committed when a captive is rendered to a third country for detention and interrogation.[40]

Congress determined that acts of torture occurring within the U.S. would be "covered by existing applicable federal and state statutes," such as those criminalizing assault, manslaughter, and murder.[41] Thus, the CAT notwithstanding, in the U.S. torture is subject to its own limitations which are contrary to the international obligations assumed by the U.S. What is clear is that these obligations pertaining to the prohibition, prevention, and punishment of torture and other forms of cruel, inhuman and degrading treatment and punishment apply no matter where the U.S., through its agents, exercises control over a person. Therefore, torture is a crime under U.S. law.

The Torture Convention Implementation Act states "whoever outside the United States commits or attempts to commit torture shall be fined…or imprisoned not more than 20 years, or both, and if death results…shall be punished by death or imprisoned for any term of years or for life."[42] In October 2008, Charles "Chuckie" Taylor, Jr., the son of the infamous Liberian dictator on trial for crimes against humanity before the Special Court for Sierra Leone seated at The Hague, became the first person convicted under 18 U.S.C. §§2340 and 2340(A) allowing the prosecution of American citizens and anyone on U.S. soil for torture committed abroad.[43] Federal District Judge Cecilia M. Altonaga, in an opinion denying dismissal of the indictment, wrote:

> It is beyond peradventure that torture and acts that constitute cruel, inhuman or degrading punishment, acts prohibited by *jus cogens,* are similarly abhorred by the law of nations. *See, e.g., Sosa v. Alvarez-Machain,* 542 U.S. 692, 732, 124 S. Ct. 2739, 159 L. Ed. 2d 718 (2004) ("[F]or purposes of civil liability, the torturer has become – like the pirate and slave trader before him – *hostis humani generis,* an enemy of all

---

[38]   CAT, *supra* note 4, at art. 3.

[39]   *See* U.S. Reservations, Declarations, and Understandings, *supra* note 15, at Understanding 2.

[40]   BARBARA OLSHANSKY, DEMOCRACY DETAINED: SECRET UNCONSTITUTIONAL PRACTICES IN THE U.S. WAR ON TERROR, 213 (2007).

[41]   *See* Sen. Rep. 103–107, at 59 (1993) (discussing legislation implementing CAT Articles 4 and 5).

[42]   18 U.S.C. §2340A(b). The Bush Administration lawyers at first erroneously argued that the Guantánamo Bay Naval Station was under Cuban sovereignty and therefore outside the jurisdiction of U.S. commitments to prevent torture. This was the beginning of misguided, if not patently erroneous arguments designed to limit the CAT's applicability, as discussed below. The CAT clearly applies on Guantánamo Base, as does U.S. federal law under Title 18 U.S. Code and the UCMJ, under Title 10 U.S. Code for U.S. military personnel and dependants, and MEJA for private contractors. *See* Chapter 5, section 5.5, *The Legal Responsibility of Private Contractors Acting on Behalf of the U.S. Government.*

[43]   *See* Elizabeth Dickinson, *Chuckie Taylor Sentenced to 97 Years,* FOREIGN POLICY, Jan. 9, 2009.

mankind.") (quoting *Filartiga v. Pena-Irala*, 630 F.2d 876, 890 (2d Cir. 1980)). Certainly the numerous international treaties and agreements, and several domestic statutes that contain varying proscriptions against torture, addressing both civil and criminal reparation, demonstrate the law of nations' repudiation of torture.

Over a century ago, the Supreme Court stated that "if the thing made punishable is one which the United States are required by their international obligations to use due diligence to prevent, it is an offense against the law of nations." *United States v. Arjona*, 120 U.S. 479, 488, 7 S. Ct. 628, 30 L. Ed. 728 (1887). In the present international community, it cannot be said that the Torture Act, legislation that criminalizes acts of torture by U.S. nationals or persons present in the United States, committed outside the United States, does not address an act made punishable by the Government's international obligations under the Convention, and which the Government is required to use due diligence to prevent. Thus, the Torture Act also finds constitutional protection as a law enacted by Congress to punish offenses against the law of nations.[44]

Somehow, what seemed so self-evident to Judge Altonaga completely escaped the Bush Administration lawyers, who gave §§2340 and 2340A an expanded meaning in the August 1, 2002 Bybee memo (authored by Yoo) to Gonzales. They relied on the federal statute's plain meaning of the term "severe" in various English language dictionaries, namely, *Webster's New International*, the *American Heritage*, and the *Oxford English*. These dictionaries define "severe" as "extreme" or "hard to sustain or endure," which connotes "such a high level of intensity that the pain is difficult for the subject to endure."[45] Neither Bybee nor Yoo, nor anyone else in the Administration referred to the negotiating history of the CAT as is required under the Vienna Convention on the Law of Treaties,[46] which the U.S. did not sign, but whose provisions it has followed in various decisions of the Supreme Court.[47] The Bybee/Yoo memorandum looked to the use of the term "severe pain" to signify ailments which placed an individual at risk of "serious jeopardy, serious impairment to bodily functions, or serious dysfunction of any bodily organ or part" in the absence of immediate medical treatment.[48] Even though the context, as well as the intent and purpose of the legislation consulted, was quite different from that of the CAT, Bybee and Yoo

---

44   United States v. Charles Emmanuel, F.Supp.2d (S.D.Fla. 2008).

45   Memorandum from Jay S. Bybee, Assistant Attorney Gen., Office of Legal Counsel, U.S. Dep't of Justice, to Alberto R. Gonzales, Counsel to the President, Standards of Conduct for Interrogation under 18 U.S.C. §§2340–2340A (Aug. 1, 2002) [hereinafter Bybee Memo].

46   Vienna Convention on the Law of Treaties, art. 31, 1155 U.N.T.S. 331 (May 23, 1969).

47   *See* RESTATEMENT (THIRD) OF THE FOREIGN RELATIONS LAW OF THE UNITED STATES.

48   Bybee Memo, *supra* note 45. This is contrary to the intent of the CAT. *See* NOWAK & MCARTHUR, THE UNITED NATIONS CONVENTION AGAINST TORTURE, *supra* note 4. For a history of the CAT and its intended purposes, see Danelius, Derby, and de la Cuesta, *supra* note 4. None of these authors were cited in any memoranda authored by Bybee, Yoo, or others in the Bush Administration.

extrapolated from that unrelated legislation what they deemed necessary for its purposes of presumably redefining torture. Thus, it redefined torture as that which produces such severity of pain or suffering that is associated with organ failure, impairment of bodily function, or death. This redefinition goes against the text and the intent and purposes of the CAT, as evidenced by its legislative history.

The same method of interpretation was used for another aspect of the torture definition, namely, severe mental pain or suffering which §2340 defines as "prolonged mental harm caused by or resulting from one of four enumerated acts."[49] Bybee and Yoo resorted to *Webster's New International* dictionary and again, found that to prolong is to "lengthen in time."[50] Thus, acts giving rise to the harm must result in some lasting damage, though the damage need not be permanent.[51]

Another August 1, 2002 memo from Yoo to Gonzales confirmed the findings contained in the first memo of that same date (which Yoo authored but which went out under Bybee's name), namely, that interrogation methods which comply with §§2340 or 2340A, as interpreted in the August 1, 2002 Bybee memo, do not violate the U.S. obligations under the CAT in reliance upon the understanding cited above. A third memo was also sent on August 1, 2001, by Bybee to John Rizzo, then Acting General Counsel to the CIA, relying on the findings contained in the August 1 memo to Gonzales. The OLC concluded that the use of the following ten interrogation techniques by the CIA would not constitute torture: 1) attention grasp, 2) walling, 3) facial hold, 4) facial slap, 5) cramped confinement, 6) wall standing, 7) stress positions, 8) sleep deprivation, 9) insects placed in a confinement box, and 10) waterboarding.[52]

These three OLC memoranda were the cornerstone of the Bush Administration's policy in dealing with certain detainees in U.S. custody, and subsequent memoranda originating in DOJ and DOD built upon them.[53] Additionally, a DOD Working Group Report on Detainee Interrogations in the Global War on Terrorism established by Secretary Rumsfeld produced two reports on March 6, 2003 and April 4, 2003, which provided an overview of

---

[49]   18 U.S.C. §2340.

[50]   Bybee Memo, *supra* note 45, at 177.

[51]   *Id.*

[52]   Memorandum from Assistant Attorney General Jay S. Bybee for John Rizzo, General Counsel of the Central Intelligence Agency, memorandum on Interrogation of al Qaeda Operatives (August 1, 2002). See also Chapter 2 for a discussion of interrogation techniques.

[53]   The Memorandum from Deputy Assistant Attorney General John Yoo to William J. Hayes II, General Counsel of the Dep't of Defense, Re: Military Interrogation of Alien Unlawful combatants Held Outside the United States, Mar. 14, 2003 [hereinafter the Yoo Memo], echoed the findings of the first August 1, 2002 memo that torture encompasses only "extreme acts," and that "severe pain" must rise to the level "associated with a physical condition or injury sufficiently serious that it would result in death, organ failure, or serious impairment of body functions." *Id.* at 38–39.

interrogation tactics that were allowed at Guantánamo. Interestingly, these reports always euphemistically use the term "may" in reference to harsh interrogation techniques. The reports incorporated substantial portions of the two Bybee/Yoo memoranda of August 1, 2002 discussing torture under §§2340 and 2340A and U.S. obligations under the CAT, including those portions regarding specific intent, severe pain or suffering, and severe mental pain or suffering.[54]

After the torture at Abu Ghraib came to light in spring 2004, and given the controversial nature of the first August 1, 2002 memo, the DOJ withdrew the memo in June 2004. Daniel Levin, Acting Assistant Attorney General, authored a new memo dated December 30, 2004, expressly rejecting the narrow interpretations of "severe pain or suffering" set forth by Yoo and Bybee in their 2002 memo.[55]

The methodology used by the OLC in determining the meaning of "severe pain or suffering" violated not only the intent of the CAT, but also this country's long and well-established jurisprudence on treaty interpretation. In so doing, they violated the Constitution's Supremacy Clause that "all treaties made, or which shall be made, under the authority of the United States, shall be the supreme law of the land."[56] The *Restatement (Third) of Foreign Relations Law of the United States* §111 mirrors the language of the Supremacy Clause by suggesting that international law and international agreements entered into by the U.S. are laws of the U.S., though the Senate must give its advice and consent, and whenever international agreements are not self-executing, national legislation is required. As a party to the CAT, the U.S. is obligated to abide by its provisions, subject to any reservations, understandings, and declarations deposited by the Senate upon ratification of the Convention.

State parties of the Vienna Convention on the Law of Treaties are to interpret the treaty in good faith in accordance with a term's ordinary meaning given their context and in light of the treaty's object and purpose.[57] To determine context, a

---

[54] Department of Defense, *Working Group Report on Detainee Interrogation in the Global War on Terrorism: Assessment of Legal, Historical, Policy, and Operational Considerations* (Apr. 4, 2003).

[55] Memorandum by Daniel Levin for James B. Comey (Dec. 30, 2004), at 8. Levin believed that Congress did not intend "severe" pain or suffering to encompass only "excruciating and agonizing pain or suffering," since that proposal was rejected by the Senate prior to ratifying the CAT for "setting too high a threshold of pain." Levin considered cases interpreting "severe physical or mental pain or suffering" under the Torture Victim Protection Act to reach the conclusion that the severity of physical pain and suffering is dependent on the frequency, duration, and intensity of the harm inflicted on the victim – "the more intense, lasting, or heinous the agony, the more likely it is to be torture." *Id.* at 9 (citing Price v. Socialist People's Libyan Arab Jamahiriya, 294 F.3d 82, 92–93 (D.C. Cir. 2002). Levin reaches the same conclusion regarding severe mental pain or suffering as that found in the August 1, 2002 memo.

[56] U.S. Const. art. VI, §2.

[57] Vienna Convention on the Law of Treaties, art. 31, 1155 U.N.T.S. 331 (May 23, 1969).

state party should look to any agreements or instruments made in concluding the treaty. While the U.S. is not a party to the Vienna Convention, the *Restatement (Third) of the Foreign Relations Law of the United States* provides similar rules of interpretation as those contained in the Convention. Section 325 of the *Restatement (Third)* is similar to Article 31 of the Vienna Convention, and it provides that an international agreement is to be interpreted "in good faith in accordance with the ordinary meaning to be given to its terms in their context and in light of its object and purpose."[58] Comment b to §325 additionally suggests that in interpreting an agreement, the context comprises not only the text but also any other agreements made in connection with the conclusion of the agreement.[59] Furthermore, at least within the context of the U.S. common law system, statutory interpretation commonly follows a path where one first looks to the plain language of a statute, and where the text is ambiguous, additional consideration should be made towards using other tools of interpretation, such as looking at the legislative history and the intent and purposes of the legislation.

1.3. INTERNATIONAL HUMANITARIAN LAW: THE GENEVA CONVENTIONS AND THE CUSTOMARY INTERNATIONAL LAW OF ARMED CONFLICT

The prohibition of torture is part of customary IHL and is binding upon all states.[60] Customary law with regard to the treatment of prisoners of war was first codified in the 1899 Hague Convention, and then in the 1907 Hague Convention and its Annexed Regulations. Most countries of the world have military or other legislation that includes either in whole or in part the norms of the Four Geneva Conventions of August 12, 1949 and the two Additional Protocols of 1977. Because the 1949 Conventions have been ratified by 194 states, they are now considered customary international law, and are thus applicable to all states irrespective of whether they are state parties to the relevant Convention.[61]

The Geneva Conventions apply to all armed conflicts of an international and non-international character.[62] The Third Geneva Convention specifically

---

[58] RESTATEMENT (THIRD) OF THE FOREIGN RELATIONS LAW OF THE UNITED STATES §325(1).

[59] *Id.* at cmt. b.

[60] *See* JEAN-MARIE HENCKAERTS & LOUISE DOSWALD-BECK, 1, 2 CUSTOMARY INTERNATIONAL HUMANITARIAN LAW (2005).

[61] *See* G.A. Res. 59/37, U.N. Doc. A/RES/59/37 (Dec. 2, 2004), noting "the virtually universal acceptance of the Geneva Conventions of 1949" and "the trend towards a similarly wide acceptance of the two Additional Protocols of 1977".

[62] *See* A MANUAL ON INTERNATIONAL HUMANITARIAN LAW AND ARMS CONTROL AGREEMENTS 1 (M. Cherif Bassiouni ed., 2000).

concerns prisoners of war and requires that detainees be treated humanely at all times,[63] and that detainees who are questioned will not be subject to any form of physical or mental coercion.[64] Article 17 of the Third Geneva Convention on Prisoners of War states specifically that, "[n]o physical or mental torture, nor any other form of coercion, may be inflicted on prisoners of war…"[65] In addition, the Convention prohibits "outrages upon personal dignity, in particular humiliating and degrading treatment."

Torture, along with murder, rape, willful destruction of public and private property, and use of civilian and POW human shields, is considered a "grave breach" of the Geneva Conventions.[66] Such "grave breaches" can only be committed by a state within the context of an international conflict. Common Article 3, which applies to conflicts of a non-international character, does not contain the same specificity,[67] but the prohibitions are the same.[68] Common Article 3 refers to transgressions of its prohibitions as "violations" and not as "grave breaches." States have certain obligations with regard to grave breaches, including: criminalizing them in their domestic laws, prosecuting or extraditing those who commit them,[69] and providing other states with judicial assistance in the investigation of them.[70]

The Geneva Conventions' prohibition against torture has been explicitly acknowledged in U.S. military training and manuals since the U.S. signed the Conventions as a High Contracting Party in 1949.[71]

High-level DOJ attorneys within the Bush Administration, none of whom were IHL experts, erroneously proffered the position that the Geneva Conventions do not apply "enemy combatants" detained in the "war on terror". In a declassified 2003 DOJ memorandum, then-Deputy Assistant Attorney General John Yoo made the outrageous claim that *no domestic or foreign law –*

---

[63]   Geneva III, *supra* note 10, at arts. 31 and 27.

[64]   *Id.*, at arts. 17 and 31.

[65]   Geneva III, *supra* note 10, at art. 17. *See also* Jordan J. Paust, *Executive Plans and Authorizations to Violate International Law*, 43 COLUM. J. TRANSNAT'L L. 811 (2005), summarizing the history of torture prohibitions.

[66]   Common Article 3 prohibits "[v]iolence to life and person, in particular murder of all kinds, mutilation, cruel treatment and torture;…outrages upon personal dignity, in particular humiliating and degrading treatment." Geneva III, *supra* note 10.

[67]   *See* Geneva I, II, III, and IV, *supra* note 10, at art. 3.

[68]   *See* Theodor Meron, *International Criminalization of Internal Atrocities*, 1995 AM. J. INT'L L. 89 (1995).

[69]   Geneva III, *supra* note 10, at arts. 129 and 146.

[70]   Geneva I, at art. 49; Geneva II, at art. 50; Geneva III, at art. 129; and Geneva IV, at art. 146, *supra* note 10.

[71]   *See* Department of the Army Field Manual 34–52, Intelligence Interrogation (Sept. 28, 1992), which states that "the Geneva and Hague Conventions and the UCMJ set definite limits on the measures which can be used to gain the willing cooperation of prisoners of war." It lists the following as examples of physical torture: electric shock; infliction of pain through chemicals or bondage; forcing an individual to stand, sit or kneel in abnormal positions for prolonged periods of time; food deprivation; and any form of beating. *Id.* at 1–8.

including the Geneva Conventions – applies to the treatment of alien unlawful enemy combatants held outside the U.S.[72] This was clearly wrong with respect to detainees in Iraq and Afghanistan, which are international conflicts in accordance with IHL. Yoo further asserted that if IHL applied, it would violate the President's power as Commander-in-Chief, and that the latter supersedes IHL.[73] The Bush Administration was intent on limiting the application of the Geneva Conventions and customary IHL to its policy of "enhanced interrogation" techniques. The claim of Presidential Executive power has absolutely no bearing on the international legal obligations of the U.S. pursuant to conventional and customary IHL. The U.S. Supreme Court, in *Hamdan v. Rumsfeld*, ruled against the Bush Administration's clearly untenable arguments of non-applicability of IHL and presidential powers trumping both international and domestic law.[74]

1.4. OTHER INTERNATIONAL LAW NORMS APPLICABLE TO THE PROHIBITION OF TORTURE

The 1948 Convention on the Prohibition of Genocide is defined in a way that includes torture if it is used with the intent to exterminate a given human group in whole or in part.[75] However, that was not the case in the policy and practices of the Bush Administration.

The European Convention on Human Rights (ECHR), ratified by 47 states, prohibits torture in Article III,[76] and the American Convention on Human Rights (ACHR), ratified by 24 states, prohibits it in Article V.[77] The jurisprudence of the European and Inter-American Courts has amply dealt with torture cases.[78]

---

[72]   *See* Yoo Memo, *supra* note 53.

[73]   *Id.*

[74]   Hamdan v. Rumsfeld, 126 U.S. 2749, 2762–69 (2006).

[75]   Convention on the Prevention and Punishment of the Crime of Genocide, Dec. 9, 1948, 78 U.N.T.S. 277 (entered into force Jan. 12, 1951), at arts. 1 and 2. 18 U.S.C. §1091 enforces the Convention with regard to U.S. nationals or within U.S. territory only. *See generally* WILLIAM A. SCHABAS, GENOCIDE IN INTERNATIONAL LAW (2000).

[76]   European Convention for the Protection of Human Rights and Fundamental Freedoms, Nov. 4, 1950, 213 U.N.T.S. 221 (1951). "No one shall be subjected to torture or to inhuman or degrading treatment or punishment." The Convention is also called the European Convention on Human Rights.

[77]   The American Convention on Human Rights (Article 5(2)), Nov. 22, 1969, O.A.S. Treaty Series No. 36, 1144 U.N.T.S. 123 (entered into force July 18, 1978). "No one shall be subjected to torture or to cruel, inhuman, or degrading punishment or treatment. All persons deprived of their liberty shall be treated with respect for the inherent dignity of the human person."

[78]   Examples of cases from the European Court of Human Rights include *Ribitsch v. Austria*, Case No. 42/1994/489/571, Judgment of the ECHR (Dec. 4, 1995); *Aksoy v. Turkey*, Case No. 21987/93, Judgment of the ECHR (Dec. 18, 1996); and *Mehmet Eran v Turkey*, Case No. 32347/02, Judgment of the ECHR (October 2008). Examples of Cases from the Inter-American Court of Human Rights include Case of Lori Berenson Mejia v. Peru, 2004 Inter-Am. Ct. H.R.

The European Court of Human Rights in *Aksoy v. Turkey* imposed the requirement to thoroughly investigate the possibility of torture "[w]here an individual is taken into police custody in good health but is found to be injured at the time of release."[79] The Court subsequently found the injuries in the case were a result of torture. Due to the "fundamental importance of the prohibition on torture" the Court imposed an obligation under Article 13 of the European Convention to conduct "thorough and effective investigations of incidents of torture."[80]

In *Assenov and Others v. Bulgaria*, the Court recognized a state's obligation to investigate torture not only under Article 13, but under Article 3 of the ECHR as well.[81] This was the first time a court recognized a failure to conduct an effective investigation as a violation of Article 3.[82] "[W]here an individual raises an arguable claim that he has been seriously ill-treated by the police... in breach of Article 3, that provision... in conjunction the State's general duty under Article 1..." requires "that there should be an effective official investigation."[83]

In *Tomasi v. France*, the Court held that difficulties inherent in investigating crimes, even terrorism, cannot place limits on the protection and respect for the physical integrity of individuals guaranteed under Article 3.[84] The Manual on Effective Investigation and Documentation of Torture and Other Cruel, Inhuman or Degrading Treatment or Punishment (the Istanbul Protocol) provides internationally recognized standards and procedures to investigate and report instances of torture.[85] Although the protocol is non-binding, states are also obligated under customary international law and the Geneva Conventions to investigate allegations of torture. These obligations include criminalizing torture, taking effective governmental action to prevent it, ensuring prompt and impartial investigations, listing torture as an extraditable offense, and ensuring that torture victims have access to redress. The Istanbul Protocol is recognized by the U.N., the European Union, and the African Commission on Human and Peoples' Rights, and the U.N. Commission on Human Rights encourages its use as a tool for governments to combat torture. Central to the Istanbul Protocol is the necessity for prompt, impartial, and effective investigations of torture. It also advises states to establish domestic investigation procedures.

(ser. C) No. 119 (Nov. 25, 2004)); Case of *Plan de Sánchez Massacre*, Case 11.763, Inter-Am. C.H.R., Report No. 31/99, I/A (2004).

[79] U.N. High Commissioner for Human Rights, Manual on Effective Investigation and Documentation of Torture and Other Cruel, Inhuman or Degrading Treatment or Punishment (August 9, 1999) [hereinafter Istanbul Protocol]; *Aksoy v. Turkey*, Case No. 21987/93, Judgment of the ECHR (Dec. 18, 1996).

[80] *Id.*

[81] *Id.*

[82] *Id.*

[83] *Id.*

[84] *Tomasi v. France*, Case No. 12850/87, Judgment of the ECHR (Aug 27, 1992).

[85] The Istanbul Protocol, *supra* note 79.

The Istanbul Protocol specifically provides doctors and lawyers with internationally recognized ethical standards and procedures to investigate and report instances of torture. It is a lawyer's duty to protect the rights of clients, promote justice, uphold human rights and fundamental freedoms, and act diligently in accordance with the law. Meanwhile, under the Protocol, physicians are to recognize its fundamental tenet, which is to "always act in the best interests of the patient, regardless of other constraints, pressures or contractual obligations."[86]

Customary IHL criminalizes "crimes against humanity,"[87] as do the statutes of the International Criminal Tribunal for the former Yugoslavia (ICTY)[88] and the International Criminal Tribunal for Rwanda (ICTR)[89] established by the United Nations Security Council, and Article 7 of the International Criminal Court (ICC).[90] "Crimes against humanity" includes torture when conducted on a widespread or systematic basis which reflect a state's policy. If torture in the U.S. was conducted on such a basis, even though the term "crimes against humanity" is not specifically included in U.S. legislation, the charge can be invoked by other countries under universal jurisdiction.[91]

International tribunals such as the ICTY, the ICTR, and the ICC have addressed torture as a substantive crime, as well as from an evidentiary perspective, namely, the inadmissibility of evidence obtained under torture. The statutes of the ICCY, ICTR, and ICC, with respect to their provisions on "war crimes" (respectively, Arts. 4, 3, and 8) and "crimes against humanity" (respectively, Arts. 3, 5, and 7) establish criminal responsibility for those who commit torture.

---

[86] *Id.*

[87] *See* M. Cherif Bassiouni, Crimes Against Humanity: Historical Evolution and Contemporary Practice (2010); Leila Nadya Sadat, Forging a Convention for Crimes Against Humanity (forthcoming, 2010); M. Cherif Bassiouni, *Crimes Against Humanity: The Case for a Specialized Convention*, 9 Wash U. Global Stud. L. Rev. (forthcoming 2010).

[88] *See generally* Statute of the International Tribunal for the Prosecution of Persons Responsible for Serious Violations of International Humanitarian Law Committed in the Territory of the Former Yugoslavia since 1991, U.N. Doc. S/25704 at 36, annex (1993) and S/25704/Add.1 (1993), adopted by the Security Council May 25, 1993, U.N. Doc. S/Res/827 (1993).

[89] Statute of the International Tribunal for Rwanda, S.C. Res. 955, U.N. SCOR, 49th Sess., 3453d mtg. at 3, U.N. Doc. S/Res/955 (1994).

[90] *See* the Rome Statute of the International Criminal Court, July 17, 1998, 2187 U.N.T.S. 90. *See also* M. Cherif Bassiouni, 1–3 The Legislative History of the International Criminal Court: Introduction, Analysis, and Integrated Text (2005).

[91] *See* Kai Ambos, *Prosecuting Guantanamo in Europe: Can and Shall the Masterminds of the "Torture Memos" be Held Criminally Responsible on the Basis of Universal Jurisdiction?*, 42 Case W. Res. J. Int'l L. 405 (2009); M. Cherif Bassiouni, *Universal Jurisdiction for International Crimes: Historical Perspectives and Contemporary Practice*, 42 Va. J. Int'l L. 81 (2001). The Crimes Against Humanity Act of 2009 was introduced by Sen. Richard Durbin in June 2009 and referred to the Senate Committee on the Judiciary.

Neither the ICTY nor the ICTR have specific provisions in their statutes on the non-admissibility of evidence obtained through torture.[92] Nevertheless, evidence obtained through torture has been excluded on of other sources of conventional and customary international law.[93] Both tribunals have provisions which state that if the probative value is substantially outweighed by the need to ensure a fair trial then the evidence can be excluded.[94] The ICTY is even more specific and states that evidence is not admissible if it is obtained by methods which cast substantial doubt on its reliability or if its admission is antithetical to the integrity of the proceedings.[95] The prohibition of torture is upheld by both tribunals and heralded as "one of the most fundamental standards of the international community."[96] The Court has also held that evidence obtained in other circumstances, less severe than torture, is inadmissible.[97] In *Brdjanin*, the Chamber stated that statements that are not made voluntarily or are obtained by oppressive conduct cannot be admitted.[98] The tribunals would and should, therefore, exclude evidence obtained through the method of torture.

A number of cases were decided by the ICTY and ICTR, including interpretations of the CAT, however, at no time did lawyers of the Bush Administration refer to that jurisprudence, as it was contrary to their positions. In the case of *Prosecutor v. Krnojelac*, the Trial Chamber stated:

When assessing the seriousness of the acts charged as torture, the trial chamber must take into account all the circumstances of the case, including the nature and context of the infliction of the pain, the premeditation and institutionalization of the ill-treatment, the physical condition of the victim, the manner and method used, and the position of inferiority of the victim. In particular, to the extent that an individual has been mistreated over a prolonged period of time, or that he or she has been subjected to various forms of mistreatment, the severity of the acts should be assessed as a whole to the extent that it can be shown that this lasting period or the repetition of the acts are interrelated, follow a pattern, or are directed to the same prohibited goal.[99]

---

92   *See* ICTY Statute, *supra* note 88, at art. 15; ICTR Statute, *supra* note 89, at art. 14.

93   *See, e.g.,* Prosecutor v. Brdjanin, Case No. IT-99-36-T, Decision on the Defense Objection to Intercept Evidence (Mar. 1, 2004), holding that with the increasing level of gravity of the violation, the likelihood that the admission would be kept out as seriously damaging increases.

94   *Id.* at Rule 89, 70.

95   *See* ICTY, *supra* note 88, at art. 14, rule 95.

96   Prosecutor v. Furundzija, Case No. IT-95–17/1, Judgment, paras. 144, 154 ff (Dec. 10, 1998).

97   *See, e.g.* Prosecutor v. Nikolic, Case No. IT-94–2-PT, Decision on Defense Motion Challenging the Exercise of jurisdiction by the Tribunal, (Oct. 9, 2002).

98   *See Prosecutor v. Brdjanin, supra* note 93.

99   Prosecutor v. Krnojelac, Judgment, ICTY Trial Chamber, Case No. IT-97–25-T (Mar. 15, 2002), at para. 182.

In direct contradiction to some of the Bush Administration lawyers' legal positions, the ICTY held that a permanent injury is not a pre-requisite for torture.[100] In *Prosecutor v. Kvocka*, the ICTY gave examples of torture as "beatings, sexual violence, prolonged denial of sleep, food, hygiene and medical assistance, as well as threats to torture, rape or kill relatives."[101] The Court aptly stated further in *Prosecutor v. Naletilic and Martinovic* that:

> There are no more specific requirements which allow an exhaustive classification and enumeration of acts which may constitute torture. Existing case law has not determined the absolute degree of pain required for an act to amount to torture. Thus, while the suffering inflicted by some acts may be so obvious that the acts amount per se to torture, in general, allegations of torture must be considered on a case by case basis so as to determine whether, in light of the acts committed and their context, severe physical or mental pain or suffering was inflicted.[102]

This jurisprudence, which is consonant with the description by scholars of similar jurisprudence in national legal systems and which conforms to common sense, shows that context, practices, and the relationship of torturer and victim, as well as the condition of the victim, are relevant factors. However, these factors can never be defined objectively because there are too many variables. Torture cases must be evaluated in a way that combines both objective and subjective factors. The Bush Administration lawyers took the opposite position, choosing instead to ignore international jurisprudence.

The jurisprudence of the ICTY and ICTR is not binding on U.S. courts with respect to matters not involving the ICTY's competence as defined by the Security Council which established the Court. However, the U.S. has fully participated in the proceedings of the ICTY and ICTR,[103] and has enacted both national implementing legislation and Surrender Agreements with the two tribunals which has allowed for surrender to their jurisdiction.[104] None of these contextual considerations or particularities were taken into account by the Bush

---

[100] Prosecutor v. Limaj et al., Judgment, ICTY Trial Chamber, Case No. IT-03–66-T (Nov. 30, 2005), at para. 236; Prosecutor v. Kvocka et al., Judgment, ICTY Trial Chamber, Case No. IT-98–30/1-T (Nov. 2, 2001), at para. 148.

[101] *Prosecutor v. Kvocka, id.*, at para. 144.

[102] Prosecutor v. Naletilic and Martinovic, Judgment, ICTY Appeals Chamber, Case No. IT-98–34-A (May 3, 2006) at para. 299.

[103] *See e.g.*, the surrender proceedings of Eliziphan Ntakirutimana to the ICTR, Ntakirutimana v. Reno, 184 F.3d 419, 428, 430 (5th Cir. 1999).

[104] National Defense Authorization Act, Public Law No. 104–106 (1996), which validated the following: Agreement on Surrender of Persons between the Government of the United States and the International Tribunal for the Prosecution of Persons Responsible for Serious Violations of International Humanitarian Law in the Territory of the Former Yugoslavia, 1911 U.N.T.S. 224 (5 Oct. 1994); Agreement on Surrender of Persons between the Government of the United States and the International Criminal Tribunal for Rwanda (24 Jan. 1994), unpublished in U.N.T.S., *reprinted in* 2 THE INTERNATIONAL CRIMINAL TRIBUNAL FOR RWANDA 391 (Virginia Morris & Michael Scharf eds., 1998). *See* Kenneth J. Harris & Robert

Administration lawyers or referred to in the memoranda that enabled the policy and practices of torture.

With regard to the ICC, admissibility of evidence is controlled by Art. 69(7) of its Statute, which makes evidence inadmissible if it is obtained by means of a violation of the Statute or internationally recognized human rights, and if the admission of the evidence would be antithetical to the integrity of the proceedings.[105] Since torture violates internationally recognized human rights and damages the integrity of the proceedings of the ICC, such evidence would not be admissible in the Court.

1.5. THE BUSH ADMINISTRATION'S CONCEPTION OF THE NON-BINDING NATURE OF INTERNATIONAL LAW AND THE TECHNIQUES OF REDEFINING THE LAW

Karl Rove, the political czar of the White House during the Bush Administration, demonstrates in his recent book, *Courage and Consequence*, how public perceptions are created and shaped.[106] Not only was he the Grey Eminence of the President (the title given to Cardinal Richelieu in the days of Louis XIV of France), but his political influence permeated the senior levels of government and reached well into the policymaking levels of the Republican Party. The making and shaping of public political perceptions encompassed the redefinition of law and legal obligations.

American neo-conservative jurists have argued in the last two decades that international law is that which states agree to, and also that from which states can exempt themselves if deemed contrary to their sovereign interests. Such a notion is not new – it follows a Hobbesian utilitarian approach whereby states are essentially bound by what they perceive to be their interests, subject to their judicious appraisal of how such judgments would impact on other states, and thus ultimately impact their own state.[107] The theory of exceptionalism which neo-conservative jurists developed was the legal support for the Bush Administration's policies and actions, such as the policy of pre-emptive use of

---

Kushen, *Surrender of Fugitives to the War Crimes Tribunals for Yugoslavia and Rwanda: Squaring International Legal Obligations with the U.S. Constitution*, 7 Crim. L.F. 563 (1996).

[105] ICC Statute, *supra* note 90.

[106] Karl Rove, Courage and Consequence: My Life as a Conservative in the Fight (2010).

[107] *See* Thomas Hobbes, On the Citizen 30 (Richard Tuck & Michael Silverthorne eds., 1998); M. Cherif Bassiouni, *Perspectives on International Criminal Justice*, 50 Va. J. Int'l L. 269 (2010), at 280.

military force as an exception to the prohibition against aggression.[108] This was
the basis for the U.S. invasion of Iraq in 2003. The invasion of Afghanistan in
2001 was also in part based on that proposition, but linked more closely to self-
defense by reason of the facts, namely, the September 11, 2001 attack on the U.S.
by al-Qaeda operatives whose leadership and organizational headquarters were
in Afghanistan.[109] There were no facts evidencing Iraq's threat to the U.S., other
than the fabricated Bush Administration claims that Iraq had weapons of mass
destruction capable of being used against the U.S., and the unproven proposition
that Iraq had connections to al-Qaeda.

In short, for these political realists, international law is binding, but not
entirely, not at all times, nor for all cases, and nor for the U.S. when it does not
deem it desirable to do so. The arguments of the supporters of this position are
more sophisticated than what is stated above, but if one de-mystifies their most
capable intellectual gymnastics, what is stated above aptly captures their
propositions.[110]

These and other arguments are not new, and it seems that every time a
particularly difficult crisis occurs involving major powers, the temptation toward
"exceptionalism" is great. In contrast, many have argued that one of the
compelling reasons for observing international law is derived from the inherent
power of legitimacy that an international law rule embodies, and that compliance
with the rule of law extends legitimacy to the complying state.[111] Thus,
compliance inures to the credit of the complying state by adding legitimacy to its
policies and actions. Moreover, when states comply with the substance and
processes required by international law, they become part of a collective
compliance stream which provides mutual reinforcement among states who are
part of that stream.[112]

The debate over non-compliance with international law has never been far
from the surface in U.S. practice or in the writings of its scholars, particularly
with respect to customary international law.[113] No one articulated it better than
John Bolton, a well-known advocate for neo-conservative rejection of

---

[108] *See* MICHAEL IGNATIEFF, AMERICAN EXCEPTIONALISM AND HUMAN RIGHTS (2006); PHILIPPE
SANDS, LAWLESS WORLD (2005); JOHN F. MURPHY, THE UNITED STATES AND THE RULE OF
LAW IN INTERNATIONAL AFFAIRS (2004). For an earlier perspective, see LOUIS HENKIN, HOW
NATIONS BEHAVE: LAW AND FOREIGN POLICY (2d ed. 1979).

[109] *See* JANE CORBIN, AL-QAEDA: IN SEARCH OF THE TERROR NETWORK THAT THREATENS THE
WORLD (2003).

[110] *See* JACK GOLDSMITH, THE LIMITS OF INTERNATIONAL LAW (2005); Eric A. Posner, *Do States
Have a Moral Obligation to Obey International Law?*, 55 STAN. L. REV. 1901 (2003). *See also*
Curtis Bradley & Jack Goldsmith, *Customary International Law as Federal Common Law: A
Critique of the Modern Position*, 110 HARV. L.R. 815 (1997).

[111] *See* THOMAS M. FRANCKE, THE POWER OF LEGITIMACY AMONG NATIONS (1990). *See also*
MARY ELLEN O'CONNELL, THE POWER AND PURPOSE OF INTERNATIONAL LAW (2009).

[112] *See e.g.*, INTERNATIONAL RULES: APPROACHES FROM INTERNATIONAL LAW AND
INTERNATIONAL RELATIONS (Robert J. Beck et al. eds., 1996).

[113] *See* Paust and others, *supra* note 6.

international law's binding effects on the U.S., when he stated on behalf of the Bush Administration: "It is a big mistake for us to grant any validity to international law even when it may seem in our short-term interest to do so, because over the long term, the goal of those who think that international law really means anything are those who want to constrict the U.S."[114]

A more intellectualized approach has been offered in the writings of Professors Jack Goldsmith and Eric Posner.[115] Their position basically discounts the legitimacy and binding nature of the international rule of law. They support their views on the proposition that state consent to a rule that does not have enforcement mechanisms to induce compliance is discretionary, thus, justifying the rejection of the binding legal effects of prior decisions made by duly constituted decision makers when there is no internal norm to support it. For these two authors, international law has no moral compass, no moral pole, no inherent legitimacy, but is at best a product of coincidences, cooperation, and coercion which brings about state compliance in some situations and not in others. There is much validity to the observation as a phenomenon that applies to large and small powers. What is questionable is whether the U.S. should follow, or worse yet, lead such a practice. This position was, however, foundational to the Bush Administration in its rejection of the applicability of the Geneva Conventions, the CAT, and other limitations deemed too binding by the legal experts advising the Administration. Goldsmith, in his book *The Terror Presidency*, as Assistant Attorney General and Head of the DOJ's Office of Legal Counsel from October 2003 to June 2004, reveals the purposes behind his and Posner's theory embodied in the limits of international law wherein he states defensively that "many people think the Bush Administration has been indifferent to wartime legal constraints. But the opposite is true: the Administration has been strangled by law, and since Sept. 11, 2001, this war has been lawyered to death. The Administration has paid attention not necessarily because it wanted to, but rather because it had no choice."[116] Goldsmith clearly reveals that the Bush Administration felt strangled by international law and was fighting against it, not because it believed that it had to comply with it legally or

---

[114] Samantha Power, *Boltonism*, NEW YORKER, March 21, 2005, at 23. *See also* Scott Horton, *State of Exception: Bush's War on the Rule of Law*, HARPER'S, July 2007, at 74; Charles Krauthammer, *The Truth About Torture*, THE WEEKLY STANDARD, Dec. 5, 2005.

[115] *See* GOLDSMITH, THE LIMITS OF INTERNATIONAL LAW, *supra* note 110; Posner, *Do States Have a Moral Obligation to Obey International Law?*, *supra* note 110.

[116] JACK GOLDSMITH, THE TERROR PRESIDENCY: LAW AND JUDGMENT INSIDE THE BUSH PRESIDENCY (2007), at 69. The book has the hallmarks of a brief for the defense, as does John Yoo's CRISIS AND COMMAND: A HISTORY OF EXECECUTIVE POWER FROM GEORGE WASHINGTON TO GEORGE W. BUSH (2010). Goldsmith is clearly the one who sought to correct things after the Bybee and Yoo memoranda of August 1, 2002, which are discussed herein. However, it took him until 2003 to change course. Also presenting a defensive position is DOUGLAS FEITH, WAR AND DECISION: INSIDE THE PENTAGON AT THE DAWN OF THE WAR ON TERRORISM (2009).

morally, but because others both in government and outside government had such a belief in international law. Goldsmith confirms that position when he advised White House Legal Counsel Alberto Gonzales that "the President can also ignore the law and act extra-legally."[117]

Goldsmith, first as Special Counsel to Secretary Rumsfeld and then as Assistant Attorney General in charge of the OLC at DOJ, carried out his mission in a way that sought to convince those inside the Bush Administration that international law was not necessarily constraining U.S. power if the U.S. sought to exempt itself from its applicability.[118] In short, if international law was not binding nor constraining, and that states could argue exceptionalism, particularly when their sovereign rights or national security interests were at stake, then the Bush Administration could rely on this foundation in order to claim either the non-applicability of the Geneva Conventions to "enemy combatants" as it defined such persons, and the CAT as it re-defined torture as proposed by Bybee and Yoo, namely, organ failure.[119] The compliance debate, founded on the undermining of the legally binding nature of international law, voided the discourse of substance and diverted it into semantics. Thus, it was not that the Geneva Conventions did not exist, did not apply, or were not binding, but that they did not apply to enemy combatants, even though no such exception exists in the Geneva Conventions. The same reasoning applied to the CAT. It was not that the CAT did not exist or was not binding, but that the definition of what constituted torture was to be found outside the convention itself. Another way of putting it is to say that the Bush Administration's lawyers exceptionalism extended to its interpretation of international law, even when it meant giving external meanings to international law norms irrespective of the words contained in these norms or their intended purposes.[120] The Bush Administration lawyers disregarded what the law *is* in favor of what they deemed that it *ought* to be.

---

[117]   *Id.* at 80. Goldsmith reports that even Gonzales was apparently dismayed. "The post-Watergate hyper-legalization and threatening that the very idea of acting extra-legally was simply off the table, even in times of crisis. The President had to do what he had to do to protect the country. And the lawyers had to find some way to make what he did legal." *Id.* at 81. For a contrary position see Allen Buchanan, *Democracy and the Commitment to International Law*, 34 Ga. J. Int'l & Comp. L. 305 (2006) at 307–08. For a review of Goldsmith and Posner's work, see Oona A. Hathaway & Ariel N. Lavinbuk, *Rationalism and Revisionisms in International Law*, 119 Harv. L. Rev. 1404 (2006). Conversely, several former legal advisers who shared their experiences in a project developed by Professors Michael P. Scharf and Paul R. Williams attested to the influence of international law in past administrations. *See* Scharf & Williams, Shaping Foreign Policy in Times of Crisis, *supra* note 6.

[118]   *Id.* at 60, 63, and 69.

[119]   Yoo memo, *supra* note 54.

[120]   This is a technique that was used by the U.S.S.R. and former 'Eastern Bloc' states under its control. In connection with a variety of internaitonal legal obligations, their argument was "yes, but". In other words, yes, there is an admission that a given international legal obligation exists, but that which is claimed to be encompassed within the obligation is not necessarily so. Surely, the neo-conservative jurists of the Bush Administration were by no means

Another technique employed by the Bush Administration jurists was to simply ignore or sidestep that which was not convenient to their thesis. In part, this may be due to the fact that American jurists' skills are honed in the art of adversarial advocacy, which is only loosely bound by sparsely enforced parameters of ethical conduct as determined by individual state Bar Associations. Legal education and legal practice hardly recognize the figure of the lawyer/advisor, meaning someone who is not giving legal advice for purposes of advocacy or support of a client's position, but with a view to providing the client under advisement, whether in the private or public sector, with an understanding of what the law stands for and where the line is to be drawn with respect to impermissible limits. It is perhaps because of this situation that the Office of Professional Responsibility in the DOJ downgraded a draft recommendation to hold Bybee and Yoo as having acted in an unprofessional manner, to describing their conduct as simply being in poor judgment.[121] However, that may be too much of an understatement for what smacks of a politically-motivated decision. Presumably, if the professional standard relied upon by those reviewing the advice given by these two jurists was predicated on standards of robust adversarial advocacy, then there might be some justification for the final conclusion which downgraded the internal recommendation of a professional misconduct finding. If, however, the standard would have been that of the attorney/advisor who has an obligation to be impartial in the representation of what the law does and does not permit, then surely the outcome would have been different. It is difficult to understand, even within an adversarial advocacy context, government lawyers who are allowed to ignore certain legal considerations which are not convenient to their position, with no professional ramifications. In the private sector, as discussed herein in Chapter 5, lawyers who advise their clients without regard to existing law are held both civilly responsible as well as in ethical violation of their professional responsibilities. For sure, if the Bush Administration lawyers' methodology, reasoning, and selectivity in choice of what sources they relied upon was used in the context of attorneys in private practice giving advice to a client seeking to avoid taxation, it

---

consciously imitating their counterparts of another generation, but it shows how similar the subversive legal techniques of jurists serving totalitarian regimes can be.

[121] *See* Memorandum for the Attorney General, Memorandum of Decision Regarding the Objections to the Findings of Professional Misconduct in the Office of Professional Responsibility's Report of Investigation Into the Office of Legal Counsel's Memoranda Concerning Issues Relating to the CIA's Use of "Enhanced Interrogation Techniques" on Suspected Terrorists, Jan. 5, 2010. The author of the report, Associate Deputy Attorney General David Margolis, wrote that while he did not believe that the written opinions of Yoo and Bybee rose to the level of "professional misconduct," his decision "should not be viewed as an endorsement of the legal work that underlies those memoranda." *Id.* at 2. *See also* Eric Lichtblau & Scott Shane, *Justice Department Report Finds John Yoo and Jay Bybee Not Guilty of Misconduct*, N.Y. Times, Feb. 19, 2010.

would most probably be deemed advice on tax evasion, which is both a potential criminal and ethical violation.

Lawyers in the Bush Administration not only distorted applicable international and domestic legislation, but also ignored relevant U.S. legal provisions which reflect a commitment to international law. U.S. policy in matters of international criminal law and torture as an international crime has its roots in post-WWII prosecutions. The U.S. then had the leading role in the establishment of the International Military Tribunal (Nuremberg),[122] the International Military Tribunal for the Far East (Tokyo),[123] prosecutions in occupied Germany under Control Council Law No. 10,[124] prosecutions in the U.S. zones of occupation in Japan, and in particular in the Yokohama class B perpetrators cases;[125] and the Military commissions in the Philippines.[126]

More recently, the U.S. has adopted the Genocide Accountability Act,[127] the Child Soldiers Accountability Act,[128] and Human Rights Enforcement Act,[129] all of which contain a provision for accountability within the U.S. for the international crimes defined in these laws. Following this trend, other draft legislation for international crimes have been introduced in the Senate, and are currently under review by Congressional judicial committees, including the Trafficking in Persons Accountability Act of 2008,[130] and the Crimes Against Humanity Act of 2009.[131] These laws, as well as the prosecutions conducted in the U.S. such as the Charles Taylor Jr. case, show that international law is

---

[122]   The International Military Tribunal at Nuremberg, created by the Agreement for the Prosecution and Punishment of Major War Criminals of the European Axis, Aug. 8, 1945; Charter of the International Military Tribunal, 59 Stat. 1544, 1546, 82 U.N.T.S. 279, 284.

[123]   International Military Tribunals for the Far East Special Proclamation: Establishment of an International Military Tribunal for the Far East, Jan. 19, 1946 T.I.A.S. No. 1589, at 3 4 BEVANS 20. Charter for the International Military Tribunal for the Far East, Apr. 26, 1946, T.I.A.S. No. 1589, at 3, 4 BEVANS 20.

[124]   Allied Control Council Law No. 10, Punishment of Persons Guilty of War Crimes, Crimes Against Peace and Against Humanity, §II(2)(e), Dec. 20, 1945, *reprinted in* TELFORD TAYLOR, FINAL REPORT TO THE SECRETARY OF THE ARMY ON THE NUREMBERG WAR CRIMES TRIALS UNDER CONTROL COUNCIL LAW NO. 10, at 250 (1949).

[125]   *Reviews of the Yokohama Class B and Class C War Crimes Trials by the Eighth Army Judge Advocate 1946–69* (United States Army, Office of the Judge Advocate General, 1981).

[126]   Japanese General Yamashita was tried before a U.S. Military Commission in the Philippines. Yamashita v. Styer, 327 U.S. 1 (1946). *See generally* A. FRANK REEL, THE CASE OF GENERAL YAMASHITA (1949).

[127]   Genocide Accountability Act of 2007, Pub. L. 110–151 §1 (Dec. 21, 2007), 121 Stat. 1821, amending Title 18 U.S.C. §1091.

[128]   Child Soldiers Accountability Act of 2008, Pub. L. 110–340 (Oct. 3, 2008).

[129]   Human Rights Enforcement Act of 2009, Pub. L. 111–122 (Dec. 22, 2009). This legislation established a section within the Criminal Division of the DOJ to enforce human rights laws, and to make technical and conforming amendments to criminal and immigration laws pertaining to human rights violations.

[130]   Introduced by Sen. Richard Durbin in June 2007, and passed the Senate in Oct. 2008, at which time it was referred to the House Judiciary committee for review.

[131]   Introduced by Sen. Richard Durbin in June 2009 and referred to the Senate Committee on the Judiciary.

enforced in the U.S. and is not as alien to the American legal system as the Bush Administration lawyers made it appear.

What is notably peculiar in the legal memoranda opinions and positions expressed in favor of the non-applicability of the Geneva Conventions and the sidestepping of the CAT, is the total absence of any mention of other relevant sources on the history of the CAT,[132] as well as relevant U.S. legislation and case law. Admittedly, from a narrow adversarial/advocacy perspective, the Bush Administration lawyers did not feel compelled to put forth arguments detrimental to their position, but surely as attorney/advisors they should have included in their opinions everything which was relevant to the issues on which they were providing a legal foundation for what has proven to be a violation of several treaties, the Constitution, and U.S. laws.

The thinking that prevailed within the Bush Administration was that compliance with international law was optional, subject to exceptions or redefinitions arising out of sovereignty exigencies or national security concerns. No matter which option someone within the Administration chose, a great deal of leeway was left for *ad hoc* decisions to be made on the basis of what best serves a given government's policy. This ultimately became the intellectual matrix within which the Bush Administration's policies evolved.

Despite the strength of international repudiation of the practice of torture, the U.S. has turned its back on such prohibitions in the name of the "war on terror." When the policy and practices put forth during the Bush Administration are brought to the bar of justice, judges may ask the government lawyers who aided in the commission of torture how much they knew of the legal subjects about which they opined. They may ask how wide the good faith margin of error should be for people – especially for those with the intellectual abilities of these attorneys – in reaching the conclusions that they did in their legal opinions. Surely it will not be easy to prove that the government attorneys in question acted with specific intent, as some crimes under the UCMJ and Title 18 require.[133] However, it will be relatively easy to show that attorneys such as Yoo possessed the general intent required by the standard of "reasonable lawyer in like circumstances" required for professional responsibility. It is especially instructive to note that individuals involved are more than average lawyers: one is a sitting federal judge, another was nominated for a federal judgeship, and another is a university professor at a prestigious law school. It would be hard for them to argue that they made a reasonable mistake of law as a defense.

---

[132] *See supra* note 4.

[133] *See* UCMJ, *supra* note 22. *See also* John Warner National Defense Authorization Act for Fiscal Year 2007, Pub. L. 109–364 (amending the UCMJ to include persons supporting the armed forces during a "declared war or a contingency operation").

1.6. THE PROHIBITION OF TORTURE UNDER U.S. LAW

While the Bush Administration lawyers applied theories of "exceptionalism" and imaginative approaches to the interpretation of international law, such techniques could not work with respect the Constitution and laws of the U.S. In that respect, they had a bigger challenge. One way to address it was to reinterpret the Constitution's "War Powers" provision,[134] and to claim that in times of war the Constitution itself gives the President full powers to act, which means that such actions cannot be in violation of the Constitution. Admittedly in times of war, former presidents have assumed greater powers, and even acted in contravention of the Constitution, but neither the legislative nor the judicial branches stopped them at the time, and these two branches subsequently restored the pendulum of separation of powers to its proper balance.[135] Never before, however, has the Eighth Amendment prohibiting "cruel, unusual and inhuman or degrading treatment or punishment" been suspended as part of Presidential war powers, nor has IHL been suspended by any wartime President. The lawyers arguing for President Bush's unrestrained war time powers to suspend all of the above and more was simply unprecedented and constitutionally untenable.

The Fourth, Fifth, Sixth and Eighth Amendments apply to such practices as prolonged detentions, coerced confessions, and torture.[136] The U.S. Supreme Court has held that Constitutional protections apply to aliens only when they are within U.S. territory.[137] Constitutional rights give rise to a separate cause of action under the Civil Rights Act of 1964.[138] The Supreme Court has thus far refrained from applying the Fourth, Fifth, and Sixth Amendment protections to U.S. public agents acting outside of U.S. territory.[139] Foreign criminal suspects

---

[134]   War Powers Resolution, Title 50 U.S.C. §§1541–48 (1973). John Yoo has written extensively on this subject after he left his position at the DOJ, see JOHN YOO, CRISIS AND COMMAND: A HISTORY OF EXECUTIVE POWER FROM GEORGE WASHINGTON TO GEORGE W. BUSH (2010; JOHN YOO, THE POWERS OF WAR AND PEACE: THE CONSTITUTION AND FOREIGN AFFAIRS AFTER 9/11 (2006). *See also* JOSEPH MARGULIES, GUANTÁNAMO AND THE ABUSE OF PRESIDENTIAL POWER 168 (2006).

[135]   This occurred during the War of Independence under President Washington, the Civil War under President Lincoln, World War II under Presidents Roosevelt and Truman, and the Vietnam War under President Johnson. *See also id.*

[136]   U.S. CONST. amends. V, VI, VIII. *See* Weems v. United States, 217 U.S. 349 (1910) applying the Eighth Amendment to punishment, and more recently, Kennedy v. Louisiana, 554 U.S. (2008) and Graham v. Florida, 560 U.S. (2010).

[137]   See Johnson v. Eisentrager, 339 U.S. 763, 784–85 (1950), wherein the Court held that where that U.S. courts had no jurisdiction over German war criminals held in a U.S.-administered German prison, because the prisoners had at no time been on American sovereign territory. *See also infra* Chapter 4, section 4.5, *Extraterritorial Application of the U.S. Constitution.*

[138]   *See* 42 U.S.C. §1841. *See, e.g.*, Griggs v. Duke Power Co., 401 U.S. 424 (1971); and Washington v. Davis, 426 U.S. 229 (1976).

[139]   *Id. See also infra* Chapter 4, section 4.5, *Extraterritorial Application of the U.S. Constitution.*

held by the U.S. are entitled to Fifth Amendment safeguards.[140] The use of "enhanced interrogation" techniques violates the Eighth Amendment protections against cruel and unusual punishment.[141]

In 2003, the U.S. ratified the Child Soldiers Protocol to the Convention on the Rights of the Child,[142] the obligations of which Bush Administration lawyers (particularly DOD lawyers and military personnel) failed to take into account with respect to the detention of juveniles held at Guantánamo, Iraq, and Afghanistan.[143]

The Constitution and the Bill of Rights prohibit cruel and unusual treatment or punishment, which includes torture and use of evidence obtained by coercion.[144] The protections extend to all persons in the United States. Torture occurring within the U.S. is prohibited under several federal statutes,[145] and under the Constitution and laws of all the states which prohibit acts such as assault, battery, manslaughter, and murder.

The War Crimes Act of 1996[146] made it a federal criminal offense for all U.S. nationals to commit any violations of Common Article 3 of the 1949 Geneva Conventions.[147] This includes murder, mutilation, cruel treatment, and torture.[148] However, in the wake of the Supreme Court decision in *Hamdan v. Rumsfeld*, which reaffirmed the applicability of the Geneva Conventions in the "war on terror,"[149] Bush Administration officials became concerned about the potential prosecution of U.S. civilian public agents, CIA officers, and former military personnel (who as a result of leaving military service are no longer subject to the UCMJ) for the mistreatment and torture of detainees in U.S. custody. The Bush Administration in 2006 drafted proposed amendments to the 1996 War Crimes

---

140   *See* OLSHANSKY, DEMOCRACY DETAINED, *supra* note 40, at 45; RONALD J. SIEVERT, DEFENSE, LIBERTY, AND THE CONSTITUTION 42 (2005). *See also* Hamdi v. Rumsfeld, 124 U.S. 2633 (2004), where the Court determined that the President could not detain a U.S. citizen as an "enemy combatant" without the "essential constitutional promises" of due process, including notice and an opportunity to be heard before a neutral decision-maker.

141   U.S. CONST. amend. VIII. *See also* Estelle v. Gamble 429 U.S. 97, 102–03 (1976).

142   United Nations Convention on the Rights of the Child, 1577 U.N.T.S. 3, *entered into force* Sep. 2, 1990; Optional Protocol to the Convention on the Rights of the Child on the Involvement of Children in Armed Conflicts, G.A. res. 54/263, Annex I, 54 U.N. GAOR Supp. (No. 49) at 7, U.N. Doc. A/54/49 (2000), *entered into force* Feb. 12, 2002.

143   *See infra* Chapter 2, section 2.6, *Interrogations of Juveniles*.

144   U.S. CONST. amend. V.

145   Title 18 U.S.C. §§1111–1122, homicide, including manslaughter; §§2340, 2340A, torture; §§111–119, assault; §§2241–48, sexual abuse; §§1501–1521, obstruction of justice; §§1961–68, Racketeer Influenced and Corrupt Organizations.

146   18 U.S.C. §2441 (2006). *See also* Exec. Order No. 13440, 72 Fed. Reg. 40707 (2007).

147   *See* Geneva I, art. 50; Geneva II, art. 51; Geneva III, art. 130; and Geneva IV, art. 147, *supra* note 10.

148   18 U.S.C. §2441 (c)(3).

149   *Hamdan v. Rumsfeld, supra* note 74.

Act.[150] The Military Commissions Act of 2006, which served primarily to establish a legal framework to prosecute detainees at Guantánamo, also included amendments to the 1996 War Crimes Act.[151] These amendments not only had a retroactive effect, but they also restricted the scope of responsibility for war crimes by adding the qualifying term of "grave breach" to the words "Common Article 3," even though the term "grave breach" applies only to conflicts of an international character and not to conflicts of a non-international character to which Common Article 3 applies.[152] This was likely deliberately intended in order to confuse the courts which would seek to distinguish between "grave breaches" and violations of Common Article 3, even though substantively they cover the same protected interests.[153]

Military personnel are subject to both criminal federal law under Title 18 of the U.S. Code, and to the UCMJ.[154] Under the UCMJ they may be court martialed for aggravated assault, dereliction of duty, mistreatment of detainees, and murder.[155] The UCMJ applies to military personnel and their dependants.

Military jurisdiction also extends to civilian contractors of the military, who are subject to federal criminal law under Title 18 of the U.S. Code pursuant to the Military Extraterritorial Jurisdiction Act (MEJA). This statutory enactment closes the jurisdictional gap over civilians operating alongside military forces outside the U.S.[156] MEJA gives U.S. courts jurisdiction over crimes that are committed on military installations by U.S. citizens or foreign nationals, including those who are subject to the UCMJ, and those civilians employed by or accompanying the military.

There is no doubt under U.S. law that evidence obtained by torture or by lesser coercive means cannot be admitted into evidence before federal or state courts, nor can such evidence be used to secure other evidence that could be

---

[150] *See* R. Jeffrey Smith, *War Crimes Act Changes Would Reduce Threat of Prosecution*, WASH. POST, Aug. 9, 2006.

[151] Pub. L. 103–366 §6(b)(2006).

[152] *Id. See* Michael Garcia, *The War Crimes Act: Current Issues* (Congressional Research Service, RL33662, U.S. Library of Congress, Jan. 22, 2009). Furthermore, the amendments purposefully left out violations which the Geneva Conventions consider to be "outrages upon personal dignity," which could include humiliations such as forced nudity or the use of dog leashes on a detainee. The amending legislation brought about a negative reaction from the ICRC, which unsuccessfully brought its concerns to the Bush Administration before the proposed legislation was sent to Congress. *See* Smith, *War Crimes Act Changes, supra* note 120.

[153] *See* THEODOR MERON, THE HUMANIZATION OF INTERNATIONAL LAW 29–38, 45–50 (2006); Theodor Meron, *The Humanization of Humanitarian Law*, 94 AM. J. INT'L L. 239, 243–47 (2000). *See also* M. Cherif Bassiouni, *The New Wars the Crisis of Compliance with the Law of Armed Conflict by Non-State Actors*, 98 J. CRIM. L. & CRIMINOLOGY 712 (2008), at 728.

[154] *See* 10 U.S.C. §47.

[155] *See* Mynda G. Ohman, *Integrating Title 18 War Crimes into Title 10: A Proposal to Amend the Uniform Code of Military Justice*, AIR FORCE L. REV. 49 (Winter 2005).

[156] *See* Military Extraterritorial Jurisdiction Act of 2000, 18 U.S.C. §3261 (2000) [hereinafter MEJA].

used in court. The doctrines of the "exclusionary rule"[157] and the "fruit of the poisonous tree"[158] enunciated by the Supreme Court, are still valid and they apply any time such tainted evidence seeks to be admitted or used in U.S. legal proceedings. These are territorial, nationality, or contextual exceptions. These legal standards apply no matter what, no matter where, and no matter whom.

1.7. OVERLAPPING LEGAL REGIMES

The U.S. is a federal system in which criminal justice is subject to the constitutions and laws of the different states, though under the overall umbrella of the U.S. Constitution. Thus, multiple criminal justice regimes exist in the 50 states. Within the federal government, there are also two principal legal regimes – Title 10 U.S.C., namely, the UCMJ which is applicable to military personnel whether inside or outside U.S. territory; and Title 18 U.S.C., provisions of which criminalize certain conduct deemed to be subject to federal law and is essentially applicable to civilians (but also to military personnel who commit non-military federal crimes), and which also apply extraterritorially to U.S. and non-U.S. citizens. Title 18, however, does not include all federal criminal laws. For reasons that defy sound policy, there is no comprehensive federal criminal code. Indeed, in addition to the federal crimes contained in Title 18, nearly every title in the U.S. Code has provisions that criminalize certain conduct domestically and extra-territorially. Moreover, in recent times, with the advent of the expanded use of private contractors under the Bush Administration, it became necessary to enact special legislation applicable to such contractors, namely, MEJA, which establishes yet another separate legal regime for these contractors (see Chapter 5, section 5.5, for a discussion of the use of private contractors).

The multiplicity of these legal regimes evidences the existence of gaps in the normative scheme and their overlap also evidences inconsistencies, thus precluding a uniform policy of addressing criminal violations depending upon when a person is deemed to be military, civilian, or private contractor, and whether the conduct is committed on U.S. territory or abroad. Sound legislative policy would require the identification of conduct being prohibited and criminalized, irrespective of whether the violators are military personnel, civilian, or private contractors; and also whether the conduct is committed inside or outside U.S. territory. Thus, for example, the UCMJ has extraterritorial applications which attach to the conduct of military personnel no matter where they are outside the territorial confines of the U.S., MEJA has some extraterritorial applications but not similar to those of the UCMJ. Title 18, with some exceptions, applies essentially to conduct committed within the U.S., with exceptions for

---

[157]   *See* Mapp v. Ohio, 367 U.S. 643 (1961).
[158]   *See* Silverthorne Lumber Co. v. United States, 251 U.S. 385 (1920).

certain extraterritorial applications with respect to crimes committed against U.S. facilities and interests outside the U.S., crimes which although committed abroad have an impact within the U.S., crimes committed abroad but against U.S. citizens, diplomats, and other protected persons, or by U.S. citizens (such as treason and non-payment of taxes).

The multiplicity of these legal regimes with their different norms and contents, as well as their different applications both territorially and extra-territorially, make it difficult to have a cohesive policy approach to the prosecution of criminal conduct which is deemed contrary to the interests and laws of the U.S. Thus, prosecutions become difficult and inconsistent as evidenced by the case involving members of the infamous private contractor security firm Blackwater USA (currently known as Xe Services LLC). In that case, the dismissal of a criminal case against members of that firm charged with indiscriminate use of force in killing 17 Iraqi civilians has had a negative effect on U.S.–Iraq relations, but has also telegraphed to the world that private contractors, like the mercenaries of one time, can act with relative impunity.[159]

The multiplicity of these overlapping regimes, with their gaps, overlaps, and content differences, makes it difficult for the pursuit of a principled approach to the prosecution of those who commit cruel, inhuman, and degrading treatment in violation of the CAT, violations of IHL, and violations of both Titles 10 and 18 of the U.S. Code. This complex domestic situation is aggravated by the fact that there are also multiple international legal regimes which also have their overlaps and gaps, particularly with respect to the distinction in IHL between conflicts of an international and non-international character, and purely internal conflicts.[160] These complexities notwithstanding, a principled policy approach should guide the decisions of the operators of the military and civilian regimes in accordance with both Titles 10 and 18 U.S. Code. In other words, the overlaps and gaps mentioned above should not become exploited by political considerations to subvert principled decisions in order to achieve political ends.

Another factor that bears consideration in connection with the above is the absence of a process in the U.S. by which to establish truth. Throughout the modern history of the U.S., the Senate has filled this void by having hearings on certain subjects and issuing reports which are akin to what is done at the international level and by other countries under the label of truth commissions.

---

[159] U.S. v. Slough *et al.*, 2009 U.S. Dist. LEXIS 121809 (D.C. Cir. 2009). *See* Charlie Savage, *Charges Against Blackwater Guards Dismissed in Iraq Killings*, N.Y. Times, Dec. 31, 2009; Ernesto Londoño, *Justice Department to Appeal Dismissal of Blackwater Indictment*, Wash. Post, Jan. 24, 2010; Fred Rosen, Contract Warriors: How Mercenaries Changed History and the War on Terrorism (2005). *See also* Chapter 5, section 5.5, *The Responsibility of Private Contractors with the U.S. Government*.

[160] *See* M. Cherif Bassiouni, *The Normative Framework of International Humanitarian Law: Overlaps, Gaps, and Ambiguities*, 8 Transnat'l L. & Contemp. Probs. 199 (1998); Bassiouni, *The New Wars and the Crisis of Compliance with the Law of Armed Conflict by Non-State Actors*, *supra* note 123.

In the last 50 years, there have been 53 truth commissions in different countries which have examined and revealed what happened in the course of domestic conflicts.[161] Considering the problems created by the overlapping U.S. legal regimes, their gaps, differences in content, and in some respect inconsistencies which have been politically exploited, it would be logical and appropriate for the Senate to conduct hearings in the nature of a truth commission to determine how the policy of torture was developed, and how the practices of torture were conducted. While Senator Patrick Leahy and Representative John Conyers floated the idea of a truth commission or a blue-ribbon investigative panel to look into the circumstances that led the Bush Administration to create its policy of torture, it has not been taken seriously by the Obama Administration as politically viable.[162]

Another device is the appointment of an independent commission of inquiry as was the case with the establishment of the 9/11 Commission.[163] Such a commission would be beneficial for this nation to understand how the torture policy developed and how it enabled the practice of torture inside and outside the U.S. in violation of treaty obligations, the U.S. Constitution, and the laws of the U.S. Many in this country and abroad would surely question why this did not occur, particularly when viewed in combination with the lack of prosecutions under Titles 10 and 18 for crimes that are well-established in U.S. law. The inference is quite likely to be that the U.S. acted with disregard for international law and its own Constitution and laws and in the pursuit of its domestic policies. The legal and political ramifications of this situation will have an impact upon the moral standing of the U.S. in the world, as well as upon its legitimacy and credibility, as described in this book.

1.8. CONCLUSION

International and U.S. law are unequivocal about the prohibition of torture. The fact that lawyers in the Bush Administration went to great lengths to misinterpret

---

[161] *See* Eric Wiebelhaus-Brahm, *Truth Commissions, in* 1 THE PURSUIT OF INTERNATIONAL CRIMINAL JUSTICE: A WORLD STUDY ON CONFLICTS, VICTIMIZATION, AND POST-CONFLICT JUSTICE (M. Cherif Bassiouni ed., 2010); PRISCILLA HAYNER, UNSPEAKABLE TRUTHS: CONFRONTING STATE TERROR AND ATROCITY (2002).

[162] *See* Jason Leopold, *Blistering Indictment Leveled Against Obama Over His Handling of Bush-Era War Crimes*, TRUTHOUT.ORG, Dec. 12, 2009. *See also* Chapter 5, section 5.2, *The Political Responsibility of Congress.*

[163] The National Commission on Terrorist Attacks Upon the United States (also known as the 9/11 Commission) was an independent, bipartisan commission created by congressional legislation in late 2002. Its mission was to prepare a complete account of the circumstances surrounding the September 11, 2001 terrorist attacks, including preparedness for and the immediate response to the attacks. The Commission, mandated to provide recommendations designed to guard against future attacks, released its final report on July 22, 2004.

and misapply the law only evidences how far they had to go to convince their peers that there was some legal loophole or gap that could be exploited to carry out illegal practices, ostensibly for a better purpose. This was no more than the Machiavellian concept of making the ends justify the means, irrespective of how clearly unlawful the means may be. To add another layer of presumptuousness to the preposterous arguments advanced about the distinction between torture and the "enhanced interrogation" techniques described in Chapter 2, the Bush lawyers intellectualized the rationalization of exceptionalism and selectivity in what they deemed to be binding or not. In the end, the spurious nature of these arguments became obvious, even though their transparency should have been obvious to many more at the time they were offered.

What should happen now is the clear denunciation of the invalidity of these arguments in order that they not be used in the future. Moreover, those who made these arguments should be held accountable, not only for their potential criminal violation of the law, but also for their ethical violations of their professional obligations.

APPENDIX 1: LEGAL DEFINITIONS

Definitions of Torture:

CAT: "Torture means any act by which severe pain or suffering, whether physical or mental, is intentionally inflicted on a person for such purposes as obtaining from him or a third person information or a confession, punishing him for an act he or a third person has committed or is suspected of having committed, or intimidating or coercing him or a third person, or for any reason …, when such pain or suffering is inflicted by or at the instigation of or with the consent or acquiescence of a public official or other person acting in an official capacity. It does not include pain or suffering arising only from, inherent in or incidental to lawful sanctions."

U.S. Federal Law (18 U.S.C. §2340 (1): "Torture means an act committed by a person acting under the color of law specifically intended to inflict severe physical or mental pain or suffering (other than pain or suffering incidental to lawful sanctions) upon another person within his custody or physical control."

Bybee Memo: "Where the pain is physical, it must be of an intensity akin to that which accompanies serious physical injury such as death or organ failure. Severe mental pain requires …lasting psychological harm as seen in mental disorders like posttraumatic stress disorder."

1949 Geneva Conventions Commentary: Torture is the "infliction of suffering on a person in order to obtain from that person, or from another person, confessions or information."

ICRC – International Humanitarian Law: "There must exist a specific purpose (such as obtaining a confession or as punishment) plus an intentional infliction of severe pain or suffering. There is no obligation for this to be instigated or consented by someone in an official capacity."

Definitions of cruel, inhuman or degrading treatment:

CAT: "Acts of cruel, inhuman or degrading treatment or punishment are those not amounting to torture when such acts are committed by or at the instigation of or with the consent or acquiescence of a public official or other person acting in an official capacity."

U.S. Federal Law: None specifically; refer instead to the U.S. Constitution and court cases for examples.

Bybee Memo: Refers only to the U.S. Constitution for 'cruel, unusual, and inhumane treatment or punishment'.

1949 Geneva Conventions Commentary: "Inhuman Treatment" includes "certain measures, for example, which cut PoWs off completely from the outside world and in particular from their families, or would cause great injury to their human dignity."

ICRC – International Humanitarian Law: For cruel or inhuman treatment, no specific purpose is necessary such as obtaining information and/or the level of pain is less than under torture although a significant level of suffering or pain must be inflicted for this category. For outrages upon personal dignity, no specific purpose is required but a significant level of humiliation or degradation is necessary.

Provisions of International Humanitarian Law

Common Article 3 of the Geneva Conventions – Non-International Conflicts

Persons not taking active part in the hostilities shall in all instances be treated humanely. The following acts are and shall remain prohibited at any time and in any place:

(a) violence to life and person, in particular murder of all kinds, mutilation, cruel treatment and torture;
(b) taking of hostages;
(c) outrages upon personal dignity, in particular humiliating and degrading treatment;
(d) the passing of sentences and the carrying out of executions without previous judgment pronounced by a regularly constituted court, affording all the judicial guarantees which are recognized as indispensable by civilized people.

Third Geneva Convention – Prisoners of War – Conflicts of an International Character

Article 12: The Party detaining the individuals is responsible for their treatment.

Article 13: Prisoners must at all times be humanely treated. An unlawful act/omission by the detaining Party resulting in death or seriously endangering the health of the PoW is a serious breach of the Convention. Measures of reprisal against PoWs are prohibited.

Article 14: PoWs are entitled in all circumstances to respect for their persons and their honor. Women shall be treated with all the regard due to their sex.

Article 16: PoWs shall be treated alike by the Detaining Power, without any adverse distinction based on race, nationality, religious belief or political opinions or any other distinction founded on similar criteria.

Article 17: Every PoW is bound to give only his or her surname, first names and rank, date of birth, and army regimental, personal or serial number. No physical or mental torture nor any other form of coercion, may be inflicted on PoWs to secure from them information of any kind whatever.

Article 5 of Protocol I

Protected persons must be protected against any threats and acts of violence and from insult. Again, no physical or moral coercive methods can be used to obtain information from these persons. All persons in this category, including those who lose their entitlement to these protections, shall be treated with humanity. (Articles 5, 27, and 31 of the Fourth Convention)

Some obligations and responsibilities of member states to the CAT:

- Take effective legislative, administrative, judicial or other measures to prevent acts of torture in any territory under its jurisdiction;
- No person can be expelled, returned or extradited to another State if there are substantial grounds to believe he or she is in danger of being tortured;
- Ensure all acts of torture are offences under its domestic criminal law;
- Establish jurisdiction over offences that are: (i) committed in any territory controlled by it including a ship/aircraft registered to that State, (ii) committed by any of its nationals, and (iii) committed to any of its nationals;
- Prohibit the use of any statements obtained by torture as evidence in any proceedings (except as against the torturer);
- Promptly and impartially investigate any complaints of torture;
- Give fair and adequate compensation for victims of torture; and
- Prevent any cruel, inhuman or degrading treatment occurring anywhere under its jurisdiction.

U.S. Constitution

Fourth Amendment: "The right of the people to be secure in their persons, houses, papers, and effects, against unreasonable searches and seizures, shall not be violated, and no Warrants shall issue but upon probable cause, supported by Oath or affirmation, and particularly describing the place to be searched, and the person or things to be seized."

Fifth Amendment guarantees that no person "…shall be compelled in any criminal case to be a witness against himself, nor be deprived of life, liberty or property without due process of law…".

Eighth Amendment: "Excessive bail shall not be required…nor cruel and unusual punishment inflicted."

Points of the Detainee Treatment Act of 2005:

- Denies the right to file a writ of *habeas corpus* by or for any prisoner at Guantánamo Bay;
- Gives the D.C. Court of Appeals, exclusive jurisdiction for any appeal of a sentence of death or imprisonment of more than ten years; although for all lesser sentences, review by the Court of Appeals is discretionary; and
- Provides procedural protection for U.S. personnel accused of improper interrogation techniques.

Regarding the Geneva Conventions

The new Army Manual 2–22.3 refers to several sources of law without stating what prevails.

The old Army Manual FM34–52 said if a conflict existed between the Geneva Conventions and any rule listed in the military manuals, the Geneva Conventions prevailed.

Miscellaneous

The new Army manual 2–22.3 clearly states the "use of torture is not only illegal but also is a poor technique that yields unreliable results, may damage subsequent questioning and may induce the person to say what he thinks the interrogator wants to hear." The new Army manual does not discuss 'force'.

The old Army manual on the use of force: from both legal and moral viewpoints, the restrictions established by international law, agreements and customs render threats of force, violence and deprivation useless as interrogation techniques

Approaching a line between permissible actions and prohibited actions – New Army Manual 2–22.3

First Method: as an interrogator, think about the same approach or technique used on a fellow soldier. In that situation, would you consider it to be an abuse?

Second Method: consider if the proposed technique would violate a law or regulation. If 'yes' is the answer to either of these questions, the technique should not be used.

Main Points of the Military Commissions Act

- Grants unprecedented and unchecked authority to the Executive Branch to label individuals, including those in the U.S. as being "unlawful enemy combatants";
- Does not allow evidence obtained through torture to be used against any defendant;
- Allows evidence obtained through coercion to be used against defendants, conditional on judicial preview;
- Allows hearsay evidence to be used unless the defendant can show it is unreliable or lacking in probative value;
- Grants the President the authority to interpret and apply the 1949 Geneva Conventions with such interpretation being published in the Federal Register;
- Denies certain rights of those in custody including the right of *habeas corpus* to challenge the legality of their detention; the principle of "fair trial" under the Geneva Conventions and human rights treaties is not met with the denial of the right of a speedy trial and rejection of sections relating to compulsory self-incrimination and pretrial investigations that generally apply in trials.
- The crimes triable by military commissions include terrorism, conspiracy, and the use of torture or cruel or inhuman treatment;
- Narrows the scope of the War Crimes Act by redefining and eliminating some crimes; and
- Restricts judicial review of the tribunals' rulings to the U.S. Court of Appeal, D.C. Circuit.

The Military Commissions Act also prohibits anyone from bringing a claim under the Geneva Conventions in lawsuits against the U.S. government or its agents.[164]

---

[164] Importantly, the Act attempts to eliminate accountability for past illegal acts and excludes several actions previously defined as criminal offences. In an interview with Jakob Kellenberger, President of the ICRC, reported that the ICRC had certain concerns and questions about the new legislation including, "[t]he very broad definition of who is an "unlawful enemy combatant" and the fact that there is no explicit prohibition on the admission of evidence attained by coercion are examples." He warned that the legislation could weaken basic guarantees given under the Geneva Conventions which are supposed to protect everybody from humiliating and degrading treatment. *See Developments in U.S. Policy and Legislation Towards Detainees: The ICRC Position* (International Committee of the Red Cross, Oct. 19, 2006).

CHAPTER 2
INTERROGATION TECHNIQUES

Some may argue that we would be more effective if we sanctioned torture
or other expedient methods to obtain information from the enemy...
What sets us apart from our enemies in this fight, however, is how we behave.
In everything we do, we must observe the standards and values that dictate
that we treat noncombatants and detainees with dignity and respect.
While we are warriors, we are also all human beings.[*]

– General David Petraeus

May 10, 2007

2.1. INTRODUCTION

Interrogation techniques and their limits have been well settled since the U.S. Army Field Manual 27–10 of 1956, which codifies international humanitarian law (IHL).[1] There is nothing in any of the armed services' field manuals or interpretations thereof between 1956 and 2001 which is contrary to IHL. The new interrogation techniques described in this chapter took matters beyond what IHL permits, and into violative practices. These new practices also violate previously established practices under the various services' field manuals. General Petraeus' quote cited above is only one of many expressed by senior uniformed military commanders. They reflect the U.S. military's correct understanding of IHL and the limits imposed by it upon interrogation techniques. By implication these statements and positions, some of which are discussed in this book, show how different these positions are from what the Bush Administration imposed. If only the senior commanders like Petraeus would have resisted the political influences of their civilian superiors, as well as other civilians in the Executive branch, our nation and its military would have been better for it.

What follows in this chapter describes the use of euphemisms and how they were employed to engage in illegal acts under certain guises intended to make them appear legal and even banal. The latter is a well-known technique of

---

[*]   From an open letter from General David H. Petraeus to servicemen in the Multi-National Force – Iraq, May 10, 2007.

[1]   U.S. Dep't of the Army, The Law of Land Warfare, Field Manual No. 27–10 (Jul. 18, 1956).

authoritarian regimes in order to induce ordinary people to commit evil acts.[2] The Nazi euphemism of the "final solution to the Jewish problem" became the rallying call for the extermination of the Jews. The euphemisms of the "war on terror," "enemy combatants" and "enhanced interrogation" became code words for permissible torture. However, to paraphrase Shakespeare, a rose by any other name is still a rose. The techniques described below and their applications to certain persons reveal how unequivocal and how horrendous the torture was. Anyone reading these facts cannot but be shocked.

2.2. THE NEW "ENHANCED INTERROGATION" TECHNIQUES

Some of the interrogation techniques that were deemed permissible and which were actually carried out include: making detainees stand for long periods of time; sleep deprivation; constant loud music; forcing a father to watch the mock execution of his 14-year old son; placing a lit cigarette in the ear of a detainee to burn his eardrum; bathing a person's hand in alcohol and lighting it on fire; shackling detainees to the floor for 18 to 24 hours, and from the top of a door frame to dislocate their shoulders; "waterboarding," which involves placing a cloth on a person's head and dousing it with water to create the sensation of drowning;[3] forcing a person to squat for periods up to and beyond 24 hours; crushing a person's bare hands and feet with boots, producing bleeding and severe hematoma; inflicting beatings with bare knuckles and hard objects, producing broken bones and lacerations; beating heads against walls; striking with the knees and boots in body locations known to cause severe pain and suffering; withholding medical treatment of the injured; and many others.[4]

---

[2]   *See* HANNAH ARENDT, EICHMANN IN JERUSALEM: A REPORT ON THE BANALITY OF EVIL (1963).

[3]   For a *Vanity Fair* article, Christopher Hitchens attempted to undergo a session of waterboarding. Here is how he described the experience: "You may have read by now the official lie about this treatment, which is that it 'simulates' the feeling of drowning. This is not the case. You feel that you are drowning because you *are* drowning – or, rather, being drowned, albeit slowly and under controlled conditions and at the mercy (or otherwise) of those who are applying the pressure." *Believe Me, It's Torture,* VANITY FAIR (August 2008). *See also* Evan Wallach, *Drop by Drop: Forgetting the History of Water Torture in U.S. Courts,* 45 COLUM. J. TRANSNAT'L L. 468 (2007).

[4]   Memorandum from William Haynes II to Donald Rumsfeld, Secretary of Defense, Counter-resistance Techniques (Nov. 27, 2002) [hereinafter JTF-GTMO Memo], listed interrogation techniques originally approved by Secretary Rumsfeld in 2002 (although this approval was rescinded in 2003). *Rumsfeld okayed abuses says former U.S. general,* REUTERS, Nov. 27, 2006. On a post outside of Abu Ghraib, a directive by Rumsfeld authorized:

    A short list, maybe 6 or 8 techniques: use of dogs; stress positions; loud music; deprivation of food; keeping the lights on, those kind of things. And then a handwritten message over to the side that appeared to be the same handwriting as the signature, and that signature

Additional torture practices documented in Iraq, Guantánamo, and Afghanistan include:[5] beating with fists, truncheon, whips, kicks, or slamming; electrical shocks with external electrodes; stretching or suspension causing tearing of ligaments, muscles or asphyxia; asphyxiation by water immersion, obstruction of airway, chest compression, or suspension; chemical burning; ligatures of the limbs or genitals; painful medical procedures such as administration of drugs or enemas; deprivation of food, water, and toilet access, shelter from cold or heat, medical care, and sleep; sensory deprivation; forcing detainee to urinate on self, masturbate, renounce religion, falsely confess or accuse, or apply the urine or feces of others; threats to the prisoner or his family; insults; denigration of the detainee's religion; mock executions; sexual degradation, including nudity and fondling; forcing a victim to watch the abuse or torture of loved one; perceptual monopolization including loud noise, immobilization, bright lights, and blindfolding; confinement in a small space; dog bites; and disorienting drugs.[6] It should be noted that prolonged solitary confinement and sensory deprivations are well-established forms of physical and psychological torture, even though the Bush Administration has attempted to

---

    was Secretary Rumsfeld's. And it said, 'Make sure this happens' with two exclamation points.'

Interview by Majorie Cohn with Brig. Gen. Janis Karpinski, TRUTHOUT.ORG, Aug. 3, 2005. Many accounts in the media, as well as the official reports released under the Freedom of Information Act request of the ACLU and the Center for Constitutional Rights, describe these and other practices. *See e.g.* Hina Shamsi, *Command's Responsibility: Detainee Deaths in U.S. Custody in Iraq and Afghanistan* (Human Rights First, Feb. 2006); Seth F. Kreimer, *"Torture Lite," "Full Bodied" Torture, and the Insulation of Legal Conscience*, 1 J. NAT'L SECURITY L. & POL'Y 187 (2005); Jane Mayer, *The Memo: How an Internal Effort to Ban the Abuse and Torture of Detainees Was Thwarted*, NEW YORKER, Feb. 27, 2006.

[5]   In a report by Physicians for Human Rights, medical evaluations using internationally accepted standards of eleven men held at Guantánamo revealed evidence of the following interrogation methods: beatings during arrest, transport and custody; deprivation of basic necessities and sanitary conditions; stress positions; isolation/sensory deprivation or bombardment; threats of harm to detainees and their families; use of extreme temperatures; electric shocks, sexual assault and physical assault; sleep deprivation; and sexual, religious and other forms of degrading treatment. *See Broken Laws, Broken Lives: Medical Evidence of Torture by U.S. Personnel and Its Impact* (Physicians for Human Rights, June 2008).

[6]   STEVEN H. MILES, OATH BETRAYED: TORTURE MEDICAL COMPLICITY AND THE WAR ON TERROR 8–9, 50–51 (2006). *See also* Steven H. Miles, *Abu Ghraib: Its Legacy for Military Medicine*, 362 LANCET 725, 728 (2004); Steven Miles, *Interview for Democracy Now, Oath Betrayed: Torture, Medical Complicity, and the War on Terror*, DEMOCRACY NOW, June 30, 2006; Army Inspector General, *Detainee Operations Inspections* (July 21, 2004); International Committee of the Red Cross, *Report on the Treatment by the Coalition Forces of Prisoners of War and Other Protected Persons by the Geneva Convention in Iraq During Arrest, Internment, and Interrogation* (ICRC, Feb. 2004). In June of 2004, the ICRC said that the physical and mental coercion of the prisoners at Guantánamo is "tantamount to torture" and the role of physicians was "a flagrant violation of medical ethics." Neil A. Lewis, *Red Cross Finds Detainee Abuse in Guantánamo: U.S. Rejects Accusations*, N.Y. TIMES, Nov. 30, 2004, at A1; George J. Annas, *Human Rights Outlaws: Nuremberg, Geneva, and the Global War on Terror*, 87 BOSTON U. L. REV. 427, 433 (2007).

portray them as benign forms of mild coercion.[7] From these examples, it is clear that torture was practiced, and those who ordered or allowed it to happen may be responsible under conspiracy to commit torture, while those who committed it are responsible for the crime of torture itself.

Some interrogation logs have been made public via the DOJ's Office of Inspector General's Report on the FBI's Involvement in Observations of Detainee Interrogations in Guantánamo Bay.[8] It is important to keep in mind that such interrogation methods were used by U.S. government or military agents on a U.S. military base – this was not an interrogation "in the field," as a part of the "extraordinary rendition" program, nor was it conducted by U.S. contractors.

The development of a policy allowing torture as an interrogation method was effected in a top-down fashion by high-ranking members of the Bush Administration, as discussed in Chapter 3. While the Army manuals governing the rules of interrogation assume the applicability of the Geneva Conventions and other U.S. and international law, on February 2, 2002, President Bush declared a "new paradigm" for the interrogation of detainees in which such laws did not apply to al-Qaeda and Taliban detainees captured in Afghanistan.[9] Due to the confusion generated by the President's declaration, untrained, inexperienced and inadequately supervised interrogators began to experiment with more aggressive interrogation techniques.[10]

---

[7]   *See* Stuart Grassin, *Psychiatric Effects of Solitary Confinement*, 22 WASH UNIV. J. L. POL'Y 325 (2006).

[8]   Email from Classified FBI Agent to Valerie Caproni, FBI Office of General Counsel (Aug. 2, 2004, 10:46 EST) (on file with author). One released report from an FBI special agent to the FBI Office of General Counsel reported that he observed a detainee bound to the floor by his arms and legs, barefoot, covered in feces in 100+ degree temperatures for over 20 hours. There was no food or water available to the unconscious detainee. In this report the FBI agent reported that present MPs, under direction of interrogators, were instructed to leave the detainee there. The revolting examples abound, and can be found in appendices two and three following this chapter.

[9]   Memorandum from George W. Bush, President, to the Vice President, Secretary of State, Secretary of Defense, the Attorney General, Chief of Staff to the President, Director of Central Intelligence, Assistant to the President for National Security Affairs, and Chairman of the Joint Chiefs of Staff, RE: Humane Treatment of Taliban and al Qaeda Detainees, Feb. 7, 2002. In this memorandum, President Bush stated, relying on the advice of the Attorney General and the DOJ, that "none of the provisions of Geneva apply to our conflict with al Qaeda in Afghanistan or elsewhere throughout the world because, among other reasons, al Qaeda is not a High Contracting Party to Geneva." He also stated in the memorandum, once again relying on the "legal conclusions of the DOJ," that "common Article 3 of Geneva does not apply to either al Qaeda or Taliban detainees, because, among other reasons, the relevant conflicts are international in scope and common Article 3 applies only to 'armed conflict not of an international character.'" *Id.*

[10]   *See* Jordan J. Paust, *Prosecuting the President and his Entourage*, 14 ILSA J. INT'L & COMP. L. 539 (2007). "The President's 2002 memorandum authorized and order the denial of treatment required by the Geneva Conventions and, therefore, necessarily authorized and ordered violations of the Geneva Conventions, which are war crimes." *Id.* at 539.

It was within this legal vacuum that U.S. Army Commander Gen. James T. Hill and others recommended to the Joint Chiefs of Staff the interrogation techniques adapted from Survival, Evasion, Resistance, and Escape (SERE) training to be used on the prisoners at Guantánamo. SERE is the training program designed, in part, to teach military personnel how to resist severe interrogation techniques by enemy forces. The methods had been 'reverse engineered' to develop an interrogation program for use by U.S. forces. In a memorandum recommending adoption of severe interrogation techniques, Hill stated that "Although I am cognizant of the important policy ramifications of some of these proposed techniques, I firmly believe that we must quickly provide Joint Task Force 170 counter-resistance techniques to maximize the value of our intelligence collection mission."[11] These techniques eventually migrated from Guantánamo to Afghanistan, and ultimately to Iraq, where the Geneva Conventions clearly applied.[12]

2.3. THE SPREAD OF SERE INTERROGATION TECHNIQUES

Although plans for implementing harsh interrogation techniques were set in motion during the summer of 2002, official requests from interrogators and commanders in Guantánamo Bay did not start moving up the chain of command to any notable extent until October 2002. In September, Haynes, Gonzales, and Addington visited Guantánamo Bay, observed some interrogations, and met with Maj. Gen. Michael E. Dunlavey, commander of JTF-170 at Guantánamo and tasked with handling interrogation operations for the DOD. In this meeting the signal was sent that interrogators should "do whatever needs to be done" to get information.[13]

On October 2, 2002, Jonathon Fredman, Counsel to CIA Counter-terrorism Center, attended a meeting at Guantánamo with Staff Judge Advocate Lt. Col. Diane Beaver, Maj. Gen. Dunlavey, and Lt. Col. Jerald Phifer in which they discussed use of harsh interrogation techniques. The discussion during this

---

[11]   Memorandum from U.S. Army Commander General James T. Hill to the Joint Chiefs of Staff, Re: Counter-Resistance Techniques, Oct. 25, 2002, at para. 4.

[12]   Hamdan v. Rumsfeld, 126 U.S. 2749, 2762–69 (2006). It should be noted that the U.S. sought legitimacy by the Security Council for its presence in Iraq. It obtained S.C. Resolution 1790 (2007) which, while giving no legitimacy to the U.S. invasion, nevertheless established that it was a conflict of an international character to which IHL applies. *See* U.N. Doc. S/Res/Es/1790 (2007). For a general discussion of the legality and legal status of U.S. forces in Iraq, *see* M. Cherif Bassiouni, *Legal Status of U.S. Forces in Iraq from 2003–2008*, 11 CHICAGO J. INT'L L. (forthcoming 2010).

[13]   *See* PHILIPPE SANDS, TORTURE TEAM: RUMSFELD'S MEMO AND THE BETRAYAL OF AMERICAN VALUES (2008). *See also* Scott Horton, *Which Came First, Memo or Torture?*, L.A. TIMES, Apr. 21, 2008.

meeting mirrors the callousness and disregard for federal and international law seen in legal memoranda emanating from DOJ. Fredman's view of boundaries of interrogation was "It is basically subject to perception. If a detainee dies, you're doing it wrong."[14] In addition, Beaver's comments coincide with the DOJ's methods of creating legal justification for harsh interrogation and torture by saying, "we'll need [legal] documentation to protect us."[15] Her comments also indicate that the methods they discussed were illegal under international and possibly U.S. law. A week later, Phifer made a request to Dunlavey for permission to use new interrogation techniques.[16] These techniques have an uncanny resemblance to methods U.S. soldiers are confronted with in SERE training.

A serious question is how exactly the SERE techniques came to be used at Guantánamo Bay.[17] The CIA had begun looking into new methods of interrogation as early as the spring of 2002.[18] With the capture of Abu Zubaydah in March 2002, the CIA contracted James Mitchell, a former Air Force psychologist to lead the interrogation team responsible for him. Mitchell's training did not include intelligence or Middle Eastern culture, however. He was a psychologist who had a background in designing and implementing the SERE program. It is not known exactly when the CIA began to apply SERE-like interrogation methods to Abu Zubaydah, but the OLC approved of 18 interrogation techniques for the CIA on August 1, 2002, in what has become known as the Bybee II memorandum.[19] The methods in this classified

---

[14] *Detainee Interrogation Techniques before the Senate Comm. on Armed Services.* 110th Cong. (2008) (Adjoining Documents Tab 7). Fredman kept his position at the CIA after Bush left office. *See* Spencer Ackerman, *Key Player in 'Enhanced' Interrogations Still at CIA*, WASH. INDEPENDENT, April 23, 2009.

[15] *Id.*

[16] Lt. Col. Jerald Phifer, Memorandum for Commander, JTF-170, *Request for Approval of Counter-resistance Strategies* (Oct. 11, 2002).

[17] The chronology of DOD's role in developing the policy of "aggressive" interrogation techniques was of particular interest to the Senate's Committee on Armed Forces. *See Senate Armed Forces Committee Inquiry into the Treatment of Detainees in U.S. Custody*, Apr. 21, 2009.

> Shortly after Secretary Rumsfeld's December 2, 2002 approval of his General Counsel's recommendation to authorize aggressive interrogation techniques, the techniques – and the fact the Secretary had authorized them – became known to interrogators in Afghanistan. A copy of the Secretary's memo was sent from GTMO to Afghanistan. Captain Carolyn Wood, the Officer in Charge of the Intelligence Section at Bagram Airfield in Afghanistan, said that in January 2003 she saw a power point presentation listing the aggressive techniques that had been authorized by the Secretary. ...From Afghanistan, the techniques made their way to Iraq.

> *Id.* at xxii-xxiii.

[18] *See* JANE MAYER, THE DARK SIDE: THE INSIDE STORY OF HOW THE WAR ON TERROR TURNED INTO A WAR ON AMERICAN IDEALS (2008), at 164.

[19] *See* Memorandum from Assistant Attorney General Jay S. Bybee, Ass't Att'y Gen., for John Rizzo, General Counsel, Central Intelligence Agency, memorandum on Interrogation of al Qaeda Operatives, Aug. 1, 2002.

memorandum allegedly match those noted in the Haynes memorandum that would be drafted in November of 2002.[20]

During September 2002, commanders at Guantánamo were brainstorming new interrogation techniques due to pressure coming from Washington for more results. These sessions were attended in part by CIA employees who at the time would have been familiar with SERE techniques after the Agency had used them on Abu Zubaydah.[21] In *Torture Team*, Philippe Sands writes that Beaver admitted that ideas from the brainstorming sessions came from all directions.[22] Those involved would get excited and suggest new ideas on what methods could be used. She even made reference to the television show *24* as a source.[23] However, even with the multitude of suggestions made, the final list of potential methods compiled by Phifer still closely resembled the one approved for the CIA months before.

In preparation for a request for new interrogation techniques, Beaver wrote a legal memorandum for Dunlavey that recommended use of SERE techniques on Guantánamo detainees.[24] She included recommendations for a few safeguards in using these techniques, but approved of harsh interrogation methods in certain circumstances. Beaver now claims that she requested further, outside review of her memorandum.[25] However, when Dunlavey made a request to Gen. Hill, he included Beaver's memorandum without further request for legal review.[26]

The request and adjoining legal memorandum moved up the chain of command to the Joint Chiefs of Staff. The memorandum was distributed to the services and the different military services provided their input, expressing concern and calling for further investigation into the methods and legal basis for using them. Adm. Dalton initiated an investigative review to pursue this vetting of the techniques.[27] However, Haynes stated that he did not want this broad review to continue, and at this point, Dalton ceased her broad investigation.[28]

---

20   JTF-GTMO Memo, *supra* note 4. *See* SANDS, TORTURE TEAM, *supra* note 13, at 184.
21   *See* SANDS, TORTURE TEAM, *supra* note 13, at 64.
22   *Id.* at 61.
23   *Id.*
24   *See* JTF-GTMO Memo, *supra* note 4.
25   *Detainee Interrogation Techniques before the Senate Comm. on Armed Services.* 110th Cong. (2008).
26   *Id.*
27   *Id.* (statement by Jane Dalton).
28   *Id.*

2.4. SELECTED CASE STUDIES OF "ENHANCED INTERROGATION" TECHNIQUES

The purpose of describing what happened in the following cases is to show: 1) how willful acts of torture, cruel, and inhuman and degrading treatment or punishment were, 2) how useless they were, and 3) how obvious they were to those who committed them (U.S. military and intelligence personnel), as well as to their superiors, who did nothing to stop these crimes under international and U.S. law, as they are required by law to do.

Abu Zubaydah

Abu Zubaydah was captured in Pakistan in March 2002, suspected of being a principal operational commander within al-Qaeda. He was wounded during his capture and initially taken to a CIA facility for medical treatment. The interrogation of Abu Zubaydah in 2002 began with two FBI special agents who began an interview process with him before CIA interrogators were available. From March until June 2002, the FBI began a rapport-building method of dealing with Abu Zubaydah to the extent that agents Ali Soufan and Steve Gaudin cleaned up after a hospitalized Abu Zubaydah following bowel movements.[29] According to Soufan, FBI's top experts on al-Qaeda and fluent in Arabic, he and Gaudin were able to gain the confidence of Abu Zubaydah with the use of proven FBI interrogation techniques. Under their supervision, Abu Zubaydah eventually identified Khaled Sheikh Mohammed as the mastermind behind the 9/11 attacks and the Jose Padilla dirty bomb plot.[30]

The arrival of CIA interrogators, specifically James Mitchell, brought a drastic change in the treatment of Abu Zubaydah. Soufan described the CIA's method of interrogation to be "borderline torture" after observing a coffin-like box that Mitchell had built for Abu Zubaydah.[31] Soufan objected directly to the CIA, but he was assured that the procedures used had been approved "at the highest levels."[32] Distressed at what was happening at the CIA "black site," Soufan described the methods of the CIA's interrogation to FBI counterterrorism Assistant Director Pasquale D'Amuro, who in turn brought the concerns to the Bureau's Director, Robert Mueller. Mueller ordered Soufan and other FBI agents

---

[29]   *See* Michael Isikoff, *Ali Soufan Breaks his Silence*, NEWSWEEK, May 4, 2009.

[30]   Ali Soufan, *My Tortured Decision*, N.Y. TIMES, April 22, 2009. Soufan was sent to Guantánamo in early 2002 to train interrogators. The attitude he received from military intelligence officers was to the effect of "You guys are cops. We don't have time for this." Isikoff, *Ali Soufan Breaks his Silence, supra* note 29.

[31]   *Review of the FBI's Involvement in and Observations of Detainee Interrogations in Guantánamo Bay, Afghanistan, and Iraq*, Department of Justice Office of Inspector General 122 (2008) [hereinafter OIG Report], at 68.

[32]   OIG Report, *id.* at 69.

home, and soon thereafter, issued a directive banning FBI personnel from participating in CIA interrogations.[33]

In August 2002, D'Amuro met with Michael Chertoff, Alice Fisher, and David Kelley of the DOJ to discuss the methods used by the CIA as well as ways the FBI may "add value" to ongoing investigations. During this meeting, D'Amuro learned that the CIA had attained a legal opinion from the DOJ that explained that certain techniques could be used. In early deliberations by the NSC Principals Committee (including Cheney, Rice, Ashcroft, and other high-level officials) over which interrogation methods would be approved for use by the CIA, Abu Zubaydah was the detainee being discussed.[34] In the Senate Armed Forces Committee's inquiry into the treatment of detainees in U.S. custody, discussions surrounding the interrogation of Abu Zubaydah played a major role in the early development of approved CIA interrogation techniques.[35] According to high-level officials whom Ron Suskind interviewed for his book, *The One Percent Doctrine*, President Bush allegedly told CIA director George Tenet "I said [Abu Zubaydah] was important. You're not going to let me lose face on this, are you?" Tenet replied "No sir, Mr. President."[36] Indeed, President Bush mentioned Abu Zubaydah's interrogation specifically in his statement to the press after the Supreme Court *Hamdan* decision, in which he admitted to the existence of CIA "black sites".[37]

Abu Zubaydah was eventually waterboarded 83 times, as acknowledged by the CIA.[38] According to the ICRC, Abu Zubaydah was the only one of the infamous fourteen "high-value" detainees in CIA custody who was subjected to every harsh interrogation technique they were able to determine had been used.[39] These included continuous solitary confinement and incommunicado detention, suffocation by water, prolonged stress standing, beatings by use of a collar, beating and kicking, confinement in a box, prolonged nudity, sleep deprivation and use of loud music, exposure to cold temperature/cold water, prolonged use of

---

[33]   *See* Isikoff, *Ali Soufan Breaks his Silence, supra* note 29.

[34]   Mark Mazzetti, *Bush Officials Linked to Debate on Interrogation Methods for Detainees*, N.Y. Times, Sep. 24, 2008.

[35]   *Inquiry into the Treatment of Detainees in U.S. Custody*, Report of the Committee on Armed Services, United States Senate, Nov. 20, 2008, at 16–19.

[36]   Ron Suskind, The One Percent Doctrine: Deep Inside America's Pursuit of its Enemies Since 9/11 (2006).

[37]   Press Release, The White House, *President Discusses Creation of Military Commissions to Try Suspected Terrorists*, Sept. 6, 2006. *See also* Transcript, *President Bush's Speech on Terrorism*, N.Y. Times, Sep. 6, 2006.

[38]   Memorandum for John Rizzo, Senior Deputy General Counsel, C.I.A., *Application of United States Obligations Under Article 16 of the Convention Against Torture to Certain Techniques that May Be Used in the Interrogation of High Value al-Qaeda Detainees*, May 30, 2005 [Bradbury Memo III].

[39]   International Committee for the Red Cross, *ICRC Report on the Treatment of Fourteen "High Value Detainees" in CIA Custody*, Feb. 14, 2007, at 9.

handcuffs and shackles, threats, forced shaving, and deprivation/restricted provision of solid food.[40]

Abu Zubaydah currently remains at Guantánamo, although his actual connections to al-Qaeda are in serious doubt. Suskind, who researched Abu Zubaydah extensively, described him as a "minor logistics man, a travel agent," and furthermore, as mentally ill.[41] The ultimate determination that Abu Zubaydah was indeed a "certifiable split personality" who knew much less than he was purported to have known was "echoed at the top of the CIA and briefed to the President and the Vice President."[42]

Joseph Margulies, a law professor at Northwestern University and Abu Zubaydah's defense counsel, wrote in a newspaper editorial:

> Today, he suffers blinding headaches and has permanent brain damage. He has an excruciating sensitivity to sounds, hearing what others do not… Partly as a result of injuries he suffered while he was fighting the communists in Afghanistan, partly as a result of how those injuries were exacerbated by the CIA and partly as a result of his extended isolation, Abu Zubaydah's mental grasp is slipping away.[43]

Mohammed Al-Qahtani

Mohammed Al-Qahtani is thought to have been the missing 20th hijacker of the 9/11 attacks. After being refused entry into the U.S. in August 2001, he went to Pakistan, where he was captured in December 2001 and eventually sent to Guantánamo Bay.

According to a DOD interrogation log which has been made public, Al-Qahtani had been subjected to 160 days of isolation in a pen perpetually flooded with artificial light.[44] He was interrogated on 48 of 54 days, for 18 to 20 hours at a stretch. He was stripped naked; straddled by taunting female guards, in an exercise called "invasion of space by a female;" forced to wear women's underwear on his head and to put on a bra; threatened by dogs; placed on a leash; and told that his mother was a whore. Al-Qahtani was also subjected to a phony kidnapping, deprived of heat, given large quantities of intravenous liquids without access to a toilet, deprived of sleep, and forced to undergo an enema. At one point, Al-Qahtani's heart rate had dropped so precipitately, to 35 beats a minute, that he required cardiac monitoring.

In November 2006, the DOD's Criminal Investigation Task Force reported that Al-Qahtani would be "unprosecutable" because of the extent to which his

---

[40]   *Id.*

[41]   *See* Suskind, The One Percent Doctrine, *supra* note 36.

[42]   *Id. See also* Dan Eggen & Walter Pincus, *FBI, CIA Debate Significance of Terror Suspect*, Wash. Post, Dec. 18, 2007.

[43]   Joseph Marguiles, *Abu Zubaydah's Suffering*, L.A. Times, Apr. 30, 2009.

[44]   *Inside the Interrogation of Detainee 063*, Time, June 12, 2005.

interrogations had risen.[45] This report was prescient, because in May 2008, charges against Al-Qahtani were dismissed without cause. Susan J. Crawford, who was appointed the Convening Authority at the Military Commissions at Guantánamo in 2007,[46] refused to refer Al-Qahtani's case to trial because his interrogations so clearly rose to the level of torture. In an interview with Bob Woodward in January 2010, she admitted:

> We tortured Qahtani. His treatment met the legal definition of torture. And that's why I did not refer the case [for prosecution]… The techniques they used were all authorized, but the manner in which they applied them was overly aggressive and too persistent… You think of torture, you think of some horrendous physical act done to an individual. This was not any one particular act; this was just a combination of things that had a medical impact on him, that hurt his health. It was abusive and uncalled for. And coercive. Clearly coercive. It was that medical impact that pushed me over the edge [to call it torture].[47]

Although charges against Al-Qahtani have been dropped, as of April 2010, he remains at Guantánamo.

Mohamedou Ould Salahi

Mohamedou Ould Salahi, a Mauritanian by birth, studied electrical engineering and ran an internet café in Germany. Previous to 9/11, U.S. authorities unsuccessfully tried to connect Salahi to a plot to blow up the Los Angeles airport. Shortly after 9/11, he was detained in Mauritania on suspicion of having ties to al-Qaeda. U.S. public agents illegally rendered Salahi to Jordan, where he was detained and tortured for eight months. He was then sent to Bagram in Afghanistan, and ultimately transferred to Guantánamo in August 2002, where he remains.[48]

When Salahi first arrived at Guantánamo, his interrogation was undertaken by the FBI, which relied on its standard rapport-building techniques. The FBI's "friendly tenor" was criticized heavily by military interrogators, however, and by May 2003, all of the Bureau's agents had left Guantánamo.[49] In July 2003, Maj. Gen. Miller sought "special project status" on behalf of the Defense Intelligence

---

[45]   *See* Bill Dedman, *Can '20ᵗʰ Hijacker' Ever Stand Trial? Aggressive Interrogation at Guantanamo May Prevent his Prosecution,* MSNBC.COM, Oct. 26, 2006.

[46]   Press Release, Dep't of Defense, *Seasoned Judge to Tapped to Head Detainee Trials,* Feb. 20, 2007. Crawford was formerly chief judge of the military's highest court, appointed by George H.W. Bush in 1991. She retired from her position as Convening Authority of the Military Commissions in January 2010.

[47]   Bob Woodward, *Detainee Tortured Says U.S. Official: Trial Overseer Cites 'Abusive Methods' Against 9/11 Suspect,* WASH. POST, Jan. 19, 2010.

[48]   *See* Press Release, ACLU, *Guantánamo Prisoner Successfully Challenges Unlawful Detention,* Apr. 9, 2009.

[49]   OIG report, *supra* note 31, at 122.

Agency for Salahi, so that he could authorize techniques not specified by the Secretary of Defense in the "Counter-Resistance Techniques in the War on Terrorism" memorandum of April 16, 2003.[50] Secretary Rumsfeld approved of this request on August 13th.[51] Following this approval, interrogators threatened the life of Salahi and his family members several times during his interrogation. He was subjected to sensory deprivation, isolation, sleep "adjustment", and 20-hour interrogations that could amount to sleep deprivation.[52] Salahi also alleged that he was subjected to extreme temperatures in a room called the "freezer," and that he was subjected to strobe lights, deprivation of clothing in front of females, sexual touching by females, and severe beatings.[53] At one point, Salahi was masked and taken on a boat ride, where he was beaten and made to overhear a conversation in Arabic between an Egyptian and a Jordanian, discussing whose country would ultimately "get him."[54] Interrogators also falsely portrayed themselves as FBI agents, a concern which was brought to FBI headquarters.

Marine Corps Lt. Col. Stuart Couch, the military lawyer originally assigned to prosecute the case against Salahi in the military commissions, determined that Salahi's confessions were so tainted by torture that they could not ethically be used against him. Couch told his supervisors that he was "morally opposed" to Salahi's treatment and for that reason he refused to participate in the prosecution.[55]

In 2005, a habeas corpus challenge to Salahi's detention was filed with the U.S. Federal District Court of the District of Columbia. On March 22, 2010, Federal District Court Judge James Robertson ruled that the U.S. could no longer continue to detain Salahi, and ordered his release.[56] The DOJ is currently appealing the decision.

---

[50]   *Id.*

[51]   *See Senate Armed Services Committee, supra* note 18, at xxii.

[52]   OIG report, *supra* note 31.

[53]   *Id.* at 124.

[54]   *Id.* at 124.

[55]   *See* Darrel J. Vandeveld, *I Was Slow to Recognize the Stain of Guantánamo*, Wash. Post, Jan. 18, 2009. Couch ultimately resigned from his posting at the military commissions.

[56]   Memorandum Order, Mohammedou Ould Salahi v. Obama et al., No. 05-CV-0569 (D.D.C., April 2010). In his order, Judge Robertson wrote:

> The government's problem is that its proof that Salahi gave material support to terrorists is so attenuated, or so tainted by coercion and mistreatment, or so classified, that it cannot support a successful criminal prosecution. Nevertheless, the government wants to hold Salahi indefinitely, because of its concern that he might renew his oath to al-Qaida and become a terrorist upon his release. That concern may indeed be well-founded… But a habeas court may not permit a man to be held indefinitely upon suspicion, or because of the government's prediction that he may do unlawful acts in the future – any more than a habeas court may rely upon its prediction that a man will not be dangerous in the future and order his release if he was lawfully detained in the first place.
>
> *Id.* at 31–32.

Khaled Sheikh Mohammed

Khaled Sheikh Mohammed, popularly known in the media as "KSM", is the highest level detainee in U.S. custody – according to the 9/11 Commission, he was the principal architect of the 9/11 attacks. Mohammed was captured in Pakistan in March 2003, and kept in secret CIA "black sites" for over three years until his transfer to Guantánamo in September 2006.

A 2005 DOJ memo released in April 2009 confirmed that Mohammed had undergone waterboarding 183 times in March 2003.[57] It is also alleged that Mohammed's children, aged six and eight, were also detained and threats against their lives used as another interrogation method to elicit information from Mohammed.[58] According to a report of the CIA's Office of Inspector General which released in August 2009, "an experienced Agency interrogator reported that the interrogators threatened Khalid Shaykh Muhammed, [saying] that if anything else happens in the United States, 'We're going to kill your children.'"[59]

The ICRC visited Guantánamo in 2006 and was allowed to interview 14 "high level" detainees, one of them being Khaled Sheikh Mohammed.[60] Its report to the CIA unambiguously concluded that the treatment that the detainees had endured amounted to torture:

> The general term "ill-treatment" has been used throughout, however, it should in no way be understood as minimising the severity of the conditions and treatment to which the detainees were subjected. Indeed, as concluded by this report, the ICRC clearly considers that the allegations of the fourteen include descriptions of treatment and interrogation techniques – singly or in combination – that amounted to torture and/or cruel, inhuman, or degrading treatment.[61]

As the most notorious detainee held at Guantánamo, how and where Khaled Sheikh Mohammed is to be tried has become a highly political issue. While Attorney General Eric Holder is committed to transferring all of the cases before military commissions to federal courts, his announcement to try Mohammed in the heart of New York City brought about a public backlash.[62] As of May 2010,

---

[57]   Steven J. Bradbury, Principal Deputy Assistant Attorney General, Dep't of Justice Office of Legal Counsel, Memorandum for John A. Rizzo, Senior Deputy General Counsel, Central Intelligence Agency, *Re: Application of United States Obligations Under Article 16 of the Convention Against Torture to Certain Techniques that may be Used in the Interrogation of High Value al-Qaeda Detainees*, May 30, 2005.

[58]   *See* Michael Melia, *Father of Pakistani Alleges U.S. Torture*, WASH. POST, Apr. 16, 2007.

[59]   Central Intelligence Agency, Office of the Inspector General, *Counterterrorism Detention and Interrogation Activities (September 2001 – October 2003)* (7 May 2004), at 42.

[60]   International Committee for the Red Cross, *ICRC Report on the Treatment of Fourteen "High Value Detainees" in CIA Custody*, Feb. 14, 2007.

[61]   *Id.* at 5.

[62]   *See* Jane Mayer, *The Trial: Eric Holder and the Battle over Khaled Sheikh Mohammed*, THE NEW YORKER, Feb. 15, 2010.

the decision of where Mohammed and others will be tried is still pending, although the appointment of a new Convening Authority of the military commissions in March 2010 does not bode well for trials before federal courts.[63]

Abd Al-Rahim Al-Nashiri

Abd Al-Rahim Al-Nashiri, a Saudi citizen, is a suspected member of al-Qaeda and is the alleged mastermind behind the 2000 bombing of the U.S.S. Cole Naval Destroyer off the coast of Yemen. He was captured by special agents of the CIA in the United Arab Emirates in November 2002, and held in secret "black sites" until March 2008, when he was moved to Guantánamo.

Al-Nashiri is the third detainee which the CIA has acknowledged having waterboarded, along with Abu Zubaydah and Khaled Sheikh Mohammed. The 2009 CIA OIG report described some of Al-Nashiri's interrogations in this way:

> 92. The debriefer assessed Al-Nashiri as withholding information, at which point [blank] reinstated [blank] hooding, and handcuffing. Sometime between 28 December 2002 and 1 January 2003, the debriefer used an unloaded semi-automatic handgun as a prop to frighten al-Nashiri into disclosing information. After discussing this plan with [blank] the debriefer entered the cell where Al-Nashiri sat shackled and racked the handgun once or twice close to Al-Nashiri's head. On what was probably the same day, the debriefer used a power drill to frighten Al-Nashiri. With [blank] consent, the debriefer entered the detainee's cell and revved the drill while the detainee stood naked and hooded. The debriefer did not touch Al-Nashiri with the power drill.
>
> …
>
> 94. During another incident [blank] the same Headquarters debriefer, according to a [blank] who was present, threatened Al-Nashiri by saying that if he did not talk, "We could get your mother in here," and "We can bring your family in here."
>
> …
>
> 97. OIG received reports that interrogation team members employed potentially injurious stress positions on Al-Nashiri. …[an Agency officer] expressed concern that Al-Nashiri's arms might be dislocated from his shoulders. …Al-Nashiri was reportedly lifted off the floor by his arms while his arms were bound behind his back with a belt.
>
> 98. [blank] interrogator reported that he witnessed other techniques used on Al-Nashiri that the interrogator knew were not specifically approved by DoJ. These included the use of a stiff brush that was intended to induce pain on Al-Nashiri and standing on Al-Nashiri's shackles, which resulted in cuts and bruises.[64]

---

[63]   In March 2010, Secretary of Defense Gates appointed Adm (Ret.) Bruce MacDonald as the new Convening Authority of the Military Commissions at Guantánamo Bay. MacDonald previously served as the Chief Judge Advocate General of the Navy. *See* Carol Rosenberg, *Obama Appoints New Chief for War Court at Guantanamo*, MIAMI HERALD, Mar. 25, 2010.

[64]   *Counterterrorism Detention and Interrogation Activities, supra* note 58, at 41–42.

Al-Nashiri has stated that any self-incriminating evidence he may have provided while in detention was entirely the result of torture during interrogations – easily believed when faced with the above admissions of the CIA. In February 2009, all charges against al-Nashiri were dropped without prejudice when President Obama suspended the military commissions for further review.[65] He remains in detention at Guantánamo until such time as the venue for his trial has been determined.

Yasser Al-Zahrani, Mani Al-Utaybi, and Salah Ahmed Al-Salami

Yasser Al-Zahrani, a Saudi citizen, was captured at the age of 17 in Afghanistan. After four years in Guantánamo, on June 9, 2006 he, along with Mani Al-Tabi, and Ali Abdullah Ahmed, died under violent and mysterious circumstances. The following morning, Guantánamo commander Rear Adm. Harry Harris declared the deaths suicides, and acts of "asymmetrical warfare."[66] None of the men had been charged with any crimes, and were not considered high-risk detainees. In fact, Al-Zahrani and Al-Tabi were close to being cleared for release from Guantánamo.[67] Investigations into their deaths by the U.S. Naval Criminal Investigative Service (NCIS) took more than two years, and its heavily redacted report, issued in August 2008, concluded that the deaths had indeed been suicides.[68] However, the strange circumstances and contradictions surrounding the deaths remained unexplained. Scott Horton wrote in *Harper's* magazine:

> According to NCIS documents, each prisoner had fashioned a noose from torn sheets and T-shirts and tied it to the top of his cell's eight-foot-high steel-mesh wall. Each prisoner was able somehow to bind his own hands, and, in at least one case, his own feet, then stuff more rags deep down into his own throat. We are then asked to believe that each prisoner, even as he was choking on those rags, climbed up on his washbasin, slipped his head through the noose, tightened it, and leapt from the washbasin to hang until he asphyxiated. The NCIS report also proposes that the three prisoners, who were held in non-adjoining cells, carried out each of these actions almost simultaneously.[69]

These were not the only anomalies surrounding the supposed suicides of Al-Zahrani, Al-Utaybi, and Al-Salami. Early in 2009, a decorated NCO of the military intelligence unit assigned to Camp Delta where the three men died came

---

[65]   *See U.S. Drops Guantanamo Charges per Obama Order*, REUTERS, Feb. 5, 2009.

[66]   *See* Scott Horton, *The Guantanamo "Suicides": A Camp Delta Sergeant Blows the Whistle*, HARPER's (February 2010).

[67]   Mark P. Denbeaux, *June 10th Suicides at Guantanamo: Government Words and Deeds Compared* (Seton Hall Law Center for Policy and Research, Aug. 21, 2006), at 6, 12.

[68]   *See* Mark P. Denbeaux, *Death in Camp Delta* (Seton Hall Law Center for Policy and Research, Dec. 2009).

[69]   *Id.*

forward with evidence that the deaths were indeed homicides, and that authorities had initiated a cover-up. Army Staff Sergeant Joseph Hickman had been on duty the night the three men died, and knew that the men had been transported to a secret "black site" at Guantánamo well before their purported suicides. Hickman, who was under orders not to speak with anyone of that night, waited until President Obama had been inaugurated to come forward with his information. He first went to Mark Denbeaux of Seton Hall University Law School, whose Center for Policy and Research had already done substantial work analyzing government reports about the deaths.[70] Denbeaux and Hickman went quietly to the DOJ with the information, expecting that under a new Administration a serious investigation would take place. To their surprise, however, DOJ undertook an investigation, but confirmed the results earlier NCIS report. Frustrated with the lack of government's lack of interest in determining the true responsibility for these deaths, Hickman went public with his story, which was published in an article by Scott Horton for *Harper's* magazine.[71] The DOD immediately issued a statement repudiating Hickman's account of the events, and the official cause of death of Al-Zahrani, Al-Utaybi, and Al-Salami remains "suicide".

Shafiq Rasul, Asif Iqbal, Rhuhel Ahmed, and Jamal Al-Harith

One of the most egregious cases torture is that of Shafiq Rasul and his co-petitioners in a civil lawsuit against Gen. Richard Myers, former Chairman of the Joint Chiefs of Staff. There is no better way of describing the case than by quoting from the petition for Writ of Certiorari presented by the petitioners in the U.S. Supreme Court:

> The complaint below was filed by four innocent British citizens who were incarcerated at Guantánamo from January 2002 to March 2004. Petitioners never took up arms against the United States, never received any military training, and have never been members of any terrorist group. They have never been charged with any crime. They were never determined to be enemy combatants.[72] Respondents are former Secretary of Defense Donald Rumsfeld and high ranking military officers who ordered and supervised petitioners' incarceration and mistreatment at Guantánamo.

> Petitioners Rasul, Iqbal, and Ahmed are boyhood friends from the town of Tipton in England. At the time they were detained, they were 24, 20 and 19 respectively. Iqbal had gone to Pakistan in September 2001 to get married. Ahmed joined him to be his best man. Rasul was in Pakistan studying computer science. All three went to

---

[70]   *See* Denbeaux, *June 10ᵗʰ Suicides at Guantanamo, supra* note 67.

[71]   Horton, *The Guantanamo "Suicides", supra* note 66.

[72]   The complaint was dismissed on respondents' motion to dismiss. Accordingly, at this stage of the proceedings, all factual allegations of the complaint must be presumed to be true. Bridge v. Phoenix Bond & Indem. Co., 553 U.S. (2008), 128 S. Ct. 2131, 2135 n.1 (2008).

Afghanistan to assist in providing relief for the humanitarian crisis that arose in 2001. In Afghanistan they were captured by Afghan warlord Rashid Dostum, who is widely reported to have delivered prisoners to U.S. forces for the purpose of collecting a per capita bounty offered by the U.S. military. Dostum delivered Rasul, Iqbal, and Ahmed into U.S. custody in late 2001.

Petitioner Al-Harith was also born and raised in England. He is a website designer in Manchester. In 2001, he traveled to Pakistan for a religious retreat. When he was advised to leave the country because of growing animosity toward the British, he booked passage on a truck to Turkey, from which he planned to fly home to England. His truck was hijacked, and Al-Harith was forcibly brought to Afghanistan and turned over to the Taliban. He was accused of being a British spy, imprisoned in isolation, and beaten by his Taliban guards. After the Taliban fled in the wake of the U.S. invasion of Afghanistan, the British Embassy's plans to evacuate Al-Harith were preempted when U.S. forces arrived at the prison and took him into custody.

All four petitioners were held and interrogated by the U.S. under appalling conditions in Afghanistan before they were transported to Guantánamo, where they were systematically tortured and abused pursuant to directives from respondent Rumsfeld and the military chain of command. For more than two years, petitioners were brutalized by conduct that included:

- repeated beatings (including with rifle butts and while shackled and blindfolded);
- prolonged solitary confinement, including isolation in total darkness;
- deliberate exposure to extremes of heat and cold;
- threats of attack from unmuzzled dogs;
- forced nakedness;
- repeated body cavity searches;
- denial of food and water;
- deliberate disruption and deprivation of sleep;
- shackling in painful stress positions for extended periods;
- injection of unknown substances into their bodies; and
- deliberate interference with and denigration of their religious beliefs and practices, including the deliberate submersion of the Koran in a filthy toilet bucket.

Petitioners were deliberately prevented from fulfilling their daily obligation to pray, as prayers were frequently interrupted by shouts, taunts, and the playing of earsplitting music over the camp public address system. The chaining of petitioners in the "short-shackling" position was not only extremely painful but also prevented them from taking the required posture for prayer. Forced nakedness violated the Muslim tenet requiring modesty, particularly during prayer. Petitioners' beards were shaved forcibly, an infringement of Muslim religious practice.

Desecration of the Koran was frequent and systematic, with numerous incidents of Korans being sprayed with high-power water hoses, splashed with urine, and thrown in the toilet bucket. These were calculated and illegal displays of disrespect toward the essential symbol of Islam.[73]

Following their release, petitioners were returned to their country of nationality, namely, the U.K., and from there sued a number of high government officials, including Secretary Rumsfeld and other military officers at Guantánamo for damages, asserting claims for torture, religious abuse, and other mistreatment. On April 24, 2009, the D.C. Court of Appeals dismissed the case on the grounds that the Constitution does not have extraterritorial application, and therefore claims arising out of the Fifth and Eighth amendments do not extend to Guantánamo Bay. The dismissal rejected the proposition that non-U.S. citizens who are outside the sovereign territory of the U.S. are entitled to constitutional rights, including due process rights. More significantly, the Court held that the defendants had a qualified immunity, based on the proposition that they had no reasonable expectation their actions would be contrary to U.S. law. Lastly, with respect to petitioners' claim under the Religious Freedom Restoration Act (RFRA),[74] the Court of Appeals found that the Act did not apply to them, not only because of the fact that the claim violations occurred outside the sovereign territory of the U.S., but that the plaintiffs did not qualify as "persons" under the Act.[75] Petition for certiorari was filed by the petitioners, but the Supreme Court rejected it on Dec. 14, 2009.[76]

This case is significant in many respects. The first involves an initial error in judgment by the U.S. military who "bought" three of the petitioners from an Afghan warlord (as they did in similar cases without due diligence), and seizing the fourth after denying him repatriation to the U.K., thus raising serious questions about the intake process. The second has to do with the judgment of the intake officers at Guantánamo and the inability to identify the innocence of those four over a period of 26 months (which raises serious questions about the judgment of those engaged in the intelligence process at Guantánamo). Third, the mistreatment used against those four persons over such a long period of time during which there had to be an awareness that these were innocent civilians caught in the web of war and greed. This raises not only the question of what would be considered elementary good judgment for intelligence officers and investigators, but also what justification would there have been to prolong the imprisonment and mistreatment of persons they had to know were innocent civilians. Could it have been fear of embarrassment? Fear of cover-up as time

---

[73] Shafiq Rasul et al. v. Richard Meyers, Air Force General et al., Petition for Writ of Certiorari, Aug. 24, 2009, at 4–7.

[74] 42 U.S.C. §2000 *et seq.*

[75] The Court held that a person must be a U.S. citizen, a permanent resident of the U.S., or physically present in the U.S. Judge Brown disagreed on that point in the context of her concurring opinion.

[76] Rasul et al. v. Myers, 09–227, *cert. denied* Dec. 14, 2009.

went on? A way of showing the superiors in the chain of command that those working at Guantánamo were diligent? Could it have been command influence from the top to keep pressing on no matter whom the victims were?

Unlike other cases discussed above, this one has an added dimension, namely, the rejection of their judicial claim under U.S. law by the D.C. Circuit Court and the refusal of the Supreme Court to grant certiorari. If ever there was a case that needed redress, even symbolically, this is the one. The fact that the U.S. legal system failed in that respect adds a tragic closing to a painful chapter.

2.5. INTERROGATIONS OF JUVENILES

It is now known that children younger than 18 years of age have been subjected to "enhanced interrogation" techniques and prolonged detentions. In a report filed by the Bush Administration in accordance with its obligations under the United Nations Committee on the Rights of the Child, the U.S. admitted to having detained 2,500 juveniles between 2002 and 2008 in its "war on terror."[77] The vast majority of these detentions were in Iraq, where in 2007 the U.S. built a special juvenile detention center to house the large youth population.[78] While the exact number of juvenile detainees may never fully be known since the DOD does not follow international law in the categorization of adults and children,[79] government records reveal that more than twenty detainees under the age of 18 had been sent to Guantánamo.[80]

Under international law, an individual is considered an adult at 18 years of age.[81] However, the DOD created its own standard for the age of maturity, 16 years of age.[82] Therefore juvenile detainees over the age of 16 were often housed with adults.[83] The DOD's definition of the age of maturity is contrary to that of

---

[77]   *See* Walter Pincus, *U.S. Has Detained 2,500 Juveniles as Enemy Combatants,* WASH. POST, May 15, 2008.

[78]   *Id.*

[79]   *See* BARBARA OLSHANSKY, DEMOCRACY DETAINED: SECRET UNCONSTITUTIONAL PRACTICES IN THE U.S. WAR ON TERROR 91 (2007).

[80]   *See* Jo Becker, *The War on Teen Terror,* SALON.COM, June 24, 2008.

[81]   *Id.*

[82]   In the U.S., the age at which adult criminal responsibility is applied varies depending on the state within which a person is charged, and the severity of the alleged crime. Many legal scholars and policy-makers have expressed alarm at the current U.S. trend of sending younger and younger offenders to adult prisons. *See, e.g.,* Jeffrey Butts & Ojmarrh Mitchell, *Brick by Brick: Dismantling the Border Between Juvenile and Adult Justice,* 2 BOUNDARY CHANGES IN CRIMINAL JUSTICE ORGANIZATIONS 167 (U.S. DOJ, National Institute of Justice, 2000). Young offenders not tried in adult courts are handled by a states' juvenile justice system, which generally provides more procedural safeguards and takes the principle of rehabilitative sanctions seriously. Also note that the Supreme Court has determined an offender must be 18 years or older to be eligible for the death penalty. *See* Roper v. Simmons 543 U.S. 551 (2005).

[83]   *See* OLSHANSKY, DEMOCRACY DETAINED, *supra* note 79, at 90.

the United Nations Convention on the Rights of the Child, which defines a child as "every human being below the age of 18 years."[84] The U.S. has not ratified that Convention, however, in June 2002, the U.S. ratified the Convention's Optional Protocol on the Involvement of Children in Armed Conflict, which obligates state parties to "take all feasible measures to ensure that persons within their jurisdiction recruited or used in hostilities contrary to [the] Protocol are demobilized or otherwise released from service. State Parties shall, when necessary, accord to these persons all appropriate assistance for their physical and psychological recovery and their social reintegration."[85]

Contrary to the provisions under the Optional Protocol, the U.S. has held detainees under the age of 15, some as young as 13 years old.[86] Human Rights Watch reported that children were even detained and interrogated as "enemy combatants."[87] Often these children experienced many of the same harsh interrogation techniques as the adult detainees.[88] Some of the detention conditions included: long periods of time in isolation; no access to family members; limited access to legal counsel; interrogations without the presence of a parent or attorney; and indefinite detentions without charges.[89] To comply with U.S. international obligations, if the government reasonably believed a child had vital information, the government should have allowed the child access to an attorney and the presence of a parent for any and all interrogations.

One such shocking example of the treatment experienced by juvenile detainees is that of Omar Khadr, who was captured at age 15 and has been held at Guantánamo since 2002.[90] Khadr was captured in Afghanistan for throwing a grenade at U.S. troops, and killing a U.S. serviceman, Sgt. Christopher Speer. The circumstances were of a military engagement between the U.S. military and the Taliban unit. The U.S. unit had killed a number of Taliban militants, to which three of Khadr's friends belonged, and according to various reports, they were all under the age of 18. It also appears that Khadr was part of that unit and was acting as a lawful combatant, as were his three deceased comrades. He was engaged in the activities of a lawful combatant, even though at the time he was a

---

84   United Nations Convention on the Rights of the Child, 1577 U.N.T.S. 3, *entered into force* Sep. 2, 1990, at Art. 1.

85   Optional Protocol to the Convention on the Rights of the Child on the Involvement of Children in Armed Conflicts, G.A. Res. 54/263, Annex I, 54 U.N. GAOR Supp. (No. 49) at 7, U.N. Doc. A/54/49 (2000), *entered into force* Feb. 12, 2002.

86   *See* OLSHANSKY, DEMOCRACY DETAINED, *supra* note 79, at 90.

87   *Id.* at 92.

88   *Id.* at 90. Amnesty International reported 13-year-old detainee Mohammed Ismail Agha was subjected to solitary confinement and sleep deprivation during his detention by the U.S. government. Mohammed Ismail Agha was held at U.S. Air Force Bagram Air Base in Afghanistan and later at Guantánamo for over a year without a charge or trial.

89   *See* OLSHANSKY, DEMOCRACY DETAINED, *supra* note 79, at 92.

90   *See* MICHELLE SHEPHARD, GUANTANAMO'S CHILD: THE UNTOLD STORY OF OMAR KHADR (2008). *See also* Carol Rosenberg, *New Court Can Silence Captives Who Tell Secrets*, MIAMI HERALD, Feb. 4, 2008.

minor. Why was he designated an unlawful enemy combatant, and why was he considered a potential terrorist threat to the U.S.? It should have been obvious at the time that there was no reason to transfer the 15-year old to Guantánamo. It became obvious after his transfer that he was neither an unlawful enemy combatant nor a threat to U.S. security.

During his detention, Khadr was subjected to prolonged solitary confinement and abusive interrogations, which included being shackled in painful positions, threatened with rape, and used as a "human mop" after he urinated on the floor during one interrogation session.[91] Currently Khadr is facing terror charges under the 2009 Military Commissions Act – to the surprise of many, he was one of the first to be so designated.[92] The Military Commissions Act does not contain any juvenile safeguards to ensure that his vulnerable status as a child is protected. If the trial proceeds, the "judge will be the first in western history to preside over the trial of alleged war crimes committed by a child. No international criminal tribunal established under the laws of war, from Nuremberg forward, has ever prosecuted former child soldiers as war criminals."[93] Instead of prosecuting him for war crimes, the U.S. should have treated Khadr as a victim and sought to rehabilitate him under its obligations under the Protocol on Child Soldiers of the Convention on the Rights of the Child.[94]

Another example is that of Mohamed Jawad, an illiterate Afghan teenager who was living in a Pakistani refugee camp when, according to his military defense counsel Maj. David Frakt, he was recruited by Afghan militia, drugged and forced to fight alongside them.[95] He was eventually captured by U.S. forces after throwing a grenade at two U.S. troops and their translator, gravely injuring them. Although there are no official documents stating Jawad's exact age, he believes he was 16 when he was taken into custody, while the U.S. military claims he was 17. Investigations undertaken by the Afghan Independent Human Rights Commission claim Jawad could have been as young as 12.[96] In any event, Jawad was certainly a juvenile when taken into custody, and should have been afforded the rights and safeguards appropriate to his age.

---

[91] *See U.S.: Stop Unfair Trial of Guantánamo Youth* (Human Rights Watch, Feb. 1, 2008).

[92] *See* Rosenberg, *New Court Can Silence Captives Who Tell Secrets, supra* note 90.

[93] *See* Andy Worthington, *Guantánamo Trials: Where Are The Terrorists?* THE HUFFINGTON POST, Feb. 8, 2008. As of March 2010, officials in the Obama Administration were reported to be quietly seeking a way to repatriate Khadr back to Canada, not having "the stomach to try a child for war crimes." *See* Steven Edwards, *U.S. Looks for Way to Return Khadr,* NATIONAL POST (Canada), Mar. 8, 2010. In April 2010, hearings into whether statements Khadr made to interrogators were made under duress, and therefore inadmissible, began at the Military Commission. *See* Richard Serrano, *Teenage Militant Case at Tribunal,* L.A. TIMES, Apr. 28, 2010.

[94] Optional Protocol, *supra* note 85.

[95] *Releasing Jawad: A Boy's Life at Guantanamo* (Human Rights Watch, Jan. 11, 2010).

[96] Sayed Salahuddin, *Afghan was Taken to Guantanamo Aged 12: Rights Group,* REUTERS, May 27, 2009.

Initially held at Bagram in Afghanistan, Jawad alleged that he was made to wear a black bag over his head, shackled and forced to stand naked for prolonged periods of time, beaten, deprived of sleep, and thrown down a flight of stairs.[97] In early 2003, he was transferred to Guantánamo, where his mental state quickly deteriorated. Interrogators found him talking to posters on his wall, and in December 2003, he attempted suicide, first by banging his head against a metal wall, and then by hanging. Just a few months after his suicide attempt, it was documented that in May 2004 Jawad was subjected to intense sleep deprivation, where he was moved from cell to cell 112 times over a 14-day period, averaging only 2–3 hours per cell.[98]

Charges were formally brought against Jawad in January 2008. By the time Frakt had been appointed as Jawad's defense counsel, Frakt said that he found him to be in an "extremely fragile mental state," and that he had "lost track of time, lost touch with reality, and suffered from severe depression."[99] In the fall of 2008, the judge at the military commission ruled that Jawad's confession was inadmissible because he had been tortured, and that in any case, throwing a grenade at U.S. troops during combat did not amount to a war crime.[100] One of the prosecutors in the case, Darrel J. Vandeveld, was so distraught over the evidence of Jawad's torture and the reluctance of his superior, Col. Morris Davis, to consider a plea deal, that he ultimately tendered his resignation.[101] However, despite the lack of charges against him, Jawad remained in detention until July 2009, when in response to a habeas corpus petition filed on behalf of Jawad by the ACLU and with the assistance of the former prosecutor, Vandeveld, U.S. District Judge Ellen Huvelle made clear that Jawad had been illegally detained and ordered the government to release him.[102]

In his early twenties, and after seven years of unlawful detention and abusive treatment, Jawad was released and repatriated to Afghanistan in July 2009. Worried that Jawad would be arrested upon his re-entry, Frakt, along with Human Rights Watch, the ACLU, and Amnesty International fundraised enough money to send a group of observers back to Kabul with him. Jawad was indeed detained again, but the lawyers accompanying him were able to successfully plead for his release with the Afghan Attorney General.[103]

---

[97] Stacy Sullivan, *Confessions of a Former Guantanamo Prosecutor* (Human Rights Watch, Oct. 28, 2008); Vandeveld, *I Was Slow to Recognize the Stain of Guantanamo, supra* note 55.

[98] Vandeveld, *id.* This was a popular form of sleep deprivation, often referred to by guards as the "frequent flyer" program.

[99] Stacy Sullivan, *The Forgotten Kid of Guantanamo* (Human Rights Watch, May 27, 2008).

[100] *See* Human Rights Watch, *Releasing Jawad, supra* note 95.

[101] *See* Sullivan, *Confessions of a Former Guantánamo Prosecutor, supra* note 97. *See also infra* Chapter 6, section 5.4, *Those Who Abided by their Professional Obligations*, for a discussion of military prosecutors who have resigned from their positions at Guantánamo.

[102] Press Release, American Civil Liberties Union, Judge Orders Release of Guantánamo Detainee Mohammed Jawad (July 30, 2009).

[103] *See* Human Rights Watch, *Releasing Jawad, supra* note 95.

Neither Khadr nor Jawad were terrorists as teenagers, but after several years of mistreatment and unjustified detention at Guantánamo, they may likely become a threat to U.S. security. On a moral level, they are human beings that the U.S. deliberately and unjustifiably destroyed in fulfillment of a policy which was both unlawful and immoral.

2.6. CONCLUSION

In August 2002, the Intelligence Science Board was created to advise the Office of the Director of National Intelligence on emerging scientific and technical issues of importance to the intelligence community. The ISB commissioned a study on "educing information," a topic which includes not only strict interrogation, but the elicitation of information and strategic debriefing. In December 2006, the ISB published a study entitled *Educing Information: Interrogation: Science and Art,* which aimed to address the lacunae of knowledge amongst lawyers, judges, legislators, policymakers and human rights advocates regarding the intelligence gathering process.[104] In an article within the study, Col. Steven M. Kleinmen, former Director of the Air Force Combat Interrogation Course and DOD Senior Intelligence Officer for Special Survival Training, wrote:

> A major stumbling block to the study of interrogation, and especially to the conduct of interrogation in field operations, has been the all-too-common misunderstanding of the nature and scope of the discipline. Most observers, even those within professional circles, have unfortunately been influenced by the media's colorful (and artificial) view of interrogation as almost always involving hostility and the employment of force – be it physical or psychological – by the interrogator against the hapless, often slow-witted subject. This false assumption is belied by historic trends that show the majority of sources (some estimates range as high as 90 percent) have provided meaningful answers to pertinent questions in response to direct questioning (i.e., questions posed in an essentially administrative manner rather than in concert with an orchestrated approach designed to weaken the source's resistance).[105]

In sum, what was done was essentially useless, and that adds insult to injury. Stupidity, and more so stubborn stupidity are aggravating factors to the crimes committed.

---

[104]   EDUCING INFORMATION, INTERROGATION: SCIENCE AND ART – FOUNDATIONS FOR THE FUTURE (Russell Swenson & Robert Fein eds., National Defense Intelligence College, 2006).

[105]   Col. Steven M. Kleinman, *KUBARK Counterintelligence Interrogation Review: Observations of an Interrogator, in* EDUCING INFORMATION, *id.,* at 95.

The "enhanced interrogation" techniques described in this chapter reveal without a doubt that there was a torture-enabling policy whose trickle-down effect was accelerated by incentives and disincentives developed at the highest level of government. Spurred by command influence, a widespread and systematic pattern of torture practices ensued. The government lawyers, as indicated in this book, sought to portray it as something else. How much physical abuse and mistreatment until one can call it torture? After how long? With what effect on the victims, and in what overall context did these acts of torture occur? Should individual circumstances be taken into account, such as the age or health condition of the person (in some cases, including 15–20 year olds)? The fact that these practices occurred over a period of seven years in so many venues (Guantánamo, Iraq, and Afghanistan), as well as in CIA "black sites" and with the use of private contractors, which for a long time were not subject to U.S. law (including immunity for private contractors in Iraq up to the date of the SOFA), can only be deemed the outcome of policy. Yet, in a most evasive decision, the U.S. Court of Appeals for the District of Columbia, shirking away from its judicial responsibility, held in 2009 in *Rasul et al. v. Myers*, that:

> The Court stressed that its decision "does not address the *content of the law* that governs petitioners' detention." *Id.* at 2277 (emphasis added). With those words, the Court in *Boumediene* disclaimed any intention to disturb existing law governing the extraterritorial reach of any constitutional provisions, other than the Suspension Clause.

> * *
> *

> There is another reason why we should not decide whether *Boumediene* portends application of the Due Process Clause and the Cruel and Unusual Punishment Clause to Guantánamo detainees – and it is on this ground we will rest our decision on remand. The doctrine of qualified immunity shields government officials from civil liability to the extent their alleged misconduct "does not violate clearly established statutory or constitutional rights of which a reasonable person would have known." *Harlow v. Fitzgerald*, 457 U.S. 800, 818 (1982).

> * *
> *

> Our vacated opinion explained why qualified immunity insulates the defendants from plaintiffs' *Bivens* claims. *Rasul I*, 512 F.3d at 665–67. *Boumediene* does not affect what we wrote. No reasonable government official would have been on notice that plaintiffs had any Fifth Amendment or Eighth Amendment rights. *Id.* at 666. At the time of their detention,[106] neither the Supreme Court nor this court had ever held

---

[106] All four plaintiffs were released more than four years before the Supreme Court decided *Boumediene*, and months before the Court held even that statutory habeas corpus jurisdiction extended to Guantánamo. *See* Rasul v. Bush, 542 U.S. 466, 483–84 (2004). The U.S. does not require government employees to anticipate future developments in constitutional law. *See* Anderson v. Creighton, 483 U.S. 635, 639 (1987); Butera v. District of Columbia, 235 F.3d 637, 652 (D.C. Cir. 2001).

that aliens captured on foreign soil and detained beyond sovereign U.S. territory had any constitutional rights – under the Fifth Amendment, the Eighth Amendment, or otherwise. The Court in *Boumediene* recognized just that: "It is true that before today the Court has never held that noncitizens detained by our Government in territory over which another country maintains *de jure* sovereignty have any rights under our Constitution." 128 S. Ct. at 2262.[107]

For the D.C. Circuit Court to hold that the Constitution does not limit the practice of torture committed abroad by U.S. public agents based on established U.S. policy is a shocking construction of due process. Worse yet, it ignores the fact that these acts of torture committed abroad were initiated by policy and directives issued in the United States. It has been well-established that the fact that a crime was perfected or completed abroad does not negate the applicability of U.S. law. Moreover, how the court could conclude that the public officials in question, some of whom were part of the torture-enabling policy discussed in Chapter 3, had no reasonable notice of the acts committed at Guantánamo and should therefore benefit from public immunity is surely the most *Alice in Wonderland* type of reasoning and conclusion that any court has ever engaged in. One is almost compelled to assume from the court's contrived reasoning that the motivation was political, namely, to shield senior government officials such as President Bush, Vice President Cheney, Secretary Rumsfeld, Attorney General Gonzales, and others from civil liability.[108]

The failure of the U.S. to acknowledge its responsibility in the torture policy and practices described above, and the failure of Congress to take appropriate legislative remedies, as well as the failure of the judiciary (particularly the Circuit Court of the District of Columbia and the U.S. Supreme Court) to provide judicial remedies, will only reinforce the moral wrong committed by the U.S. and undermine this nation's legitimacy and credibility internationally. From a policy perspective, the cumulative effect of all of this will be to engender not only despair about the U.S. among the 1.4 billion Muslims in the world, but a great

---

[107] The Supreme Court wrote in *Rasul I* that no one had reason to suppose that Guantánamo was within the territorial sovereignty of the U.S. *See* 512 F.3d at 666–67. The agreement giving the U.S. an indefinite lease recognized that the lessor, the Republic of Cuba, retained ultimate sovereignty. *See* Agreement Between the United States and Cuba for the Lease of Lands for Coaling and Naval Stations, Feb. 23, 1903, U.S.-Cuba, T.S. No. 418, art. III. The Supreme Court recognized this in Vermilya-Brown Co. v. Connell, 335 U.S. 377, 381 (1948). *See also* Immigration and Nationality Act, 8 U.S.C. §1101(a)(38). In fact, before *Boumediene*, it was clearly established that "[w]ho is the sovereign, *de jure* or *de facto*, of a territory is not a judicial, but is a political question, the determination of which by the legislative and executive departments of any government conclusively binds the judges... of that government." Oetjen v. Cent. Leather Co., 246 U.S. 297, 302 (1918) (quoting Jones v. United States, 137 U.S. 202, 212 (1890)); Vermilya-Brown, 335 U.S. at 380; *see also* Lin v. United States, No. 08–5078, slip op. at 8–9 (D.C. Cir. April 7, 2009).

[108] *See* Jordan J. Paust, *Civil Liability of Bush, Cheney, et al. for Torture, Cruel, Inhuman, and Degrading Treatment and Forced Disappearance*, 42 CASE W. RES. J. INT'L L. 359 (2009). Professor Paust makes a compelling case for civil liability.

deal of anger as well, which in turn will cause many disaffected young Muslims in all parts of the world to seek revenge in one way or another. In a perverse way, the policy and practices designed to combat terrorism are likely to lead to more terror violence against the U.S. Thus, instead of enhancing the security of the U.S., the policy and practices of the Bush Administration and the weak remedies and responses of the Obama Administration simply place the U.S., its citizens, and its interests in more significant harm's way than it has been at any other time in its history. The acts described in this chapter show how evil the acts of torture were. "Enhanced interrogation" techniques were torture. How this great nation could have engaged in these practices and how we can ignore these facts is beyond belief.

On April 15, 2010, the United Nations Human Rights Council adopted a resolution which unequivocally states that the prohibition against torture is non-derogable, that it must be protected under all circumstances, and that no states of emergency or claim relating to a war-like condition can ever be advanced as justification. The Resolution explicitly states in paragraph 1 that it:

> *condemns* all forms of torture and other cruel, inhuman or degrading treatment or punishment, including through intimidation which are and shall remain prohibited in any time and at any place, whatsoever and can thus never be justified, and calls upon all States to implement fully the *absolute* prohibition of torture and other cruel, inhuman, or degrading treatment or punishment." (emphasis added)[109]

In case the point is not clear, this statement is directed against the U.S. Then again, the U.S. has well-established its exceptional status, and it now appears that the Obama Administration, notwithstanding its change in style from its predecessors, is nonetheless following in some of its footsteps.

---

[109]   U.N. Doc. A/HRC/1319 (15 April 2010).

APPENDIX 2: INTERROGATION METHODS

FM 34–52 Standard Methods for Military Interrogations prior to 2002	**Use of incentives** **Rapport building** **Rationalize detainee's feelings of guilt** **Flattery and exoneration from guilt** **Emotional Love** **Fear down** **Incentives Short term** – Cigarettes, meals, showers **Incentives Long term** – Repatriation, **Asylum** **Futility to resist** **Emotional Hate** – Encouraging resentment and disloyalty **Fear up** – This is to maintain a level of fear, not induce long term stress. **Silence** – short term silence **"We all know"** – Interrogator acts as if they know everything already so that lying is futile. **Establish Identity** **Repetition of Questions** **Rapid Fire Questions** **Change of Scene** – Take EPW to more comfortable surrounding to relax them.
FBI Interrogation Methods	**Based on rapport building.** The primary concern for organizations such as the FBI, in addition to gathering intelligence, is to gain evidence for future interrogations.
Adopted SERE techniques in JTF-GTMO memo (November 2002)	Category I Yelling Deception

	Category II Prolonged standing Stress positions Falsified reports Isolation Change of Scene 20 hour interrogations Removal of Clothing Forced Grooming Use of Phobias Category III Threat of death or severe pain to detainee or his/her family. Exposure to Cold Weather/Water Waterboarding Mild physical contact (poking, pushing)
October 5, 2002 – Pre-JTF-GTMO Memo – Guantánamo Army Interrogations	**Sleep Deprivation** – including yelling, strobe lights, "body placement discomfort" (possibly variations of stress positions). **Sensory Overload** **Yelling/Screaming until detainee 'broke'** **Insults** **Fear Up – Harsh** **Insulting/Squatting over Qur'an** **Good cop/Bad Cop** **Dogs in Interrogation room** -claimed to be a military idea to exploit Arab fear of dogs.
October 8, 2002 – Gen. Dunlavey requests from SOUTHCOM 19 new techniques not available in FM 34–52. These are divided into three categories and are eventually approved in the Rumsfeld memo	The methods in this request match the methods used following Secretary General Rumsfeld's signing of the JTF-GTMO. These are described below under 'Post JTF-GTMO Memo'

Post JTF-GTMO Memo and VOCO–Guantánamo Army Interrogations Army Interrogations	**20 hour interrogations** **Repeatedly pouring water on head** **Stress positions** **Holding detainee down while female straddled him.** **Humiliation – places women's underwear on detainee's head.** **Insulting family** **Leashing and leading detainee like dog** **Forced physical training** **Removal of Clothing** **Forced Grooming** **Use of Phobias** **Threat of death or severe pain to detainee or his/her family** **Exposure to Cold Weather/Water** **Waterboarding** **Mild physical contact**
April 2002 – Addington, Flanigan, Haynes, Gonzales meet to discuss what sorts of pain could be inflicted on Zubaydah by CIA. CIA sent a "wish-list" of "stress-techniques". Spring 2002 – CIA invited Martin Seligman to give a lecture on SERE techniques.	**Stress positions** **Isolation** **Sensory deprivation** **Death threats** **Stripping detainee**
CIA Mid-2002 to 2003	**Extreme Temperatures** **Sexual Humiliation** **Prolonged standing** **Sleep deprivation** **Waterboarding** **Punching** **Slapping** **Insults** **Denying medication** **Extreme temperature exposure**
CIA – Asadabad, Afghanistan June 2003	**Severe beating of detainee, resulting in death.**
Army (Intelligence, MP) – Iraq – August 15, 2003	**Physical abuse (strikes to body)** **Threatening to kill detainee** **AR 15–6 Disciplinary Proceedings (Dec. 12, 2003)**
Army Afghanistan – July 2003–2004	**Sleep Deprivation**

Army – GTMO November 2003	**Hooding** **Physical Abuse** *See* Memorandum for Chief of Staff, U.S. Central Command. Nov. 14, 2003 Subject: Allegation of Mistreatment From T.J. Keating, VADM, U.S. Navy
CIA 2003 – Bagram AB	**'Softening up' detainees (beatings)** **Use of MP to 'soften up' detainees** **Exposure to extreme temperatures**
Army MI – Abu Ghraib, October 2003 These actions were encouraged by MI and reported to officers. CIA involvement also noted.	**Forced nudity** **Humiliation** **Isolation** **Sensory deprivation** **Stress positions** **Verbal threats** **Severe beatings** **Sleep deprivation** **Harsh up** **Unsanitary conditions** **Sexual abuse** **Hostage taking** **Use of work dogs to 'Fear up' detainees** **Sexual abuse/Humiliation** **Stress positions** **Sleep deprivation**

APPENDIX 3: DETENTION RELATED ABUSES OCCURRING ACROSS MULTIPLE LOCATIONS[*]

Abuses	Guantánamo	Afghanistan	Iraq	CIA Detention
Beatings Including "Walling"	– Some detainees reported physical assaults.[1] For example, a young detainee refused to accompany a guard to the interrogation room and was so severely beaten that he had to be hospitalized.[2] – Immediate Reaction Force (IRF) teams, a kind of in-house riot squad, regularly were called in to punish a detainee for even minor infractions, like keeping a piece of string in	– Detainees were often assaulted while being transferred from their cells to the interrogation rooms.[5] – A detainee at Bagram reported an episode of abuse in which he was kicked repeatedly in the abdomen, causing painful swelling. It took him six months to recover, and during this time he was frequently denied medical attention.[6]	– Detainees were stripped, beaten, yelled at, spit on, and used as target practice for paintball.[8] – Soldiers punched, slapped, and kicked detainees, slammed them into walls and jumped on their naked bodies.[9] – A British interrogator reported seeing a detainee who had been beaten so severely by a Special Mission Unit Task Force that his back was nearly	– Some detainees, throughout the initial weeks or months of their imprisonment, suffered beatings several times a day consisting of punches, kicks, slaps, and beating with a cable.[11] – One detainee reported that when interrogators perceived him to be uncooperative, he was placed against a wall and punched and slapped in the face, body, and head.[12]

[*] This chart is the work product of the International Center for Transitional Justice, U.S. Accountability Project. It was written by Carolyn Patty Blum and Lorna Peterson, and was originally published in: Carolyn Patty Blum, Lisa Magarrell & Marieke Wierda, *Criminal Justice for Criminal Policy: Prosecuting Abuses of Detainees in U.S. Counterterrorism Operations* (New York: International Center for Transitional Justice, 2009), *available at*: http://www.ictj.org/static/Publications/ICTJ_USA_CriminalJustCriminalPolicy_pb2009.pdf. Abuses are listed in alphabetical order, with a panel for detainee deaths appearing last. The locations in this chart track the order in which they appear in the text of the paper. Examples included in this chart are representative, but in no way inclusive of all of the recorded abuses or all abuses that detainees experienced in any known location.

Abuses	Guantánamo	Afghanistan	Iraq	CIA Detention
	his cell. The IRF teams are known to beat, squash, smash, sit on, and beat detainees' heads on the floor.[3] According to some sources, this practice continues to be used at Guantánamo.[4]	– Another detainee at Kandahar reported that his guards beat him severely, including kicks to the head that caused the loss of four teeth and a swelling so large it had to be removed by camp doctors.[7]	broken, his nose was broken, and he had two black eyes and multiple contusions on his face.[10]	– Some detainees had collars placed around their necks that interrogators used to slam the detainees' heads against the wall, a practice known as "walling."[13] – Khaled el-Masri was brutally beaten while being transferred from the custody of Macedonian police to the hands of individuals who flew him to Afghanistan, where the CIA imprisoned him.[14]
Confinement in Boxes or Cages	– In the first several months after the prison opened, prisoners were housed in open-air cages similar to dog kennels, which exposed them to the elements.[15]	– Detainees in Bagram were kept in cages and in compartments made of barbed wire and blankets.[16] – A detainee in Kandahar reported seeing another detainee tied up "like a package" with belts inside a coffin-like crate, which was sealed before the prisoner was carried away.[17]	– A detainee in Abu Ghraib described his cell as a 1.5-by-2.5-meter cage with a smaller cage inside. He was at times locked in the smaller cage.[18]	– Abu Zubaydah was placed in a cramped box in which he could not sit comfortably; this caused his existing wounds to open and bleed.[19] Interrogation plans also allowed for placing an insect in the box with the prisoner.[20] – Detainees were locked in a "dog box" one cubic meter in size.[21]

Abuses	Guantánamo	Afghanistan	Iraq	CIA Detention
Exploitation of Need for Medical Care and Medical Professional Involvement in Torture	– One detainee reported being placed in isolation in a very cold cell without a blanket, where he was denied medical treatment despite regular vomiting and blood in his urine.[22] – As punishment for a hunger strike, Lakhdar Boumediene was placed in solitary confinement and denied treatment for a foot injury.[23] – Another detainee whose mental health deteriorated rapidly after imprisonment was restrained and given only water and blankets as "privileges." While he was interrogated, he was also put on a sleep deprivation regimen; all of these caused further deterioration of his health.[24]	– One prisoner who was held in Bagram and Kandahar developed a large black and blue swelling in his abdomen after being kicked during an interrogation. Although he was given surgery against his will, the swelling did not subside for six months, and he was given no medical care.[26] – Detainees reported receiving forced medication before interrogation sessions.[27] – While Murat Kurnaz was suspended five days by the arms in various positions, doctors repeatedly came to examine him.[28]	– Soldiers allowed a guard, rather than a doctor, to stitch up a detainee's wound when he was injured after being slammed against his cell wall.[29] – Detainees held at Abu Ghraib were denied medical care for wounds inflicted by soldiers.[30] – While held in a U.S.-controlled camp, one detainee reported being denied necessary medicine for diabetes and angina.[31]	– Medical personnel were present and involved in the CIA interrogations of Khalid Sheikh Mohammed and Abu Zubaydah in a secret detention center in Thailand.[32] – American doctors were present in CIA detention sites and saw prisoners on a regular basis.[33]

Abuses	Guantánamo	Afghanistan	Iraq	CIA Detention
	– A detainee held in Camp X-Ray reported that medical personnel were present during IRF squad beatings to make sure there were no injuries.[25]			
Extended Isolation	– Detainees were kept in isolation in an extremely cold environment and short-shackled to the floor.[34] – Mohamed al-Qahtani was kept in isolation for six months [35] – Camp 6 was modeled on U.S. "supermax" prisons. Detainees are kept in total isolation; they are locked in their rooms for a minimum of 22 hours a day, with the possibility of two hours of recreation time in a yard with no view to the outside.[36]	– Detainees were routinely subject to extended isolation in prison camps at Kandahar and Bagram.[37]	– Detainees were held in isolation for extended periods of time, up to two or three weeks. The conditions of isolation included being kept naked in very hot or very cold small rooms.[38] – In a small room at Abu Ghraib referred to as "the hole," detainees were held in total isolation and total darkness.[39]	– Detainees were kept in continuous solitary confinement throughout detention, most for more than three years.[40] – Guards were typically masked and didn't communicate with detainees.[41]

Abuses	Guantánamo	Afghanistan	Iraq	CIA Detention
Extremes of Light and Dark	– Detainees were subject to fluorescent lighting 24 hours a day.[42] – Conversely, some detainees noted that they were forced into total darkness, especially during isolation.[43] – A detainee who was subject to complete darkness in isolation during several months of interrogation reported that he began hearing voices.[44] – One detainee said the lights in his cell were left on continuously for the entire half-year he was kept in an isolated "brig."[45] – During transfer to Guantánamo, detainees were forced to wear blackout goggles along with earmuffs or earplugs.[46]	– Detainees were hooded when transferred to the prisons and during initial processing.[47] – An FBI interviewer reports finding a detainee sitting on the ground, blindfolded with ear coverings for sensory deprivation.[48] – Around-the-clock floodlights kept prisoners in Bagram awake.[49]	– In some prison camps, some detainees were kept hooded during the first 24 hours of imprisonment, while others were hooded during interrogation or for extended periods while locked in their cells.[50] – Some detainees were held in completely dark cells and were deprived of light at all times.[51]	– Detainees were hooded prior to transport and kept hooded throughout travel, ranging anywhere from one to 30 hours.[52] – Khaled el-Masri was held in Afghanistan in a dark cellar with no light source.[53]

Abuses	Guantánamo	Afghanistan	Iraq	CIA Detention
Forced Nudity	– Removal of clothing was used during interrogation and as a form of punishment, akin to the removal of a comfort item.[54] – Detainees were regularly strip-searched as a part of interrogation and forced to stand naked in front of female interrogators.[55] – Military interrogators stripped Mohamed al-Qahtani in front of a woman during the course of his interrogation.[56]	– A detainee held in Kandahar reported being stripped after his initial interrogation at the camp and was denied clothes thereafter.[57] – Prisoners at Kandahar and Bagram had their clothes cut off with scissors when they arrived at the prison. They were kept naked in front of each other and female soldiers.[58]	– Prisoners were forced to strip and remain in their cells naked for days at a time.[59] – Detainees were regularly photographed and videotaped while naked.[60] – Detainees were held in cells and marched around the camp naked in view of and escorted by female MPs.[61]	– Most of the detainees interviewed by the ICRC reported being forced to endure extended nudity, some for weeks or months at a time.[62]
Military Dogs	– Detainees were threatened with having guards' dogs unleashed on them.[63] – During an interrogation of al-Qahtani, a dog was first agitated by its handler, and then brought into the interrogation room where it	– Dogs were used during the movement of detainees and as a way of exerting control.[65] – Barking dogs were often present during detainee intake at prison camps.[66]	– Unmuzzled military working dogs were used to frighten detainees. At least one detainee was bitten and severely injured by a dog.[67] – The use of dogs on detainees at Abu Ghraib was approved by officials	– Inadequate information is currently available on the treatment of prisoners held at CIA "black sites" and the possible use of dogs in those facilities.

Abuses	Guantánamo	Afghanistan	Iraq	CIA Detention
	barked, snarled, and nearly bit him.[64]		and resulted in abusive use of dogs to frighten detainees.[68]	
Religious Abuse	– Many accounts indicate guards desecrated the Qur'an by writing on it, throwing it, or stepping on it. One incident provoked a mass suicide attempt after an interrogator threw a detainee's Qur'an on the floor and stomped on it.[69] – During interrogation of one detainee, an interrogator would squat over the Qur'an provided to the detainee in order to elicit a reaction.[70] – Detainees were deprived of clothing, sometimes in the presence of female guards, which violates Islamic teachings that proscribe	– Detainees reported incidents of the desecration of the Qur'an at Kandahar and Bagram, including throwing it on the ground, sitting on it, and spitting in it. In one case, a soldier kicked the Qur'an into the hands of another soldier, who threw it into a latrine.[74] – Detainees were not allowed to pray together.[75]	– Detainees report that they were forcibly shaved as punishment.[76] – One detainee reports being forced to pray while naked.[77] – Detainees at Abu Ghraib and other prisons in Iraq report desecration of the Qur'an such as ripping off the cover, dropping it on the ground or into dirty water.[78]	– Access to the Qur'an was denied to all the detainees at points throughout their imprisonment, sometimes in response to their lack of cooperation with interrogators.[79] – Some detainees were not allowed to pray.[80] – One detainee kept in constant light could not figure out the proper times to pray or the direction of Mecca.[81]

Abuses	Guantánamo	Afghanistan	Iraq	CIA Detention
	nudity as an impure state.[71] – Soldiers in Camp Delta banged on the cell doors with sticks while detainees tried to pray.[72] – Mohamed al-Qahtani was prevented from praying during interrogation. Interrogators used the opportunity to pray as a bartering tool in exchange for compliance.[73]			
Sexual Abuse	– Female guards frequently conducted full body searches of prisoners and/ or watched as prisoners showered and toileted. – One female interrogator performed a lap dance on a detainee.[82] – Female interrogators acted in sexually provocative ways; they stripped in view	– In Kandahar, a prisoner was forced to insert a finger into his own anus in front of female soldiers and other prisoners as he was being processed into the facility.[89] – Detainees reported terrifying strip searches and body cavity searches, often in the presence of	– Naked male detainees at Abu Ghraib were forced to wear women's underwear.[91] – Detainees were forced to assume sexually degrading positions.[92] – Soldiers sodomized prisoners with chemical lights, nightsticks, or broomstick handles.[93]	– Al-Nashiri was threatened with sodomy and the arrest and rape of his family.[97] – At least one detainee rendered to a foreign country was subject to genital mutilation.[98]

Abuses	Guantánamo	Afghanistan	Iraq	CIA Detention
	of a detainee, inappropriately touched prisoners, and invaded their personal space.[83] – At least one prisoner was forced to watch pornographic images.[84] – Prisoners were threatened with homosexual rape.[85] – One prisoner was forced to wear a bra and woman's thong on his head.[86] – A female interrogator stroked a prisoner's arms, squeezed his genitals to cause pain, and bent his thumbs back during Ramadan, a month when it is forbidden for Muslims to touch people of the opposite gender.[87] – A female interrogator assaulted a detainee by wiping dye from a red magic marker on the	female soldiers, as well as female soldiers watching and laughing as detainees showered.[90]	– Soldiers forced men into sexual positions for photographing, including forced masturbation or arranging naked men in piles.[94] – One soldier raped a female detainee.[95] – A photograph captured one detainee being led on a leash by a female guard.[96]	

Abuses	Guantánamo	Afghanistan	Iraq	CIA Detention
	detainee's shirt and telling the detainee that the red stain was menstrual blood.[88]			
Sleep Deprivation	– Detainees were deprived of sleep through the use of flashing lights, loud music, fans, banging on cells, and other noises.[99] – Another technique for sleep deprivation, nicknamed the "frequent flyer program," involved forcing the detainee to switch cells constantly in order to disrupt his sleep cycle and disorient him so that he would be unable to resist his interrogator.[100] – One prisoner was subject to interrogation for 18 to 20 hours a day for 48 days, allowing for only four hours of rest.[101]	– Bright, flashing lights, loud music, and waking detainees up every 15 minutes during their sleep period were techniques used as punishment or as part of interrogation strategies.[102]	– Detainees were subject to loud music or recordings of a baby crying, extended periods of being shackled in a standing position, sometimes while hooded, and being awakened repeatedly and taken in for interviews in order to prevent detainees from sleeping.[103] – A detainee at Abu Ghraib reported soldiers banging on cell doors.[104] – The soldier who placed the hooded detainee on a box with wires attached to fingers, toes, and penis reported that her job was to "keep detainees awake."[105]	– Detainees report being shackled with arms in the air, which prevented sleep.[106] – One detainee was suspended for two weeks with only two or three breaks to lie down.[107] – Stress positions were combined with lengthy interrogation sessions, loud music, and blasting cold air to deprive detainees of sleep.[108] – A detainee held in a CIA detention site in Afghanistan reported constant loud music and guards waking him up every half-hour.[109]

Abuses	Guantánamo	Afghanistan	Iraq	CIA Detention
Stress Positions, Including Suspension	– One detainee reported that when interrogated, he was forced to sit chained to a chair for 18 to 20 hours at a time, which caused extreme back pain.[110] – Detainees were short-shackled by their legs and arms to eyebolts in the middle of the floor, forcing them to crouch or lie in a fetal position for extended periods.[111] – Even after short-shackling ostensibly was banned in GTMO, detainees continued to report its use.[112]	– Detainees were restrained with their arms behind their backs or chained to a wall for long periods of time.[113] – Detainees report being suspended from their arms, sometimes with arms behind them, or hung upside-down for hours or even days.[114]	– The special operations facility at Camp Nama, contained a torture cell nicknamed the "Black Room." It was a windowless, jet-black garage-sized space, barren except for several 18-inch hooks on the ceiling left over from Hussein's era.[115] It was outfitted with floor-to-ceiling speakers. Most detainees were held there in painful stress positions, subjected to sleep deprivation by use of strobe lights, cold water, and rap or rock music at deafening levels.[116] – At Mosul, prisoners were routinely subject to forced kneeling in the mud, sometimes for hours longer than the approved time of 45 minutes.[117]	– Detainees were stripped naked and then shackled to the ceiling by their hands.[119] – This treatment might last continuously for several days or occur regularly over the course of several months.[120] – Two detainees were shackled in this position for seven consecutive days at one point, and one noted that he was only given short respites from this position over the course of two to three weeks.[121] – One detainee reported being kept chained to a chair in a seated position for two to three weeks, while being provided only with water and a nutrient drink.[122]

Abuses	Guantánamo	Afghanistan	Iraq	CIA Detention
			– Many detainees at Abu Ghraib reported stress positions. For example, one detainee was often shackled in his cell with one arm raised in the air and the other tied to his ankle. He was also lifted off the ground by his arms, which were tied behind his back. This type of suspension happened to him four or five times and resulted in dislocated shoulders.[118]	– Detainees were painfully shackled or hung from a pole.[123]
Temperature Extremes	– The military regularly subjected detainees to temperature extremes by turning air conditioning up full blast and/or leaving detainees without blankets or other coverings.[124] – Detainees were left short-shackled to the floor in extremely cold rooms.[125]	– A detainee in Kandahar was kept with other prisoners in an extremely hot tent for the first 20 days of his imprisonment, which made him very sick.[128] – During the cold winters, the two-blanket ration was inadequate to protect	– FOB Tiger used a shipping container to detain prisoners with temperatures as high as 115 to 145 degrees Fahrenheit.[130] – One FBI agent reported seeing a detainee shivering during an interrogation in a	– One detainee reports that clothes would be given and taken away from him, depending on his level of cooperation with interrogators.[134] – While nude, detainees were doused with cold water or placed in a cell that was kept extremely cold.[135]

Abuses	Guantánamo	Afghanistan	Iraq	CIA Detention
	– Detainees were also kept short-shackled in very hot rooms, occasionally for days and without food, water, or access to hygiene facilities.[126] – At Camp X-Ray, the first unit built at Guantánamo, the cells had concrete floors and open-air sides composed of chain-link fencing, which exposed detainees to the elements.[127]	detainees against the cold.[129]	cold room with the air conditioner turned up.[131] – Detainees at Abu Ghraib were held in isolation in very hot or very cold rooms.[132] – One detainee reported having his clothes soaked in water and being denied blankets once the temperatures began to drop.[133]	– Blankets were often denied to detainees.[136]
Threats	– Detainees reported being threatened by interrogators,[137] including transfer to countries with well-known records of human rights abuses.[138] – One prisoner was presented with false documents stating that his mother would be transferred to	– Threats of physical or mental torture or death and harm to family members were used to frighten detainees.[145] – One detainee reported being forced to pile on top of other naked detainees and threatened with death if he moved.[143]	– Male detainees were threatened with rape.[145] – One detainee was threatened with a loaded 9-mm pistol.[146] – Detainees report being told their wives or children would be raped and tortured while women's and children's voices were	– Detainees report being threatened with various forms of ill-treatment, including waterboarding, electric shocks, infection with HIV, sodomy, and the arrest and sexual assault of family members.[148] – An interrogator threatened Abd al-Rahim al-Nashiri by

Abuses	Guantánamo	Afghanistan	Iraq	CIA Detention
	Guantánamo for interrogation if he did not give them the information they wanted.[139] – One detainee was told that if he didn't talk, he would "disappear down a deep dark hole" where worse things than physical torture would happen, his documents would be shredded, and no one would know where he had gone.[140] – Chinese intelligence officials were granted access to interrogate Uighur detainees, who were subjected to sleep deprivation throughout the process. This was carried out by the Chinese interrogators or by U.S. military personnel at the behest of the Chinese.[141]	– At least four detainees were threatened with death at gunpoint.[144]	audible in the background.[147]	racking a handgun close to his head and firing up a power drill while al-Nashiri stood hooded and naked.[149] – CIA interrogators also threatened detainees with the death of their families or led them to believe family members would be raped or otherwise abused.[150]

Abuses	Guantánamo	Afghanistan	Iraq	CIA Detention
Torture- Other Extreme Forms	– Mohamed al-Qahtani was subject to multiple abusive interrogation techniques at once. Twenty-hour interrogation sessions were combined with stress positions, cold temperatures, forced physical training, and dousing with cold water. Interrogations involved humiliation techniques such as being led by a dog leash and forced to perform dog tricks, stripping in front of a woman, being straddled by a female interrogator, being forced to wear a bra and women's underwear on his head, forced prayer to an idol shrine, being told he had homosexual tendencies, threats to tell other prisoners he became	– A former Guantánamo prisoner who was held in Afghanistan described the use of water torture, electric shock, and other extreme forms of torture in detention centers. While imprisoned in Kandahar, he was personally forced to endure water torture, electric shock, hanging by his arms for five days, and severe beatings.[152] – While detained at Bagram, Mohammad Jawad was thrown down a stairwell while hooded and shackled.[153]	– FBI agents report being present during water torture in which prisoners had water forced down their throats while cuffed and on their knees.[154] – One detainee was placed naked and hooded on a box with wires attached to his fingers, toes, and penis to simulate electric torture.[155] – FBI agents also reported actual electrical torture, possibly using a Taser.[156] – Soldiers broke chemical lights and poured the phosphoric liquid on detainees.[157] – Detainees were burned by being placed on hot surfaces such as truck beds or jeep hoods. Resulting injuries were sometimes so severe that the detainees required prolonged	– Three detainees described being waterboarded, which involves strapping the detainee to an inclined board, placing a cloth over the entire face, and pouring water onto the cloth in order to cause the sensation of drowning.[159] – Government sources indicated that one prisoner was waterboarded 83 times and another for 183 times, far in excess of even what was authorized for the CIA interrogation program.[160] – Waterboarding was combined with other abusive practices such as nudity in the presence of female interrogators.[161]

Abuses	Guantánamo	Afghanistan	Iraq	CIA Detention
	aroused during searches, and being forced to dance with a male interrogator.[151]		hospitalization in military custody.[158]	
Death	– Although there are no reports of killings in Guantánamo, the circumstances of detainee deaths in the facility remain mysterious. One detainee died of colon cancer, a treatable form of cancer had it been detected and treated earlier with proper medical screening.[162] – Five suicides have occurred at Guantánamo, about which very little public information has been released.[163]	– Two deaths in Bagram occurred in December 2002. Military intelligence agents and police inflicted multiple beatings and blunt-force strikes to the bodies of Dilawar and Habibullah, who both died as a result. The killings were graphically described in nearly 2,000 pages of documents.[164] – In June 2003, Abdul Wali, an Afghan farmer who had voluntarily turned himself in to U.S. authorities to clear his name, was beaten and died three days later. CIA contractor David Passaro had interrogated Wali, and according to	– One high-ranking general from Hussein's air force was violently beaten, put into a sleeping bag head-first, wrapped with a cord, and rolled from side to side while a soldier sat on him. He died as a result.[168] – In another incident, only after relatives submitted photographs of the bruises, cuts, and marks on the body of a former Iraqi army officer did DOJ indicate that the death was a homicide.[169] – The body of one victim was depicted in one of the Abu Ghraib photographs. Navy SEALS and the CIA captured Manadel	– In December, 2002, a CIA official, working at a secret facility near Kabul, referred to as the "Salt Pit," ordered a detainee to strip naked, dragged him around on the rocky ground, and left him restrained and naked overnight in the cold. He died that night, probably as a result of hypothermia.[173]

Abuses	Guantánamo	Afghanistan	Iraq	CIA Detention
		prosecutors, beat him with his hands and a flashlight and kicked him very forcefully in the groin.[165] – In March 2003, U.S. soldiers mistakenly arrested a group of eight Afghan National Army soldiers. They were taken to the U.S. base at Gardez. U.S. soldiers severely beat the soldier-prisoners, and one died as a result. The others exhibited heavy bruises and described being punched, kicked, hung upside down, hit with sticks and cables, soaked in cold water, and forced to lie in the snow. They were also subject to electroshocks.[166] – Another Afghan detainee died at Gardez in September 2004. The U.S. military claimed he died of	al-Jamadi; they detained and tortured him in a small area known as the "Romper Room" at the Baghdad Airport. He was transferred to Abu Ghraib as a "ghost prisoner." CIA agents ordered military police to suspend him while he was hooded. When guards attempted to reposition him, they found his body hanging limp and gushing blood. His body was packed in ice and wrapped in a body bag in order to facilitate the next day's charade of putting him into an orange uniform, laying him on a gurney with an IV, and wheeling him out as if he were ill.[170] – One detainee died of asphyxiation during an interrogation. Evidence of	

Abuses	Guantánamo	Afghanistan	Iraq	CIA Detention
		snakebite, but his family claims that the body was bruised.[167]	lunt- force trauma to his arms and legs was discovered upon examination of the body.[171] – Several other detainees are documented to have died in custody.[172]	

Endnotes

[1] Office of the Inspector General, Oversight and Review Division, *A Review of the FBI's Involvement and Observations of Detainee Interrogations in Guantanamo Bay, Afghanistan and Iraq* (May 2008), at 174–179 [hereinafter *FBI Report*]; Physicians for Human Rights, *Broken Laws, Broken Lives: Medical Evidence of Torture by US Personnel and Its Impact* (2008), at 47, 57, 63.

[2] Laurel Fletcher & Eric Stover, The Guantanamo Effect: Exposing The Consequences of U.S. Detention and Interrogation Practices 75 (2009). This incident triggered a hunger strike. *Id.*, at 75.

[3] Physicians for Human Rights, *Broken Laws, Broken Lives, supra* note 2, at 57.

[4] Jeremy Scahil, *Little Known Military Thug Squad Still Brutalizing Prisoners at Gitmo Under Obama*, Alternet.org, May 15, 2009; Jonathan Goetz & Britta Sandberg, *Freed Guantanamo Detainees Claim Abuse Continues Under Obama*, S.F. Sentinel, Jul. 21, 2009.

[5] Fletcher & Stover, The Guantanamo Effect, *supra* note 3, at 33.

[6] Physicians for Human Rights, *Broken Laws, Broken Lives, supra* note 2, at 62.

[7] *Id.*, at 47.

[8] Human Rights Watch, *"No Blood, No Foul:" Soldiers' Accounts of Detainee Abuse in Iraq* (2006), at 11, 19.

[9] Major General Antonio Taguba, *Article 15–6, Investigation of the 800th Military Police Brigade*, report of inquiry made at the request of Lt. Gen. Ricardo S. Sanchez, January 2004, at 16 [hereinafter *Taguba Report*].

[10] Senate Armed Services Committee, *Inquiry Into the Treatment of Detainees in U.S. Custody*, 110th Cong., 2d sess., 2008, 163 [hereinafter *Senate Armed Services Committee Report*].

11   International Committee of the Red Cross, *ICRC Report on the Treatment of Fourteen "High Value Detainees" in CIA Custody* 13 (February 2007) [hereinafter *ICRC 2007 Detainee Report*]; NYU School of Law, Center for Human Rights and Global Justice, *On the Record: U.S. Disclosures on Rendition, Secret Detention and Coercive Interrogation* (2008), at 15.

12   *ICRC 2007 Detainee Report, id.* at 13.

13   *Id.*, at 12. This technique is called "walling." Steven G. Bradbury, Memorandum, *Re: Application of United States Obligations Under Article 16 of the Convention Against Torture to Certain Techniques that May Be Used in the Interrogation of High Value al Qaeda Detainees*, 30 May 2005, 7 [hereinafter *Bradbury Memo of May 30, 2005*].

14   James Meek, *They Beat Me from All Sides*, GUARDIAN, Jan. 14, 2005.

15   Center for Constitutional Rights, *Report on Torture and Cruel, Inhuman and Degrading Treatment of Prisoners at Guantanamo Bay, Cuba* 14 (2006).

16   Physicians for Human Rights, *Broken Laws, Broken Lives, supra* note 2, at 51, 62.

17   MURAT KURNAZ, FIVE YEARS OF MY LIFE: AN INNOCENT MAN IN GUANTANAMO 65 (2007).

18   Physicians for Human Rights, *Broken Laws, Broken Lives, supra* note 2, at 25.

19   *ICRC 2007 Detainee Report, supra* note 12, at 14.

20   Jay S. Bybee, *Interrogation of Al Qaeda Operative [Abu Zubaydah]*, Memorandum for John Rizzo, August 1, 2002, at 3.

21   Center for Human Rights and Global Justice, *On the Record, supra* note 12, at 15.

22   Physicians for Human Rights, *Broken Laws, Broken Lives, supra* note 2, at 63.

23   Goetz & Sandberg, *Freed Guantanamo Detainees Claim Abuse Continues Under Obama, supra* note 5.

24   Physicians for Human Rights, *Broken Laws, Broken Lives, supra* note 2, at 8.

25   *Id.*, at 57.

26   *Id.*, at 62.

27   Ian Pannell, *Ex-Detainees Allege Bagram Abuse*, BBC NEWS, Jun. 24, 2009.

28   KURNAZ, FIVE YEARS OF MY LIFE, *supra* note 18, at 73–76.

29   *Taguba Report, supra* note 10, at 17.

30   Physicians for Human Rights, *Broken Laws, Broken Lives, supra* note 2, at 8, 37.

31   *Id.*, at 33.

32   *Bradbury Memo of May 30, 2005, supra* note 14, at 8; Sheri Fink, *Do CIA Cables Show Doctors Monitoring Torture?*, SALON.COM, May 28, 2009.

33   NYU School of Law, Center for Human Rights and Global Justice, *Surviving the Darkness: Testimony from the U.S. "Black Sites"* 21–29 (2007).

34   FLETCHER & STOVER, THE GUANTANAMO EFFECT, *supra* note 3, at 63–65.

35   Albert T. Church III, *Review of Department of Defense Detention Operations and Detainee Interrogation Techniques* (Mar. 7, 2005) at 169 [hereinafter *Church Report*].

36   Amnesty International, *USA: Cruel and Inhuman: Conditions of Isolation for Detainees at Guantanamo Bay* (2007).

37   *FBI Report, supra* note 2, at 227.

38   *Senate Armed Services Committee Report*, supra note 11, at 216.

39   *Id.*

40   *ICRC 2007 Detainee Report, supra* note 12, at 7; Special Rapporteur Dick Marty, *Secret Detentions and Illegal Transfers of Detainees Involving Council of Europe Member States: Second Report,* report prepared for the Council of Europe Parliamentary Assembly Committee on Legal Affairs and Human Rights, Doc. 11302 rev., 49. The CoE Report describes initial four month regimens of isolation that included no exposure to natural light, interaction only with masked, silent guards, constant white noise, shackling, forced nudity, intermittent delivery and inadequate amounts of food, among other abuses.

41   *ICRC 2007 Detainee Report, supra* note 12, at 8.

42   Center for Constitutional Rights, *Report on Torture and Cruel, Inhuman and Degrading Treatment, supra* note 16, at 17.

43   *Id.*

44   *Senate Armed Services Committee Report,* supra note 11, at 140.

45   *FBI Report, supra* note 2, at 81.

46   Fletcher & Stover, The Guantanamo Effect, *supra* note 3, at 37.

47   *FBI Report, supra* note 2, at 223.

48   *Id.*

49   Fletcher & Stover, The Guantanamo Effect, *supra* note 3, at 27.

50   *FBI Report, supra* note 2, at 254.

51   *Id.,* at 256.

52   *ICRC 2007 Detainee Report,* 6.

53   David Charter, *An Innocent Man's Five Months in CIA 'Salt Pit,'* Times (London), Dec. 6, 2005.

54   *FBI Report, supra* note 2, at 199–200. Comfort items were such basics as blanket, mattress, toothbrush or the Qu'ran. Camp Delta Standard Operating Procedures (March 1, 2004), at §4–20.

55   Dep't of Defense, *Schmidt-Furlow Report, Army Regulation 15–6: Final Report Investigation into FBI Allegations of Detainee Abuse at Guantanamo Bay, Cuba Detention Facility* (Apr. 1, 2005), 19–20 [hereinafter *Schmidt-Furlow Report*].

56   *FBI Report, supra* note 2, at 102.

57   Physicians for Human Rights, *Broken Laws, Broken Lives, supra* note 2, at 3.

58   *Id.,* at 47; Fletcher & Stover, The Guantanamo Effect, *supra* note 3, at 24–29.

59   *Taguba Report, supra* note 10, at 16; *FBI Report, supra* note 2, at 251.

60   *Taguba Report, supra* note 10, at 16.

61   *Senate Armed Services Committee Report, supra* note 11, at 213.

62   *ICRC 2007 Detainee Report, supra* note 12, at 14.

63   Physicians for Human Rights, *Broken Laws, Broken Lives, supra* note 2, at 63.

64   *FBI Report, supra* note 2, at 84.

65   *Id.,* at 230.

66   Fletcher & Stover, The Guantanamo Effect, *supra* note 3, at 25.

[67] *Taguba Report, supra* note 10, at 17.

[68] Josh White, *Detainee in Photo with Dog Was a 'High-Value' Suspect*, WASH. POST, Mar. 13, 2006.

[69] FLETCHER & STOVER, THE GUANTANAMO EFFECT, *supra* note 3, at 55.

[70] *FBI Report, supra* note 2, at 83.

[71] Physicians for Human Rights, *Broken Laws, Broken Lives, supra* note 2, at 47.

[72] Physicians for Human Rights, *Broken Laws, Broken Lives, supra* note 2, at 58.

[73] Dep't of Defense, *Interrogation Log Detainee 063*, 23 Nov. 2002 – 11 Jan. 2003, reprinted in *Inside the Interrogation of Detainee 063*, TIME, June 12, 2005.

[74] FLETCHER & STOVER, THE GUANTANAMO EFFECT, *supra* note 3, at 30.

[75] Physicians for Human Rights, *Broken Laws, Broken Lives, supra* note 2, at 83.

[76] *FBI Report, supra* note 2, at 261.

[77] Physicians for Human Rights, *Broken Laws, Broken Lives, supra* note 2, at 42.

[78] Richard A. Serrano & John Daniszewski, *Dozens Have Alleged Qu'ran's Mishandling*, L.A. TIMES, May 22, 2005.

[79] *ICRC 2007 Detainee Report, supra* note 12, at 20.

[80] *Id.*

[81] Center for Human Rights and Global Justice, *Surviving the Darkness, supra* note 34, at 25.

[82] *Church Report*, 174–176; Center for Constitutional Rights, *Report on Torture and Cruel, Inhuman and Degrading Treatment, supra* note 16, at 24.

[83] Physicians for Human Rights, *Broken Laws, Broken Lives, supra* note 2, at 63; FLETCHER & STOVER, THE GUANTANAMO EFFECT, *supra* note 3, at 66.

[84] *FBI Report, supra* note 2, at 102–3.

[85] Center for Constitutional Rights, *Report on Torture and Cruel, Inhuman and Degrading Treatment, supra* note 16, at 25.

[86] *Schmidt-Furlow Report*, 19–20.

[87] *FBI Report, supra* note 2, at 175.

[88] *Church Report*, 55.

[89] Physicians for Human Rights, *Broken Laws, Broken Lives, supra* note 2, at 47.

[90] *Id.*, at 51; FLETCHER & STOVER, THE GUANTANAMO EFFECT, *supra* note 3, at 22.

[91] *Taguba Report, supra* note 10, at 16.

[92] *Id.*, at 19.

[93] Tony Lagouranis and Allen Mikaelian, *Fear Up Harsh: An Army Interrogator's Dark Journey Through Iraq* (New York: NAL Caliber 2007), 137.

[94] *Taguba Report, supra* note 10, at 17.

[95] *Id.*

[96] Michael Scherer & Mark Benjamin, *Dehumanization*, SALON.COM, Mar. 14, 2006.

[97] *ICRC 2007 Detainee Report, supra* note 12, at 17.

[98] Center for Human Rights and Global Justice, *On the Record, supra* note 12, at 15.

99 *FBI Report, supra* note 2, at 190–91; FLETCHER & STOVER, THE GUANTANAMO EFFECT, *supra* note 3, at 64–65; Physicians for Human Rights, *Broken Laws, Broken Lives, supra* note 2, at 58. Some detainees were subject to 24/7 blaring of rap music or tapes of babies crying, Barney the dinosaur, or loud insistent cat meowing. Moustafa Bayoumi, *Disco Inferno,* THE NATION, Dec. 26; Center for Constitutional Rights, *Report on Torture and Cruel, Inhuman and Degrading Treatment, supra* note 16, at 18.

100 *FBI Report, supra* note 2, at 183; *United States v. Jawad,* 1 Nat'l Inst. Of Mil. Just., Mil. Comm'n R. 334 (Military Commission Hearing, 2008) (D-008 Ruling on Defense Motion to Dismiss – Torture of Detainee).

101 *Schmidt-Furlow Report,* 17; *FBI Report, supra* note 2, at 102.

102 *FBI Report, supra* note 2, at 224–25.

103 *Id.,* at 256.

104 Physicians for Human Rights, *Broken Laws, Broken Lives, supra* note 2, at 42.

105 *Taguba Report, supra* note 10, at 18.

106 *ICRC 2007 Detainee Report, supra* note 12, at 11.

107 *Id.*

108 *Id.,* at 11, 15; Greg Miller, *Memos Shed Light on CIA Use of Sleep Deprivation,* WASH. POST, May 10, 2009.

109 Center for Human Rights and Global Justice, *Surviving the Darkness, supra* note 34, at 21.

110 Physicians for Human Rights, *Broken Laws,* 58.

111 *Schmidt-Furlow Report,* 27.

112 FLETCHER & STOVER, THE GUANTANAMO EFFECT, *supra* note 3, at 62–63.

113 *Id.,* at 24; *FBI Report,* 167.

114 Kurnaz, *Five Years of My Life,* 73–76; Fletcher & Stover, *Guantanamo Effect,* 24.

115 Eric Schmitt & Carolyn Marshall, *In a Secret Unit's Black Room, A Grim Portrait of U.S. Abuse,* N.Y. TIMES, Mar. 19, 2006.

116 Human Rights Watch, *No Blood, No Foul,* 9.

117 Lagouranis & Mikaelian, *Fear Up Harsh,* 89.

118 Physicians for Human Rights, *Broken Laws, Broken Lives, supra* note 2, at 25, 76–7.

119 *ICRC 2007 Detainee Report, supra* note 12, at 11.

120 *Id.*

121 *Id.*

122 *Id.,* at 18.

123 Center for Human Rights and Global Justice, *On the Record, supra* note 12, at 15.

124 *FBI Report, supra* note 2, at 184–185; FLETCHER & STOVER, THE GUANTANAMO EFFECT, *supra* note 3, at 63; Physicians for Human Rights, *Broken Laws, Broken Lives, supra* note 2, at 58.

125 FLETCHER & STOVER, THE GUANTANAMO EFFECT, *supra* note 3, at 63–65.

126 *FBI Report, supra* note 2, at 180.

[127] *Church Report*, 101.

[128] Physicians for Human Rights, *Broken Laws, Broken Lives, supra* note 2, at 80.

[129] Fletcher & Stover, The Guantanamo Effect, *supra* note 3, at 27.

[130] Human Rights Watch, *No Blood, No Foul*, 25–34. See also reports of similar abuses at Camp Mercury, Eric Schmitt, *Three in 82nd Airborne Say Beating Iraqi Prisoners was Routine*, N.Y. Times, Sep. 24, 2005 (Ian Fishback, a soldier based there, went public with his story).

[131] *FBI Report, supra* note 2, at 260.

[132] *Senate Armed Services Committee Report*, supra note 11, at 216.

[133] Physicians for Human Rights, *Broken Laws, Broken Lives, supra* note 2, at 18.

[134] *ICRC 2007 Detainee Report, supra* note 12, at 19.

[135] *Id.*, at 15.

[136] *Id.*

[137] Physicians for Human Rights, *Broken Laws, Broken Lives, supra* note 2, at 58, 63.

[138] Center for Constitutional Rights, *Report on Torture and Cruel, Inhuman and Degrading Treatment, supra* note 16, at 18–19.

[139] *Schmidt-Furlow Report*, 26, ex. 72.

[140] *Id.*, at 25.

[141] *FBI Report, supra* note 2, at 183–184 n. 134.

[142] Fletcher & Stover, The Guantanamo Effect, *supra* note 3, at 36.

[143] *Id.*, at 25.

[144] Pannell, "Ex-Detainees Allege Bagram Abuse."

[145] *Taguba Report, supra* note 10, at 17.

[146] *Id.*

[147] Physicians for Human Rights, *Broken Laws, Broken Lives, supra* note 2, at 18.

[148] *ICRC 2007 Detainee Report, supra* note 12, at 8; Center for Human Rights and Global Justice, *On the Record*, 15.

[149] Central Intelligence Agency Office of Inspector General, *Counterterrorism Detention and Interrogation Activities (September 2001-October 2003)*, special review, May 7, 2004, at 42 [hereinafter *CIA Report*].

[150] *Id.*, at 42–43.

[151] *FBI Report, supra* note 2, at 102–3. Susan Crawford, convening authority of the military commissions, publicly stated that Al Qahtani's treatment was torture and, because of it, withdrew the indictment against him. Bob Woodward, *Detainee Tortured Says U.S. Official*, Wash. Post, Jan. 14, 2009.

[152] Kurnaz, *Five Years of My Life*, 69–76.

[153] Bob Herbert, *How Long is Long Enough?*, N.Y. Times, 29 June 2009.

[154] *FBI Report, supra* note 2, at xxv-xxix.

[155] *Taguba Report, supra* note 10, at 17.

[156] *FBI Report, supra* note 2, at 243–44.

157   *Taguba Report, supra* note 10, at 17.
158   *FBI Report, supra* note 2, at 242.
159   *ICRC 2007 Detainee Report, supra* note 12, at 10.
160   *Bradbury Memo of May 30, 2005*, 37. The CIA program authorized waterboard use for two 'sessions' per day of up to two hours, where water could be applied up to six times for ten seconds or longer. In a 24 hour period, a detainee could be subjected to up to twelve minutes of water application, and the waterboard was authorized to be used on as many as five days during a 30-day approval period. *Id.*
161   *ICRC 2007 Detainee Report, supra* note 12, at 11.
162   Carlotta Gall and Andy Worthington, "Time Runs Out for an Afghan Held by U.S. Detention Unjustified, Karzai Officials Say," *New York Times*, February 5; Carol Rosenberg, "Pentagon: Cancer killed Guantanamo Detainee," *Miami Herald*, December 30, 2007; John Chandler and Currey Hitchens, "A Cancer on Body Politic," *Atlanta Journal-Constitution*, March 9, 2008.
163   William Glaberson & Margot Williams, "Officials Report Suicide of Guantanamo Detainee," *New York Times*, 2 June 2009.
164   Tim Golden, *Brutal Details of 2 Afghan Inmates' Deaths*, New York Times, May 20, 2005.
165   Human Rights First, *Command's Responsibility: Detainee Deaths in U.S. Custody in Iraq and Afghanistan*, (Human Rights First, February 2006), 14.
166   Human Rights Watch, *News: U.S.: Failure to Provide Justice for Afghan Victims*, February 14, 2007.
167   *Id.*
168   Human Rights Watch, *The Road to Abu Ghraib* (New York: Human Rights Watch, 2004), 28.
169   *Id.*, at 29. The detainee had been held by US Special Forces at FOB Rifles. This report also included the account of the murder of a Baath party official who was strangled and kicked in the chest before death.
170   Seymour M. Hersh, *Torture at Abu Ghraib*, New Yorker, May 10, 2004; Human Rights First, *Command's Responsibility*, 11–12 (detailed account of the killing).
171   *FBI Report*, 238.
172   Physicians for Human Rights and Human Rights First, *Leave No Marks: Enhanced Interrogation Techniques and the Risk of Criminality* (Physicians for Human Rights, 2007), 15–16; Human Rights First, *Command's Responsibility*, 17, 21–26.
173   Dana Priest, *An Afghan prison stirs doubts on CIA*, Washington Post, March 6, 2005.

APPENDIX 4: MILITARY RESPONSES TO INTERROGATION TECHNIQUES

Memorandum for UN and Multilateral Affairs Division (J-5), Joint Staff (Attn: CDR Lippold) from Col. Donald Richburg, USAF. Subject: Counter-resistance techniques (Nov. 4, 2002)

Col. Richburg's memo expresses concern over the interrogation techniques requested by commanders at GTMO in October 2002. He notes that certain methods requested may be considered torture and use of others could preclude criminal prosecution.

AF Planner Joint Action Brief Sheet from Thomas Randall. Subject: Counter-Resistance Techniques (Nov. 1, 2002)

Thomas Randall's brief sheet notes concern that interrogation techniques requested by commanders at GTMO in October 2002 could be torture and suggests further legal review.

Assessment of JTF-170 Counter-Resistance Strategies and the Potential Impact on CITF Mission and Personnel, Major Sam McCahon, Chief Legal Advisor, Division Chief, Plans Policy and Integration, DOD CITF

A Critical memo sent to the commander of CITF in response to GTMO commander's requested methods of interrogations in 2002. McCahon strongly recommends against using Category III techniques for several reasons, including exposure to criminal liability.

Memorandum for Legal Counsel to Chairman, Joint Chiefs of Staff. Subject: SJS 02–06697

Includes a CITF legal opinion by John Ley and OTJAG email.

Memorandum for the Office for the Army General Counsel from John Ley. Subject: Review – Proposed Counter-resistance Techniques

Notes that Category III methods in 2002 GTMO request for new interrogation techniques are illegal under Federal law and UCMJ. Recommends against use of new methods.

Memorandum for the Director for Strategic Plans and Policy Directorate, Joint Staff from Capt. D.D. Thompson, U.S. Navy. Subject: Navy Planner's Memo WRT Counter-resistance techniques (Nov. 4, 2002)

Recommends further legal and policy review of techniques requested in October 2002 from GTMO. Notes international scrutiny of techniques of interrogation methods are *inadvertently* disclosed to ICRC.

Memorandum from Headquarters United States Marine Corps to Joint Staff. Subject: Counter-Resistance Techniques. (Nov. 4, 2002)

Express of concern regarding GTMO interrogation techniques requested in October 2002, noting that several Category II and III techniques are illegal under Federal Law.

Memorandum for SAF/JC from Maj. Gen. Jack Rives, USAF. Subject: Final Report and Recommendations of the Working Group to Assess the Legal, Policy, and Operational Issues Relating to Interrogation of Detainees Held by the U.S. Armed Forces in the War on Terrorism (Feb. 5, 2003)

Critiques the 2003 working group's recommended interrogation methods, calling the most extreme to be illegal under US and international law. Also suggests that the newly recommended techniques are a reversal of US military policy.

Memorandum for SAF/GC from Maj. Gen. Jack Rives, USAF. Subject: Comments on Draft Report and Recommendations of the Working Group to Assess the Legal, Policy, and Operational Issues Relating to Interrogation of Detainees Held by the U.S. Armed Forces in the War on Terrorism (Feb. 6, 2003)

Reiteration of General Rives legal, policy, and moral concerns in the Working Groups new interrogation methods.

Memorandum for General Counsel of the Air Force from BG Kevin Sandkuhler, USMC. Subject: Working Group Recommendations on Detainee Interrogations (Feb. 27, 2003)

Sandkuhler observes that the OLC does not have the interest of servicemen in mind when it created its legal memos concerning interrogation techniques. He recommends that the Working group addresses servicemen's concerns when authorizing interrogation techniques. He notes concern about servicemen criminal liability, treatment of captured servicemen, and maintaining pride, honor and self-respect.

Memorandum for the Air Force General Counsel from Admiral Michael Lohr, U.S. Navy. Subject: Comments on the March 6, 2003 Detainee Interrogation Working Group Report (Mar. 13, 2003)

Recommends changes to the Working Group paper so that it notes that certain techniques would constitute illegal torture.

Memorandum for General Counsel of Air Force from Admiral Michael Lohr, U.S. Navy. Subject: Working Group Recommendations Relating to Interrogation of Detainees (Feb. 6, 2003)

Lohr expresses further concern over the Working Group Recommendations. Asks, "Is this the 'right thing' for U.S. military personnel?"

Memorandum for General Counsel of the Department of the Air Force from Maj. Gen. Thomas Romig, U.S. Army. Subject: Draft Report and Recommendations of the Working Group to Assess the Legal, Policy, and Operational Issues Relating to Interrogation of Detainees Held by the US Armed Forces in the War on Terrorism (Mar. 3, 2003)

Criticizes the OLC legal arguments regarding enhanced interrogation and torture. Recommends that military personnel be involved in further vetting of recommended techniques.

Gen. Merrill McPeak et al. as Amici Curiae Supporting Petitioner, *Hamdan v. Rumsfeld*, 548 U.S. 557 (2006) (No. 05–184)

Senior military officials argue that the Geneva Conventions apply to captured al-Qaeda and Taliban fighters. In addition, the President may not deny Geneva protections. Finally, the Military Commissions formed to try Hamdan violate the Geneva Conventions.

Memorandum for Inspector General, Department of Navy from Alberto Mora, Dept. of Navy General Counsel. Subject: Statement for the Record: Office of General Counsel Involvement in Interrogation Issues (July 7, 2004)

Alberto Mora recounts his discovery of harsh interrogation techniques at GTMO on December 17, 2002 and narrates his attempts to halt the use of these methods in the following months.

Email to Sam McCahon, Mallow Brittain, Thomas Blaine, Johnson Scott, Smith David from Mark Fallon. Subject: Counter Resistance Strategy Meeting Minutes (Oct. 28, 2002)

Mark Fallon's email reflects his reaction to the October meeting at GTMO discussing the use of harsh interrogation techniques. He describes methods such as water-boarding as 'shocking the conscience' and notes that "this looks like the kinds of stuff Congressional hearings are made of."

CHAPTER 3
THE TORTURE-ENABLING POLICY AND ITS TRICKLE-DOWN EFFECTS

3.1. INTRODUCTION

In the U.S., as well as in all democratic governments, the making of legal policy is a legislative prerogative. It is Congress which passes laws, and entrusts their fair and correct application to the Executive branch, and their interpretation to the Judicial branch. The making of the torture-enabling policy was in some respect a subversion of the legislative powers of Congress. The Bush Administration, under the euphemistic guise of interpreting the law, simply re-wrote the law. But it did not do so by means of an Executive Order or by rules and regulations enacted pursuant to federal legislation which authorizes it. Instead, it used a variety of subterfuges which are described in this chapter. Even though some of these were quite transparent as to their purpose of violating the Constitution and laws of the U.S., as well as international law, the Bush Administration was able to slip its plan past the Legislative and Judicial branches by means of a variety of governmental memoranda which were issued by government lawyers in different agencies so as to create what is described in this chapter as an enabling policy with a very clear trickle-down effect designed to produce practices which would otherwise be illegal.

Even though the subterfuge was transparent to so many, it was not met with much if any opposition by the Legislative branch, or for that matter by the Judicial branch, whose role in this case would not have been to oppose governmental policy, but simply to interpret it as being in violation of the Constitution and laws of the United States. The failure of these two branches of government to carry out their constitutional responsibilities is what allowed the Executive branch to abuse its power and subvert the law. Aided and comforted by a certain segment of the American public, and undeterred by any opposition from the legal profession or the opposing political party, the Bush Administration proceeded with its torture-enabling policy.

3.2. THE MAKING OF THE POLICY

The institutionalization of torture started with the setting in motion of policy and practices by Vice President Cheney and his legal collaborators – his Chief of Staff, David Addington and DOD General Counsel, William J. Haynes III – who, in turn, influenced then While House Legal Counsel Gonzales, Bybee in the DOJ, and Secretary Rumsfeld. These men formed a powerful inner circle from which the torture policy emanated.[1] To better understand the policy, it is necessary to examine the practices carried out under it. This includes use of the "enhanced interrogation" techniques described earlier in Chapter 2, as well as the practices carried out in the CIA's "black sites" and "extraordinary rendition" program (*infra* Chapter 4), whereby surrogate states carried out torture for the benefit of the U.S. on persons kidnapped by the CIA and forcefully (and unlawfully) delivered to the surrogate state. The outsourcing of torture was also supplemented by private contractors (*infra* Chapter 5). Appendices 3 and 4 herein describe these practices in Guantánamo, Iraq, Afghanistan, and elsewhere. The widespread and systematic nature of these practices carried out in so many places over such a long period evidence the policy that brought them about.

The trickle-down effect of the torture policy was achieved when the civilian leadership of the DOD bypassed the Judge Advocates General of the various branches of the military, as well as some non-lawyer senior military officers, whose understanding of IHL and sense of honor led them to oppose such practices by the U.S. military.[2] Surely, these honorable men and women in uniform who opposed torture also considered the consequences of such practice if enemies of the U.S. would do the same to American POWs, even though reprisals are prohibited under IHL.[3]

It is important to understand the history of mass crimes in their different settings; namely, that such crimes occur when policy is established at the top and its effects cause a down-stream multiplier effect. To cause large-scale compliance with unlawful or questionable requests, it is necessary to create systematic

---

[1]   *See* PHILIP ZIMBARDO, THE LUCIFER EFFECT: UNDERSTANDING HOW GOOD PEOPLE TURN EVIL (2008) for the trickle-down effect of command decision. *See also* ERVIN STAM, THE ROOTS OF EVIL: THE ORIGINS OF GENOCIDE AND OF GROUP VIOLENCE (1989); JAMES WALLER, BECOMING EVIL: HOW ORDINARY PEOPLE COMMIT GENOCIDE AND MASS KILLING (2002); HANNAH ARENDT, EICHMANN IN JERUSALEM: A REPORT ON THE BANALITY OF EVIL (1963).

[2]   *See generally* KAREN GREENBERG, THE LEAST WORST PLACE: GUANTANAMO'S FIRST 100 DAYS (2009), which explains the efforts of a group of career Marine officers who tried, and ultimately failed, to stop the efforts of the Pentagon to implement new harsh interrogation techniques and bypass the Geneva Conventions. Amongst those holding opposing views were Deputy Judge Advocate General of the Air Force Albert Mora, Maj. Gen. Jack. L. Rives, Navy Rear Adm. Michael Lohr, Navy Rear Adm. John B. Hutchins, as well as Army Legal Counsel John Ley, USAF Col. Donald Richburg, and Navy Capt. D.D. Thompson, Special Assistant to CNO for JCS Matters, U.S. Navy.

[3]   On the prohibition of reprisals, see FRITS KALSHOVEN, BELLIGERENT REPRISALS (2005).

conditions that eliminate or reduce opposition by providing incentives for compliance. In addition, the appearance of legality has to be conveyed, and that is why legal schemes developed by willful jurists become necessary. Finally, to bring the general public around to support or at least tolerate the policy and its consequential practices, it is necessary to create the perception of dehumanization of the victims of the unlawful policy.[4]

The military JAG lawyers and others in the military who opposed the torture-enabling policy had to face politically-appointed civilian lawyers in the DOD, the DOJ, and the White House who used their legal talent and their political authority to subvert the law.[5] The process was systematic, and it was achieved by: compartmentalizing decision-making; sidestepping military command and control; separating organs and personnel addressing the issues of torture; and creating a new judicial institution, the Military Commissions, with lesser legal standards of due process and fairness than the Constitution provides and euphemistically labeling a new category of persons as "enemy combatants," to whom the protection of the Geneva Conventions were denied. This was accompanied by creating a jurisdictional gap or black hole for the unlawful practice of "extraordinary rendition" and "black sites" operated by the CIA; and permitting unlawful practices by private contractors without judicial oversight. In so doing, some of these government lawyers may have violated the law[6] and the ethics of the legal profession, undermining the Constitution and the laws of

---

[4]   *See supra* note 1.

[5]   Regarding the OLC's position on customary international law, Army Major General Thomas J. Romig, Judge Advocate General wrote:

> The OLC opinion states further that customary international law cannot bind the U.S. Executive Branch as it is not part of federal law. As such, any presidential decision made in the context of the ongoing war on terrorism constitutes a 'controlling' Executive act; one that immediately and automatically displaces any contrary provision of customary international law. This view runs contrary to the historic position taken by the U.S. Government concerning such law and, in our opinion, could adversely impact DOD interests worldwide. On the one hand, such policy will open us to international criticism that the 'U.S. is a law unto itself'. On the other, implementation of questionable techniques will very likely establish a new baseline for acceptable practice in this area, putting our new service personnel at far greater risk and vitiating many of the POW/detainee safeguards the U.S. has worked hard to establish over the past five decades.

> Memorandum for General Counsel of the Dep't of the Air Force, Subject: Draft Report and Recommendations of the Working Group to Access Legal, Policy and Operational Issues Related to Interrogation of Detainees Held by the U.S. Armed Forces in the War on Terrorism (March 3, 2003).

[6]   U.S. v. Lee, 106 U.S. 196, 220 (1882). "No man in this country is so high that he is above the law. No officer of the law may set that law at defiance with impunity. All the officers of the government, from the highest to the lowest, are creatures of the law, and are bound to obey it." *See also, 11 Op. Atty Gen.* 297, 299–300 (1865). Attorney General Speed recognized that the laws of war and the laws of nations "are of binding force upon the departments and citizens of the Government" and neither Congress nor the Executive can "abrogate them or authorize their infraction." *Id.*

the U.S., which they had sworn to uphold as members of the legal profession.[7] Such legal advisors may include Jay S. Bybee (then Assistant Attorney General and now a federal judge), Alberto Gonzales (then White House Counsel and subsequently Attorney General),[8] William J. Haynes II (then General Counsel, DOD, and who was even nominated for a federal judgeship by President Bush), and John Yoo (then Deputy Assistant Attorney General and now a professor at the University of California, Berkeley). Many other government lawyers contributed to the enterprise and helped to execute it. These lawyers used their legal talents to justify highly questionable propositions, some which were slightly more than fig-leaf cover-ups for torture.[9] The legal opinions issued and

---

[7]   *See* Bradley Wendel, *The Torture Memos and the Demands of Legality*, 12 LEGAL ETHICS 107 (2009); Peter Marguiles, *Foreword: Risk, Deliberation and Professional Responsibility*, 1 J. NAT'L SEC. L & POL'Y 357 (2005); Mary Cheh, *Should Lawyers Participate in Rigged Systems? – The Case of the Military Commissions*, 1 J. NAT'L SEC. L & POL'Y 375 (2005); George C. Harris, *The Rule of Law and the War on Terror: The Professional Responsibilities of Executive Branch Lawyers in the Wake of 9/11*, 1 J. NAT'L SEC. L & POL'Y 409 (2005); Kathleen Clark, *Ethical Issues Raised by the OLC Torture Memorandum*, 1 J. NAT'L SEC. L & POL'Y 455 (2005); Aaron R. Jackson, *The White House Counsel Torture Memo: The Final Product of a Flawed System*, 42 CAL. W. L. REV. 149 (2005).

[8]   Gonzales, as White House Legal Counsel, argued that the Geneva Conventions did not apply to Taliban detainees:

> As you have said, the war against terrorism is a new kind of war. It is not the traditional clash between nations adhering to the laws of war that formed the backdrop for GPW. The nature of the new war places a high premium on other factors, such as the ability to quickly obtain information from captured terrorists and their sponsors in order to avoid further atrocities against American civilians, and the need to try terrorists for war crimes such as wantonly killing civilians. In my judgment, this new paradigm renders quaint some of its provisions requiring that captured enemy be afforded such things are commissary privileges, scrip (i.e., advances of monthly pay), athletic uniforms, and scientific instruments.

David Wippman, *Introduction: Do New Wars Call for New Laws? in* NEW WARS, NEW LAWS? APPLYING THE LAW OF WAR IN 21ST CENTURY CONFLICTS 11 (David Wippman & Matthew Evangelista eds. 2005), *citing* Memorandum from Alberto R. Gonzales to President Bush (January 25, 2002). The Attorney General has the responsibility to "raise hard legal and constitutional questions whenever a president it tempted to overreach the limits of his authority." *Id.* Instead, Gonzales acted more like "President Bush's personal legal strategist, doing everything in his power to justify Bush's apparent desire to authorize torture, deny detainees access to the write of habeas corpus, and order unlawful electronic surveillance and institute legal proceedings that defy due process of law." *Id.*

[9]   The legal opinions and other government memoranda prepared by these legal advisors appear in THE TORTURE PAPERS: THE ROAD TO ABU GHRAIB (Karen J. Greenburg & Joshua L. Dratel eds., 2005). *See e.g.*, Memorandum from John C. Yoo, Deputy Assistant Attorney Gen., & Robert J. Delahunty, Special Counsel, Office of Legal Counsel, U.S. Dep't of Justice, to William J. Haynes II, Gen. Counsel, Dep't of Defense, Application of Treaties and Laws to al Qaeda and Taliban Detainees (Jan. 9, 2002) [hereinafter Yoo/Delahunty Memo]; Memorandum from Jay S. Bybee, Assistant Attorney Gen., Office of Legal Counsel, U.S. Dep't of Justice, to Alberto R. Gonzales, Counsel to the President, and William J. Haynes II, Gen. Counsel, Dep't of Def., Application of Treaties and Laws to al Qaeda and Taliban Detainees (Jan. 22, 2002); Memorandum from Alberto R. Gonzales, Counsel to the President, to George W. Bush, Decision Re Application of the Geneva Convention on Prisoners of War to the Conflict with Al Qaeda and the Taliban (Jan. 25, 2002); Memorandum from Jay S. Bybee, Assistant Attorney

government memoranda drafted were presented in order to allow the Bush Administration to establish a policy that these legal advisors knew or should have known was likely to constitute a violation of U.S. and international law.[10]

Gen., Office of Legal Counsel, U.S. Dep't of Justice, to Alberto R. Gonzales, Counsel to the President, Standards of Conduct for Interrogation under 18 U.S.C. §§2340–2340A (Aug. 1, 2002) [hereinafter Bybee Memo]; Letter from John C. Yoo, Deputy Assistant Attorney Gen., Official of Legal Counsel, U.S. Dep't of Justice to Alberto R. Gonzales, Counsel to the President (regarding "the views of our Office concerning the legality, under international law, of interrogation methods to be used... on captured al Qaeda operatives."); Memorandum from William J. Haynes, II, Gen. Counsel, U.S. Dep't of Def. to Donald Rumsfeld, Sec'y of Def., U.S. Dep't of Def., Counter-resistance Techniques (Nov. 27, 2002); Memorandum from William J. Haynes II, Gen. Counsel, U.S. Dep't of Def. to Mary L. Walker, Gen. Counsel, Dep't of the Air Force, Working Group to Assess (Interrogation Issues) (Jan. 17, 2003); Memorandum from John C. Yoo, Assistant Deputy Attorney Gen., Office of Legal Counsel, U.S. Dep't of Justice, for William J. Haynes II, Gen. Counsel, U.S. Dep't of Def. (Mar. 14, 2003), elaborating on the legality of interrogation methods authorized for the DOD, and arguing that military interrogations of al-Qaeda detainees were not subject to the strictures of federal laws prohibiting assault because of executive wartime authority to override such laws, and because federal and international laws were inapplicable to such extraterritorial interrogations.

It should be noted that the Bybee memo was disregarded by the Bush Administration because it was so obviously flawed and in contradiction with Art. 1 of the CAT and with Title 18 U.S.C. §2340. An amended position was developed in the Memorandum from Daniel Levin, Acting Assistant Attorney Gen., Office of Legal Counsel, U.S. Dep't of Justice, to James B. Comey, Deputy Attorney Gen., Office of Legal Counsel, U.S. Dep't of Justice, Regarding Legal Standards Applicable Under 18 U.S.C. §§2340–2340A (Dec. 30, 2004).

Senior government officials, including the President, relied on these memoranda and issued their own directives. *See* Memorandum from Donald Rumsfeld, Sec'y of Def., Dep't of Def. to Chairman of the Joint Chiefs of Staff, Status of Taliban and Al Qaeda (Jan. 19, 2002); Letter from John Ashcroft, Attorney Gen., U.S. Dep't of Justice to President George W. Bush (Feb. 1, 2002), discussing the DOJ's position on why the Geneva Conventions did not apply to al-Qaeda and Taliban detainees; Memorandum from President George W. Bush to Vice President Dick Cheney et al., Humane Treatment of al Qaeda and Taliban Detainees (Feb. 7, 2002); U.S. Dep't of Def., Military Commission Order No. 1: Procedures for Trials by Military Commissions of Certain Non-United States Citizens in the War Against Terrorism (Mar. 21, 2002); Memorandum from Donald Rumsfeld, Secretary of Defense to James T. Hill, Commander of the U.S. Southern Command, Counter-Resistance Techniques in the War on Terrorism (Apr. 16, 2003) [hereinafter Rumsfeld Memo]. Again, all of these memoranda can be found in THE TORTURE PAPERS, *id.*

[10]   *See* Michael D. Ramsey, *Toward a Rule of Law in Foreign Affairs*, 106 COLUM. L. REV. 1450, 1451, 1453, 1458–61, 1466, 1480–72 (2006); Jordan J. Paust, *Above the Law: Unlawful Executive Authorizations Regarding Detainee Treatment, Secret Renditions, Domestic Spying, and Claims to Unchecked Executive Power*, 2 UTAH L. REV. 345, 398 (2007), describing his interpretations as "a jurisprudence of a right-winged flock that is not 'conservative' or originalist, but a historical, autocratic, and ideological at base. It is also clearly not strict constructionist." Paust goes on to note: "The blueprint for its adherents reflects a willingness to ignore the Founders' and Framers' most relevant majority and uniform views... the text and structure of the Constitution, and overwhelming judicial opinions for more than 200 years, and pretends that if a few professors with an extremist agenda disagree legal limits somehow disappear and the content of law can be recast merely through anti-contextualist ideological debate." *Id.* at 398. Paust refers to this affliction as "Westlaw-phobia" where "professors who offer sometime sophistic speculation about important aspects of the reach of law or who, having discovered alleged controversy or uncertainty among themselves, assume that the content of the law is

The supposed justification for these measures was that they were need in a new type of war, the "war on terrorism," another euphemism that was conveniently used to lead to torture, and to its public acceptance as both necessary and justified.[11] Terrorism, however, has been practiced throughout history, and the world has had much experience with it since the 1960s. This is not a new phenomenon, and the U.S. as well as other countries have had ample experience in dealing with it over the years. The euphemism was intended to convey the impression that the U.S. is facing a new kind of threat requiring new methods – thus, the "enhanced interrogation" techniques. As transparent as that scheme was, it worked, at least for a while.

The Bush Administration pursued the "war on terror" for three reasons: 1) the President and his advisors did not know how better to cope with the aftermath of 9/11; 2) it was, in their judgment, the best way to protect the U.S. from future terrorist attacks; and 3) it created opportunities to expand Presidential powers. The means to achieve these ends was the rationalization or justification of torture, because in times of war, as these lawyers erroneously saw it, the President has no Constitutional limitations. This same rationale was used for wiretaps ordered without going through the established legal procedures, namely, the FISA Court.[12] The White House was testing the powers of the Presidency by torturing individuals perceived to be actual or potential terrorists. Most Americans could not identify with foreigners believed to constitute a threat to the security of the U.S., and viewed the Bush Administration's measures as acceptable. As a consequence, policies and practices were established for constitutionally unchecked Presidential powers. Congress was in part bypassed, although it

---

    no longer extant and discoverable." *Id.* at 399. For a comprehensive analysis of these and other official U.S. documents, see Evan J. Wallach, *The Logical Nexus Between the Decision to Deny Application of the Third Geneva Convention to the Taliban and al Qaeda and the Mistreatment of Prisoners in Abu Ghraib*, 36 CASE W. RES. J. INT'L L. 541 (2004).

[11]   From Wippman, *Introduction, supra* note 8:

    The U.S. notion of an open-ended war on terrorism has other very broad implications. The United States has asserted the right to use military force against terrorists wherever they can be found, with or without the consent of the government on whose territory they may be located. Civilians (including terrorists) suspected of criminal acts must ordinarily be apprehended; to attack them militarily outside the context of an ongoing armed conflict could be construed as an illegal summary execution. Indeed, the United States has in the past criticized Israel for engaging in the "targeted killing" of Palestinian militants. But as National Security Adviser Condoleezza Rice stated following a 2002 U.S. attack on suspected al Qaeda operative in Yemen, "we're in a new kind of war, and we've made it very clear that this new kind of war [will] be fought on different battlefields."

    Id. at 4.

[12]   Shortly after 9/11, President Bush secretly approved a new surveillance program which allowed the National Security Agency to monitor U.S. citizens' international email messages and phone calls without first obtaining warrants under the Federal Intelligence Surveillance Act (FISA). In March 2010, the Federal District Court of San Francisco ruled that the program was illegal. *See* Charlie Savage & James Risen, *Federal Judges Finds N.S.A. Wiretaps Were Illegal*, N.Y. TIMES, Mar. 31, 2010.

adopted the PATRIOT Act which legitimized new limitations on Constitutional rights and curtailed the judiciary's constitutional review process.[13]

3.3. THE TRICKLE-DOWN EFFECT FROM THE WHITE HOUSE

History reveals that leaders who abuse their powers rarely implicate themselves so clearly that their responsibility can subsequently be established. Those who order wrongful acts are usually cautious enough to conceal themselves behind innuendos and other means that can eventually shield them from being held accountable. Organized crime leaders, mafia dons, tyrannical regime leaders, and others have perfected the art of obfuscating truth and of concealing themselves behind what has come to be euphemistically called "plausible deniability," which makes it impossible to prove the commission of a crime beyond a reasonable doubt.

Decision makers and other high ranking officials have no need to explicitly plan out and specifically order actions that would directly tie them to the infractions of those who would execute them. All that is needed is a broad policy and a chain of command that can effectuate a trickle-down effect. The Bush Administration, particularly the Vice President's office, possessed all these requirements. As a result, senior members of the Administration could establish a policy of torture whose consequences would reach far below their rank without implicating themselves in the process.

The goal of the Bush Administration became clear within days of the attacks of September 11, 2001 and continued to develop as the CIA and the military began to detain suspects. CIA representatives meeting with Bush Administration officials insisted that it would be necessary to work outside the bounds of the Geneva Conventions in order to secure actionable intelligence.[14] The policy goal became clear: extract actionable intelligence by creating the opportunity to do so via legally questionable methods.

The carefully worded memoranda perpetuated in the early days of the "war on terror" were wolves in sheep's clothing. "The vice president's counsel proposed that President Bush issue a carefully ambiguous directive. Detainees would be treated humanely and, to the *extent appropriate and consistent with military necessity*, in a manner consistent with the principles of" the Geneva Conventions (emphasis added).[15] A superficial reading of that policy statement seems benign. However,

---

13   Uniting and Strengthening America by Providing Appropriate Tools Required to Intercept and Obstruct Terrorism (USA PATRIOT) Act of 2001, Pub. L. No. 107–56, §804, 115 Stat. 272, 377 (2001) (codified at 18 U.S.C.A. §7(9)(A) (2001)).

14   Barton Gellman, Angler: The Cheney Vice Presidency (2008) at 174.

15   *Id.* at 176.

the phrase "consistent with military necessity" gave a vast amount of wiggle room in what further policies the Bush Administration would promote in the future.

The next logical step was for the Bush Administration to claim a high level of military necessity to broaden the government's purported legitimate use of force in interrogations. In the months following the September 11 attacks, the public fear of further attacks allowed the White House a policy of "military necessity" to ensure national security with public support. However, as understood in international humanitarian law, this does not constitute "military necessity".

The White House explicitly asserted that *torture* would not be used in extracting intelligence from suspected terrorists and other detainees. "It was a syllogism informed by the same old claim of unlimited power. 'Torture' was *defined* as what 'we do not condone,' as Bush put it. Whatever Bush did permit, Alberto Gonzales said, 'does not constitute torture.'"[16] Thus the term "enhanced interrogation" evolved. The effect of narrowing the definition of torture and legitimizing so-called "enhanced interrogation" techniques served two purposes. First, it insulated the high-ranking officials of the Bush Administration from criminal responsibility. Second, it would have a socio-psychological effect on lower-ranking officials, including military personnel, and civilian agents. This was the method used by the Bush Administration, which was designed to shield its senior members from responsibility.

Addington, Gonzales, Bybee, Yoo, and Flanigan fashioned the early torture memoranda that first created new parameters for "enhanced interrogation" while also legitimizing methods that an ordinary person would consider unlawful or morally wrong. "Yoo claimed without limitation that the president could disregard laws and treaties prohibiting torture, war crimes, warrantless eavesdropping, and confinement without a hearing. The breadth of his language was stunning."[17]

When these memoranda and suggestions for "enhanced interrogation" techniques filtered down the chain of command, a disturbing mechanism was put in place. Through a series of steps, a trap formed that allows low-level subordinates to fall into a pattern of behavior an outside observer would see as abhorrent. An extended, bureaucratic chain of command acts as a fiendish filter device that creates this trap. Philip Zimbardo, in his book *The Lucifer Effect,* summarizes this device by breaking it into ten elements.[18] Briefly stated, they are:

1. Arranging a contractual obligation to control behavior in a pseudo-legal fashion.
2. Giving participants meaningful roles.

---

[16]   *Id.* at 193.
[17]   *Id.* at 137.
[18]   Zimbardo, The Lucifer Effect, *supra* note 1.

3. Presenting basic rules that make sense before actual use but then can be used arbitrarily to justify mindless compliance.
4. Altering semantics of the act, the actor, and the action.
5. Creating opportunities for the diffusion of responsibility from the actor.
6. Starting the path toward evil with a small insignificant first step.
7. Providing small gradual steps towards the ultimate evil act.
8. Gradually changing the nature of the authority from just to unjust.
9. Making exit costs for the actor.
10. Offering an ideology or big lie.[19]

Each of these steps enabled the trickle-down effect through the Bush Administration's government chain of command giving rise to torture. The first two steps mentioned above were inherently built into the chain of command. Military servicemen are bound to follow orders and they were placed under pressure to attain information from detainees. There was explicit pressure from the very top of the chain of command to get results. Failure to attain these results would, as the Bush Administration propagated, have negative results for both the interrogator and the U.S. as a whole. The high-level stakes brought about by the Vice President's office eventually affected even Col. Diane Beaver, who authored parts of the Rumsfeld memo and claimed to not have been under pressure. At insinuation that al-Qaeda had the smallpox virus, Beaver stated, "To me, it just brought home that I could be in a place where if al-Qaeda could bring smallpox in, that what al-Qaeda would do."[20]

The methods eventually approved by Secretary Rumsfeld met the criteria of step three in Zimbardo's analysis.[21] The Yoo memo and interrogation methods at first glance almost seem restrained, but the actual exercise of these methods clearly shows the depravity of such a policy. The interrogation techniques evolved from a series of steps starting with minor abuses of detainees, and progressed to third and forth tier categories of actions that are far more aggressive. The language in the memoranda provided to interrogators gave rise to these tactics by being ambiguous regarding the limits of the purported permissible techniques.

The torture memoranda fulfilled steps four and five of Zimbardo's list. Those prepared by Yoo, Bybee, Gonzales, Addington, and Flanigan (and others) twisted the semantics of what torture is. In addition, they diffused the responsibility of the actor by dismissing restrictions provided by international and domestic law.

---

[19]   ZIMBARDO, THE LUCIFER EFFECT, *supra* note 1, at 274. The steps enumerated here result from the 1961 Milgram Experiment in which the subject of the experiment was to submit increasingly painful electric shocks to a "patient" in a dummy memory experiment. The experiment showed subjects' willingness to expose others to dangerous high-level shots through the progressive machinations of the experimenting authority. *See* STANLEY MILGRAM, OBEDIENCE TO AUTHORITY: AN EXPERIMENTAL VIEW (1974).

[20]   GELLMAN, ANGLER, *supra* note 14, at 186.

[21]   *See* Rumsfeld Memo, *supra* note 9.

The memoranda did not stop there, however. Because advice from the OLC is authoritative within the Executive Branch, the memoranda created by Yoo and others essentially created an *ex ante* pardon for anyone who followed the OLC's advice, thus creating a perceived level of immunity for all parties involved in potentially unlawful conduct.[22]

The development of the steps described above was accompanied by dehumanization of the enemy in order to condition public opinion and dampen opposition to torture. Dehumanization occurs whenever some "human beings consider other human beings to be excluded from the moral order of being a human person."[23] Under this condition it becomes possible for a normal person to perform acts of "destructive cruelty."[24] Along with the other factors described above, dehumanization was part of the policy of torture.

Finally, according to Zimbardo, such a mechanism requires a "big lie" for any subordinate to cling to. The big lie here was two-fold. First the White House continually perpetuated the myth that the behavior that it approved of and implicitly encouraged was *not* torture. The second part of the ideology was that such extreme levels of interrogation are necessary to attain actionable intelligence and maintain national security. Neither of these assertions is true.[25]

In addition to the fulfillment to the steps described above there was one other major tool: fear. "Fear is the State's psychological weapon of choice to frighten citizens into sacrificing their basic freedoms and rule-of-law protections in exchange for the security promised by the all-powerful government."[26] One highly visible form of fear-mongering were the Department of Homeland Security's color-coded threat levels, which were originally designed to notify and mobilize citizens, and became a fixture on many news television programs. The vague and impractical warnings only served to elevate fear and, by this, provide popular support for the Bush Administration and its actions.[27]

The policy developed by the Bush Administration, especially the office of the Vice President, did not require an overt order to torture any detainees to obtain actionable intelligence; instead "there were no winks, no nods. Nothing more than a statement of plain fact: Qahtani might know something vital."[28] The nature of the bureaucratic chain of command served as a more than adequate mechanism to allow a top-level official set in motion the trickle-down effect that creates a multiplier effect and mutates the initial directive into something that

---

22   GELLMAN, ANGLER, *supra* note 14, at 177.
23   ZIMBARDO, THE LUCIFER EFFECT, *supra* note 1, at 307.
24   *Id.*
25   *See* Office of the Inspector General, *A Review of the FBI's Involvement in and Observations of Detainee Interrogations in Guantanamo Bay, Afghanistan, and Iraq,* at 171 (May 2008) [hereinafter OIG Report].
26   ZIMBARDO, THE LUCIFER EFFECT, *supra* note 1, at 430.
27   *Id.* at 431.
28   GELLMAN, ANGLER, *supra* note 14, at 185.

ends up being far more malicious. Any leader with even the vaguest conception of this phenomenon may use it to his own benefit while insulating himself from any direct implication for the crimes committed. The history of every abusive regime in the world demonstrates that these steps have been followed in development of abusive practices which include genocide, crimes against humanity, torture, and other human rights violations.

3.4. SEEKING TO ESTABLISH "PLAUSIBLE DENIABILITY"

Bits and pieces of what is akin to a conspiracy are emerging, and the separate dots of the plan are being connected between what are now commonly called the "torture memos" and the practices that ensued. For example, *N.Y. Times* story by Scott Shane, David Johnston, and James Risen showed that the position of the Bush Administration and the DOJ was that the President has unlimited authority in a time of war, which basically meant that he was not constrained by the Constitution, and that he could commit a violation of the Constitution, U.S. criminal laws, the UCMJ and international law because he was acting within his own sphere of constitutional powers. Thus, even if he explicitly ordered what amounts to torture by any other description, the President would be within his constitutional prerogatives, and thus not legally accountable.[29] It follows that those who followed the President's directives would have a complete defense for any acts with the presidential directives, even if they would be otherwise deemed illegal.

When this absurd and unlawful position became public, the reaction was in part negative. A gradual softening of the position followed, and, ultimately, in a DOJ legal opinion in December 2004, the Bush Administration in effect abandoned its assertion. However, when Alberto Gonzales became Attorney General in February 2005, the DOJ issued another opinion – this one secret – that authorized the CIA to engage in the same practices outside the U.S. which the Administration was backing down from using within the U.S. Quite clearly, a clash had developed between on one side, Deputy Attorney General James Comey (who served as acting Attorney General while Attorney General John Ashcroft was hospitalized) and legal counsel Jack Goldsmith, and on the other, Alberto Gonzales, the Vice President, and his Chief of Staff David Addington. The memoranda distributed to the CIA in 2005 have since been released, revealing DOJ lawyers' attempts to continually create avenues for the CIA to interrogate suspects with methods amounting to torture. Those penned by

---

[29]   *See* Scott Shane, David Johnston & James Risen, *Secret U.S. Endorsement of Severe Interrogations,* N.Y. TIMES, Oct. 4, 2007; David Johnston & Scott Shane, *Debate Erupts on Techniques used by C.I.A.,* N.Y. TIMES, Oct. 5, 2007.

Deputy Assistant Attorney General Steven Bradbury, again asserted the legality of techniques such as "waterboarding." Bradbury not only considered and approved of individual techniques, but also condoned the pervasive, continual combinations of methods, providing practically no guidance as to if or when these could culminate into torture.[30]

The purpose of the DOJ's legal opinions was to give legal protection or cover to the President and senior officials, as well as to members of the Executive Branch carrying out executive orders. In other words, these legal opinions were designed to relieve subordinates of the President, acting in his capacity as Commander-in-Chief, of the responsibility of committing war crimes and other crimes under international and U.S. law. However, as the legality of different legal opinions comes to be questioned, those who may one day face prosecution will find it difficult to use them as a defense. As stated by the U.S. Supreme Court, "orders given by the executive" or executive "instructions cannot change the nature of the transaction, or legalize an act which, without those instructions, would have been a plain trespass" of the law.[31] In IHL, as well as under the UCMJ, a subordinate has the obligation to refuse to obey an order that is manifestly illegal. The legal opinions in question were intended to address this issue as well, by giving the compliant subordinate the argument that the order was not "manifestly unlawful" because it was backed by the DOJ.[32] However, once some of these opinions were withdrawn and substituted with others which contradicted the original opinions, the new opinions should have been a clear warning to any subordinates that they were unreliable and that the techniques referred to as "enhanced interrogation" techniques were in reality torture.

Some individuals who were involved in this process must have subsequently realized that, notwithstanding these memos and the secrecy of the Bush Administration's policy and practices, they were exposed to criminal responsibility. Persons such as the then President, the Vice President, the Attorney General, the Chief-of-Staff of the Vice President, the legal counsels to the DOJ, the general counsel to the DOD, and others who contributed to the web of orders, directives, and instructions under which torture was committed may

---

[30]   *See* Memorandum for John Rizzo, Senior Deputy General Counsel, C.I.A., Application of 18 U.S.C. §§2340 to Certain Techniques That May Be Used in the Interrogation of a High Value al-Qaeda Detainee (May 10, 2005) [Bradbury Memo I]; Memorandum for John Rizzo, Senior Deputy General Counsel, C.I.A., Application of 18 U.S.C. §§2340 to the Combined Use of Certain Techniques in the Interrogation of High Value al-Qaeda Detainees (May 10, 2005) [Bradbury Memo II]. Bradbury's authoring of these memoranda facilitates a clearly criminal behavior, and are blatantly erroneous in their interpretation of severe physical and mental pain and suffering. *See* Jordan J. Paust, *The Second Bybee Memo: A Smoking Gun,* THE JURIST (April 22, 2009).

[31]   Little v. Barreme, 6 U.S. 170 (1804). *See also* In Ex parte Orozco, 201 F. 106, 111–12 (W.D. Tex. 1912). The court recognized that conduct resting "merely upon an order directed by the President" was illegal and cannot "be sustained in a court of justice."

[32]   *See* LAWRENCE P. ROCKWOOD, WALKING AWAY FROM NUREMBERG (2007).

be subject to criminal prosecution in the U.S. In addition to U.S. prosecutions, they may also be subject to prosecution in any country that is a signatory to the CAT, as well as the Geneva Conventions, both under the general theory of universal jurisdiction[33] and under the conventions which the U.S. has committed itself.

To answer for the eventuality of his responsibility, Jack Goldsmith published *The Terror Presidency*,[34] a book setting forth his role as legal counsel for the DOJ. He described altering two prior legal opinions, including the most abhorrent and clearly erroneous one issued by Yoo. Goldsmith, now a professor at Harvard, describes himself, Deputy Attorney General James Comey, and Attorney General John Ashcroft as being in opposition to Gonzales when he was White House Legal Counsel and later Attorney General, as well as to David Addington, the Chief-of-Staff for Vice President Cheney.

As more facts are discovered and the emerging pattern of a conspiracy becomes clearer, it will be possible to ascertain the truth. However, as discussed in Chapter 6, the Obama Administration has yet to pursue the option of a full investigation. Some individuals within the Bush Administration, such as Cheney, Addington, Haynes, and Yoo, continue to defend their positions and their actions, which without a full investigation will remain unchallenged.

3.5. THE SPREAD OF "ENHANCED INTERROGATION" TECHNIQUES FROM GUANTÁNAMO TO AFGHANISTAN AND IRAQ

Immediately after the attack of 9/11, the legal framework was being developed for sidestepping the Geneva Conventions, the CAT, and federal laws. Building upon legal memoranda written by the DOJ (Yoo), President Bush released a memorandum asserting the power to suspend the Third and Fourth Geneva Conventions as between the U.S. and Afghanistan, and further asserting that the Conventions did not apply to the Taliban or al-Qaeda members.[35] In addition, the DOJ was releasing memoranda dismissing any concerns about Fifth and Sixth Amendment protections.[36]

Some of the most damning evidence of the Bush Administration's push to set the stage for harsh, torturous interrogations comes in the form of memoranda

---

[33] M. Cherif Bassiouni, *Universal Jurisdiction for International Crimes: Historical Perspectives and Contemporary Practice*, 42 VA. J. INT'L L. 81 (2001).

[34] JACK GOLDSMITH, THE TERROR PRESIDENCY: LAW AND JUDGMENT INSIDE THE BUSH PRESIDENCY (2007).

[35] Memorandum to Alberto Gonzales, from Jay Bybee, Status of Taliban Forces Under the Fourth Geneva Convention (Feb. 7, 2002).

[36] Memorandum to William Haynes II, from Jay Bybee, *Potential Legal Constraints Applicable to Interrogations of Persons Captured by US Forces in Afghanistan.* (Feb. 26, 2002).

penned by Yoo and Bybee in the DOJ on August 1, 2002 and March 14, 2003,[37] as well as a memorandum from the DOD authorizing interrogators to use SERE-derived techniques (the "JTF-GTMO" memo).[38] In very brief summary, the DOJ memoranda used what amounts to legal gymnastics to argue that the interrogation techniques being used at Guantánamo Bay (the same ones endorsed by the DOD) do not violate federal or international law. It set a preposterously high standard for torture, stating that the pain inflicted during interrogation "[m]ust be equivalent in intensity to the pain accompanying serious physical injury, such as organ failure, impairment of bodily function, or even death."[39] This standard is used nowhere else in the world; under the Geneva Conventions, absolutely no physical harm is allowed, so there is no question about the "level" of pain. The CAT used the term "severe" because it was recognized that in apprehending and detaining people, a police office uses legitimate force. The CAT drafters did not want any kind of physical harm to be included (such as occurs, for example, if handcuffs are too tight). Since 1984 not a single country in the world has interpreted the CAT in this way, nor has the Committee Against Torture interpreted it differently. The American position is therefore unique and unusual in comparison to interpretations around the world.

The memoranda went on to argue that the President has complete discretion in decisions regarding military conflict. The March 14, 2003 memorandum essentially states that the President is free to override any international treaty in order to conduct his war on terror. It also goes to great lengths to argue that any U.S. law forbidding harsh or torturous techniques would not apply to Guantánamo Bay. Even if one would argue that these were simply memoranda and not a direct authorization to inflict torture and inhumane treatment on detainees, other factors still lend to the theory that high-ranking members of the DOJ as well as others in the Administration are culpable for illegal interrogation methods at Guantánamo Bay, Iraq, Afghanistan, and elsewhere.

First and foremost, beginning immediately after the 9/11 attacks, those involved in developing the policy of torture specifically circumvented military, DOJ, and DOS officials who disagreed with their legal and policy decisions. In September 2001, the DOS Ambassador-at-Large for War Crimes, Pierre Prosper, was asked to head an inter-agency task force to review and make legal recommendations for how to undertake the inevitable detentions of those captured in the wake of the attacks. The group included the general counsels of

---

[37] Yoo and Bybee memoranda, *supra* note 9.

[38] Memorandum from William Haynes II to Donald Rumsfeld, Secretary of Defense, Counter-resistance Techniques (Nov. 27, 2002) [JTF-GTMO memo].

[39] Memorandum to Alberto R. Gonzales, Counsel to the President, and William J. Haynes II, Gen. Counsel, Dep't of Def., from Jay S. Bybee, Assistant Attorney Gen., Office of Legal Counsel, U.S. Dep't of Justice, *Application of Treaties and Laws to al Qaeda and Taliban Detainees.* (Jan. 22, 2002).

the White House, Office of the Vice President, NSC, DOS, Office of the Secretary of Defense, Chairman of the Joint Chiefs of Staff, and the intelligence agencies.[40] The task force had worked for nearly two months when President Bush issued a Military Order defining the legal framework in which those captured in the "war on terror" would be detained.[41] Unbeknownst to the members of the task force, a group of advisors known as the "War Council" had been working in parallel, with their own tailored advice for the Executive (see *supra* section 3.7, *The Decision Makers and Senior Executors of the Torture-Enabling Policy*). The War Council was composed of Addington, Haynes, Gonzales, Bybee, Yoo, and Flanigan, and seemed intent on remaining an insular entity so that dissenting legal and policy opinions would not contradict their views on Presidential authority or permissible interrogation techniques. The Military Order came as a complete surprise not only to Prosper and the task force, but to Secretary of State Colin Powell and the Joint Chiefs of Staff of the military as well – principal officials who should not have been excluded in the design of such an important policy directive with wide-ranging implications for the military.[42]

On December 27, 2001, Secretary Rumsfeld announced the decision to use Guantánamo Bay as the primary detention center. Detainees who were being held in Afghanistan and elsewhere were to be moved there in the first few weeks of January 2002, and there was a scramble to establish the legal framework for their custody. On January 9, DOS Legal Advisor William H. Taft IV was sent a 40-page memo drafted by Yoo and Delahunty of DOJ's OLC, and given one day to respond to Haynes with any comments.[43] Taft and his team of lawyers at DOS were shocked by the fundamentally flawed understandings of IHL contained in the memo, which they believed amounted to a complete abandonment of the U.S.' obligations under the Geneva Conventions. They moved quickly to counteract the War Council's attempt to re-write basic international law, and on January 11, the same day that detainees were arriving at Guantánamo, Taft sent his lengthy rebuttal to Yoo, with copy to Gonzales.[44] According to Karen Greenberg:

> In barely restrained disbelief, Taft's memo and its cover letter, referred to [Yoo and Delahunty's] Draft Memorandum as "seriously flawed," "incorrect," "incomplete," and "fundamentally inaccurate" in both its analyses and conclusions. The OLC memo was also "procedurally impossible," "unsound," at points based on arguments that were "completely irrelevant," and ignorant about political concepts such as "failed

---

40   *See* GREENBERG, THE LEAST WORST PLACE, *supra* note 2, at 2.

41   George W. Bush, Military Order – Detention, Treatment and Trial of Certain Non-Citizens in the War on Terror, Nov. 13, 2001.

42   *See* GREENBERG, THE LEAST WORST PLACE, *supra* note 2, at 3.

43   Yoo/Delahunty memo, *supra* note 9.

44   Memorandum to John Yoo, Office of Legal Counsel, Dep't of Justice, from William H. Taft IV, Legal Advisor, Dep't of State, *Your Draft Memorandum of January 9* (Jan. 11, 2002).

states" and even about the Taliban, as well as about legal protocols such as reciprocity and treaty suspension. ...The memo forcefully argued that...the OLC had distorted the historical record as well as misstated legal precedents and applicable rules.[45]

Shortly thereafter, Secretary Powell himself penned a similar memo to Gonzales, but by that time the arguments were moot – according to top DOS officials, Bush had already decided to abandon the rule of the Geneva Conventions before the Yoo/Delahunty memo had even been sent to Taft.[46] The DOS had lost its primacy as the Administration's advisors on matters involving international law.

While the War Council and DOS battled in Washington, the legal team on the ground at Guantánamo were at a loss for how to proceed with the incoming detainees. In situations involving prisoners of war, the International Committee of the Red Cross, which has the responsibility to ensure compliance with the Geneva Conventions, must be contacted immediately. Guantánamo's commander, Brig. Gen. Michael Lehnert, a man who worked tirelessly throughout his tenure at the detention center to preserve the law of Geneva and the dignity of the detainees, had already requested the authorization to contact the ICRC from the Pentagon and been denied.[47] With no legal directive forthcoming from Washington regarding the official status of the detainees, SOUTHCOM's staff Judge Advocate, Col. Manuel Supervielle, took it upon himself to do so, and was reprimanded by the Pentagon for the decision.[48]

Some months later, after the November 2002 JTF-GTMO memo was released, high-ranking members of the Army, Air Force, Navy, and Marines wrote memoranda highlighting their concerns about the interrogation techniques listed in it.[49] These concerns were dismissed, and Secretary Rumsfeld approved the memo in December 2002. Haynes, prior to Rumsfeld's approval, quashed a broad based investigation Rear Adm. Jane G. Dalton initiated with members of

---

[45]   *See* GREENBERG, THE LEAST WORST PLACE, *supra* note 2, at 54.

[46]   Memorandum from Colin L. Powell, Sec'y of State, U.S. Dep't of State to Alberto R. Gonzales, Counsel to the President, Draft Decision Memorandum for the President on the Applicability of the Geneva Conventions to the Conflict in Afghanistan (Jan. 26, 2002). *See* GREENBERG, THE LEAST WORST PLACE, *supra* note 2, at 156; Jane Mayer, *Outsourcing Torture: The Secret History of America's "Extraordinary Rendition" Program*, THE NEW YORKER (Feb. 8, 2005).

[47]   GREENBERG, THE LEAST WORST PLACE, *supra* note 2, at 57.

[48]   *Id.* at 62.

[49]   *Id.* Army Legal Counsel John Ley argued that the "Army interposes significant legal, policy and practical concerns regarding most of Category II and all of Category III techniques proposed." John Ley, *Memorandum for the Office of the Army General Counsel, Subject: Review – Proposed Counter-Resistance Techniques* (undated). "The Air Force has serious concerns regarding the legality of many of the proposed techniques, particularly those under Category III. Some of these techniques could be construed as "torture," as that crime is defined by 18 U.S.C. §2340. ... The Level III techniques will almost certainly result in any statements obtained being declared as coerced and involuntary, and therefore inadmissible." Donald E. Richburg, Colonel, USAF, Memorandum from Headquarters U.S. Air Force to Joint Staff: Review of SOUTHCOM/GTMO Request for Techniques (Nov. 4, 2002). All of the techniques in Category II and one Category III technique, "waterboarding," were approved.

the armed services.[50] Haynes also intentionally relied on and pushed forward Col. Beaver's incomplete legal memo as a means for justifying SERE techniques at Guantánamo, even when several people such as Dalton pointed out its inaccuracies.[51] As explained, he assured Dalton that the methods could be performed humanely and legally.

It is important to note that members of the DOJ were in regular communication with interrogators throughout this time period. This is the most evident in the War Council meetings that occurred during the time that the new "enhanced interrogation" techniques were being developed. Although their main concern was to drive policy that would expand the President's Executive power while addressing issues arising from the "war on terror," the way in which they strove for this goal was to empower the President to use any methods necessary in detaining and interrogating suspected terrorists. Later, in early 2003, there is no evidence Secretary Rumsfeld or any of his allies took any steps to narrow the DOD 'General Counsel's Working Group Report on Detainee Interrogations in the Global War on Terrorism' after Staff Judge Advocates from the Army, Navy, Air Force, and Marines expressed grave concerns regarding the policies and legal opinions described therein.[52]

Even if certain methods were not specifically authorized, reports of illegal interrogations were consistently coming in from interrogation sites to the DOJ and DOD.[53] If this were the case, the DOJ would be condoning the use of torture, if not encouraging it. The FBI informed DOJ about concerns over the interrogations of Mohammad Al-Qahtani and members of the DOJ were well aware of the abusive interrogations occurring.[54] As described below, the ICRC submitted concerns about detainee mistreatment to high-ranking officers.[55] Commanders were receiving reports of abuse as they were occurring, not simply after the fact.

The SERE techniques migrated fairly rapidly from Guantánamo Bay to Afghanistan and Iraq, where the Geneva Conventions clearly applied.[56] Secretary Rumsfeld released his initial memorandum on the use of these techniques on December 2, 2002. By the summer of 2003, mere months later, Capt. Carolyn

---

[50]   *Detainee Interrogation Techniques before the Senate Comm. on Armed Services.* 110th Cong. (2008) (Statement by Jane Dalton). See also the Appendices at the end of Chapter 2.

[51]   *Id.*

[52]   General Counsel's Working Group Report on Detainee Interrogations in the Global War on Terrorism: Assessment of Legal, Historical, Policy, and Operational Considerations, March 6, 2003 and April 4, 2003.

[53]   *See* OIG Report, *supra* note 25, at 107. *See also* Greg Jaffe & David Cloud, *Officials in Iraq Knew Last Fall Of Prison Abuse – Red Cross Report Was Seen By U.S. Military Leaders Two Months Before Inquiry*, Wall St. J., May 19, 2004, at A1.

[54]   *See* OIG Report, *supra* note 25, at 77, 84.

[55]   *See* Jaffe & Cloud, *Officials in Iraq Knew Last Fall Of Prison Abuse, supra* note 53. *See also infra* Chapter 5, section 5.6, *Low-level Prosecutions.*

[56]   *See* Hamdan v. Rumsfeld, *infra* note 84.

Wood, a military intelligence officer, was using SERE techniques at Bagram Air Base, Afghanistan. In Army Criminal Investigation Department (CID) investigations, there are references of an interrogator being sent back to the U.S. to serve as a SERE instructor, implying that she already had a level of expertise in SERE interrogation methods.[57] Furthermore, Maj. Gen. Geoffrey Miller, the commander of Guantánamo Bay and its interrogators, had been sent to by high-ranking commanders to Abu Ghraib to "Gitmo-ize" the facility and teach new interrogation techniques.[58] Miller's involvement seems directly related to several detainee abuses at Abu Ghraib, where military intelligence, under the direction of Col. Thomas Pappas, Capt. Wood, and with the support of Gen. Barbara Fast, kept detainees in isolation for long periods of time.[59] When an interrogator asked Miller about how to maintain control of the detainees, he said, "You have to treat these detainees like dogs."[60]

With a mindset of "releasephobia," senior officers ensured detainees at Abu Ghraib were improperly held without a review board to determine their status. The officers had a genuine fear of releasing these detainees because any released prisoners would be inclined to tell others what was happening and the officers knew they would bear the blame. Furthermore, the officers knew that most detainees were Afghan and would return to their home country, where a cultural tradition of revenge meant that the families of prisoners would likely take revenge on any American they encountered. Finally, people who have been treated as these detainees were are likely to commit violent acts, therefore the officers felt that no one could be set free without dire consequences. Brig. Gen. Karpinski explained that the Combat Status Review Tribunals (CSRTs) often resembled kangaroo courts that would determine a detainee to be an unlawful combatant with the flimsiest of reasons. The policy was also reflected in the comments of Maj. Gen. Wojdakowski, the second most senior general in Iraq at the time: "I don't care if we have 15,000 innocent civilians, we are winning the war."[61]

---

[57]　United States Army Criminal Investigation Command, Case No. CID259–80255, Document No. 28198.

[58]　*See* JORDAN J. PAUST, BEYOND THE LAW: THE BUSH ADMINISTRATION'S UNLAWFUL RESPONSES IN THE "WAR" ON TERROR (2007), at 26. Secretary Rumsfeld sent Maj. Gen. Geoffrey Miller to Iraq in August 2003 to ensure "that coercive interrogation tactics used at Guantánamo were used in Iraq." Brig. Gen. Janis Karpinski confirmed in an August 2005 interview that Miller was sent to Iraq in 2003 "to use a template from Guantánamo Bay to 'Gitm-oize' the operations at Abu Ghraib." *See also* Jeffrey Smith, *Memo Gave Intelligence Bigger Role, Increased Pressure Sought on Prisoners*, WASH. POST, May 21, 2004. Karpinski was reduced to the rank of Colonel as a result of an Army Inspector General investigation into prisoner abuse, and was the only general punished for detainee abuse at Abu Ghraib. *See also* Taguba Report, app. 45, at 190.

[59]　*Id.*

[60]　*Id. at 129.*

[61]　*Id. at 171.*

In terms of actual interrogation policy, Lt. Gen. Sanchez, commander of the U.S. occupation forces in Iraq, made frequent changes to interrogation guidelines that created ambiguity as to what methods were actually authorized. The result was an atmosphere of tolerance as to what techniques were used. Rather than create a clear policy that would protect detainees' rights, Sanchez conveyed a policy of "do what needs to be done and ask for authorization if you need to."

Wojdakowski also apparently knew of detainee abuses in February 2004 due to an ICRC report describing a number of them.[62] Wojdakowski, Pappas, and Col. Mark Warren were present at this meeting, according to Karpinski.[63] This indicates that the highest-ranking officers in Iraq knew of the unlawful abuses far earlier than they had claimed in congressional hearings.[64]

Within the CIA, requests by agents to use "enhanced interrogation" techniques were routed to Deputy Director for Operations James Pavitt. Permission from Pavitt was necessary for minor abuses to such methods as strikes to the body, sleep deprivation, and humiliation. However, officials higher in the Bush Administration were aware of the "extraordinary rendition" program. Cheney, Addington, Bybee, Yoo, and Gonzales were involved with discussions with the CIA over interrogations and renditions in the months following 9/11. CIA agents suggest that it was the prodding of these men that urged the CIA to further adopt techniques such as torture and rendition to countries that use torture.[65] CIA Director Tenet described "enhanced interrogation" techniques in detail to high-level officials including Cheney, Powell, Rice, and Ashcroft.[66] Not long after these discussions, Addington, Yoo, and Bybee would draft the legal memoranda that would provide a shield to the CIA to conduct unlawful actions seemingly without fear of legal backlash. Coming as it did from the Office of General Counsel, the government officials involved in these practices had every reason to believe this legal advice to be reliable. Consequently, as mentioned above, the CIA pursued new, harsh interrogation techniques at Guantánamo and CIA "black sites" with complete disregard for domestic or international law.[67]

The graphic pictures of Abu Ghraib are a stark reminder of the type of practices that were carried out as a result of these policies, and they exemplify the types of actions that fall within the prohibition of the Third Geneva

---

[62]   Report of the International Committee of the Red Cross (ICRC) on the Treatment by the Coalition Forces of Prisoners of War and Other Protected Persons by the Geneva Conventions in Iraq During Arrest, Internment and Interrogation (February 2004).

[63]   *See* Douglas Jehl, *The Struggle for Iraq: Military Contradictions*, N.Y. TIMES, May 14, 2004.

[64]   *See* Jaffe & Cloud, *Officials in Iraq Knew Last Fall Of Prison Abuse, supra* note 53.

[65]   *Id.* at 120.

[66]   *Id.* at 144.

[67]   *See* Memorandum for John Rizzo, Acting General Counsel of the C.I.A., Interrogation of al-Qaeda Operative (Aug. 1, 2002), finding that use of SERE techniques, including waterboarding and repetitively throwing detainees against a wall would not constitute an illegal act. *See also* Bradbury Memoranda I, II, *supra* note 30.

Convention, as well as the definition of and prohibition against torture found in the CAT and U.S. law.[68] Tragically, over 200 persons have been reported dead in U.S. custody as a result of interrogation techniques ensuing from the policy and practices approved by the government lawyers working for the Bush Administration.[69]

3.6. CURTAILING DUE PROCESS AS A WAY OF CONCEALING THE PRACTICE OF TORTURE

A cornerstone of the torture-enabling policy of the Bush Administration was to curtail judicial review. This was accomplished by displacing federal jurisdiction and the UCMJ's processes and replacing them with military commissions, and by removing the right of access to habeas corpus by Guantánamo detainees.

---

[68] On February 15, 2006, additional photos of abuse at Abu Ghraib were released by Australia's Special Broadcasting Service. *See* Robert H. Reid, *More Photos Emerge of Abuse*, CHI. TRIB., Feb. 16, 2006; Erich Follath et al., *America's Shame: Torture in the Name of Freedom*, SPIEGEL, Feb. 20, 2006.

> They are photos that make your blood run cold. They take your breath away. They turn your stomach. They are photos that make you wonder what kinds of human beings would do these things to other human beings. They trigger anger, disgust and shame. One photo shows a prisoner being sandwiched between two stretchers, like some perverse ad for a burger. In another, a disoriented detainee, his body smeared with an unidentified substance, stumbles down a prison corridor. A third image depicts a hooded man waiting helplessly on a stool, with electric cables attached to his body. There are many more – and they all show prisoners being deliberately humiliated for their captors' amusement, men stripped naked and forced into submission. But it's not just humiliation – the photos also depict physical pain. In one photo, an American soldier kneels on the back of a naked Iraqi prisoner, a puddle of blood indicating rough treatment. In another, a prisoner bows deeply, servant-like, in front of an American military officer: Uncle Tom's Cabin in the Middle East.
>
> …
>
> The crimes committed by U.S. soldiers in the name of freedom and human rights, documented in unalterable photographs, appear to confirm the suspicion that America's true aim is something entirely different – that the U.S. is primarily interested in imposing its own world order and preserving its dominance.
>
> In short, for the U.S., the most powerful and influential global power ever, the images from Abu Ghraib – and the ongoing debate over the legality of its prison camp at Guantánamo –have produced a moral catastrophe that's likely to endure for a very long time.

> *Id.*

[69] For reports on the torture victims and investigative outcomes as of 2006, see Hina Shamsi, *Command's Responsibility: Detainee Deaths in U.S. Custody in Iraq and Afghanistan* (Human Rights First, Feb. 2006). *See also* Anthony R. Jones & George R. Fay, *Investigation of Intelligence Activities at Abu Ghraib* (Aug. 2004), which indicated that the DOD's interrogation policies "confused Army and civilian interrogators at Abu Ghraib… and were not completely consistent with Army doctrine… as a result interrogators at Abu Ghraib, employed non-doctrinal approaches that conflicted with other DOD and Army regulatory, doctrinal, and procedural guidance." Wallach, *The Logical Nexus, supra* note 10, at 624.

The arguments for military commissions are not without precedent or justifiable foundations, if these commissions offer those tried before them at least the same guarantees as those afforded by the UCMJ and subject to habeas corpus review. However, the establishment of military commissions where the elementary rights of defense are curtailed and the elementary standards of fairness are removed, coupled with the bar to habeas corpus, places these proceedings in violation of the Constitution. Whether this was done in good faith is a matter to be judicially determined. If it was done to further the overall policy of enabling torture, then it supports the theory of criminal conspiracy.

After the Supreme Court's decision in *Hamdi v. Rumsfeld*,[70] that a U.S. citizen has a right to be notified that he has been classified as an enemy combatant and to challenge that classification, and in *Rasul v. Bush*,[71] that a non-U.S. citizen can also challenge the legality of his or her detention based on the federal habeas corpus statute,[72] the DOD established the Combatant Status Review Tribunal (CSRT),[73] which in theory gave each Guantánamo detainee notice of the factual basis for his detention and classification as an enemy combatant.[74] CSRT determinations of enemy combatant status and prosecutions of detainees at Guantánamo commenced under the Military Commissions Act of 2006.[75] Khaled Sheikh Mohammed, a high level detainee who was transferred to Guantánamo from a "black site" and whose CSRT transcript was released, claimed in the process of his interrogation that he was involved in 31 criminal plots – something highly unlikely to be accurate – and he also claimed abusive treatment. His confession is, according to Col. Dwight Sullivan, "a textbook example of why we shouldn't allow coercive methods."[76]

While the CSRTs ruled that at least 38 detainees should be released,[77] many felt that the CSRTs were no more than a sham. There is evidence that detainees who were initially found not to be enemy combatants were retried until a

---

[70]   Hamdi v. Rumsfeld, 542 U.S. 507, 533 (2004).

[71]   Rasul v. Bush, 542 U.S. 466 (2004).

[72]   28 U.S.C. §2241 (2000).

[73]   *See* Jane Mayer, *A Deadly Interrogation*, THE NEW YORKER, Nov. 14, 2005.

[74]   558 detainees went through the CSRT process. *See* U.S. Dept. of Defense, List of Detainees Who Went Through Complete CSRT Process, *available at* www.dod.mil/pubs/foi/detainees/ detainee_list.pdf (last visited January 15, 2010).

[75]   U.S. Military Commissions Act of 2006 [hereinafter MCA], Pub. L. 109–3666, 120 Stat. 2600 (codified in scattered sections of 10 and 18 U.S.C.).

[76]   Dept. of Defense, Office for the Administration Review of the Detention of Enemy Combatants at U.S. Naval Base Guantánamo Bay, Cuba, Summary of Evidence for Combatant Status Review Tribunal for Khalid Shaykh Muhammad (Feb. 8, 2007); Verbatim Transcript of Combatant Status Review Tribunal Hearing for Khalid Shaykh Muhammad, ISN #10024 (March 10, 2007).

[77]   David A. Martin, *Judicial Review and the Military Commissions Act: On Striking the Right Balance*, 101 AM. J. INT'L L. 344, 350 (2007); David A. Martin, *Offshore Detainees and the Role of Courts After Rasul v. Bush: The Underappreciated Virtue of Deferential Review*, 2 B.C. THIRD WORLD L.J. 125, 141–143 (2005).

Tribunal did indeed judge them as an unlawful enemy combatant.[78] In the CSRT cases reviewed by a Seton Hall University School of Law report, the government did not produce witnesses in any hearing, nor documentary evidence to the detainee prior to the hearing in 96 percent of the cases. Moreover, the only evidence presented was a "summary of the evidence," and decisions of the Tribunal were made on the same day in 81 percent of cases. While the procedures recommended that the government have an attorney present at the hearing, detainees were denied this right. When a detainee was found not to be an enemy combatant, he was not told of the decision or informed of later hearings.[79] During one detainee meeting with a "personal representative" (because detainees were denied the right to counsel), the detainee was notified that the CSRT proceeding was his opportunity to contest his categorization as an enemy combatant; that the government had already found him to be an enemy combatant at multiple levels of review; that the government's finding was based on classified evidence that he could not see; and that the tribunal must presume that the secret classified evidence was reliable and valid.[80] It is also worth noting that the government did not produce a single witness – military or civilian – during the unclassified portion of the detainee's tribunal proceedings.[81] Moreover, during the proceeding, any information that a confession or information relating to the detainee's status was coerced was not taken into consideration.

As indicated above, following *Hamdi* and *Rasul*, in December of 2005 the Detainee Treatment Act (DTA) was enacted by Congress. It narrowed the federal habeas statute in that "no court, justice, or judge shall have jurisdiction to hear or consider… an application for a writ of habeas corpus filed by or on behalf of an alien detained by the Department of Defense at Guantánamo Bay, Cuba."[82] The DTA did not expressly include torture, but prohibited cruel, inhuman or degrading treatment or punishment "prohibited by the Fifth, Eighth, and Fourteenth Amendments to the Constitution of the United States."[83]

In June of 2006, after determining that the DTA did not apply to cases pending before it, the Supreme Court rejected the Bush Administration's military commission system to try detainees as unconstitutional, relying on the UCMJ in

---

78   *See* Mark Denbeaux & Joshua Denbeaux, *No-Hearing Hearings, CSRT: The Modern Habeas Corpus?* 3 (Seton Hall Public Law Research Center, Dec. 13, 2006). *See also* Karen J. Greenberg, *Guantánamo Is Not Prison: 11 Ways to Report on Gitmo without Upsetting the Pentagon* (Center on Law and Security, Mar. 9, 2007), quoting Rear Admiral Harry B. Barris Jr. " Today, it is not about guilt or innocence. It's about unlawful enemy combatants… And they are all unlawful enemy combatants."

79   *See* Denbeaux & Denbeaux, *No-Hearing Hearings, id.* at 2–3.

80   *Id.* at 5.

81   *Id.* at 21.

82   Pub. L. No. 109–148, Div. A, tit. 10, 119 Stat 2739, §1005(e)(1)(2005) (codified at 42 U.S.C. §2000dd (2006), 10 U.S.C. §801, 28 U.S.C. §2241).

83   *Id.*

Hamdan v. Rumsfeld.[84] In *Hamdan,* the Supreme Court overruled the lower court's holding that Common Article 3 of the Geneva Conventions did not apply to the conflict with al-Qaeda.[85] Common Article 3's prohibition on the "passing of sentences and carrying out of executions without previous judgment pronounced by a regularly constituted court affording all the judicial guarantees which are recognized bas indispensable by civilized peoples"[86] was determined by the Supreme Court to be required by §821 of the UCMJ. President Bush had determined that Common Article 3 did not apply to the conflict with al-Qaeda and the Taliban because they were international in character. He also said that the Geneva Conventions did not apply because neither al-Qaeda nor the Taliban were party to them.[87] The Supreme Court found that the Bush Administration's interpretation of the Geneva Conventions was incorrect.[88]

In response to June 2006 *Hamdan* decision, the President returned to Congress with a sense of urgency for the creation of new military commissions. In a White House address of September 6, 2006, he noted that "a small number of suspected terrorist leaders and operatives captured during the war have been held and questioned outside the U.S., in a separate program operated by the Central Intelligence Agency."[89] He stated: "As soon as Congress acts to authorize the military commissions I have proposed, the men our intelligence officials believe orchestrated the deaths of nearly 3,000 Americans on September the 11th, 2001, can face justice."[90] The next month in October 2006, the Military Commissions Act of 2006 was enacted,[91] and by February 2007, the first three detainees' cases began. The Military Commissions Act of 2006 allows the U.S. to use military tribunals in lieu of federal courts to prosecute detainees for war crimes. The Act expressly authorizes military commissions; codifies the Bush Administration's positions in *Hamdan* which alters the ability of detainees to bring writs of habeas corpus;[92] denies detainees the right to bring private actions under the Geneva Conventions; enhances the executive branch's power of treaty

---

[84]   Hamdan v. Rumsfeld, 126 U.S. 2749, 2762–69 (2006).

[85]   *Id.* at 2793–98.

[86]   *Id.* at 2795, *citing* Common Article 3 of the Geneva Conventions.

[87]   George W. Bush, Memorandum: Humane Treatment of Al Qaeda and Taliban Detainees, para. 2(a) (Feb. 7, 2002).

[88]   *Hamdan v. Rumsfeld, supra* note 84, at 2795.

[89]   Press Release, The White House, President Discusses Creation of Military Commissions to Try Suspected Terrorists, Office of the Press Secretary (Sept. 6, 2006).

[90]   *Id. See also* David A. Martin, *Judicial Review and the Military Commissions Act: On Striking the Right Balance,* 101 AM. J. INT'L L. 344, 352 (2007).

[91]   Pub. L. No. 109–366, 120 Stat. 2600 (2006) (to be codified at 10 U.S.C. §§948a-950w). *See also* David Scheffer, *Introductory Note to Military Commissions Act of 2006,* 45 ILM 1241 (2006).

[92]   The MCA states:

> No court, justice, or judge shall have jurisdiction to hear or consider an application for a writ of habeas corpus filed by or on behalf of an alien detained by the United States who has been determined by the United States to have been properly detained as an enemy combatant or is awaiting such determination.

MCA, *supra* note 75, §7(a), amending 28 U.S.C. §2241(e).

interpretation; eliminates reliance on foreign or international sources of law;[93] and avoids the Common Article 3 definition of a criminal act.[94] It also provides that statements obtained under any technique stopping short of torture can be admitted at the trial.[95] The Act narrows the definition of crimes that are prosecutable under the War Crimes Act, thus precluding future criminal responsibility of government officials.[96] According to Senator John Cornyn, through the Military Commissions Act "Congress will finally accomplish what it sought to do through the [Detainee Treatment Act] last year. It will finally get the lawyers out of Guantánamo Bay."[97]

Essentially, with the Military Commissions Act, a new list of "grave breaches" of the Geneva Conventions was created that omits "degrading and humiliating treatment" and "the passing of sentences… without previous judgment pronounced by a regularly constituted court affording all the judicial guarantees."[98] These developments, however, are contrary to the U.S. commitment to the Geneva Conventions, violate customary international law, and are additional smokescreens to hide that torture took place.

On April 30, 2007, the Supreme Court denied certiorari for two Guantánamo prisoners, Salim Ahmed Hamdan, a one-time driver for Osama bin Laden, and Omar Khadr, a 15-year old Canadian charged with killing an army medic, neither of whom are U.S. citizens.[99] Both Hamdan and Khadr were challenging the legality of the military commissions.[100] However, the military judges in the military tribunal dropped all war crimes charges against Hamdan and Khadr for lack of jurisdiction because the defendants were labeled as "enemy combatants," instead of "unlawful enemy combatants."[101] To date, Hamdan and Khadr are the

---

[93] *But see,* Curtis A. Bradley, *The Military Commission Act, Habeas Corpus, and the Geneva Conventions,* 101 AM. J. INT'L L. 342 (2007); Curtis A. Bradley, *The* Charming Betsy *Canon and Separation of Powers: Rethinking the Interpretive Role of International Law,* 86 GEO. L.J. 479 (1998), discussing Murray v. Schooner Charming Betsy, 6 U.S. 64, 118 (1804) (stating that "an act of Congress ought never to be construed to violate the law of nations if any other possible construction remains"). *See also* RESTATEMENT THIRD OF THE FOREIGN RELATIONS LAW OF THE UNITED STATES §114 (1987).

[94] *Id.*

[95] Christian M. DeVos, *Mind the Gap: Purpose, Pain, and the Difference between Torture and Inhuman Treatment,* 14 HUM. RTS. BRIEF 4 (Winter 2007).

[96] Title 18 U.S.C. §2241 (2000).

[97] *See* BARBARA OLSHANSKY, DEMOCRACY DETAINED: SECRET UNCONSTITUTIONAL PRACTICES IN THE U.S. WAR ON TERROR 162 (2007); 152 Cong. Rec. S10262 (daily ed. Sept. 27, 2006), S10403.

[98] *The Military Commission Act of 2006: A New System of Law and Order in the "War on Terror,"* INT'L L. REV. 8, 9 (2006).

[99] Hamdan v. Gates, 552 U.S. 994 (2007); Khadr v. Bush, 587 F.Supp.2d 225 (D.D.C. 2008). *See also,* Amy Goldstein, *Justices Against Refuse Guantánamo Bay Cases,* WASH. POST, May 1, 2007, at A4.

[100] *Id.*

[101] *See* David Morgan, *White House under pressure over Guantánamo ruling,* REUTERS, June 5, 2007.

only two individuals in Guantánamo Bay that have been charged with war crimes since the Military Commission Act was passed.[102]

Several detainees have been put on trial under the MCA. On March 26, 2007, David Hicks, an Australian, was the first among the Guantánamo prisoners to be tried under the new military commission system. In exchange for a nine-month sentence to be served in his native country, he pleaded guilty to one charge of material support for terrorism.[103] His plea bargain was widely reported to have been a political deal brokered between Vice President Cheney and then Australian Prime Minister John Howard, who was facing a difficult re-election campaign in a country where the continued detention of Hicks was extremely unpopular.[104]

On June 11, 2007, in *Al-Marri v. Wright*,[105] the Fourth Circuit ruled that the President could not declare civilians present in the U.S. to be "enemy combatants," nor could they be held by the military indefinitely. The Court held that "[t]o sanction such presidential authority to order the military to seize and indefinitely detain civilians, even if the president calls them 'enemy combatants,' would have disastrous consequences for the Constitution – and the country... We refuse to recognize a claim to power that would so alter the constitutional foundations of our republic."[106] On June 29, 2007, the Supreme Court granted certiorari at the end of its term to review whether Guantánamo detainees could appeal to the federal court system regarding their indefinite detention.[107] The Court held on June 12, 2008 that §7 of the Military Commissions Act of 2006 was unconstitutional because it purported to abolish the writ of habeas corpus despite the fact that the Constitution permits suspension of that writ only "in Cases of Rebellion or Invasion." As a result, Guantánamo detainees accused of

---

[102] *See* Andrew O. Selsky, *Judges at Guantánamo Throw out Two Cases*, CHI. TRIB., June 5, 2007.

[103] *See* Bruce Zagaris, *Australian David Hicks Pleads Guilty After U.S. Threatens Military Defense Counsel*, 23 INT'L ENFORCEMENT L. REPORTER 185 (May 2007); Josh White, *Australian's Guilty Plea is First at Guantánamo*, WASH. POST, Mar. 27, 2007, at A1.

[104] *See Cheney 'Struck Hicks Deal' with PM*, THE AUSTRALIAN, Oct. 26, 2007; Scott Horton, *The Plea Bargain of David Hicks*, HARPER'S (April 2007); *Hicks 'Silenced' Before Election*, THE AGE (Australia), Apr. 5, 2007. David Hicks came under the influence of militant ideology at a young age, first traveling to Albania to fight alongside the Kosovo Liberation Army, then later alongside the Lashkar-e-Taiba in Pakistan and al-Qaeda in Afghanistan. Hicks was captured in Afghanistan in December 2001, and transferred to Guantánamo in early 2002. By the time he was prosecuted before a military commission in 2005, the wars in Afghanistan and Iraq had become unpopular in Australia, and the international indignation over the practice of torture by U.S. public agents was at its peak. Bringing Hicks home to face justice in Australia became a cause in that country and an issue which PM Howard had to address during the elections. *See PM Faces Internal Pressure Over Hicks Trial*, SYDNEY MORNING HERALD, Aug. 3, 2005.

[105] Al-Marri v. Wright, 487 F.3d 160 (4th Cir. 2007).

[106] *Id.* at 29.

[107] *See* William Glaberson, *Supreme Court to Hear Guantánamo Detainees' Case*, N.Y. TIMES, June 29, 2007.

being "enemy combatants" have the right to challenge the validity of their detention in a full-fledged U.S. federal court proceeding.[108]

As argued by Stephen Vladeck in the ABA National Security Law Report, the conclusion that the detainees have a constitutional right to petition for writs of habeas corpus does not necessarily mean they have substantive rights to enforce those petitions.[109] Justice Anthony Kennedy in the *Boumediene* decision and Justice Stephen Breyer's dissent in the case's initial certiorari hearing[110] illustrate how the Detainee Treatment Act only gave the D.C. Circuit the power to decide whether "the standards and procedures specified by the Secretary of Defense for Combatant Status Review Tribunals", and "to the extent the Constitution and law of the United States are applicable, whether the use of those standards and procedures to make the determination is consistent with the Constitution and laws of the United States."[111] A detainee could not argue to the D.C. Circuit that there was no authority for his detention without arguing the CSRT violated due process.[112]

Beyond denying the right to habeas corpus, President Bush also maintained that he had the right to preventatively detain persons indefinitely. The Supreme Court has not yet ruled on this underlying assertion that the President can preventatively detain persons; however it is a policy that has been reaffirmed by the Obama Administration which has defended its right to preventively detain members of al-Qaeda.[113]

In addition to denying detainees the due process guaranteed under U.S. law, the Bush Administration attempted to intimidate lawyers offering pro bono assistance to Guantánamo detainees. Charles Stimson, as Deputy Assistant Secretary of Defense for Detainee Affairs at the Pentagon, declared in a statement that "Corporate CEOs seeing this should ask firms to choose between lucrative retainers and representing terrorists."[114] Stimson made a similar statement during a radio interview to the effect that companies should take their business to other law firms that do not represent suspected terrorists.[115] Stimson then listed over a dozen major law firms he thought should be boycotted, but was subsequently asked to resign to quiet the controversy stirred up by his remarks.

---

[108] Boumediene v. Bush, 128 S. Ct. 2229 (2008).

[109] *See* Stephen I. Vladeck, *Reflecting on Boumediene: The Substance of Habeas and the Futility of Exhaustion*, 30 ABA COMM. ON LAW AND NAT'L SEC. LAW REPORT 1 (2008), at 7.

[110] Boumediene v. Bush, 127 S. Ct. 1478, 1479, *cert. denied* (2007) (Breyer, J., dissenting).

[111] *See* Vladeck, *Reflecting on Boumediene, supra* note 109, at 7.

[112] *Id.*

[113] *See* Respondent's Memorandum Regarding the Government's Detention Authority Relative to Detainees Held at Guantanamo Bay, *In Re Guantanamo Bay Detainee Litigation*, Misc. No. 08–442 (D.D.C. 2009); Jonathan Tracy, *Detention and Prosecution of Alleged Terrorists and Combatants*, 16 HUM. RTS. BRIEF 51 (2009).

[114] *See* Marjorie Cohn, *First They Came for the Lawyers*, AFTERDOWNINGSTREET.ORG, Jan. 15, 2007.

[115] *See* John Heilprin, *Pentagon Disavows Law Firm Boycott Call*, CHI. TRIB., Jan. 14, 2007.

In February 2010, this argument was revived when Liz Cheney (the daughter of the former Vice President) and her organization, *Keep America Safe*, released a video which questioned the loyalty of DOJ lawyers who had previously worked on behalf of Guantánamo detainees, and in a McCarthy-esque turn of events, demanded that the Attorney General release the names of those who had done so, referring to them as the "al-Qaeda Seven".[116]

On January 22, 2009, President Obama signed Executive Orders directing the closure of the Guantánamo Bay detention facilities within a year and the immediate case-by-case review of the detainees still held at the facility.[117] By the time the DOJ Guantánamo Detainee Review Panel completed its work in January 2010, there were approximately 196 remaining in detention.[118] While the recommendations have yet to be released publicly, it has been widely reported that 35 detainees will face prosecution in federal courts or military commissions, and approximately 100 will likely be transferred to other countries.[119] Most troubling, however, was the decision to hold the remaining 50 detainees indefinitely, having been determined to be too dangerous to release, yet without enough evidence against them to be tried in court – even in before the more conviction-friendly military commissions.[120] Most of the 600 or so detainees

---

[116] *See* John Schwartz, *Attacks on Detainee Lawyers Split Conservatives*, N.Y. TIMES, Mar. 9, 2010.

[117] Exec. Order No. 13,492, Review and Disposition of Individuals Detained at the Guantánamo Bay Naval Base and Closure of Detention Facilities, 74 Fed. Reg. 4,897 (Jan. 27, 2009). The Task Force, comprised of officials from the DOD, the DOS, the DOJ, the Department of Homeland Security, as well as agencies such as the CIA and the FBI, completed its work in January 2010, and Attorney General Holder forwarded the recommendations to President Obama for his approval.

[118] The Task Force, comprised of officials from the DOD, the DOS, the DOJ, the Department of Homeland Security, as well as agencies such as the CIA and the FBI, completed its work in January 2010, and Attorney General Holder forwarded the recommendations to President Obama for his approval. As of February 2010, the report had not been publicly released. *See* Peter Finn, *Justice Task Force Recommends about 50 Guantanamo Detainees to be Held Indefinitely*, WASH. POST, Jan. 22, 2010.

[119] Since Obama took office, 44 Guantánamo Bay detainees have been repatriated or resettled in third countries, including 11 in Europe. However, the issue of resettlement is often complicated. Approximately 60 of the remaining 196 detainees are from Yemen, a country which the U.S. considers too unstable an environment to promote proper rehabilitation. Seven other detainees are Chinese Uighurs, who would likely face detention and possibly torture if repatriated to China. While the Obama Administration is in the process of finding third-party countries to accept the Uighurs, the detainees are currently fighting in U.S. federal court for their right to be settled within the U.S. The U.S. Supreme Court orginally granted certiorari in *Kiyemba v. Obama* to determine whether it is within the power of the judicial branch to order the release of detainees into the U.S. However, in March 2010, after resettlement offers from Switzerland and Palau, the Supreme Court dismissed the case and ordered the U.S. Court of Appeals for the District of Columbia to reconsider the case. Kiyemba v. Obama, 555 F.3d 1022 (D.C. Cir. 2009). *See* Adam Liptak, *Supreme Court Refuses Ruling on Chinese Uighurs Held at* Guantánamo, N.Y. TIMES, Mar. 2, 2010.

[120] *See* Finn, *Justice Task Force Recommends about 50* Guantánamo *Detainees to be Held Indefinitely, supra* note 118.

who have already been released had been erroneously arrested to begin with, and should have been released long before. Instead, it is likely they were kept in detention to cover up the erroneous arrests and the torture or other cruel treatment inflicted upon them, in the hope that the public would overlook it due to the passage of time. The lengthy detentions were also used to extract pledges from those released not to disclose how they were treated, surely a shameful situation, if not an illegal one.[121]

In October 2009, President Obama signed into law the National Defense Authorization Act for Fiscal Year 2010, which included the Military Commissions Act of 2009.[122] While the legislation sought to remedy the defects of the 2006 Act, it retained the basic structure of the military commissions and failed to address many substantive rule of law concerns.[123] While evidence obtained through torture or otherwise coerced interrogations has been made inadmissible, the Secretary of Defense retains the right to enact rules which permit coerced statements and hearsay evidence. The term "unlawful enemy combatant" has been replaced with "unlawful enemy belligerent," – little more than a cosmetic legal makeover. Under the new law, defendants have the right to attend their entire trial and examine all evidence presented against them, to cross-examine witnesses against them, and to call their own witnesses.

As of March 2010, the Obama Administration is continuing to maneuver through the political maze of how best to bring to trial many of the remaining detainees at Guantánamo Bay.[124] Six detainees, including Khaled Sheikh Mohammed, have been transferred to the federal court system, and more than a dozen are still slated to be tried before the military commissions.[125] It is unclear whether convictions under the military commissions will be easier to obtain than through the traditional civilian or military court systems, which provide procedural and substantive protections to the accused.

---

[121]   Many of the released detainees reported that they had to sign statements saying that they were not tortured. They also reported that they were that they were threatened with re-arrest if they made statements about treatment they may have received or witnessed. For example, David Hicks' plea agreement stipulated that he not speak to the media for one year nor take legal action against the U.S., and that he withdraw allegations that the U.S. military abused him while in detention. *See supra* notes 103–04.

[122]   National Defense Authorization Act for Fiscal Year 2010.

[123]   *See* Warren Richey, *Obama Endorses Military Commissions for Guantánamo Detainees,* Christian Science Monitor, Oct. 29, 2009.

[124]   *See* Jane Mayer, *The Trial: Eric Holder and the Battle Over Khaled Sheikh Mohammed,* The New Yorker, Feb. 15, 2010; Charlie Savage, *Senator Proposes Deal on Handling of Detainees,* N.Y. Times, Mar. 3, 2010.

[125]   *See* Human Rights Watch, *The Guantanamo Trials, available at* www.hrw.org/en/features/ guantanamo (last visited Feb. 10, 2010).

3.7. THE DECISION MAKERS AND SENIOR EXECUTORS OF THE TORTURE-ENABLING POLICY

There are many published accounts of how persons listed below interacted and coordinated their actions, but only a thorough investigation can establish these linkages. Some assumed a more visible role than others, but it appears that the leadership was in the hands of Vice President Cheney, who on February 14, 2010 stated on television that he was "a big supporter of waterboarding... and of the enhanced interrogation techniques."[126] This is an "admission against interest" which can be used against him in civil and criminal cases. Others, like Wolfowitz and Feith had a less visible role, although Feith's book, *War and Decision*, revealed his influence on Maj. Gen. Miller, Guantánamo's first commanding officer, who subsequently assumed command over the Abu Ghraib prison in Iraq.[127]

As National Security Advisor, Condoleezza Rice coordinated government agencies' reports and summarized them, with policy options submitted to the NSC Principals Committee. The Principals Committee meetings were summarized by the NSC staffers under Rice's overall supervision and are covered by Executive privilege, but some summaries or parts thereof have been reported as declassified, and have also been reported to be highly sanitized. No disagreement with the "enhanced interrogation" techniques, including waterboarding, are recorded in those minutes. Also, no substantive legal issues were reportedly recorded in the minutes, even though other sources indicate Secretary Powell's position that the Geneva Conventions applied and that some of the "enhanced interrogation" techniques were in violation of them. No substantive discussions of the CAT seem to have taken place.

<u>National Security Council Principals Committee</u>

President
George W. Bush (2001–09)

Vice President
Dick Cheney (2001–09)

National Security Advisor
Condoleezza Rice (2001–05)
Stephen Hadley (2005–09)

---

[126] Interview with Jonathan Karl, *This Week*, ABC News, Feb. 14, 2010.
[127] Douglas Feith, War and Decision: Inside the Pentagon at the Dawn of the War on Terrorism (2009).

Secretary of State
Colin Powell (2001–05)
Condoleezza Rice (2005–09)

Attorney General
John Ashcroft (2001–05)
Alberto Gonzales (2005–07)
Michael Mukasey (2007–09)

Secretary of Defense
Donald Rumsfeld (2001–06)
Robert Gates (2006-present)

Deputy Secretary of Defense
Paul Wolfowitz (2001–05)

Under Secretary of Defense for Policy
Douglas Feith (2001–05)

CIA Director
George Tenet (2001–04)
Porter Goss (2004–05)
Michael Hayden (2006–09)

<u>Bush Administration Lawyers, *aka* "War Council"</u>

White House Counsel
Alberto Gonzales (2001–05)

Deputy White House Counsel
Tim Flanigan (2001–02)

Legal Advisor / Chief of Staff to Vice President Cheney
David Addington (2001–05 / 2005–09)

DOD General Counsel
William J. Haynes II (2001–2008)

Assistant Attorney General and Head of DOJ's Office of Legal Counsel

Jay Bybee (2001–03)
Jack Goldsmith (2003–04)

Daniel Levin (Acting 2004–05)
Stephen Bradbury (Acting 2005–07)

Deputy Assistant Attorneys General
John Yoo (2001–03)
Patrick Philbin (2001–03 OLC / 2003–05 National Security)
Robert Delahunty (Special Counsel, 2001–03)

CIA Acting General Counsel
John Rizzo (2001–08)

Agencies Involved				
White House	DOD	DOJ	DOS	CIA

3.8. CONCLUSION

Bureaucracies are characterized by a pyramidal structure where authority flows from the top and filters down through various decision making layers. The extent to which there are internal legal filters and external checks and balances varies from system to system. The more integrated government structures are, the more likely they are to be decisively affected by decisions emanating from the top. In societies where authority is not only practiced but valued, the impact of decisions made at the top are more likely to reach the base with less interference and with greater speed. This is why authoritarian regimes tend to have similarities in their decision making processes and thus, in their impact. Democratic societies differ in that the rule of law system has the capacity to block decisions which violate the national constitution and laws of that state.

The U.S. government's bureaucratic structure has similar characteristics to those of other governments, although with different cultural and legal characteristics. Although this book is not the place to discuss theories of government, decision making processes, or their impact within a bureaucratic structure, it is nonetheless useful for the reader to bear in mind the characteristics of the federal government and the political dynamics within which it operates. Washington, D.C. phrases like "Washington politics" or "Washington *tout court*" are popular euphemisms which reflect the peculiarities of the national government's system, its bureaucracy, and other factors which condition both the system as a whole, and the way in which it functions. What happened during the Bush Administration has demonstrated a new vulnerability which had not heretofore been contemplated, namely, the ability of the Vice President working from a position of power vis-à-vis the President to assemble a team of ideologically-motivated lawyers in order to establish a policy, which was put into action even though the policy and the practices violated international law, the Constitution, and U.S. law.

What this experience has demonstrated is how easy it is to subvert the legal system of the U.S., and to implement a policy that violates international law, the Constitution, and U.S. law, with no accountability. The constitutional framework of checks and balances within the American political system proved to be ineffective. The Executive branch simply took over, with the acquiescence of the Legislative branch and the restraint, if not timidity, of the Judicial branch. Similar swings of the pendulum have occurred under other presidents such as Lincoln and Roosevelt, to name two famous wartime presidents. In the end, these excesses are curbed and the constitutional pendulum swings back to its more traditional and historically acknowledged position.

That so much which represents such clear violations of our social values and our legal order could be accomplished by so few in such a short period of time evidences how frail our legal order is, and perhaps how superficial our social values are, particularly at vulnerable times. Nevertheless, it has to be encouraging to see that the pendulum does swing back from certain extreme positions to more centrist ones which reflect traditional social values and the well-established historic legal order which has prevailed in this country for over 200 years. The vulnerabilities of the system mentioned above are counterbalanced by the genius of recovery that follows. As American legal and social history reveals, this nation finds ways of correcting its past errors, even though it may take far too long to arrive at this better way, as in the cases of slavery, racial and gender discrimination, labor exploitation, and many other abuses – and now, torture.

What remains, however, is to fully understand the political, social, and psychological mechanisms that brought about the subversion of the system so that the American people become more aware of what happened and how, and thus less likely to allow a recurrence of the same phenomenon in the future. We also need to assess how and why it was so easy to create the trickle-down effect which is described in this chapter, and also the role of command influence through incentives and disincentives which made possible the implementation of the policy described in this book. Lastly, no lesson is really learned without accountability. Those responsible for the violations that have occurred must be held accountable, whether they are at the highest levels of political decision-making or as executors of their policy.

CHAPTER 4

THE PRACTICE OF "EXTRAORDINARY RENDITION" AND THE USE OF "BLACK SITES" BY THE CIA

> *If you want a serious interrogation, you send a prisoner to Jordan.*
> *If you want them to be tortured, you send them to Syria. If you want someone to*
> *disappear, never to see them again, you send them to Egypt.*[*]
> – Former CIA agent Robert Baer

4.1. INTRODUCTION

On September 17, 2001, within a week after the 9/11 attacks in the U.S., President Bush signed a secret Presidential finding which put the onus on the CIA to "create paramilitary teams to hunt, capture, detain, or kill designated terrorists almost anywhere in the world."[1] The pressure from the White House on the CIA to produce intelligence and to capture terror suspects was intense. However, the Agency is not the business of detention or interrogation (which are essentially police functions), and in response to the political pressure from the White House, the CIA created a network of covert prisons or "black sites" in military bases around the world,[2] and undertook the practice of "extraordinary rendition," whereby a detainee in custody of the CIA is handed over to a third-party country for interrogation.[3] While it is already clear that responsibility will fall heavily on the CIA, and that some of its agents will be disciplined and even

---

[*]   *Mystery Flights*, BBC THIS WORLD (2007).

[1]   *See* Jane Mayer, *The Black Sites: A Rare Look Inside the CIA's Secret Interrogation Program*, THE NEW YORKER, Aug. 13, 2007.

[2]   *See* Mark Danner, *U.S. Torture: Voices from the Black Sites*, N.Y. REVIEW OF BOOKS, Apr. 9, 2009; Leila Nadya Sadat, *Ghost Prisoners and Black Sites: Extraordinary Rendition Under International Law*, 37 CASE W. RES. J. INT'L L. 309 (2006); Elizabeth Sepper, *The Ties that Bind: How the Constitution Limits the CIA's Actions in the War on Terror*, 81 N.Y.U. L. REV. 1805 (2007); Dana Priest, *CIA Holds Terror Suspects in Secret Prisons*, WASH. POST, Nov. 2, 2005.

[3]   *See* Leila Nadya Sadat, *Extraordinary Rendition, Torture, and Other Nightmares from the War on Terror*, 75 GEO. WASH. L. REV. 1200 (2007); Margaret L. Satterthwaite, *Rendered Meaningless: Extraordinary Rendition and the Rule of Law*, 75 GEO. WASH. L. REV. 1333 (2007); David Weissbrodt & Amy Bergquist, *Extraordinary Rendition and the Torture*

prosecuted, as has already occurred abroad (see infra Chapter 5), the initiator of the order, George W. Bush, will almost certainly avoid responsibility. Moreover, his civilian political appointee lawyers will also most likely evade criminal responsibility. The story repeats itself – those who obey the orders get caught and held responsible, while those who give them walk away unscathed. This is a heavy price to pay for those in the military and the CIA whose lives are dedicated to serving their nation, when they are ill-led and asked to commit crimes by demagogical politicians and their cronies who do not have the expectation of impunity, but who have the arrogance and callousness of ordering loyal Americans to commit crimes for which they will be held accountable.

4.2. LEGAL PREMISES

The CIA detention and interrogation practices were designed by lawyers and CIA planners in reliance on a number of considerations including: the common practice of torture in certain countries' intelligence and police agencies with which the CIA had close relations; the readiness of these countries (such as Egypt, Pakistan, Jordan, Morocco, and even Syria) to torture persons that the CIA wants interrogated; the assumption that the CIA could unlawfully seize certain persons in certain countries (i.e. Italy, Germany, Bosnia, Macedonia) with the participation or tacit approval of these countries' intelligence agencies and forcefully and clandestinely move them to other countries; and the use of airfields in certain countries as transit for the unlawful human cargo (i.e. U.K., Spain, Poland, Italy, and Germany).

The basic legal assumption for both the practice of "extraordinary rendition" and the use of "black sites" is that if certain acts are committed outside the U.S. and the persons seized and transferred for torture are not U.S. citizens, then the acts in question are not crimes in the U.S. The lawyers exploited a gap in the jurisprudence of the Supreme Court which does not extend U.S. Constitutional protections under the Fourth, Fifth, Sixth, and Eighth amendments extraterritorially, particularly when those affected are non-U.S. citizens. This approach strictly construes the Constitution as providing rights applicable in the U.S. and perhaps abroad, but only to U.S. citizens. It does not construe the Constitution as establishing legal limitations on U.S. public agents acting no matter where.

Over the last 50 years, the Supreme Court in a number of decisions has ruled that the Constitution does not extend extraterritorially, and as a consequence that which is prohibited by the Constitution in the U.S. does not apply

---

Convention, 46 Va. J. Int'l L. 585 (2006); Jane Mayer, *Outsourcing Torture: The Secret History of America's "Extraordinary Rendition" Program*, The New Yorker, Feb. 14, 2005.

extraterritorially. The four major decisions on point are *Reid v. Covert*,[4] *Wilson v. Girard*,[5] *Verdugo v. Urquidez*,[6] and *United States v. Alvarez-Machain*.[7]

The Supreme Court has historically been reluctant to extend constitutional rights extraterritorially and also reluctant to extend constitutional restraints on U.S. public agents extraterritorially. There are valid arguments to sustain this position, but there is also a policy argument expressed by the Second Circuit highlighted in *United States v. Toscanino*, namely, that the Supreme Court's narrow rulings on what was essentially jurisdictional grounds left a wide door open for what several cases referred to as egregious illegal practices by U.S. public agents.[8] The Supreme Court has never directly addressed whether the Constitution limits illegal conduct by U.S. public agents outside the territory of the U.S. While some argue that its position on the non-applicability of the Constitution extraterritorially is all-encompassing, others, including this writer, argue that it does not cover conduct which is illegal under U.S. law when perpetrated by U.S. public agents abroad, and when the fruits of that illegal conduct are to be used in the U.S. legal system. Another policy argument is the preservation of the integrity of the U.S. system by extending certain limitations to U.S. public agents abroad, whether that conduct is directed against U.S. or non-U.S. citizens.[9] The Second Circuit in *Toscanino* added another limitation, namely, that the U.S. public agents' conduct is egregious or that the conduct "shocks the conscience."[10] The threshold test is therefore different than when applied in the U.S. whenever a public agent violates a given Constitutional standard (i.e., unreasonable search and seizure under the Fourth Amendment, or evidence obtained by coercion in violation of the Fifth Amendment). This was

---

[4]   Reid v. Covert, 354 U.S. 1 (1957), addressing the non-applicability of the right to trial by jury, Sixth Amendment extraterritorially.

[5]   Wilson v. Girard, 354 U.S. 524 (1957).

[6]   United States v. Verdugo-Urquidez, 494 U.S. 259 (1990), on the non-applicability of the Fourth Amendment, unreasonable search and seizure extraterritorially.

[7]   United States v. Alvarez-Machain, 504 U.S. 655 (1992), on the recognition of valid U.S. jurisdiction over a person abducted abroad and brought by force to the U.S., a position previously taken in Ker v. Illinois, 11 9 U.S. 436 (1886) and Frisbie v. Collins, 342 U.S. 519 (1952). For kidnapping as a substitute to lawful extradition, see M. CHERIF BASSIOUNI, INTERNATIONAL EXTRADITION IN U.S. LAW AND PRACTICE (5th ed. 2007), at 273–375; but see *United States v. Alvarez-Machain*, rejecting the defendant's claim that the extradition treaty in effect between the U.S. and Mexico prohibited the U.S. from forcibly abducting a fugitive within the borders of Mexico. The Supreme Court, however, subsequently upheld Alvarez-Machain's right to file an action under the Alien Tort Claims Act, and to obtain damages for the kidnapping. *See* Sosa v. Alvarez-Machain, 542 U.S. 692 (2004).

[8]   United States v. Toscanino, 500 F.2d 267 (2d Cir. 1974).

[9]   This writer argued before the Fifth Circuit in Escabedo v. United States, 623 F.2d 1098 (5th Cir. 1980) that evidence secuired by torture in Mexico should not be allowed in U.S. courts on the basis of public policy, in that torture is inherently offensive to U.S. public policy and to the Constitution. The Fifth Circuit rejected the argument, but this was before the U.S. ratified the CAT.

[10]   *Toscanino, supra* note 8, at 273, citing Rochin v. California, 342 U.S. 165 (72 S.Ct. 205, 96 L.Ed. 183) (1952).

a higher threshold, but a threshold nonetheless. The Second Circuit subsequently renewed its *Toscanino* ruling in *United States ex rel Lujan v. Gengler*,[11] while other Circuits also did the same or rejected the *Toscanino* approach in connection with forceful seizures of persons abroad and bringing them before U.S. courts.[12]

The policies supporting the extension of Constitutional limitations on U.S. public agents' conduct abroad are: the preservation of the integrity of U.S. legal processes, deterrence of public misconduct, and the continued protection of U.S. citizens no matter whether they are from official misconduct by U.S. public agents. All three policies, however, stop short of encompassing within their reach unlawful extraterritorial conduct by U.S. public agents when the victim is not a U.S. citizen. However, these policies should cover such conduct against non-U.S. citizens whenever their evidentiary fruits are to be used in U.S. legal proceedings. Even so, there is some legal leeway for U.S. public agents – the CIA in this case – to kidnap non-U.S. citizens abroad, and to forcefully transfer them to another state that would engage in acts of torture against them. It cannot be assumed that the Supreme Court would extend constitutional limitations abroad when the evidence obtained is not going to be used in U.S. courts.[13] That is something for Congress to legislate or for the President to take action upon by Executive Order.

The use of "black sites" raises a particular issue with respect to the extraterritorial application of the Constitution, insofar as those sites are effectively under U.S. control. They are no different than U.S. military bases in foreign countries. As a rule, the U.S. negotiates a Status of Forces Agreement (SOFA) with the country in which it has military bases in order to preserve U.S. jurisdiction over the personnel on that base. However, in the case of the "black sites" there were no SOFA agreements, or for that matter any other legitimate agreements between the U.S. and the sovereign state within which these "black sites" were located. They were there because the CIA had developed a secret cooperation arrangement with the local intelligence services, allowing it to use a certain location as a facility to secretly interrogate persons usually illegally flown into the given country. It can therefore be said that the "black sites" are illegal facilities controlled by a foreign government, namely, the U.S. in the country in which they are located. The question is therefore one of attribution and agency relationship. The CIA is an agency of the U.S. government and its operatives are agents of the U.S. for purposes of any conduct abroad that they engage in. In other words, if a CIA agent violates the laws of another country, the civil responsibility is attributed to the U.S., thus a foreign state which has been negatively affected by the work of U.S. public agents may have a claim against the U.S. government. This was the case of *Nicaragua v. U.S.* before the International

---

[11]   United States Ex Rel. Lujan v. Gengler, 550 F.2d 62 (2d Cir. 1975).
[12]   *See* Bassiouni, International Extradition, *supra* note 7, at 273–347.
[13]   *See supra* note 8.

Court of Justice and where the Court ruled against the U.S. for the actions of the paramilitary organization of the Contras, as well as covert CIA actions against Nicaragua.[14] Should "black sites" be considered foreign territory under the control of the U.S., the Constitution would apply. The Supreme Court in a recent case involving Iraq probably anticipated this situation and ruled that in Iraq, U.S. military bases are not considered U.S. territory, and therefore the Constitution does not extend to it.[15] Nevertheless, it is valid to raise the question, particularly because the Supreme Court is likely to rule differently with respect to U.S. military bases in Iraq in accordance with the U.S.–Iraq SOFA agreement.[16]

Against this legal backdrop, the CIA felt legally free from Constitutional restraints. However, while this gap arises under U.S. Constitutional law, it does not arise under the CAT which applies to the public officials of state parties, without geographic limitation. The policy underpinning the CAT is not jurisdictional, but the universal prohibition of torture. This was evidenced in the Charles Taylor, Jr. case in which the extraterritorial reach of the 1994 Torture Convention Implementation Act was applied. Taylor, an American citizen and son of the infamous Liberian dictator presently facing trial in The Hague for crimes against humanity, was sentenced to 147 years in prison for acts of torture committed in Liberia.[17] In a decision overruling the defendant's petition to dismiss, Federal District Judge Cecilia M. Altonaga, wrote:

> As to Defendant's second argument, that the Torture Act is presumed not to reach conduct that occurred extraterritorially, the argument finds no support from the plain words used in the statute, the starting and ending point here for any inquiry into its extraterritorial reach. Generally, courts are to presume that legislation of Congress is meant to apply only within the territorial jurisdiction of the United States. *See E.E.O.C. v. Arabian American Oil Co., 499 U.S. 244, 248, 111 S. Ct. 1227, 113 L. Ed. 2d 274 (1991).* That presumption, however, ceases to exist where a contrary intent appears. *Id.; see also Foley Bros. v. Filardo, 336 U.S. 281, 285, 69 S. Ct. 575, 93 L. Ed. 680 (1949)* (presumption that "legislation… is meant to apply within the territorial jurisdiction of the United States" may be invoked "unless a contrary intent appears").[18]

---

[14]   Military and Paramilitary Activities (Nicar. v. U.S.), 1986 I.C.J. 14 (June 27).

[15]   *See* Munaf v. Geren, 128 S.Ct. 2207 (2008).

[16]   Agreement Between the United States of America and the Republic of Iraq on the Withdrawal of United States Forces from Iraq and the Organization of Their Activities during Their Temporary Presence in Iraq ("Iraq SOFA") (Dec 14, 2008). *See* M. Cherif Bassiouni, *Legal Status of U.S. Forces in Iraq from 2003–2008*, 11 CHICAGO J. INT'L L. (forthcoming 2010).

[17]   *See* Elizabeth Dickinson, *Chuckie Taylor Sentenced to 97 Years*, FOREIGN POLICY, Jan. 9, 2009.

[18]   United States v. Charles Emmanuel, F.Supp.2d (S.D. Fla. 2008).

It should be noted that extraterritorial legislation for crimes in addition to torture exist in connection with genocide,[19] child soldiers,[20] the human rights accountability act,[21] as well as under a draft statutes presently under review by Congress on trafficking in persons[22] and crimes against humanity.[23] President Bush signed all three existing legislations. The fact that these acts are committed outside of the U.S. does not bar prosecution in the United States.

Considering the torture committed as part of the "extraordinary rendition" program conducted under the Bush Administration, and possibly still ongoing under the Obama Administration, it would be appropriate for the President to issue an Executive Order prohibiting such a practice.[24] Moreover, even in the absence of such an Executive Order, the practice is in violation of the CAT and other international and regional human rights treaties, placing U.S. public agents under the CAT's universal jurisdiction for other states to prosecute them, as well as the territorial states where the abduction took place. This was evidenced by the prosecution of U.S. public agents and their conviction in Italy, as described later in this chapter. Similar proceedings were initiated in Germany[25] and France,[26] and yet another investigation is ongoing in Spain pursuant to the CAT.[27] Judge Baltasar Garzón, a Spanish Investigative Judge, has initiated a criminal investigation against six members of the Bush Administration – Gonzales, Addington, Haynes, Bybee, Yoo, and Flanigan. The investigating complaint he issued is based on the jurisdictional authority under the CAT, the

---

[19]   Genocide Accountability Act of 2007, Pub. L. 110–151 §1 (Dec. 21, 2007), 121 Stat. 1821, amending Title 18 U.S.C. §1091.

[20]   Child Soldiers Accountability Act of 2008, Pub. L. 110–340 (Oct. 3, 2008).

[21]   Human Rights Enforcement Act of 2009, Pub. L. 111–122 (Dec. 22, 2009). This legislation established a section within the Criminal Division of the DOJ to enforce human rights laws, and to make technical and conforming amendments to criminal and immigration laws pertaining to human rights violations.

[22]   Trafficking in Persons Accountability Act of 2008, introduced by Sen. Richard Durbin in June 2007, and passed the Senate in Oct. 2008, at which time it was referred to the House Judiciary committee for review.

[23]   Crimes Against Humanity Act of 2009, introduced by Sen. Richard Durbin in June 2009 and referred to the Senate Committee on the Judiciary.

[24]   *See* Karen DeYoung, *CIA Director Panetta Says Agency is No Longer Operating Secret Prisons*, WASH. POST, Apr. 9, 2009. While Panetta was referring to the closure of secret detention facilities abroad, the Obama Administration has not yet ruled out the practice of "extraordinary rendition".

[25]   *See* Bruce Zagaris, *Germany Charges 13 CIA Operatives in el-Masri Rendition Probe*, 23 INT'L ENFORCEMENT L. REPORTER 131 (April 2007); *No Justice for El-Masri: Germany Drops Pursuit of CIA Kidnappers*, SPIEGEL ONLINE, Sep. 24, 2007.

[26]   *See* Doreen Caravajal, *Groups Tie Rumsfeld to Torture in Complaint*, N.Y. TIMES, Oct. 27, 2007.

[27]   *See* Marlise Simons, *Spanish Court Weighs Inquiry on Torture for 6 Bush-Era Officials*, N.Y. TIMES, Mar. 29, 2009, at A6.

Geneva Conventions, and the claims of six Spanish citizens who alleged that they were tortured at Guantánamo.[28]

The difference between the use of "black sites" and the practice of "extraordinary rendition," is that in "extraordinary rendition" a U.S. public agent commits an act which may or may not constitute a violation of U.S. law while the ultimate violation is committed by agents of the state to whom the detainee has been surrendered. In the use of "black sites," the violation is committed by U.S. public agents in a foreign country, but in an area which has been selected by U.S. public agents as one under their control. The ultimate violation is not only committed by U.S. public agents, but on foreign territory under these public agents' control. From a policy perspective, it could be argued that those areas selected by U.S. public agents, even though in a foreign country, are under their effective control and could be analogized to U.S. military bases, even without an official agreement between the U.S. and the host country, such as a SOFA. However, there are informal agreements between U.S. public agents and the public agents of the host country. These are subtle factual and legal distinctions, but they are nonetheless so superficial that it could be argued that in such cases, the Constitution and laws of the U.S. apply to U.S. public agents operating in these "black sites" *qua* bases. It should also be noted that on occasion the "black sites" are used simply as a transit point to deliver persons to another state, and thus may be considered part of the "extraordinary rendition" as opposed to being considered a separate category.

4.3. THE USE OF SECRET DETENTION CENTERS – THE "BLACK SITES"

Institutionalized torture under the guise of the "war on terror" occurred not only at the hands of the military, but also by two additional categories of operatives; members of the CIA and civilian contractors of the DOD. These operatives have been reported to have engaged directly in acts of torture, and to

---

[28] *See* Dwyer Arce, *Paper Chase: Spain Judge Garzon Beginning Investigation of Suspected Guantanamo Torture*, JURIST, Jan. 31, 2010. Notably, Retired Colonel Lawrence Wilkerson, former Chief of Staff of Secretary of State Colin Powell, in discussing the way in which Rumsfeld bypassed General Richard Myers, Chairman of the Joint Chiefs of Staff, and relied instead on the civilian lawyers in the Administration, said of their culpability, "Haynes, Feith, Yoo, Bybee, Gonzales and – at the apex – Addington, should never travel outside the U.S., except perhaps to Saudi Arabia and Israel. They broke the law; they violated their professional ethical code. In future, some government may build the case necessary to prosecute them in a foreign court, or in an international court." *See* Richard Norton-Taylor, *Top Bush Aides Pushed for Guantanamo Torture*, THE GUARDIAN, Apr. 19, 2008.

have caused others engaged in torture either at their behest or for their benefit, with their knowledge.[29]

As mentioned earlier, the pressure on the CIA to find and capture those responsible for the 9/11 attacks was intense. At the time the Agency already had a list of high-level suspects, but as their mandate grew, so did the number of those caught within their net. According to Jane Mayer, "What began as a program aimed at a small, discrete set of suspects – people against whom there were outstanding foreign arrest warrants – came to include a wide and ill-defined population that the Administration terms "illegal enemy combatants.""[30]

It is not known whether this program was initiated by Bush's Presidential finding of September 2001 directed to the CIA, as it remains classified. The significance of this Presidential finding is that it directed the CIA to engage in interrogations for which it was unprepared, as this has not been part of its primary mission. Because the CIA did not maintain any prison facilities, it had to rely on a network of allied countries to provide locations where it could detain and interrogate terror suspects. Tyler Drumheller, a former chief of European operations at the C.I.A., was reported to have stated:

> The agency had no experience in detention. Never. But they insisted on arresting and detaining people in this program. It was a mistake, in my opinion. You can't mix intelligence and police work. But the White House was really pushing. They wanted *someone* to do it. So the C.I.A. said, 'We'll try.' George Tenet came out of politics, not intelligence. His whole modus operandi was to please the principal. We got stuck with all sorts of things. This is really the legacy of a director who never said no to anybody.[31]

Although the CIA has never publicly disclosed any detailed information about these so-called "black sites," the acquiescence of at least eight countries has been identified, including Thailand, Afghanistan, Morocco, Poland, Romania, and others.[32]

It is assumed that the CIA used the services of private contractors in the maintenance of these "black sites" as well as in its "extraordinary rendition" program, and that raises issues of criminal and civil liability with respect to these

---

[29]   *See* Jordan J. Paust, *Above the Law: Unlawful Executive Authorizations Regarding Detainee Treatment, Secret Renditions, Domestic Spying, and Claims to Unchecked Executive Power*, 2 UTAH L. REV. 345, 398 (2007). A previously secret CIA memo, uncovered during a CIA civilian contractor's prosecution, created three exceptions for CIA personnel to use restraints prohibited by the Geneva Conventions. *See also* Priti Patel, *A Wider Torture Loophole?*, L.A. TIMES, Aug. 18, 2006, at B11.

[30]   *See* Mayer, *Outsourcing Torture, supra* note 3.

[31]   *See* Mayer, *The Black Sites, supra* note 1. After his retirement from the CIA, Drumheller wrote a book detailing the damage the Bush Administration wrought on U.S. intelligence practics. TYLER DRUMHELLER, ON THE BRINK: AN INSIDER'S ACCOUNT OF HOW THE WHITE HOUSE COMPROMISED AMERICAN INTELLIGENCE (2006).

[32]   *See* Priest, *CIA Holds Terror Suspects in Secret Prisons, supra* note 2.

contractors. It is also unclear what rules of interrogation the CIA was to work under, and whether the September 17, 2001 Presidential finding exempted public agents from any limitations arising under U.S. law. If that is the case, then the question of the President's personal responsibility arises. The issue would be can a President order U.S. public agents to engage in criminal acts in violation of the Constitution and laws of the U.S., provided that those acts are committed abroad? If nothing else, such an order is in the nature of a command issued in the U.S., and thus implicates the responsibility of the President under Title 18 U.S.C., even though the completed criminal act is to be completed outside the territory of the U.S. That is a distinct legal issue from the responsibility of public agents and private contractors carrying out such an order outside the U.S.

On July 20, 2007, President Bush issued an Executive Order interpreting Common Article 3 of the Geneva Conventions as it applied to the CIA's program of detention and interrogation.[33] In the Order, President Bush reiterated and reaffirmed his statement of February 7, 2002 that Common Article 3 did not apply to members of al-Qaeda, the Taliban, or associated forces. It reaffirmed and reinforced his authority as President and Commander-in-Chief of the U.S. military forces to interpret the meaning and application of Common Article 3, and said that this should be treated as authoritative for all purposes of U.S. law as well as U.S. obligations under international law. Although no details of the CIA's detention and interrogation program were provided in the Order, it set out certain guidelines for the CIA not to engage in murder, torture, cruel or inhuman treatment, or willful and outrageous acts of personal abuse due to humiliate or degrade someone in a manner that is so serious to be deemed beyond the bounds of human decency. Under this order, President Bush also assigned to the Director of National Intelligence the function given to him by the Military Commissions Act §6(c)(3). This function is the President's obligation to take action to ensure compliance with the prohibition of cruel, inhuman, or degrading treatment.

4.4. INTERNATIONAL AND DOMESTIC LAWS PROHIBITING THE USE OF "EXTRAORDINARY RENDITION"

Unlawful seizure of an individual occurs when state officials where the individual is present act with the connivance of another state to effectuate the surrender of the individual to either the first state, or to a third state.[34] Such cases are extremely difficult to document, since they presuppose the complicity of those

---

[33]   Exec. Order No. 13400, Interpretation of the Geneva Conventions' Common Article 3 as Applied to a Program of Detention and Interrogation Operated by the Central Intelligence Agency, July 20, 2007.

[34]   *See* BASSIOUNI, INTERNATIONAL EXTRADITION, *supra* note 7, at 273–375.

who could bring the matter to the attention of the judiciary, such as agents of state where the kidnapping or unlawful arrest took place.[35] In most states an unlawfully seized individual does not have standing to raise such issues before international or national courts, except for the right of individual petition before the European Commission on Human Rights, the Inter-American Commission on Human Rights, and the U.N. Human Rights Committee under the Optional Protocol to the International Covenant on Civil and Political Rights.[36]

"Extraordinary rendition" occurs where a citizen is kidnapped or illegally arrested and then transferred to the authorities of another state, where he or she may be tortured.[37] The CIA employs this technique when it kidnaps, sequesters, and transfers non-U.S. nationals and delivers them to governments whose secret services engage in their torture in order to obtain information of interest to the CIA.[38] Such an act by U.S. agents is in violation of the CAT, Article 3, which states:

1. No State Party shall expel, return ("refouler") or extradite a person to another State where there are substantial grounds for believing that he would be in danger of being subjected to torture.

2. For the purpose of determining whether there are such grounds, the competent authorities shall take into account all relevant considerations including, where applicable, the existence in the State concerned of a consistent pattern of gross, flagrant or mass violations of human rights.[39]

Thus, state parties cannot extradite or surrender by other means such as "extraordinary rendition" a person to another state which is known or reasonably believed to subject persons to torture. The U.S. practice of "extraordinary rendition" is therefore a violation of the CAT.[40] Prior to the National Defense

---

35 *Id.*

36 *Id.*

37 *Id.* at 292.

38 *See* HOWARD BELL, BUSH, THE DETAINEES, AND THE CONSTITUTION: THE BATTLE OVER PRESIDENTIAL POWER IN THE WAR ON TERROR 78 (2007). "[A]n April 2006 report issued by the European Parliament concluded that Air CIA had flown 1,000 undeclared flights over European territory since 2001." "Many times these planes stopped to pick up terrorism suspects who had been kidnapped to take them to countries that use torture." *See also* Dan Bilefsky, *European Inquiry says C.I.A. Flew 1,000 Flights in Secret*, N.Y. TIMES, Apr. 27, 2006; Stephen Grey, *CIA Prisoners "Tortured" in Arab Jails*, BBC NEWS, Feb. 8, 2005 (providing comments by Michael Scheuer, a 22-year veteran of the CIA, on the rendition practices of the CIA). In February 2006, the House International Relations Committee of Congress defeated three resolutions which would have required investigations into these practices. JAMES RISEN, STATE OF WAR: THE SECRET HISTORY OF THE CIA AND THE BUSH ADMINISTRATION (2006).

39 CAT, Dec. 10, 1984, 1465 U.N.T.S. 85, at art. 3.

40 *See* BASSIOUNI, INTERNATIONAL EXTRADITION, *supra* note 7, at 273–375. It could be argued that "extraordinary rendition" of detainees to countries in which torture is regularly practiced "…Does not violate U.S. obligations under the CAT because, at the time of ratification, the

Authorization Act for 2005 (the McCain Amendment), the CAT could be interpreted as applying only to acts committed outside the territorial jurisdiction of the U.S., thus allowing acts of extradition or kidnapping to fall outside the jurisdiction of the CAT if they were initiated at a U.S. facility abroad. However, pursuant to §1089 of the McCain Amendment, the "territorial jurisdiction" of the U.S. was limited to territories and possessions of the U.S.; thus the CAT then applied to acts that occur at U.S. facilities. Because 18 U.S.C. §2340A also criminalizes conspiracies to commit torture outside the U.S., it arguably could also apply in situations where a U.S. national conspired to transfer an individual outside a U.S. territory so that he might be tortured.[41] However, the PATRIOT Act once again expanded the special maritime and territorial jurisdiction of the U.S. to include:

> premises of any diplomatic, consular, *military*, or other United States government missions or entities in foreign states, including the buildings, part of the buildings, and land appurtenant or ancillary thereto, or used for the purposes of these missions or entities, irrespective of ownership.[42]

This means that all the locations mentioned above can be deemed part of the territorial jurisdiction of the U.S., and, thus, these locations are no longer outside the territorial jurisdiction of the U.S., rendering the CAT provisions inapplicable.[43]

Federal criminal statutes may nonetheless trigger criminal responsibility for the practice of "extraordinary rendition" committed within U.S. jurisdiction. In addition, the provisions of the UCMJ apply to actions of U.S. military personnel, regardless of their location. CIA personnel have been engaged in interrogations in Guantánamo Bay, Iraq (Abu Ghraib and other detention facilities), and

---

U.S. appended an understanding that 'substantial grounds' under Article 3(1) means that it is 'more likely than not' that a person would be tortured. Yet, because the 'more likely than not' standard is frame as an 'understanding' as opposed to a 'reservation' to the torture convention, presumably it was not intended to actually modify US obligations under the treaty." Leila Sadat, *Extraordinary Rendition, Torture and Other Nightmares from the War on Terror*, 75 GEO. WASH. L. REV. 1200, 1207 (2007), at 1221. Sadat goes on to note that "…[A]ll treaties must be interpreted in accordance with their 'object and purpose,' and an 'understanding' that was inconsistent with that object and purpose would presumably be tantamount to an illegal reservation to the treaty in question. Were an 'actual knowledge' standard to be read into the CAT, it would contravene the pain language of the treaty and undermine its broad, humanitarian purpose…" *Id.* at 1221–1222.

41   *See* John Garcia, CRS Report RL32438, *UN Convention Against Torture (CAT): Overview and Application to Interrogation Techniques* (Congressional Research Service, Library of Congress, Jan. 25, 2006).

42   Uniting and Strengthening America by Providing Appropriate Tools Required to Intercept and Obstruct Terrorism (USA PATRIOT) Act of 2001, Pub. L. No. 107–56, §804, 115 Stat. 272, 377 (2001) (codified at 18 U.S.C.A. §7(9)(A) (2001)).

43   *Id.*

Afghanistan (Bagram, Kandahar, and other free-fire bases),[44] as admitted by President Bush in 2006.[45] Until 2007, a legalistic interpretation of U.S. law would be that these interrogations are not subject to the UCMJ, because Congress has not declared war and the CIA are not military personnel, although they accompanied U.S. military forces and operated on U.S. bases. However, the John Warner National Defense Authorization Act for Fiscal Year 2007 was passed and replaced the word "war" in the UCMJ with "declared war or a contingency operation" in order to expand jurisdiction over non-military personnel who support the armed forces.[46]

Despite the applicability of these laws to CIA personnel, "extraordinary rendition" is intended to take advantage of the jurisdictional loopholes in Title 18 U.S.C. violations by selecting victims who are not U.S. citizens, kidnapping them outside the territory of the U.S., and delivering them to yet another state. Moreover, by not directly involving any U.S. public agent in the torture, plausible deniability is advanced by the CIA.[47]

If it is possible to establish a connection in terms of knowledge or reasonable forseeability between the CIA agents who deliver such victims to foreign government agents and the subsequent torture by these governments, then clearly these CIA agents who act outside U.S. territory have committed an international crime under the CAT and can be prosecuted under this convention in any country that can exercise jurisdiction upon them. As indicated above, they could also be prosecuted under the UCMJ. Regardless of how many times the territorial jurisdiction of the U.S. gets reinterpreted, some law or other applies to the crimes of torture or extraordinary rendition committed by U.S.

---

44   The CIA's Inspector General, John L. Helgerson, issued a classified report in 2004. *The New York Times* reported: "A classified report issued last year by the CIA's Inspector General warned that interrogation procedures approved by the Agency after the Sept. 11 attacks might violate some provisions of the international Convention Against Torture, current and former intelligence officials say. The previously undisclosed findings from the report, which was completed in the spring of 2004, reflected deep unease within the C.I.A. about the interrogation procedures, the officials said." Douglas Jehl, *Report Warned C.I.A. on Tactics in Interrogation*, N.Y. TIMES, Nov. 9, 2005, at A1. A heavily redacted version of the report was released to the ACLU in August 2009 under the organization's ongoing FOIA case.

45   Press Release, The White House, *President Discusses Creation of Military Commissions to Try Suspected Terrorists*, Sept. 6, 2006.

46   John Warner National Defense Authorization Act for Fiscal Year 2007, Pub. L. 109–364.

47   BELL, BUSH, THE DETAINEES, AND THE CONSTITUTION, *supra* note 34, at 77 (2007). Under the Special Access Program, the CIA and the U.S. military can bring outside interrogators from foreign countries. For example, in September 2002, a Chinese interrogator was brought in to interrogate ethnic Uighur detainees at Guantánamo. However, it delivers these individuals to countries that according to DOS Country Reports on Human Rights Practices, systematically engage in torture (Egypt, Morocco, Saudi Arabia, and Uzbekistan are countries where torture is a common occurrence and have been 'receiving countries' for extraordinary rendition). The *Country Reports on Human Rights Practices* are submitted annually by the DOS to the U.S. Congress in compliance with §§116(d) and 502B(b) of the Foreign Assistance Act of 1961 (FAA), and §504 of the Trade Act of 1974. *See* David Weissbrodt & Amy Bergquist, *Extraordinary Rendition: A Human Rights Analysis*, 19 HARV. HUM. RTS. J. 123, 129 (2006).

agents: within U.S. territory, it is federal criminal law; outside U.S. territory, the CAT; and with regard to acts committed by agents of the U.S. military, the UCMJ.

In addition to obligations under the CAT, "extraordinary rendition" is considered a violation of customary international law, as reflected in both the International Convention for the Protection of All Persons from Forced Disappearance[48] and the Inter-American Convention on the Forced Disappearance of Persons,[49] even though the U.S. has not acceded to either one of these two conventions. The International Convention defines forced disappearance as:

> ... the arrest, detention, abduction or any other form of deprivation of liberty by agents of the State or by persons or groups of persons acting with the authorization, support or acquiescence of the State, followed by a refusal to acknowledge the deprivation of liberty or by concealment of the fate or whereabouts of the disappeared person, which place such a person outside the protection of the law.[50]

The Inter-American Convention defines forced disappearance as:

> the act of depriving a person or persons of his or their freedom, in whatever way, perpetrated by agents of the state or by persons or groups acting with the authorization, support, or acquiescence of the state, followed by an absence of information or a refusal to acknowledge that deprivation of freedom or to give information on the whereabouts of that person thereby impeding his or her recourse to the applicable legal remedies and procedural guarantees.[51]

Although the U.S. is not a signatory to the International Convention, the prohibitions contained therein have long been considered part of customary international law.[52] The International Convention, like the Inter-American Convention, does not provide for any exceptions to the prohibition on kidnappings, and nor does it allow states to claim any "exceptional circumstances whatsoever, whether a state of war or a threat of war, internal political instability

---

[48] International Convention for the Protection of All Persons from Forced Disappearance, General Assembly Resolution, U.N. Doc. A/Res/61/177 (20 December 2006).

[49] Inter-American Convention on the Forced Disappearance of Persons, June 9, 1994, 33 I.L.M. 1529 (1994).

[50] International Convention, *supra* note 48, at Art. 2.

[51] Inter-American Convention, *supra* note 49, at Art. II.

[52] What constitutes customary international law and how it is recognized as applicable to the U.S. is a subject of debate among academics reflecting not only different perspectives on the relationship between international law and U.S. law, but also ideological perspectives. For a more expansive view, see Jordan J. Paust, *Customary International Law and Human Rights Treates are Law of the United States*, 20 MICH. J. INT'L L. 301 (1999). For a contrary position, see *See also* Curtis Bradley & Jack Goldsmith, *Customary International Law as Federal Common Law: A Critique of the Modern Position*, 110 HARV. L.R. 815 (1997).

or any other public emergency, may be invoked as a justification for enforced disappearance."[53] The International Convention also requires an up-to-date register of all persons held at every place of detention and requires the register be available to family members and legal counsel of the detainees.[54]

The International Convention is a reflection of the evolution of international reactions against this type of practice in tyrannical regimes, particularly as they have been practiced in Latin America and in some Asian and African countries. These types of regimes have engaged in the practice of what is euphemistically referred to as making a person "disappear," which simply means to assassinate. International human rights law has been unable for decades to bring a stop to these practices, and that is why they have been criminalized, as is the case with other persistent human rights violations whose elimination has proven to be difficult by non-criminal means, such as torture. Enforced disappearance usually involves torture, and it ultimately results in death. It also inflicts psychological pain and suffering on the members of the family of the victim, as well as members of the community. For obvious reasons, the U.S. has elected not to sign on to the International Convention, but as the prohibition of its practices becomes more recognized in customary international law, it will become binding upon the U.S., notwithstanding its decision not to accede.

It should also be noted that kidnapping and transferring of persons from one country to another, even though occurring outside of the territorial jurisdiction of the U.S., is almost always likely to occur within the territorial jurisdiction of another state. Since kidnapping is a crime under the laws of all countries of the world, and since many countries have ratified the CAT or have provisions within their criminal laws criminalizing torture, actions by CIA operatives and private contractors would constitute a crime under the laws of the state where the kidnapping or torture took place.[55]

As Professor Jordan Paust reminds us, "the *Restatement of the Foreign Relations Law of the United States* recognizes, 'causing the disappearance of individuals' is absolutely prohibited under international law (RESTATEMENT, §702c); constitutes a violation of the customary human rights of the persons who disappear (RESTATEMENT §702, cmnts a, c, n); and constitutes a violation of a peremptory prohibition *jus cogens* (RESTATEMENT, cmnt n).[56] The U.S. Army also recognizes that 'causing the disappearance of individuals' is a violation of customary international law."[57]

---

[53]   International Convention, *supra* note 48, at Art. 1.

[54]   *Id.* at Art. 17.

[55]   For example, the European Convention for the Prevention of Torture and Inhuman or Degrading Treatment or Punishment, C.E.T.S. no. 126, *entered into force* 1 February 1989.

[56]   JORDAN J. PAUST, BEYOND THE LAW: THE BUSH ADMINISTRATION'S UNLAWFUL RESPONSES IN THE "WAR" ON TERROR 36–38 (2007).

[57]   *See e.g.* U.S. DEP'T OF ARMY, OPERATIONAL LAW HANDBOOK 39–40 (2003).

The practice of summary, arbitrary, and extrajudicial executions is of the same nature as enforced disappearance and torture.[58] It involves illegal conduct by public agents resulting in the disappearance and subsequent assassination of an individual based exclusively on the abuse of power of the Executive branch. For all practical purposes, enforced disappearance, summary and extrajudicial executions, and torture resulting in death are all on the same continuum, the distinctions between them having more to do with the manner in which the unlawful conduct is carried out. Abusive governments and those that have on occasion resorted to these practices have resisted their criminalization, for example, the elaboration of the CAT, which was consistently opposed by a number of major governments. While the U.S. was supportive of the CAT, as mentioned above it has been opposed to the International Convention for the Protection of All Persons from Forced Disappearance, as well as the counterpart Inter-American Convention, and it has consistently blocked efforts within the U.N. for the development of a convention against summary, arbitrary, and extrajudicial executions.

The practice of extrajudicial execution has infamously been used by Israel in the targeted assassination of Palestinians. Israel argues that it is a form of self-defense and that the practice actually produces less harm because targeted assassination of political and military persons who engage in acts of violence against Israel is a way of saving Israeli lives.[59] The U.S. has done the same for the last decade or so, mostly in Pakistan and Yemen, by using drones. The same self-defense argument is relied upon by the U.S., as is the argument that the practice saves more lives than it takes. Far from indicating that its practice may be reduced, the U.S. has in the last few years increased its use.[60]

---

[58]   *See* Principles on the Effective Prevention and Investigation of Extra-Legal, Arbitrary, and Summary Executions, E.S.C. Res. 1989/65, U.N. ESCOR Supp. No. 1, at 52, U.N. Doc. E/1989/89 (1989); United Nations Manual on the Effective Prevention and Investigation of Extra-Legal, Arbitrary and Summary Executions, U.N. Doc. E/ST/CSDHA/.12 (1991).

[59]   *See e.g.*, Amos Guiora, *What Makes a Targeted Attack Legal or Illegal: The Experience of a Former IDF Advisor*, FOREIGN POLICY, Jul. 13, 2009, discussing the legality of targeted assassinations as "based on an expansive articulation of the concept of pre-emptive self defense, intelligence information, and an analysis regarding policy effectiveness." *See also* Amos Guiora, *Anticipatory Self-Defence and International Law – A Re-evaluation*, 13 J. CONFLICT & SECURITY L. 3 (2008). Professor Guiora, who now teaches at the University of Utah, served as a Lt. Col. and legal advisor in the Israel Defense Forces.

[60]   *See* Robert Mackey, *Drone Strikes are Legal, U.S. Official Says*, N.Y. TIMES, Mar. 26, 2010, referring to Harold Hongjuh Koh, DOS Legal Adviser. As Dean of Yale Law School, Koh was an outspoken critic of the Bush Administration's policies on detention and interrogation. However, as DOS Legal Adviser to the Obama Administration, he may on occasion see the role of his office as providing legal support for the Administration. This is essentially the argument raised earlier about whether government lawyers are essentially independent legal advisors irrespective of political decisions, or whether they are advocates as non-governmental lawyers are in the context of adversary legal relations. *See* MICHAEL P. SCHARF & PAUL R. WILLIAMS, SHAPING FOREIGN POLICY IN TIMES OF CRISIS: THE ROLE OF INTERNATIONAL LAW

The question of whether the practices of enforced disappearance and extrajudicial, summary and arbitrary executions are part of customary international law and are binding on the U.S. is more of a formal technical legal question than a substantive one. These practices are prohibited by a variety of international human rights law instruments, as well as by the Constitution and U.S. laws contained in Titles 10 and 18 U.S.C. However, technical legal arguments are interposed to the applicability of these prohibitions, including, as discussed herein, whether the Constitution applies extraterritorially and jurisdictional limitations contained in Titles 10 and 18 U.S.C. The various gaps and overlaps contained in both international law and U.S. law (also discussed herein) provide for an opportunity to use certain voids and ambiguities in the positive law to avoid its application. Nevertheless, it would be hard to argue that these practices do not violate the spirit of both international law and U.S. law, and that if placed in the proper contextual legal application, they would also be specific violations of the positive law. They are unquestionably morally offensive to the values reflected in both international and U.S. law. It should be noted, as discussed in Chapter 6, that the Obama Administration has done nothing to change these practices as engaged in during the Bush Administration, and that enforced disappearances and summary or arbitrary executions still continue to occur by U.S. public agents abroad.

4.5. EVIDENCE OF THE USE OF "EXTRAORDINARY RENDITION" AND CRIMINAL RESPONSIBILITY ABROAD

There are several well-documented cases of the CIA's "extraordinary rendition" program which are now the subject of investigations and/or prosecutions abroad. One of the most notorious cases is that of Binyam Mohamed, an Ethiopian

---

AND THE STATE DEPARTMENT LEGAL ADVISOR (2010). In a speech before the American Society of International Law, Koh discussed the practice of targeted assassinations:

U.S. targeting practices, including lethal operations conducted with the use of unmanned aerial vehicles, comply with all applicable law, including the laws of war. …In particular, this Administration has carefully reviewed the rules governing targeting operations to ensure that these operations are conducted consistently with law of war principles, including: First, the principle of distinction, which requires that attacks be limited to military objectives and that civilians or civilian objects shall not be the object of the attack; and Second, the principle of proportionality, which prohibits attacks that may be expected to cause incidental loss of civilian life, injury to civilians, damage to civilian objects, or a combination thereof, that would be excessive in relation to the concrete and direct military advantage anticipated.

Id. In April 2010, President Obama made the unprecedented decision of authorizing the targeted assassination of an American citizen, Anwar Al-Awlaki – a influential cleric living in Yemen with alleged ties to al-Qaeda. *See* Scott Shane, *U.S. Approves Targeted Killing of American Cleric*, N.Y. TIMES, Apr. 6, 2010.

national and British resident, who was first apprehended in Pakistan in April 2002. He was held without trial for nearly seven years before his release to the U.K. in February 2009, when all charges of terrorism against him were dismissed. A victim of the CIA's "extraordinary rendition" program, Mohamed was moved between secret "black sites" in Pakistan, Morocco, and Afghanistan for the first two years after his apprehension, then ultimately to Guantánamo in September 2004.

During his years of detention, Mohamed was repeatedly tortured and subjected to beatings which resulted in broken bones and loss of consciousness. According to the ACLU, "During one incident [in Morocco], Mohamed was cut 20 to 30 times on his genitals. On another occasion, a hot stinging liquid was poured into open wounds on his penis as he was being cut. He was frequently threatened with rape, electrocution and death. He was forced to listen to loud music day and night, placed in a room with open sewage for a month at a time and drugged repeatedly."[61] Conditions in U.S.-run detention centers were little better. Again, according to the ACLU:

> In Kabul, Mohamed's captors repeatedly hit his head against the wall until he bled. He was thrown into a tiny cell measuring barely more than two meters in either direction and chained to the floor. Despite the extreme cold, he was given only shorts and a thin shirt to wear and a single blanket as thin as a sheet… Mohamed was fed meals of raw rice, beans and bread sparingly and irregularly. He was kept in almost complete darkness for 23 hours a day and made to stay awake for days at a time by loud music and other frightening and irritating recordings, including the sounds of 'ghost laughter,' thunder, aircraft taking off and the screams of women and children.[62]

In 2007, the Intelligence and Security Committee – a committee of U.K. parliamentarians appointed by the Prime Minister and reporting directly to the Prime Minister – published its report into U.K. involvement in rendition, including in Mohamed's case.[63] The report was subject to extensive redaction before publication, but did, however, confirm that an agent of the U.K. security service had interviewed Mohamed while he was detained in Pakistan.

In May 2008 lawyers for Mohamed filed suit in the U.K. in an attempt to secure disclosure of any information in the possession of the U.K. government

---

[61] *See* ACLU, *Biography of Plaintiff Binyam Mohamed, available at* www.aclu.org/national-security/biographhy-plaintiff-binyam-mohamed (last visited Feb. 15, 2010).

[62] *Id.*

[63] Intelligence and Security Committee, Chair, The Rt. Hon. Paul Murphy, MP, *Rendition*, Presented to the Parliament by the Prime Minister by Commander of Her Majesty, July 2007. In July 2010, Prime Minister David Cameron announced the appointment of an independent inquiry into allegations that British security services colluded with the CIA in the rendition and torture of terrorism suspects. *See* John F. Burns, *Britain Pledges Inquiry into Torture*, N.Y. Times, Jul. 6, 2010.

which might support Mohamed's claims to have been tortured. In October 2009, the British High Court ordered officials to make public a secret seven-paragraph summary of American intelligence files describing Mohamed's treatment in custody. The British Foreign Office appealed that ruling, claiming that revealing the information would damage U.S.-British intelligence cooperation. However, in February 2010, the British Court of Appeal rejected that claim, and upheld the ruling ordering the disclosure of secret intelligence about Mohamed's detention.[64] While the seven paragraphs do not go into any detail regarding interrogation techniques used on Mohamed, they clearly state that he was "subjected to cruel, inhuman and degrading treatment by the United States authorities."[65]

Binyam Mohamed and other victims of the CIA's "extraordinary rendition" program brought a civil case against Jeppesen Dataplan, Inc., a U.S. subsidiary of Boeing based in California, in May 2007.[66] The lawsuit alleges that Jeppesen knowingly provided extensive flight services that enabled the CIA to carry out the renditions of Binyam Mohamed, Abou Elkassim Britel, Ahmed Agiza, Muhammad Bashmilah, and Bisher al-Rawi. The Obama Administration has regrettably continued the Bush Administration's legal defense in this matter, urging the Ninth Circuit Court of Appeals to dismiss the case by asserting the "state-secrets privilege" on behalf of the U.S. government and Jeppesen Dataplan.[67]

In Italy and Germany, two cases came to light where U.S. agents have been indicted for their roles in the kidnappings and renditions of terror suspects. In February 2003, CIA agents kidnapped an Egyptian cleric, Hassan Mustafa Osama Nasr (also known as Abu Omar), in the city of Milan, Italy, with the help of Italian police and intelligence agents and surrendered him to Egyptian police authorities. In Egypt he was detained and tortured, including rape, beatings, and electric shocks, for over a year.[68]

When these actions were discovered in 2005, Italian Judge Guido Salvini, following judicial investigations based on wire-tapping, issued warrants for the arrest of 22 persons said to be CIA agents for violations of both Italian and international law. In addition to these 22 arrest warrants, Italian investigative judges issued four other arrest warrants for three CIA agents and a U.S. Lieutenant Colonel who was commander of the security forces at the U.S. Aviano Air Base (Italy). Ultimately, nine Italians and 26 Americans were indicted.[69]

---

[64]   *See* Richard Norton-Taylor, *Binyam Mohamed Torture Evidence Must be Revealed, Judges Rule*, GUARDIAN, Feb. 10, 2010.

[65]   *Id.*

[66]   Mohamed et al. v. Jeppesen Dataplan, Inc., 579 F.3d 943 (9th Cir. 2009).

[67]   *See* Dahlia Lithwick, *Why is the Obama Administration Clinging to an Indefensible State-Secrets Doctrine?*, SLATE, Feb. 10, 2010.

[68]   John Crewdson of the *Chicago Tribune* was the most thorough journalist investigating this story. *See* John Crewdson, *Italy: CIA Email Ties Agents to Abduction*, CHI. TRIB., Jan. 20, 2006; John Crewdson & Alessandra Maggiorani, *Italians Press for Extradition of CIA Agents*, CHI. TRIB., Nov. 11, 2005. *See also Italy Seeks Arrests in Kidnapping Case*, N.Y. TIMES, Dec. 24, 2005, at A5.

[69]   *Id.*

On November 4, 2009, Italian Judge Oscar Maggi – judge of the fourth Criminal Section, Court of Milan – convicted 22 suspected as CIA agents and their aides and two Italian AISE (military secret service) officers for Nasr's abduction and illegal surrender to Egypt.[70] The Americans indicted were convicted *in absentia*, after the Italian and U.S. governments blocked efforts to extradite them from the U.S. Three other CIA agents of U.S. citizenship, including the former station chief in Rome, were dismissed due to diplomatic immunity since they had been listed as U.S. diplomats. The former Director of the Italian Military Secret Service and his deputy, as well as other three AISE officers, were dismissed because Article 202 of the Italian Code of Procedure states that in the case of "state secrets" which prevents an accused from presenting exculpatory evidence, that accused should be dismissed from the case. The Italian Constitutional Court confirmed this in its decision No. 106 of March 11, 2009.

CIA agents moved Nasr, who was illegally seized in Milan, with support from the Italian Military Secret Service to the U.S. Aviano Air Base (Italy) where he was put on a plane and flown to the U.S. Ramstein Air Base (Germany). From there he was flown to Egypt, presumably on a CIA covertly registered plane, where he was imprisoned, interrogated, tortured, and abused. In April 2004, after more than one year of imprisonment and apparently with serious harmful consequences arising out of the torture, he was placed under house arrest. Nasr was then found by Egyptian police authorities to have made several calls to his relatives in Italy confirming he had been subjected to torture and other inhuman and degrading treatments. This led to his second imprisonment by Egyptian police.

While Nasr's arrest, detention, torture, and re-imprisonment are contrary to Egypt's Constitution and laws, its secret police exercise ample powers in violation of the law and without effective judicial control. This is the principal reason why the CIA chose Egypt for such an unlawful transfer, as well as Syria, Morocco, and Pakistan for similar transfers. This is the first trial and conviction by any domestic criminal justice system in connection with the U.S. "extraordinary rendition" program. It is an assertion of the rule of law over unlawful CIA activities abroad, whereby torture by surrogates is effectuated.

Germany issued arrest warrants for 13 CIA agents on January 31, 2007, for the mistaken kidnapping of a German citizen, Khaled El-Masri, in Macedonia.[71] El-Masri was captured at the Macedonian border by Macedonian police and

---

[70] Rachel Donadio, *Italy Convicts 23 Americans for C.I.A. Renditions*, N.Y. Times, Nov. 4, 2009. Robert Seldon Lady, the CIA's former head of station in Milan, received a sentence of eight years; 22 others received sentences of five years each, and two others received sentences of three years for aiding and abetting.

[71] *See* Mark Landler, *German Court Challenges C.I.A. over Abduction*, N.Y. Times, Feb. 1, 2007, at A1; Bruce Zagaris, *Germany Charges 13 CIA Operatives in el-Masri Rendition Probe*, 23 Int'l Enforcement L. Reporter 131 (April 2007).

detained there for three weeks, and was reportedly interrogated by CIA agents.[72] He was then passed off to CIA agents at the Macedonian airport and flown to Kabul, Afghanistan, where he was secretly detained for nearly five months and eventually released.[73] The U.S. then informed Germany that it had mistakenly arrested El-Masri.[74] Germany instituted a parliamentary investigation and took initial steps toward the criminal prosecution of the CIA agents.[75] However, in September 2007, the German Ministry of Justice decided not to forward to the U.S. extradition requests based on the January arrest warrants, because of the negative response by the U.S. Administration and the potential political fallout.[76] In 2008, El-Masri filed suit in Germany to force the pursuit of the extradition requests.[77]

In the U.S., El-Masri filed a civil action against the CIA, the dismissal of which was affirmed by the Fourth Circuit in 2007.[78] In April 2008, the ACLU filed a petition with the Inter-American Commission on Human Rights (IACHR) on behalf of El-Masri, requesting that the Commission declare that the extraordinary rendition program violates the American Declaration of the Rights and Duties of Man; to find the U.S. responsible for violating El-Masri's rights under that declaration; and to recommend that the U.S. publicly acknowledge and apologize for its role in violating El-Masri's rights to be free from arbitrary detention and torture.[79]

Other countries have initiated investigations into U.S. "extraordinary rendition" operations on their territories, and the level of complicity of their own governments. The Council of Europe conducted an in-depth investigation into the involvement of European countries in U.S.-led "extraordinary rendition" operations, and its findings were published in a scathing report condemning

---

[72] *See* Weissbrodt & Bergquist, *Extraordinary Rendition, supra* note 47.

[73] *Id.* at 124. *See also* Don Van Natta et al., *Germany Weighs if it Played Role in Seizure by U.S.,* N.Y. TIMES, June 2, 2006, at A1.

[74] *See* Souad Mekhennet & Craig Smith, *German Spy Agency Admits Mishandling Abduction Case,* N.Y. TIMES, June 2, 2006 at A8. El-Masri was mistaken for another Khaled al-Masri on a terrorist watch list. *Id.*

[75] Van Natta et al., *Germany Weighs if it Played Role in Seizure by U.S., supra* note 73. German investigations are looking into the possibility that the German government was a "silent partner" of the U.S. in the abduction and rendition of El-Masri. *Id.*

[76] *See No Justice for El-Masri, Germany Drops Pursuit of CIA Kidnappers,* SPIEGEL ONLINE, Sep. 24, 2007.

[77] *See German Sues for CIA Extradition,* BBC.COM, Jun. 9, 2008.

[78] El-Masri v. United States, 479 F.3d 296, 313 (4th Cir. 2007). The dismissal was based on the U.S. assertion of the state secrets privilege, which the Court agreed precluded it from reviewing the practice of "extraordinary rendition" because of the classified information that would have to be revealed in the case of such a review. *Id.* The Supreme Court denied certiorari in the case. *See* ACLU Press Release, *Supreme Court Declines Case of Innocent CIA Kidnapping Victim Khaled El-Masri,* Oct. 9, 2007.

[79] *See* Press Release, ACLU, *Innocent Victim of CIA Extraordinary Rendition Program Takes Case to International Tribunal,* Apr. 9, 2008. The IACHR accepted the petition in September 2009, and as of February 2010, the Obama Administration has yet to file its response.

both the U.S. and European countries, referring to the practice as the "'outsourcing' of torture."[80] The Council of Europe adopted resolutions criticizing the use of "extraordinary rendition" and torture by the U.S., as illustrating a flagrant disregard for international law.[81]

The European Parliament also criticized the U.S. for kidnapping and illegally detaining prisoners, approving a report about fifteen E.U. countries which aided the CIA in their "extraordinary rendition" program.[82] The interrogation of al-Qaeda suspects in those countries included harsh treatment, months of solitary confinement, shackling, and sleep deprivation.[83]

---

[80]   Council of Europe Parliamentary Assembly, Committee on Legal Affairs and Human Rights, *Alleged Secret Detentions in Council of Europe Member States*, AS/Jur (2006), Jan. 22, 2006. *See also* Priest, *CIA Holds Terror Suspects in Secret Prisons, supra* note 2.

[81]   Council of Europe, Res. 1539 (2007) (The United States of America and international law).

2. The Parliamentary Assembly recognizes that the United States remains strongly committed to a significant number of international legal norms, particularly those that promote economic interests. However, especially since the events of 11 September 1002, and in pursuit of its so-called "war on terror", the American administration has inappropriately and unilaterally disregarded certain key human rights and humanitarian legal norms considered by it to be overly constraining or otherwise inappropriate in view of the perceived new situation. In so doing, it has done a disservice to the cause of justice and rule of law and has tarnished its own hard-won reputation as a beacon in defending human rights and in upholding well-established rules of international law.

3. More specifically, the United States:

3.1. continues unlawfully to detain persons in Guantánamo and elsewhere (see Assembly Resolutions 1340 (2003) and 1433 (2005)), in flagrant breach of its international obligations, in particular under the UN International Covenant on Civil and Political Rights, the UN Convention against Torture and Other Cruel, Inhuman or Degrading Treatment or Punishment, the 1949 Geneva Conventions as well as other rules of international humanitarian law with respect to the treatment of persons captured or detained in the context of an international armed conflict;

3.2. has maintained– at least until very recently – a "spider's web" of secret detention centers and unlawful inter-state transfer routes, often in collaboration with countries notorious for their use of torture (see Assembly Resolution 1507 (2006)), a behavior which is incompatible with UN and Council of Europe human rights standards;

3.3. by negotiating bilateral immunity agreements with parties and non-parties to the statute of the International Criminal Court (ICC), and exercising considerable pressure on some countries to enter into such agreements, has attempted to undermine the effectiveness of this body, which has jurisdiction over the international crime of genocide, war crimes and crimes against humanity when states are unwilling or unable to investigate or prosecute crimes;

3.4. despite recent encouraging national judicial findings, including those of its Supreme Court, has not made any efforts to abolish the death penalty (see Assembly Recommendation 1760 (2006)).

Id.

[82]   European Parliament, *Report on the Alleged use of European Countries by the CIA for the Transportation and Illegal Detention of Prisoners,* 2006/2200(INI), Temporary Committee on the alleged use of European countries by the CIA for the transportation and illegal detention of prisoners, Rapporteur: Giovanni Claudio Fava (Jan. 26, 2007).

[83]   *Id.*

4.6. THE PERFUNCTORY "DIPLOMATIC ASSURANCES": A TRANSPARENT FIG LEAF

In February 2005, high-level U.S. officials defended the "extraordinary rendition" program by claiming that it was U.S. policy to seek and secure assurances from the receiving state that a rendered person would be treated humanely upon return.[84] Persons subject to such renditions have no ability to challenge the legality of their transfers, including any assurances against torture or ill treatment that the U.S. government may have been proffered by a receiving state. The use of assurances against torture is provided for under the CAT.[85] The U.S. Attorney General, in consultation with the Secretary of State, determines whether the assurances are 'sufficiently reliable' to allow the transfer in compliance with the obligations of the U.S. Once assurances are approved, any claims a person has under the convention will not be given further consideration by U.S. authorities. The reliability assessment of the assurances is not reviewable by a court.[86]

One such case is that of Maher Arar, a Canadian citizen of Syrian origin who was sent to Syria from the U.S., where he was tortured and detained for over 11 months.[87] After apprehending Arar in transit from Tunisia through New York to Canada in 2002, U.S. authorities flew him to Jordan, where he was driven across the border and handed over to Syrian authorities. The U.S. has claimed that prior to Arar's transfer it had obtained assurances from the Syrian government that Arar would not be subjected to torture.[88] Despite these assurances, when Arar was released without charge from Syrian custody ten months later he credibly alleged that he had been beaten by security officers in Jordan and tortured repeatedly, often with cables and electrical cords. The U.S. has not explained why it sent Arar to Syria rather than to Canada, where he resided and was a citizen, or why it believed Syrian assurances to be credible in light of the many DOS reports condemning Syria as a country where torture occurs.[89] A Canadian investigation revealed that the Canadian government knew that the U.S. would ship Arar to Syria to be tortured, and admitted to having provided the questionable intelligence that led the U.S. to detain him in the first place.[90] Arar was cleared of all terrorism accusations by the Canadian investigation and was

---

84   *Still at Risk: Developments Regarding Diplomatic Assurances Since April 2004* (Human Rights Watch 2005).

85   *See* 8 CFR §208.18 (c).

86   *See* Human Rights Watch, *Still at Risk, supra* note 84.

87   Arar v. Ashcroft, 414 F. Supp. 2d 250, 253–55 (E.D.N.Y. 2006).

88   The U.S. argued that the assurances received from Syria that Arar would not be tortured made the rendition perfectly legal. *Arar,* 414 F. Supp. 2d, 253–55.

89   *See* DOS, *Country Reports on Human Rights Practices, supra* note 47.

90   *See* Ian Austen, *Canada suspected U.S. plan for Muslim,* CHI. TRIB., Aug. 10, 2007. The Canadian government gave Arar and his family $9.75 million in compensation and an apology.

granted compensation in a civil suit in Canada, although the U.S. continues to refuse to admit its wrongdoing in his case.[91]

In a candid, but damning moment, Attorney General Gonzales admitted that diplomatic assurances against torture are unreliable. "We can't fully control what a country might do. We obviously expect a country to which we have rendered a detainee to comply with their representation to us…If you're asking me, 'Does a country always comply?' I don't have to answer that."[92] What is particularly jarring is that the U.S. government gives and receives assurances in the context of extradition on a routine basis, and would never accept such assurances as given by the states who took part in "extraordinary rendition" practices. For the DOS and other government agencies, as well as President Bush, to claim they believed these assurances were in good faith is utterly deceiving, because assurances such as these would never have been accepted in the context of normal extradition practice.

4.7. CRIMINAL RESPONSIBILITY FOR ACTS PERFORMED AS PART OF THE "EXTRAORDINARY RENDITION" PROGRAM

While the exact number of prisoners detained in the CIA program is unknown, by 2004 it was estimated that at least 100 had been held in facilities operated by the agency in undisclosed locations around the world.[93] The ICRC repeatedly asked for access to these facilities and was denied. In September 2006, President Bush announced that the last 14 prisoners held in CIA facilities were being transferred to military detention at Guantánamo Bay, but it seems clear that many had been in CIA custody at some point before that. Human Rights Watch has identified 21 people who were almost certainly held in CIA facilities.[94]

CIA officers have been reported to be concerned about facing criminal charges since the Supreme Court's rejection of the Bush Administration's interpretation of Common Article 3 in *Hamdan*; some have even taken out professional liability insurance in case of future legal fees.[95] Ever since the 1960s

---

[91]   *See Canada's Good Example*, N.Y. TIMES, Jan. 30, 2007.

[92]   *See Gonzales: U.S. Has Little Control over Foreign Prisoner Torture*, ASSOCIATED PRESS, Mar. 7, 2005.

[93]   *See* John Hendren, *CIA May Have Held 100 'Ghost' Prisoners*, L.A. TIMES, Sep. 10, 2004.

[94]   *Extraordinary Rendition, Extraterritorial Detention, and Treatment of Detainees: Restoring Our Moral Credibility and Strengthening Our Diplomatic Standing*, Testimony by Tom Malinoski, Human Rights Watch Washington Advocacy Director, U.S. Senate Committee on Foreign Relations July 26, 2007.

[95]   Jane Mayer, *A Deadly Interrogation*, THE NEW YORKER, Nov. 14, 2005. *See also* A. John Radsan, *The Collision between Common Article Three and the Central Intelligence Agency*, 56 CATH. UNIV. L. REV. 959, 994 (2007); R. Jeffrey Smith, *Worried CIA Officers Buy Legal Insurance*, WASH POST, Sept. 11, 2006.

the CIA has operated under limitations that required permission, either via Executive Order or Presidential Directive, to conduct covert operations. However, in August 2009, Attorney General Eric Holder appointed a special prosecutor, John Durham, to investigate the CIA and private contractors it hired to determine whether they had gone beyond the Executive Order and the legal opinions of the General Counsel and the DOJ's Office of General Counsel.[96] The danger with Holder's position is that it tends to legitimize whatever might be contained in the Executive Order, which is still secret, as well as the opinions and guidelines of the CIA General Counsel and the DOJ Office of General Counsel.[97] It could well be that the orders gave the CIA special authorization to engage in "extraordinary rendition" and "enhanced interrogation" techniques. The question thus arises as to whether President Bush can be held accountable as Commander-in-Chief issuing instructions to paramilitary operatives in the field. As to the CIA operatives, they would be accountable if the orders they received are "manifestly unlawful." In this case, the CIA operatives have a legal obligation to not follow the orders under international law, the Geneva Conventions, and the U.S. law. Since the CIA is not part of the military, the operatives would be charged with violating the CAT and state criminal statutes as evidenced by two cases involving such prosecution of CIA personnel in Italy and Germany.[98] However, they could not be tried under the UCMJ since they are not in the military, though many are former military personnel.

The investigation as it now stands places the bar too low by not examining the lawfulness or unlawfulness of the Executive Order and the Bush Administration's legal opinions. Furthermore, by only investigating the treatment toward the detainees that went beyond the scope of the guidelines that had been laid out in memoranda and reports, there is concern that this mandate implicitly legitimizes written instructions which lowered the bar and violate international conventions, treaties, and the Constitution and laws of the U.S.

Even if the Bush Administration could claim ignorance about torture at Abu Ghraib, Bagram, or Guantánamo before these practices were publicly disclosed, it cannot do so with the "extraordinary rendition" program. President Bush signed a secret Presidential Finding that authorized the CIA to create paramilitary teams which could obtain or eliminate terrorists almost anywhere

---

[96]   *See* Carrie Johnson, *Holder Hires Prosecutor to Look into Alleged CIA Interrogation Abuses*, WASH. POST, Aug. 25, 2009. In March 2009, the Senate Intelligence Committee also ordered a one-year review of the CIA's detention program, see James Rowley, *CIA Prisons to be Evaluated in One-Year Review by Senate Panel*, BLOOMBERG, Mar. 5, 2009.

[97]   *See* Michael Isikoff & Mark Hosenball, *Will Holder Probe on CIA Detainee Abuse Fall Flat?*, NEWSWEEK, Aug. 24, 2009. *See also* Jane Mayer, *The Trial: Eric Holder and the Khalid Sheikh Mohammed Trial*, THE NEW YORKER, Feb. 15, 2010.

[98]   *See supra* notes 58–65.

in the world.[99] Thus the Executive branch was not only aware of, but actively directing the program. As stated by Jane Mayer:

> Accurately or not, Bush Administration officials have described the prisoners' abuses at Abu Ghraib and Guantánamo as the unauthorized actions of ill-trained personnel, eleven of whom have been convicted of crimes. By contrast, the treatment of high value detainees has been directly, and repeatedly, approved by President Bush. The program is monitored closely by the C.I.A. lawyers, and supervised by the agency's director and his subordinates at the counterterrorism center.[100]

Additional legal memoranda made public by the Obama Administration in 2009 further bolster evidence of knowledge within the Bush Administration. One memorandum addressing "extraordinary rendition," signed by Bybee, distorts both domestic and international laws that serve to proscribe extradition to states that are likely to torture these extradited persons. The memorandum asserts, "… the United States is free from any constraints imposed by the Torture Convention in deciding whether to transfer detainees that it is holding abroad to third countries."[101] It further indicates that under the Geneva Conventions the U.S. need not go to great lengths to ensure extradited prisoners will not be tortured. With regard to domestic law, the memorandum describes the domestic law as "amount[ing] to little more than placatory policy statements."[102] The overarching theme of this and the other disclosed memoranda is that the President is not limited by established laws when fighting terrorists.[103] They tend to show that the Bush Administration's lawyers went beyond any legal reasonableness in justifying expanded use of Executive power in carrying out instances of "extraordinary rendition".

The use of highly suspect interrogation methods by the CIA and host countries on detainees subject to "extraordinary rendition" continues to be a subject of much concern, even after President Bush's Executive Order requiring that the CIA follow international standards in the treatment of prisoners.[104] The DOJ's subsequent explanations to Congress regarding the CIA's authorized interrogation methods reveal that the CIA continues to have much latitude in determining what interrogation methods may be used when the purpose is to

---

[99] *See* Mayer, *The Black Sites*, *supra* note 1. *See also* Press Release, ACLU, *CIA Provides Further Details on Secret Interrogation Memos*, Jan. 10, 2007.

[100] *See* Mayer, *Deadly Interrogation*, *supra* note 95.

[101] Memorandum for William J. Haynes II from Jay Bybee, Re: The President's Power as Commander in Chief to Transfer Captured Terrorists to the Control and Custody of Foreign Nations (March 13, 2002).

[102] *Id.*

[103] *See* David Savage, *Bush Administration Memos on Presidential Powers Stun Legal Experts*, L.A. Times, Mar. 4, 2009.

[104] This Executive Order was issued in the wake of the Supreme Court decision that held that Common Article 3 of the Geneva Conventions applies to all U.S. prisoners. *See* Hamdan v. Rumsfeld 126 S. Ct. 2749 (2006).

prevent terrorism.[105] Surely, the international condemnation of "extraordinary rendition" evidences the unlawful nature of the activity, placing the U.S. in the embarrassing position of being caught in the commission of officially sanctioned criminal activity which may have infringed upon the sovereignty of other states. In any event, it exposes CIA agents to criminal responsibility under the laws of foreign countries when they were acted pursuant to orders from their own government, believing those orders to be lawful. If such public agents are prosecuted in a foreign country, their defense will be that they followed the orders of their superiors, who based their orders on the legal advice of U.S. government lawyers. If the legal opinions of these government lawyers were to be presented to a foreign criminal court, they would hardly withstand the scrutiny of an average judge or prosecutor. That this advice induced the CIA to send its agents to engage in kidnappings overseas, landing in different countries for refueling, holding kidnapped persons on foreign soil, using force and possibly even torture, and delivering them to an ultimate destination country for the ostensible purpose of coercive interrogation, including torture, is irresponsible to say the least. How can any legal advisor opine that a member of the CIA could engage in a crime in the territory of another country and not be subject to its criminal jurisdiction? If that was not part of the explicit legal advice given to the CIA, it is unimaginable how senior officials in that agency would put their agents, who are U.S. citizens serving their country, in harm's way. Not only were the providers of legal advice in this case misleading their superiors, but they have as a result of it placed CIA agents in positions of having violated the laws of other countries as well as their own.[106]

---

[105]   *See* Mark Mazzetti, *Letters Give C.I.A. Tactics a Legal Rationale*, N.Y. TIMES, Apr. 27, 2008. These letters confirm that the CIA used questionable interrogation methods, and justified their use on the theory that torture is a specific intent crime, as propounded in earlier memoranda.

[106]   *For example*, 18 U.S.C. §114 states: "Whoever, within the special maritime and territorial jurisdiction of the United States and with the intent to torture [as defined in §2340], maim, disfigure, bite, cuts or slits the nose, ear, or lip or cuts out or disables the tongue, or puts out or destroys an eye, or cuts off or disables a limb, or any member of another person; or [w] hoever... with like intent, throws or pours upon another person any scalding water, corrosive acid, or caustic substance [s]hall be fined under this title or imprisoned not more than twenty years, or both." 18 U.S.C. §114 (2000). *See also* 18 U.S.C. §1111(c)(6) (2000). There is also civil liability for torture under the Torture Victim Protection Act, which also defines torture in a manner consistent with the CAT and with 18 U.S.C. §2340. *See* Torture Victim Protection Act, 28 U.S.C. §1350 (2000). There have been a number of cases under the Torture Victim Protection Act establishing liability for its perpetrators. It should also be noted that the Alien Tort Claims Act provides for a civil remedy. *See* 28 U.S.C. §1350 (2000). Importantly, the Foreign Sovereign Immunities Act of 1976 as amended in 1996, specifically states that torture is an exception to the immunity of a foreign state from prosecution or adjudication before a U.S. Court. 28 U.S.C. §1605(a)(7)(2000). Lastly, the Foreign Affairs Reform and Restructuring Act of 1988 grants the Secretary of State the power not to surrender by means of extradition or by other means a person to a country where he/she is likely to be tortured in violation of the CAT. Foreign Affairs Reform and Restructuring Act of 1988, Pub. L. No. 105–277, §2242, 112 Stat. 2681, 822 (1998). *See also* DOS regulations on the subject which include a definition

Further evidencing the President and the Bush Administration's awareness of the prohibition of torture even in connection with other matters, as if intending to prepare an eventual defense against institutionalized torture, is the inclusion of a specific provision on torture in U.S. legislation signed by the President on May 11, 2005 – the bill for emergency supplemental appropriations for defense, the global war on terror, and tsunami relief for the fiscal year ending Sept. 20, 2005, in which §6057(a)(1) provides:

> None of the funds appropriated or otherwise made available by this Act shall be obligated or expended to subject any person in the custody or under physical control of the United States to torture, or cruel, inhuman or degrading treatment or punishment, that is prohibited by the Constitution, laws, or treaties of the United States.[107]

In September 2006, President Bush publicly disclosed for the first time the existence of CIA detention centers abroad, the so-called "black sites," and announced that all of the detainees that were held in them had been transferred to Guantánamo in anticipation of their prosecutions before military commissions.[108] In April 2009, however, CIA Director Leon Panetta issued a

---

of torture at 8 C.F.R. §208.18(a)(1) (2006). There have been a number of cases by several circuits dealing with that issue, all of which have the former Attorney General Ashcroft as a defendant. *See e.g.*, Wang v. Ashcroft, 320 F.3d 130 (3d Cir. 2003); Al-Najjar v. Ashcroft, 257 F.3d 1262 (11th Cir. 2001); Sackie v. Ashcroft, 270 F. Supp. 2d 596 (E.D. Pa. 2003). Lastly, the Torture Victim Relief Act of 1998 defines torture in much the same terms as Title 18 U.S.C. §2340, and authorizes the President to provide grants for the rehabilitation for the victims of torture. 22 U.S.C. §2152 (2000).

[107] Emergency Supplemental Appropriations Act for Defense, The Global War on Terror, and Tsunami Relief, H.R. Res. 1268, 109th Cong. §6057(a)(1) (2005). Section 6057(b)(1) further refers to the definition of torture as contained in 18 U.S.C. §2340.

[108] White House Press Release, *supra* note 41. In his speech, President Bush discussed the closure of the "black sites" in relation to the Supreme Court decision in *Hamdan, supra* note 91:
> The current transfers mean that there are now no terrorists in the CIA program. But as more high-ranking terrorists are captured, the need to obtain intelligence from them will remain critical – and having a CIA program for questioning terrorists will continue to be crucial to getting life-saving information.
> Some may ask: Why are you acknowledging this program now? There are two reasons why I'm making these limited disclosures today. First, we have largely completed our questioning of the men – and to start the process for bringing them to trial, we must bring them into the open. Second, the Supreme Court's recent decision has impaired our ability to prosecute terrorists through military commissions, and has put in question the future of the CIA program. In its ruling on military commissions, the Court determined that a provision of the Geneva Conventions known as "Common Article Three" applies to our war with al Qaeda. This article includes provisions that prohibit "outrages upon personal dignity" and "humiliating and degrading treatment." The problem is that these and other provisions of Common Article Three are vague and undefined, and each could be interpreted in different ways by American or foreign judges. And some believe our military and intelligence personnel involved in capturing and questioning terrorists could now be at risk of prosecution under the War Crimes Act – simply for doing their jobs in a thorough and professional way.
> *Id.*

statement to CIA personnel, wherein he stated that the "CIA no longer operates detention facilities or black sites, and has proposed a plan to decommission the remaining sites."[109] The question arises as to whether President Bush's claimed order to close the "black sites" was actually issued, or was he merely deceiving the American people? If that is the case, and these "black sites" continued to exist until 2009, then clearly any claim of good faith on the part of President Bush would be negated by the deceptive public announcement.

Of all the decisions and directives issued by President Bush, it seems that the finding of September 17, 2001 authorizing the CIA practices described in this chapter is the one most likely to raise the implication of his direct personal criminal responsibility for commanding and soliciting the commission of a crime by U.S. public agents. Such conduct occurring within the U.S. therefore constitutes a crime in the U.S., even though the completed act is to take place outside the U.S. irrespective of whether the completed act is or is not deemed a crime under U.S. law. For sure, the finding violates the Geneva Conventions and the CAT, notwithstanding President Bush's characterization of certain persons as "enemy combatants" who are not entitled to the protection of the Geneva Conventions. The Supreme Court in *Hamdan* held that the Geneva Conventions do apply to detainees, and this is what caused President Bush to publicly announce that he had ordered the "black sites" closed.[110] Thus, assuming he acted in good faith before *Hamdan*, even though that is doubtful, but nevertheless possible, his failure to effectively close the "black sites" after *Hamdan* and after his public announcement would evidence his intent that these crimes be committed. Interestingly enough, none of the commentators who criticize the Bush Administration for its torture practices and "extraordinary rendition" have addressed this legal issue, which could turn out to be the legal Achilles' heel of President Bush. However, that presupposes the existence of a political will by the Obama Administration to prosecute a former president of the U.S., and that is highly unlikely.

4.8. EXTRATERRITORIAL APPLICATION OF THE U.S. CONSTITUTION

The framers of the Constitution did not contemplate the extraterritorial application of Constitutional rights, for the simple reason that in 1787 there were very few instances in which a state, other than an empire, extended its laws extraterritorially. Nevertheless, the framers were quite conscious of the existence of international law and indeed quite respectful of it. Suffice it to mention that in 1789 the U.S. Congress passed the Alien Tort Claims Act, which to date is one of

---

[109]   *See* Randall Mikkelsen, *CIA Says Shuttering Detention Black Sites*, REUTERS, Apr. 9, 2009.

[110]   *See* White House Press Release, *supra* note 41; *see also supra* note 95.

the most advanced national laws providing a remedy for an international law violation.[111] In addition, well before the 1800s the U.S. dealt with issues of extradition and surrender. The 1825 Extradition Act was in fact signed to present unlawful seizures and surrenders of individuals to foreign powers by the Executive branch without a legislative basis and the right to judicial review.[112] That, too, demonstrated extraordinary foresight as well as great sensitivity for the rule of law in international affairs. A great debate occurred in the U.S. around the case of *In Re Robins*[113] when the Executive branch surrendered to Great Britain a man who had escaped from a British 'Man of War' vessel on which he was placed by force.[114] A series of subsequent cases proved that the Supreme Court opposed such extrajudicial seizures by the Executive branch.[115] The Supreme Court rejected then what is today euphemistically called today "extraordinary rendition."[116] In the *Antelope* case, Chief Justice John Marshall wrote a seminal opinion on the applicability of international law.[117]

From a technical perspective, none of these cases dealt with the extraterritorial application of the Constitution. However, since the 1800s, the U.S. has consistently developed legislation applicable extraterritorially, covering every field of law ranging from anti-trust to securities and exchange matters, including criminal law and a variety of aspects of trade law.[118] There is therefore an interesting disconnect between the consistent extension of extraterritorial application of U.S. laws on the one hand, and on the other, the non-extension extraterritorially of U.S. constitutional rights (except to U.S. citizens in areas where the U.S. exercises control, such as military bases and diplomatic facilities).

Interestingly, as early as 1789, the U.S. provided a legislative remedy subject to the U.S. judiciary from extraterritorial violations of international law, deemed part of what the Constitution calls the "Supreme Law of the Land."[119] Nevertheless, over the years, U.S. courts have consistently rejected the notion that the Constitution applies extraterritorially, except for U.S. citizens on territory under U.S. control. What the Supreme Court, and for that matter lower federal courts, have seldom addressed is the extraterritorial application of the Constitution and the limitation on the actions of U.S. public agents abroad. As discussed below, a number of these cases have involved a reverse "extraordinary

---

[111] Alien Tort Claims Act, 28 U.S.C. §1350 (2000).

[112] 1825 Extradition Act. *See* BASSIOUNI, INTERNATIONAL EXTRADITION, *supra* note 7, at 49.

[113] In re Robins, 27 F. Cas. 825 (D.S.C. 1799) (No. 16175).

[114] *Id.*

[115] *See* In re Kaine, 55 U.S. (14 How.) 103 (1852); and In re Metzger, 17 F. Cas. 232 (S.D.N.Y. 1847) (No. 9,511); 46 U.S. (5 How.) 176 (1847).

[116] *See* BASSIOUNI, INTERNATIONAL EXTRADITION, *supra* note 7, at 289.

[117] The Antelope, 23 U.S. 66 (1825).

[118] *See* INTERNATIONAL CRIMINAL LAW: A GUIDE TO U.S. PRACTICE AND PROCEDURE (M. Cherif Bassiouni & Ved P. Nanda eds., 1987).

[119] U.S. CONST. Art. 6, Clause 2, "This Constitution …and all Treaties made, or which shall be made, under the Authority of the United States, shall be the supreme Law of the Land."

rendition" in the form of foreign abductions by U.S. public agents in order to bring persons to trial within the U.S. The reluctance of the Supreme Court to extend the Constitution to U.S. public agents acting abroad as a constitutional limitation on the power of such agents, irrespective of territoriality, is different from the extension of Constitutional rights in the sense of privileges in an extraterritorial context other than to U.S. citizens. For example, a U.S. citizen abroad has the right to vote in U.S. elections, and thus the right to vote which attaches to citizenship can be exercised extraterritorially, just as the obligation of U.S. citizens abroad not to engage in treason applies extraterritorially.

If certain Constitutional rights attach to U.S. citizens extraterritorially, it would be reasonable to assume that certain Constitutional limitations also apply to U.S. public agents acting abroad. Thus, such limitations that exist under the Fourth, Fifth, Sixth and Eighth Amendments would be interpreted as limitations on the power of U.S. public agents who are U.S. citizens when acting extraterritorially against other U.S. citizens. If that were accepted as policy, then it would be logical to extend that to non-U.S. citizens as well. This would ensure that the integrity of the law is carried out by public agents in the name of the U.S. government, irrespective of where they may be. This has not been the case, however, as described above, and U.S. public agents have been permitted by the Supreme Court and Circuit Courts to kidnap non-U.S. citizens abroad, even mistreating them and torturing them, engaging in unreasonable searches and seizures, and obtaining coerced confessions – all of which is usually intended to be used to be used as evidence in U.S. courts. In cases where this has occurred, U.S. courts have found different reasons not to apply the exclusionary rule and to consider admissible such evidence obtained in violation of the Constitution. Foreign seizures have also been upheld as valid.

The "extraordinary rendition" program of the CIA is, in legal terms, the reverse engineering of U.S. kidnappings abroad to bring non-U.S. citizens to the U.S. for trial. Having obtained validation from the Supreme Court as recently as 1992 in *Alvarez-Machain* where the kidnapping of a Mexican doctor in Mexico was found by the Supreme Court as not being in violation of the U.S.-Mexico extradition treaty. Curiously in that case, as well as in many "extraordinary rendition" cases, it was discovered that Dr. Alvarez-Machain had not committed the crime which the DEA believed him to have committed, and the California District Court dismissed the charges against him.[120] Considering the number of known cases in which the CIA, FBI, and DEA engage in foreign kidnappings of persons who turn out to be innocent of the alleged accusations brought by officials of these agencies, requiring some judicial review as policy, either before or after the fact, would not be unreasonable. However, federal courts, including the Supreme Court, notwithstanding their professed distance from political judgments, have consistently condemned the spirit of the Constitution, avoiding

---

[120]   See *United States v. Alvarez-Machain, supra* note 7.

extending Constitutional rights and limitations extraterritorially, even by analogy, to existing laws and Supreme Court decisions. The most recent example is a 2009 decision by the Supreme Court in which the Court did not extend extraterritorial applicability of the Constitution to U.S. military bases in Iraq where two U.S. citizens, both with dual Iraqi/U.S. citizenship, were detained by U.S. forces and were summarily surrendered to Iraqi officials without going through the U.S.-Iraq extradition treaty.[121] The decision, authored by Chief Justice Roberts, takes a step backwards in the applicability of U.S. Constitution extraterritorially to U.S. citizens on an overseas U.S. military base:

> *Eisentrager* and *Verdugo-Urquidez* were thought to be the controlling Supreme Court cases on the Constitution's application to aliens abroad. *Eisentrager* rejected a habeas petition brought by German nationals imprisoned at a United States military base in Germany. 339 U.S. at 778. The Court held that these alien prisoners, who "at no relevant time were within any territory over which the United States is sovereign," were not entitled to invoke the protection of the writ or the Fifth Amendment. *Id.* The Court referred nine times to the decisive fact that the alien prisoners were, at all relevant times, outside sovereign U.S. territory. *See id.* at 777–78.

> "[E]mphatic" is how the Court later described its rejection of the claim that aliens outside the sovereign territory of the United States are entitled to due process rights. *Verdugo-Urquidez*, 494 U.S. at 269 (citing *Eisentrager*, 339 U.S. at 770). Following *Eisentrager*, the Court in *Verdugo-Urquidez* concluded that the Fourth Amendment did not protect nonresident aliens against unreasonable searches or seizures conducted outside the sovereign territory of the United States. *Id.* at 274–75. The majority noted that although American citizens abroad can invoke some constitutional protections, *id.* at 270 (citing *Reid v. Covert*, 354 U.S. 1 (1957) (plurality opinion)), aliens abroad are in an altogether different situation. *Id.* at 271. The long line of cases dealing with constitutional rights of both lawful resident aliens and illegal aliens establishes "only that aliens receive constitutional protections when they have come within the territory of the United States and developed substantial connections with this country." *Id.* (citing *Plyler v. Doe*, 257 U.S. 202, 212 (1982) (The provisions of the Fourteenth Amendment "are universal in their application, *to all persons within the territorial jurisdiction…*") (emphasis added in *Verdugo-Urquidez*); *Kwong Hai Chew v. Colding*, 344 U.S. 590, 596 n. 5 (1953) ("The Bill of Rights is a futile authority for the alien seeking admission for the first time to these shores. But *once an alien lawfully enters and resides in this country* he becomes invested with the rights guaranteed by the Constitution to all people within our borders.") (emphasis added in *Verdugo-Urquidez*)). Those cases could not help an alien who, like Verdugo-Urquidez and plaintiffs in this case, had at no relevant time been in the country and had "no previous significant voluntary connection with the United States," *id.*

---

[121] *See Munaf v. Geren, supra* note 15.

As *Rasul I*, 512 F.3d at 666, points out, the law of this circuit also holds that the Fifth Amendment does not extend to aliens or foreign entities without presence or property in the United States. *See People's Mojahedin*, 182 F.3d at 22; *32 County Sovereignty Comm. v. U.S. Dep't of State*, 292 F.3d 797, 799 (D.C. Cir. 2002); *see also Jifry v. FAA*, 370 F.3d 1174, 1182 (D.C. Cir. 2004), *cert. denied*, 543 U.S. 1146 (2005); *Pauling*, 278 F.2d at 254 n.3. We applied this line of authority to Guantánamo during plaintiffs' detention. In *Al Odah v. United States*, 321 F.3d 1134 (D.C. Cir. 2003), we held that federal habeas jurisdiction does not extend to Guantánamo and noted that "[w]e cannot see why, or how, the writ may be made available to aliens abroad when basic constitutional protections are not." *Id.* at 1141. The Supreme Court reversed that decision (on statutory grounds) only after plaintiffs' release. *Rasul*, 542 U.S. at 483–84.[122]

4.8.1. LEGAL ANALYSIS OF THE NON-APPLICABILITY OF THE U.S. CONSTITUTION – EXTRATERRITORIALLY

The abduction and unlawful seizure of persons abroad raises constitutional and human rights questions. The basic questions in this regard are whether the Constitution has extraterritorial effect, as the Supreme Court held in *Reid v. Covert*,[123] what specific provisions of the Constitution apply extraterritorially, and to whom.[124] Indeed, it is doubtful that the Supreme Court will extend in the same manner the guarantees of the Fourth, Fifth, Sixth, Eighth, and Fourteenth Amendments extraterritorially, as it has in domestic criminal proceedings. The question is, however, still recurring. The Fifth Circuit in *Escobedo v. United States*[125] rejected an argument raised by this writer that evidence secured by torture in Mexico should be barred in the U.S.

The Second Circuit, in *Rosado v. Civiletti*,[126] came to the same conclusion for different reasons. In *Rosado*, the court acknowledged that the petitioners, U.S.

---

[122] *Rasul v. Meyers, supra* note 49, at 4–9.

[123] *Reid v. Covert*, 354 U.S. 1 (1957).

[124] *See* Christopher L. Blakesley & Dan E. Stigall, *The Myopia of U.S. v. Martinelli: Extraterritorial Jurisdiction in the 21st Century*, 39 Geo. Wash. Int'l L. Rev. 1, 4 (2007); Stephen A. Saltzburg, *The Reach of the Bill of Rights Beyond the Terra Firma of the United States*, 20 Va. J. Int'l L. 741 (1980); Paul B. Stephan, *Constitutional Limits on International Rendition of Criminal Suspects*, 20 Va. J. Int'l L. 777 (1980). *See also* Johnson v. Eisentrager, 339 U.S. 763 (1950); Bruce Bryan, Note, *The Constitutional Rights of Nonresident Aliens Prosecuted in the United States*, 3 Fordham Int'l L.J. 221 (1980), discussing the contacts an alien must have with the U.S. to entitle him to benefit from U.S. Constitutional rights.

[125] *Escobedo v. United States*, 623 F.2d 1098 (5th Cir. 1980).

[126] *Rosado v. Civiletti*, 621 F.2d 1179 (2d Cir. 1980). *See also United States v. Fernandez-Morris*, 99 F. Supp. 2d 1358 (S.D. Fla. 1999); Jordan Paust, *The Unconstitutional Detention of Prisoners by the United States, Under the Exchange of Prisoners Treaties, in* International Aspects of Criminal Law 204 (Richard B. Lillich ed., 1981); Abraham Abramovsky, *A Critical Evaluation of the American Transfer of Penal Sanctions Policy*, 61 Wis. L. Rev. 25 (1980); M. Cherif Bassiouni, *Perspectives on the Transfer of Prisoners Between the United States and Mexico and the United States and Canada*, 11 Vand. J. Transnat'l L. 249 (1978).

citizens arrested and convicted in Mexico, "have demonstrated that their convictions, under the laws of the sovereign state of Mexico, manifested a shocking insensitivity to their dignity as human beings and were obtained under a criminal process devoid of even a scintilla of rudimentary fairness and decency."[127] Nevertheless, the Second Circuit, essentially for policy reasons, did not follow this observation to its logical conclusion and refused to issue a writ of *habeas corpus* freeing the petitioners who elected to be transferred from Mexico to serve their Mexican sentences in the U.S. under the U.S.-Mexico Treaty on the Execution of Penal Sentences. The Second Circuit stated:

> Indeed, because the statutory procedures governing transfers of these prisoners to United States custody are carefully structured to ensure that each of them voluntarily and intelligently agreed to forego his right to challenge the validity of his Mexican conviction, and because we must not ignore the interests of those citizens still imprisoned abroad, we hold that the present petitioners are estopped from receiving the relief they now seek.[128]

In general, the Fourth Amendment applies extraterritorially only with respect to the conduct of a U.S. agent against a U.S. citizen.[129] It does not apply to the conduct of a private citizen of the U.S. or a foreign agent against a citizen of the U.S.[130] In addition, the Fourth Amendment does not apply extraterritorially to the conduct of a U.S. agent against an alien unless the acts are egregious enough to fall within the exception set out in *United States v. Toscanino*.[131]

---

[127] *Id.*

[128] *Id.*

[129] The Constitution applies to all actions taken abroad by the U.S. government against its citizens. Reid v. Covert, 354 U.S. 1, 5 (1956). In *Reid*, the Court stated, "The United States is entirely a creature of the Constitution. Its power and authority have no other source. It can only act in accordance with all the limitations imposed by the Constitution." *Id.* at 6.

[130] Stonehill v. United States, 405 F.2d 738, 743 (9th Cir.), *cert. denied*, 395 U.S. 960 (1969), holding Fourth Amendment does not apply to conduct by foreign officials. The Fourth Amendment is only directed at the U.S. government, not foreign governments. The exclusion from U.S. courts of evidence obtained by foreign officials through searches that violate the Fourth Amendment would not deter such conduct by those officials. Brulay v. United States, 383 F.2d 345, 348 (9th Cir.), *cert. denied*, 389 U.S. 986 (1967). *See generally* Jordan Paust, *Constitutional Limitations on Extraterritorial Federal Power: Persons, Property, Due Process and the Seizure of Evidence Abroad, in* M. CHERIF BASSIOUNI & VED P. NANDA, INTERNATIONAL CRIMINAL LAW: A GUIDE TO U.S. PRACTICE AND PROCEDURE 449 (1987).

[131] In *Toscanino, supra* note 8, the defendant, an Italian citizen, was convicted of conspiracy to import and distribute narcotics. He appealed, alleging that he had been forcibly abducted from Uruguay, where he resided, by foreign officials who were paid by the U.S. government. In addition, he alleged that after his capture, he had been taken to Brazil, where he was tortured by Brazilian authorities under the direction of U.S. agents, and that he was eventually drugged and put on a commercial flight to the U.S. He was arrested on the aircraft when it landed. The district court had relied on the *Ker-Frisbie* rule, refusing to conduct any inquiry into the means by which he had been brought to the U.S., to convict him. The Second Circuit held that Toscanino was at least entitled to a hearing on his claims, stating, "[W]e view due process as now requiring a court to divest itself of jurisdiction over

If an abduction abroad results in the seizure of evidence, the Fourth Amendment applies to conduct by a U.S. agent or by a foreign agent under the direction of the U.S. government against a U.S. citizen.[132] Thus, evidence collected in this manner would be inadmissible in U.S. courts.[133]

The Fourth Amendment does not apply to conduct by a U.S. agent against an alien, or by a foreign agent against a U.S. citizen, if the conduct does not fall within the *Toscanino* exception.[134] The U.S. Supreme Court made this clear in 1990 in the case of *United States v. Verdugo-Urquidez*.[135] In that case, the Court held that the Fourth Amendment does not apply to U.S. agents' search and seizure of property owned by an alien and located in a foreign country.[136] The

---

    the person of a defendant where it has been acquired as the result of the government's deliberate, unnecessary and unreasonable invasion of the accused's constitutional rights." *Id.* at 275.

[132]   In United States v. Verdugo-Urquidez, No. 86–0107-JLI-Crim., Amended Memorandum and Order of Feb. 18, 1987, the Court stated:

    In the context of a warrantless search, conducted by U.S. military personnel, of a U.S. citizen's apartment in post-war occupied Austria, the First Circuit discussed a relevant hypothetical: For present purposes we assume, and we think it is probably so, that the protection of the Fourth Amendment extends to U.S. citizens in foreign countries under occupation by our armed forces. [citations omitted]... For example, suppose A, a citizen of the U.S., goes to Germany to take employment in a civilian capacity under the High Commissioner. He is suspected of having previously transported stolen goods in interstate commerce, in violation of 18 U.S.C. Section 2314. Agents of the F.B.I. without any search warrant, break into A's dwelling in Germany, ransack the place, find and seize the alleged stolen goods. Upon a subsequent prosecution of A in the U.S. for that offense, it can hardly be doubted that the evidence so obtained would be excluded as the product of a search and seizure forbidden by the Fourth Amendment. And this would be so, even though no judicial officer had been authorized to act on an application for a warrant. Obviously, Congress may not nullify the guarantees of the Fourth Amendment by the simple expedient of not empowering any judicial officer to act on an application for a warrant. If the search is one which would otherwise be unreasonable, and hence in violation of the Fourth Amendment, without the sanction of a search warrant, then in such a case, for lack of a warrant, no search could lawfully be made."

    Best v. United States, 184 F.2d 131, 138 (1st Cir.), *cert. denied*, 340 U.S. 939 (1951). In *Best*, the Court ultimately held that the Fourth Amendment permitted the warrantless search, given the drastic circumstances of the immediate post-war military occupation of Austria. *Id.* at 138–41. The initial example discussed by the *Best* Court, however, remains relevant to foreign searches conducted in the absence of a state of war, and has been cited with approval by the Second Circuit. *Toscanino*, 500 F.2d at 280. .

[133]   *Toscanino*, 500 F.2d at 276.

[134]   *Id.* at 275. Permitting the use of evidence illegally seized abroad by a foreign agent or a private citizen to obtain a conviction in the U.S. is similar to the "silver platter" doctrine that developed in the wake of the Supreme Court's decision in *Wolf v. Colorado*, in which the Court held that the exclusionary rule did not apply to the states under the Fourteenth Amendment. As a result, evidence illegally obtained by federal agents, which would be excluded in a federal prosecution, could be passed to state officials "on a silver platter" for use in a state prosecution. 338 U.S. 25 (1949), *overruled by Mapp v. Ohio*, 367 U.S. 643 (1961).

[135]   *United States v. Verdugo-Urquidez*, 494 U.S. 259 (1990).

[136]   *Id.* at 261. *See also* Abramovsky, *A Critical Evaluation of the American Transfer of Penal Sanctions Policy*, *supra* note 111; Emmanuel Kijo Bentil, Note, *United States v. Verdugo-*

issue arose out of Mexican Federal Judicial Police and DEA agents' search of Verdugo-Urquidez' homes in Mexico and seizure of certain documents found there.

At the District Court, Verdugo-Urquidez moved to suppress evidence seized during the searches of his Mexican homes. The Court granted his motion, holding that the Fourth Amendment applied and that the DEA failed to justify the warrantless searches.[137] The Ninth Circuit Court of Appeals affirmed.[138] The Appellate Court concluded that "'[t]he Constitution imposes substantive constraints on the federal government, even when it operates abroad.'"[139] The dissent argued that the Fourth Amendment does not apply extraterritorially to aliens, as it is expressly limited to "the people" of the U.S.[140]

The Court found the reasoning of the dissent persuasive and noted that while the protections of the Fifth and Sixth Amendments extend to "person," some amendments specifically apply to "the people" of the U.S.[141] The Court, while recognizing the limits of this argument, nonetheless said that:

> [w]hile this textual exegis is by no means conclusive, it suggests that 'the people' protected by the Fourth Amendment, and by the First and Second Amendments, and to whom rights and powers are reserved in the Ninth and Tenth Amendments, *refers to a class of persons who are part of a national community or who have otherwise developed sufficient connection with this country to be considered part of that community.*[142]

The Court also noted that there is "no indication that the Fourth Amendment was understood by contemporaries of the Framers to apply to activities of the U.S. directed against aliens in foreign territory or in international waters."[143] Because Verdugo-Urquidez was not of "a class of persons who are part of a national community," but rather "a citizen and resident of Mexico with no voluntary attachment to the United States, and the place searched was located in

---

Urquidez: The U.S. Supreme Court's Effort to Halt the Trade in Illegal Drugs, 15 N.C. J. INT'L L. & COM. REG. 511 (1990).

[137]   Verdugo-Urquidez, 494 U.S. at 259.
[138]   *Id.*
[139]   *Id.* (citations omitted).
[140]   *Id.* at 264.
[141]   *Id.* at 265.
[142]   *Id.* (emphasis added).
[143]   *Id.* at 267.

Mexico… The Fourth Amendment has no application."[144] After *Verdugo-Urquidez*, there is no question as to the inapplicability of the Fourth Amendment protections to aliens abroad.

In these cases, however, the Fifth Amendment guarantee of due process does apply.[145] Due process under the Fourteenth Amendment has been held to require the exclusion of evidence obtained by the government in a manner that "shocks the conscience."[146] In addition, a U.S. court, under its inherent supervisory powers, could exclude evidence as violative of public policy because of the manner in which it was obtained.[147] Such general due process violations are reflected in the egregious conduct standard set out in *Toscanino*.[148]

In the event an indictment is returned in the U.S. against an individual, whether a U.S. citizen or not, a given court in the U.S. would have jurisdiction. In such cases, the Fourth Amendment applies, as do the Federal Rules of Criminal Procedure. Consequently, if a U.S. agent goes abroad to unlawfully seize, or procure the seizure of, a person or evidence, such conduct would violate Rule 41 of the Federal Rules of Criminal Procedure. In such a case, the court should exercise its inherent powers of supervision to suppress evidence illegally obtained.[149]

Nevertheless, the suppression of evidence would not invalidate the criminal jurisdiction of the court over the defendant brought before it, though illegally,

---

[144]   *Id.* at 274–75.

[145]   *Id.*

[146]   *Id.*

[147]   The supervisory power of the courts to exclude evidence in order to maintain civilized standards in the administration of criminal justice was set out in *Weeks v. United States*, 232 U.S. 383 (1914), *overruled by* Mapp v. Ohio, *supra* note 134.

[148]   *Toscanino, supra* note 8.

[149]   The inherent power theory was used in *Berlin Democratic Club v. Rumsfeld*, 410 F. Supp. 144 (D.D.C. 1976). The plaintiffs were a group of U.S. citizens living in West Germany, who claimed in their suit that U.S. military personnel had conducted warrantless electronic surveillance of their political meetings and other activities. The defendants argued that the clause was inapplicable overseas because there was no U.S. magistrate authorized to issue an overseas warrant. The Court acknowledged that Rule 41(a) of the Federal Rules of Criminal Procedure restricts the power of a magistrate to warrants that authorize the seizure of persons or property within his district, but stated: Rule 41(a) cannot limit or restrict the dictates of the Constitution to the United States, …particularly when the Supreme Court has held those dictates applicable overseas. Reid v. Covert, 354 U.S. 1 (1957). The Court's authority over federal officials is sufficient to require an official to present for approval in the U.S. a warrant for a wiretap overseas. 410 F. Supp. at 160. *See also* United States v. Williams, 617 F.2d 1063, 1099 (5th Cir. 1980) *(en banc) (concurring opinion).*

under the *Ker-Frisbie* rule,[150] affirmed by the Supreme Court in *Alvarez-Machain*.[151]

4.9. CONCLUSION

There are two fundamental questions which arise in connection with the practices described above. The first and foremost is a policy question, and the second is a narrower legal one. The policy question is in turn divided in two aspects – whether it advances the standing and interests of the U.S. to engage in these practices, and to what extent the U.S. wishes to have other countries emulate our exceptionalism and to rely on narrow technical interpretations of law as a way of achieving goals which may be illegal or disruptive to world order. How credible is the U.S. as the world's leading power to argue, "do as I say, and not as I do"? Should countries invade others under false pretenses, as we did in Iraq? Should torture continue to be practiced in so many countries which claim that it is necessary to insure national security? How far can other states go in emulating our conduct? For example, can Americans be kidnapped by agents of a given state and tortured in their own "black sites" because they perceive them to be involved in illegal acts?

---

[150] At first glance, the *Ker-Frisbie* rule appears similar to the rule of non-inquiry. Under the rule of non-inquiry, a U.S. court may not inquire into 1) the manner in which a requesting state secures evidence sufficient to establish "probable cause" in order to make an extradition request of the U.S.; 2) the processes by which a foreign criminal conviction is obtained; and 3) the treatment to which the relator may be subject upon extradition to the requesting state. Both doctrines limit the extraterritorial application of the Constitution. However, the rule of non-inquiry is distinguishable on one essential basis: it does not subject an individual to criminal conviction by a U.S. court. Thus, even if unconstitutional acts have occurred prior to a foreign state's request of extradition, or even if such acts may occur after the relator has been extradited, the criminal justice processes and standards of the U.S. have not been perverted by these acts. Failure to exclude evidence seized abroad in violation of the Fourth Amendment, and failure to release a defendant who has been forcibly abducted, allows complete disregard for the basic standards of fairness and decency that underlie the U.S. Constitution. The *Ker-Frisbie* rule has been used in Congress as a justification for the abduction abroad by the U.S. of suspected terrorists. In introducing the Terrorist Prosecution Act of 1985, S. 1429, Senator Specter, its sponsor, stated:

> In many cases, the terrorist murderer will be extradited or seized with the cooperation of the government in whose jurisdiction he or she is found. Yet, if the terrorist is hiding in a country like Lebanon, where the government, such as it is, is powerless to aid in his removal, or in Libya [sic], where the Government is unwilling, we must be willing to apprehend these criminals ourselves and bring them back for trial. We have the ability to do that right now, under existing law. Under current constitutional doctrine, both U.S. citizens and foreign nationals can be seized and brought to trial in the United States without violating due process of law.

S. 1429, 99th Cong., 1st Sess., 131 Cong. Rec. S9431 (daily ed. July 11, 1985). For the text of the Terrorist Prosecution Act, see *id.*

[151] United States v. Alvarez-Machain, *supra* note 7.

In response to the first question, there is no doubt that the U.S. has discredited itself by the use of these practices, and has placed itself at the same moral level as the worst violators of human rights in the world. While this is only anecdotal, I have personally heard comments by senior persons in countries such as Egypt, Syria, Iraq, Morocco, Jordan, and Afghanistan, who have all commented that after this period, it would be hypocritical for the U.S. to accuse other states of torture at the United Nations. Indeed, there is a disconnect between the annual DOS *Country Reports on Human Rights Practices* which condemns states for acts of torture and other forms of cruel, inhuman, and degrading treatment or punishment,[152] and yet, when for tactical reasons it suits the purposes of the CIA or the DOD, such practices are solicited from these very same states. The outcome is loss of international credibility and loss of the high moral ground. The long-term implication for inter-governmental relations is hard to assess, but sure to haunt us for decades to come.

More troubling is the impact that these unlawful practices, rationalized by American exceptionalism, may have on those in the Muslim world. If CIA agents and private contractors can engage in targeted assassinations, torture resulting in death, and other forms of cruel and degrading treatment, then why should others, specifically our enemies, not do the same? In other words, if the U.S. military can destroy towns and villages in Iraq, Afghanistan, and Pakistan, why should our enemies in these countries not have similar targets in the U.S. or abroad? The moral barrier between committing and not committing a crime is frequently supported by the pragmatic argument of mutuality. When that fails, there is little left to act as inducement for compliance. Compliance with prohibitions such as those discussed throughout this book is in large part predicated on the assumption that the opposing side will also comply. Thus, one side's breach is another side's license to do the same. Compliance with the law throughout history and irrespective of culture has always been predicated on the assumption that the law is the same for all, and that all are equal before the law. The policy and practices described herein have not only breached this unarticulated social contract, but it has done so in such a blatant, cruel, and arrogant way that it has enhanced the likelihood that others will respond in kind. An entire book could be written on the negative policy implications arising out of these practices, and how detrimental they are to the standing and leadership of the U.S. throughout the world.

As to the legal considerations discussed in this book, they reflect an amazingly narrow perspective for a nation whose legal system has prided itself on reflecting the needs of the times. Those with a limited understanding of the role of law in society transformed the understanding of the Constitution and U.S. laws into narrow positivistic interpretations. Loopholes and gaps in the law were instrumentalized in order to achieve results which are contrary to both the spirit

---

[152]   DOS *Country Reports on Human Rights Practices, supra* note 45.

and letter of the law. This approach is not only narrow, but myopic, with potential harmful consequences on institutional respect for the rule of law.

Furthermore, the use of mercenaries under the guise of "private contractors" to engage in intelligence gathering, military activities, and security activities very much akin to military missions is highly questionable in terms of public policy. The exercise of military and police powers have historically been left to the state which is the repository of public policy and public trust. It has taken centuries for societies to learn the lesson that the making and execution of public policy is the highest form of public trust, and that it cannot be contracted away to the lowest bidder whose interest is profit.

History is full of examples where authoritarian regimes have voided the law of its substantive meaning and reduced it to technicalities used by those in power to achieve their intended goals. Whether in Nazi Germany or Stalinist Russia, or in so many similar regimes of different shades and colors, those whom the regime in question seeks to eliminate are conveniently charged with the violation of some law which is interpreted in a narrow or technical manner, but which is always devoid of substantive content. In some respects, what happened in connection with the practice of "extraordinary rendition" and the use of "black sites" is of the same ilk. Government lawyers simply interpreted constitutional and other legal norms by giving them a technical meaning without regard to substantive content. The practices in question occurred because government lawyers were able to argue that the Constitution does not apply extraterritorially and thus that CIA agents, private contractors, and other operatives were neither bound by the Constitution outside the territorial confines of the U.S., nor constrained by the protections offered by these instruments. Even the distinction between U.S. and non-U.S. citizens was eroded, as evidenced by the targeting for assassination of U.S. citizens abroad.[153] One would have hoped that the substantive content of constitutional and legal protections would have been considered in connection with the practices described, as well as their value-oriented goals, in order to conclude that there are limits to what U.S. public agents and those working either under direct contract with the U.S. government or as its foreign surrogates should be permitted to do.

Novel situations will always arise that the law may not have anticipated. For example, there is no legislation that applies to the behavior of U.S. public agents who may be operating in outer space or on the moon, but that should not prevent conscientious government lawyers from being able to extend the same principles and rules of law which operate within the confines of the U.S. territory to areas beyond it, if the substance of certain limitations on public actions are best served by such an extension. Instead, the Bush Administration lawyers interpreted the Constitution and the laws in artful ways which relied on the letter of the law, as opposed to its substance. Consequently, if a person could not be tortured in the

---

[153] *See* Shane, *U.S. Approves Targeted Killing of American Cleric,* supra note 60.

U.S., that person would be delivered to another country to be tortured there, and if a U.S. public agent could not engage in torture in the U.S., that person was found to be able to do so in a "black site" abroad. If all else failed, a contract would be issued to a private contractor whose task would be ambiguously defined, but who would read between the lines and know what to do, which would otherwise be in violation of the Constitution and laws of the U.S. To a large extent, the technique of using surrogates or contractors to do unlawful acts, or to commit them on a territory which would be deemed, technically, not subject to U.S. law, is no different than for example the technique used by organized crime, when the mafia don makes it understood that someone has to disappear somewhere outside his territory. Whether the orders are carried out by immediate subordinates, farmed out to friends or allies, or contracted out, the goal is to produce the desired result without leaving legal traces.

Because of the technicalities of the law discussed in this chapter, these government lawyers and those who followed their instructions will have a plausible deniability argument to the effect that they had a reasonable belief that they operated within the confines of the letter of the law. It may be difficult to describe this hairsplitting argument which to some may appear as being more philosophical or moral than legal. However, if one reads the jurisprudential history of the due process clauses of the Fifth and Fourteenth Amendments, it is clear that what characterizes due process is not only process, but also substance.

Generations of jurists and others who have studied the American legal system have learned to appreciate the meaning of substantive due process and the substantive content of procedural due process. The 1952 Supreme Court decision in *Rochin v. California*, where the Court found that pumping the stomach of a person for purposes of extracting evidence to be used against him was a violation of due process, even though technically one could argue that this was not a "search and seizure" in the traditional sense of entering a premise in order to seize an object.[154] What is similar between the two forceful entries of a person's body and a person's premises is the unlawful means and the instrumental import of their purposes. Seizure of evidence from someone's stomach is similar to seizing evidence from someone's home. In this case, however, the means were found to be "shocking to the conscience." What else can we say about the practices described earlier in Chapter 2? Yet nowhere in the decisions of U.S. courts concerning these practices have these words been used. It seems as if what was "shocking to the conscience" in 1952 is now acceptable, including repetitive waterboarding. What has changed since then? Our collective conscience or its absence – because the victims were Muslim. Perhaps had the Bush lawyers been guided by this understanding of the law, they would have found that for American agents to kidnap people and deliver them to surrogate states for torture is also "shocking to the conscience," and in the nature of a legal violation

---

[154]   *See Rochin v. California, supra* note 10.

which is simply accomplished by means that the letter of the law had not yet specified, even though the substance of the law prohibiting these practices is unequivocally established. Another argument is found in *Griswold v. Connecticut*, where the Supreme Court found the Constitution as having a "penumbra" of rights, such as the right of privacy.[155] The limits placed by the Constitution on certain public acts, and the protections of certain rights should not therefore be seen as geographically circumscribed.

It is not only the Bush lawyers whose responsibility (if not legal, surely moral) is at stake in the situations described in this chapter. The responsibility of those at the highest decision-making level of the CIA and other involved government agencies is also in question. Moreover, one has to ask the question of how it was possible for fellow Americans (and perhaps more importantly, fellow human beings) to have committed these horrendous acts of torture upon others without even the reasonable certainty that such persons had in any way committed a crime or constituted a real and present danger to the security of others in the U.S.

It is uncertain as to whether in 2010 the practices described in this chapter have completely stopped – certainly not with regard to targeted assassinations, the use of which as discussed earlier has been increased. It is certainly very troublesome, however, to see that no accountability has been pursued, whether against those who established the policy, those who made it possible to be carried out, and those who actually carried out these inhumane acts. These practices are more than the commission of international crimes, human rights violations, and violations of U.S. law – they are a breach of public trust, with policy implications that are detrimental to U.S. interests at both home and abroad.

---

[155]   Griswold v. Connecticut, 381 U.S. 479 (1965).

CHAPTER 5

RESPONSIBILITY: POLITICAL, LEGAL, AND ETHICAL CONSIDERATIONS

> *…the fact is that we violated the laws of land warfare in Abu Ghraib. We violated the tenets of the Geneva Convention. We violated our own principles and we violated the core of our military values. The stress of combat is not an excuse, and I believe, even today, that those civilian and military leaders responsible should be held accountable.*[*]
>
> – Maj. Gen. Antonio Taguba

5.1. INTRODUCTION

Perhaps the most important characteristic of a democracy is its system of government, whose functioning is based on the rule of law. Some even argue that the ultimate difference between tyranny and democracy is the rule of law. History has all too often revealed that the rule of law is the difference between barbarism and civilization.

The rule of law means different things to different people, including jurists. However, all would agree that it is more than legal process and formalities. It is also about substance. Enforcement gives meaning and substance to the rule of law, much as equal and fair application of the law are indispensible to the attainment of predictable and consistent outcomes.

The different functions allocated to branches and bodies of government are expected to operate in the manner in which they were established. Without it, the edifice of the rule of law comes tumbling down. As the Legislative branch acquiesced in the policy and practices of torture without asserting its constitutional prerogatives, and as the Judicial branch shied away from its supervisory and enforcement role, a few in the Executive branch were able to subvert the rule of law. The very fact that eight years later steps have been taken to redress the situation proves that it was obviously wrong. We found the courage needed to put a halt to it, and yet, we still lack the courage to seek the truth about what happened and to bring the perpetrators to justice. It seems that raw politics

---

[*]   Seymour M. Hersh, *Annals of National Security: The General's Report*, THE NEW YORKER, Jun. 25, 2007.

in Washington are still more influential than moral, social, and legal values combined.

When the truth is not uncovered, and when violators of the Constitution and laws of the U.S. are not investigated, and where appropriate, prosecuted, then there is a fundamental flaw in the American legal system which undermines its democratic form of government. Without the rule of law applying fairly and equally to all, irrespective of the political status of the violator of the law, the U.S. is no more than the many governments which we criticize.

5.2. THE POLITICAL RESPONSIBILITY OF CONGRESS

The role of Congress in allowing the Bush Administration's torture policy to develop and be carried out is particularly troubling. The acquiescence of Congress in the first few years after 9/11 was evident in its frequent authorization of many of the Bush Administration's policies. A bipartisan group of Congresspersons was briefed repeatedly on the CIA's use of harsh interrogation methods, including waterboarding, in 2002 and 2003. At that time, there were no protests on the part of the briefed Congresspersons, but rather "not just approval, but encouragement."[1] With regard to the Guantánamo detainees, Congress' practically blind-passed the Detainee Treatment Act (DTA) and the Military Commissions Act (MCA). These are but two examples of its complicity in denying fair hearings to detainees, many of whom were alleging torture at the hands of the U.S.[2] Subsequent Congressional attempts to curb the Bush Administration's torture policy were unconstitutionally thwarted by controversial Presidential signing statements and vetoes. Congress, at the urging of many leading Senators, including John McCain (a Republican) and Richard Durbin (a Democrat), adopted a resolution which the House of Representatives endorsed;[3] this innocuous resolution urged nothing more than following existing

---

[1]   Joby Warrick & Dan Eggen, *Hill Briefed on Waterboarding in 2002*, WASH. POST, Dec. 9, 2007.

[2]   *See* Kristine A. Huskey, *Standards and Procedures for Classifying "Enemy Combatants": Congress, What Have You Done?*. 43 REX. INT'L L.J. 41, 44 (2007), noting Congress' lack of understanding about the processes approved in the DTA and MCA, and the fact that CSRTs had already been conducted for the vast majority of detainees upon passage of those acts. While both the Detainee Treatment Act and the Military Commissions Act (which amended the DTA) claim on their face to require that that '…no individual under the control of the U.S. government shall be subject to cruel, inhuman or degrading treatment or punishment,' both denied some detainees the right to bring writs of habeas corpus before U.S. courts. *See* 42 U.S.C. §2000dd (2006); U.S. Military Commissions Act of 2006 [hereinafter MCA] Pub. L. 109–3666, 120 Stat. 2600. The U.S. Supreme Court has since determined that such detainees do indeed have this constitutional right. *See* Boumediene v. Bush, 128 S. Ct. 2229 (2008).

[3]   President Bush signed into law H.R. 2863, the Department of Defense Emergency Supplemental Appropriations to Address Hurricanes in the Gulf of Mexico and Pandemic Influenza Act of 2006, Pub L. No. 109–148, 119 Stat. 2680 (2005). Title 10 of Division A of the

U.S. law. More particularly, it required the military to follow its own field manuals and other regulations and procedures, and to close the jurisdictional gap with respect to private contractors and CIA operatives in respect to overseas torture.[4] One would not think that it would take Congressional action to remind the Bush Administration, particularly the civilian leadership in the DOD, that it should apply U.S. law and military regulations. In response, President Bush threatened to veto any bill containing such language, and Cheney lobbied strongly against it, while the Administration and the Congressional Republican leadership sought to change or eliminate this language.[5] When in the end the text was adopted, the President announced that, in essence, he would continue to do what he was doing if he felt that it was in the best interests of the U.S., and claimed the right to ignore relevant laws adopted by Congress pursuant to the Constitution's separation of powers.[6] Bush commented that "it is for the president – not Congress or the courts – to determine when the provisions of the [McCain Amendment] interfere with his war-making powers, and when they do, he will freely ignore the law"[7] – an astonishing position since it permits the President to

---

Act is the Detainee Treatment Act of 2005, commonly referred to as the "McCain Amendment." §§1001–1006 [hereinafter, the McCain Amendment]. That text does not use the term torture. It merely provides that those in the custody or control of the DOD shall be subject only to interrogation techniques included in the U.S. Army Field Manual, §1002(a). Section 1003(a) specifically states that no individual in the custody of the U.S. government shall be subject to cruel, inhuman or degrading treatment or punishment. Quite clearly, the government lawyers whose opinions the Bush Administration relied upon had disregarded or ignored the plain language and meaning of that U.S. Army Field Manual. In signing the Bill, President Bush issued a statement calling into question the legislation's binding effect. The statement says that the Bush Administration will construe the Detainee Treatment Act "in a manner consistent with the Constitutional authority of the President to supervise the unitary Executive Branch and as Commander in Chief, and consistent with the Constitutional limitations on the judicial power." *See* Press Release, White House, President's Statement on Signing of H.R. 2863, the "Department of Defense, Emergency Supplemental Appropriations to Address Hurricanes in the Gulf of Mexico, and Pandemic Influenza Act, 2006" (Dec. 30, 2005). In that statement, the President not only challenges the binding effect of the legislation, but also challenges the judicial branch in questioning his interpretation. *Id.* In short, the President clearly indicates that he is neither bound by legislation, nor by judicial decision, irrespective of what the Constitution provides. *Id.* The President, obviously on the advice of government lawyers, that Presidential powers in time of war, as defined by the President and not by virtue of a Congressional Declaration of War as provided for by the Constitution, has absolute powers which neither Congress nor the Supreme Court can limit.

4   *Id.*

5   *See* Eric Schmitt, *House Defies Bush and Backs McCain on Detainee Torture*, N.Y. Times, Dec. 15, 2005.

6   "The executive branch shall construe provisions in the Act... in a manner consistent with the President's constitutional authority... " *See* Press Release, White House, *supra* note 3; Charlie Savage, *Bush Could Bypass New Torture Ban*, Boston Globe, Jan. 4, 2006.

7   Dahlia Lithwick, *Presidential Signing Statement are more than just Executive Branch Lunacy*, slate.com, Jan 30, 2006; Erin Louise Palmer, *Reinterpreting Torture: Presidential Signing Statements and the Circumvention of U.S. and International Law*, 14 Hum. Rts. Brief 21, 23 (Fall 2006).

nullify Acts of Congress. Such a practice is no different in substance from those dictatorial regimes in which the chief executive overrides established law at will.

As evidenced by Congress's enactment of the McCain Amendment, the Bush Administration could not claim ignorance or lack of warning regarding Congressional expectations of detainee treatment. This is significant with respect to the criminal responsibility of those who ordered the commission of torture in violation of U.S. and international law. Throughout the Bush Administration's efforts in having government lawyers issuing legal opinions, one could make the assumption that all of them acting individually, and not in concert, had a good faith, reasonable belief that their advice and legal opinions were within the bounds of the law and subject to their professional responsibilities. However, when a rider is added to legislation such as the Defense Appropriation Bill, which is unrelated to the subject matter of these lawyers' advice but whose thrust is to exonerate from responsibility those acting pursuant to this advice, it raises a question about their reasonable good faith belief in the first place. When one tries to cover up for previous action, it is difficult to assume that such previous action was done without any expectation of wrongdoing. The relevance of this legislation is that it addressed the reasonable good faith belief of these actors. The adoption of the anti-torture language within the Defense Appropriation Bill certainly indicated that Congress viewed "cruel, inhuman, and degrading treatment or punishment" to be a violation of domestic and international law.

After the Democratic Party won a majority of both houses of Congress in the 2006 elections, there were a number of hearings by both the Armed Forces and Judicial Committees which cast new light on what happened, however, there was no legislative activity to remedy the violations caused by prior legislation and by the Bush Administration's policy and practices.[8] While numerous bills were

---

[8]　The following were hearings made by the House Committee of the Judiciary: Jun. 19, 2007, Subcommittee on Crime, Terrorism, and Homeland Security, on *War Profiteering and Other Contractor Crimes Committed Overseas*; Jun. 26, 2007, Subcommittee on the Constitution, Civil Rights, and Civil Liberties, on *Habeas Corpus and Detentions at Guantanamo Bay*; Oct. 18, 2007, Subcommittee on the Constitution, Civil Rights, and Civil Liberties, on *Rendition to Torture*; Nov. 8, 2007 Subcommittee on the Constitution, Civil Rights, and Civil Liberties, on *Torture and the Cruel, Inhuman, and Degrading Treatment of Detainees: The Effectiveness and Consequences of "Enhanced" Interrogation*; Dec. 20, 2007, Full Committee, on *Applicability of Federal Criminal Laws to the Interrogation of Detainees*; Feb. 18, 2008, Subcommittee on the Constitution, Civil Rights, and Civil Liberties, on *DOJ's Office of Legal Counsel*; Apr. 11, 2008, Letters from Conyers to George Tenet, Daniel Levin (former Ass't AG), Douglas Feith, John Ashcroft, and David Addington, to appear before the Committee; May 6, 2008, Subcommittee on the Constitution, on *From the Department of Justice to Guantanamo Bay: Administration Lawyers and Administration Interrogation Rules* (series, May 6, June 18, June 26, July 15, and July 17, 2008); June 5, 2008, Judiciary Subcommittee on the Constitution, Civil Rights, and Civil Liberties, and the Committee on Foreign Affairs' Subcommittee on International Organizations, Human Rights, and Oversight, on *Extraordinary Rendition Practices (U.S. Dep't of Homeland Security inspector General Report OIG-08-18)*. The following were hearings by the Senate Judiciary Committee: Jul. 11, 2006, Full Committee, on *Hamdan v. Rumsfeld: Establishing a Constitutional Process*; Sep. 25, 2006, Full Committee, on *Examining Proposals*

floated, none came to fruition. For example, a bill titled the "Torture Outsourcing Prevention Act" was introduced in the House of Representatives in March 2007; it would explicitly prohibit "the return or other transfer of persons by the United States, for the purpose of detention, interrogation, trial, or otherwise, to countries where torture or other inhuman treatment of persons occurs, and for other purposes."[9] No action was taken on this proposed legislation.[10] In early 2008, both houses of Congress passed a bill prohibiting the CIA's use of harsh interrogation techniques, including waterboarding, which is known to have been used against a number of U.S. prisoners.[11] This bill was promptly vetoed by President Bush, however, who claimed the bill would have "taken away one of the most valuable tools on the war on terror."[12] His veto provided the clearest signal that his Administration condoned torture, and that Congress was incapable of acting as a check on his Executive power.

Congress also facilitated the Bush Administration's efforts to limit the criminal responsibility of military and civilian personnel arising under the 1996 War Crimes Act, which was amended by the 2006 Military Commissions Act (MCA). These Amendments not only had a retroactive effect, but they also restricted the scope of responsibility for war crimes by defining more narrowly what such crimes are. The WCA §2441g(c)(3) extended the meaning of a "war crime" to any violation of the Geneva Conventions' Common Article 3. The Military Commissions Act amended this provision by adding the qualifying term of "grave breach" to the words "Common Article 3," even though the term

---

to Limit Guantanamo Detainees' Access to Habeas Corpus Review; May 22, 2007, Full Committee, on *Restoring Habeas Corpus: Protecting American Values and the Great Writ*; Oct. 2, 2007, Full Committee, on *Preserving the Rule of Law in the Fight Against Terrorism*; Dec. 11, 2007, Subcommittee on Terrorism and Homeland Security, on *The Legal Rights of Guantanamo Detainees: What Are They, Should They Be Changed, and Is an End in Sight?*; Jun. 4, 2008, Full Committee, on *Improving Detainee Policy: Handling Terrorism Detainees within the American Justice System*; Jun. 10, 2008, Full Committee, on *Coercive Interrogation Techniques: Do They Work, Are They Reliable, and What Did the FBI Know About Them?*; Jul. 16, 2008, Full Committee, on *How the Administration's Failed Detainee Policies Have Hurt the Fight Against Terrorism: Putting the Fight Against Terrorism on Sound Legal Foundations*; May 13, 2009, Subcommittee on Administrative Oversight and the Courts, on *What Went Wrong: Torture and the Office of Legal Counsel in the Bush Administration*; June 9, 2009, Subcommittee on the Constitution, on *The Legal, Moral, and National Security Consequences of 'Prolonged Detention'*; Feb. 26, 2010, Full Committee, *The Office of Professional Responsibility Investigation into the Office of Legal Counsel Memoranda*.

9   H.R. 1352, introduced 3/6/2007. The Bill, introduced by Rep. Ed Markey, had 60 co-sponsors.

10   Other legislative efforts included a Bill introduced in the Senate which sought to restore habeas corpus rights to detainees held by the U.S., prohibit the use of torture evidence, and narrow the definition of "enemy combatant." The Restoring the Constitution Act S576, was introduced in February 2007 by Sen. Christopher Dodd.

11   David M. Herszenhorn, *Bill Curbing Terror Interrogators is Sent to Bush, Who Has Vowed to Veto It,* N.Y. Times, Feb. 14, 2008.

12   *Id.*

"grave breach" applies only to conflicts of an international character and not to conflicts of a non-international character to which Common Article 3 applies.[13]

More importantly, the Detainee Treatment Act[14] is referred to in the MCA as a statutory defense to any criminal prosecution under the WCA. The relevant provision of the DTA states:

> In any civil action or criminal prosecution against an officer, employee, member of the Armed Forces, or other agent of the United States Government…engaging in specific operational practices, that involve detention and interrogation of aliens who the President or his designees have determined are believed to be engaged in or associated with international terrorist activity…and that were officially authorized and determined to be lawful at the time that they were conducted, it shall be a defense that such officer, employee, member of the Armed Forces, or other agent did not know that the practices were unlawful and a person of ordinary sense and understanding would not know the practices were unlawful. Good Faith reliance on advice of counsel should be an important factor, among others, to consider in assessing whether a person of ordinary sense and understanding would have known the practices were unlawful.[15]

The MCA provision referring to the DTA covers conduct beginning on September 11, 2001 and through December 30, 2005 (the date the MCA was enacted):

> Section 1004 of the Detainee Treatment Act of 2005…shall apply with respect to any criminal prosecution that…relates to actions occurring between September 11, 2001 and December 30, 2005.[16]

The provisions clearly evidence the Bush Administration's knowledge of the potential exposure to criminal prosecution by its senior officials and the subordinates who carried out their orders, which necessitated their amendments and the introduction of retroactive statutory defenses. Congress went along, and in effect, statutorily covered up for the Bush Administration.

Congress, however, went further by allowing the legal use of tortured confessions in violation of the Constitution. The MCA's §948r(b) excludes statements obtained by means of torture, and §948r(c) and (d) permit the admission of coerced statements where the degree of coercion is disputed, allowing the military judge in the commissions to decide whether or not to admit the statement, based on whether the statement was obtained either before or after the date of the DTA's enactment.

Thus one standard is that if a coerced statement was obtained after the DTA entered into effect, the military judge can use discretion in admitting the

---

[13]   Public Law 103–366 §6(b)(2006).

[14]   Detainee Treatment Act of 2005, 42 U.S.C. §2000(dd); Public Law 109–148, §1004(a)(2005).

[15]   *Id.*

[16]   *Id.* at §8(b).

statement, provided that the interrogation methods used to obtain the statement did not amount to cruel, inhuman or degrading treatment as defined in §1003 of the DTA. That provision states:

> (d) Cruel, inhuman, or degrading treatment or punishment defined- In this section, the term "cruel, inhuman, or degrading treatment or punishment" means the cruel, unusual, and inhumane treatment or punishment prohibited by the Fifth, Eighth, and Fourteenth Amendments to the Constitution of the United States, as defined in the United State Reservations, Declarations and Understandings to the United Nations Convention Against Torture and Other Forms of Cruel, Inhuman or Degrading Treatment or Punishment done at New York, December 10, 1984.[17]

Clearly, this legislative double-talk was intended to create purposeful ambiguity to both allow coerced statements to be used in the Military Commissions, and inferentially to give those who used coercion a leg to stand on in defending any illegal acts they may have performed. Congress was therefore a party to the Bush Administration's policy, but unlike members of the Administration and those subordinates who carried out the order of their superiors, no members of Congress can be held criminally accountable for adopting ambiguous legislation which can be used in a way that permits the possible commission of a crime. However, there is surely a moral responsibility that no one in any official capacity can avoid by ambiguity.

There have been numerous CIA and other briefings to Congressional committees and to Congressional leaders, including House Speaker Nancy Pelosi (a Democrat) and others as early as September 2002.[18] They would be hard put to answer questions about what they knew, what they were specifically briefed on, and why they failed to oppose at the time what is now fairly well established as constituting violations of IHL, the U.S. Constitution, and U.S. laws. This may explain why Congressional hearings or a special commission have not been convened to address the overall issue of what happened during the Bush Administration, and why it is unlikely that this will occur while the present incumbents are in office. Political responsibility is rarely self-imposed, even by the best of politicians, though it must be noted that several members of Congress, particularly Senator Leahy and Congressman Conyers, have taken the lead in holding hearings which have consistently brought new facts to life.[19]

---

[17] Public Law 109–148, §1003(d)(2005).

[18] Joby Warrick & Dan Eggen, *Hill Briefed on Waterboarding in 2002: In Meetings, Spy Panels' Chiefs Did Not Protest, Officials Say*, WASH. POST, Dec. 9, 2007.

[19] *See supra* note 8.

5.3. THE LEGAL RESPONSIBILITY OF THOSE WHO ESTABLISHED THE POLICY AND SENIOR COMMANDERS WHO IMPLEMENTED IT

The law of command responsibility is well established both in international humanitarian law and in U.S. military law.[20] The only questions which arise in this context are of a factual nature, though some who hold civilian positions of oversight over the military may argue that they are not in the chain of command. One of the most significant issues in the law of command responsibility is that of command influence. Whenever it arises, it materializes itself essentially under the guise of disputed facts. It is one of these unfortunate realities that exists in every organizational structure, particularly in the military, where career advancement is so much dependent upon superiors' evaluation, and thus encourages compliance with the wishes of those in command.

As discussed earlier in Chapter 3, the enabling policy was developed at the highest levels of civilian government, namely the office of the Vice President. From there, it seeped into the Defense DOD with the contributions of Rumsfeld and legal counsel Haynes, who had previously been on the VP's staff and was closely associated with the policy, as well as AGs Ashcroft and Gonzales (with the latter being in the loop at the time he was counsel to the president before assuming the post of AG), and through the OLC, particularly Bybee and Yoo, who as discussed earlier may well have received their orders directly from the VP's office. The trickle-down effect as discussed above relied essentially on the military structures command and control system, which extends to such organizations as the CIA (whose staff is made mostly of former military personnel). This meant that the policy was carried out through the military and paramilitary bureaucratic and personnel structures which place a high premium on obedience to superior orders, and thus places those in command in a position

---

[20]   For history of command responsibility, see M. CHERIF BASSIOUNI, CRIMES AGAINST HUMANITY: HISTORICAL EVOLUTION AND CONTEMPORARY APPLICATION (2010). *See also* Major William H. Parks, *Command Responsibility for War Crimes*, 62 MIL. L. REV. 1 (1973).

Article 28 of the Statute of the ICC establishes the responsibility of commanders and other superiors. Rome Statute of the International Criminal Court, U.N. Doc. A/Conf.183/9 (July 1, 2002). For the legislative history of the ICC, see 1 THE LEGISLATIVE HISTORY OF THE INTERNATIONAL CRIMINAL COURT (M. Cherif Bassiouni ed., 2005).

For the non-applicability of the defense of "obedience to superior orders," see BASSIOUNI, CRIMES AGAINST HUMANITY, *id.* It must be noted that the defense of "obedience to superior orders" was rejected in Article 7 of the IMT's charter and Article 6 of the IMTFE's charter, but it can be considered in mitigation of punishment. *See generally*, NICO KEIJZER, MILITARY OBEDIENCE (1978); LESLIE C. GREEN, SUPERIOR ORDERS IN NATIONAL AND INTERNATIONAL LAW (1976); YORAM DINSTEIN, THE DEFENSE OF "OBEDIENCE TO SUPERIOR ORDERS" IN INTERNATIONAL LAW (1965); EKKEHART MÜLLER-RAPPARD, L'ORDER SUPERIEUR MILITAIRE ET LA RESPONSIBILITE DU SUBORDINNE (1965). It was also specifically eliminated in the statutes of the International Criminal Tribunals for the former Yugoslavia and Rwanda, see *infra* Chapter 1.

to exercise a high degree of influence over their subordinates. Moreover, the incentives and disincentives of reward and punishment in promotion and assignments are very real motivating factors for those operating within these structures.

The issue of command responsibility in this case arises in two ways. The first is the positive actions of commanders such as issuing direct orders, but also their failures to investigate violations when they become aware of them and their failures to take the necessary and appropriate actions to correct situations which constitute a violation of military law both under IHL and the UCMJ. As experience indicates, proof of the first category of command responsibility, namely, the issuance of orders is usually much easier unless the orders are verbal or communicated in a way that allows the superior officer to plausibly argue that he/she was misunderstood. The second category of command responsibility based on failure to act is also usually more difficult to prove, for obvious reasons. However, both are unquestionably well established as a basis for criminal responsibility of those in the command hierarchy. Whether and how this can also extend to civilians who are in the political hierarchy as opposed to the chain of command is probably the big loophole in the law of military command responsibility.

In establishing command responsibility, there is the question of whether a commander can be held to a standard of "he should have known" as opposed to whether a "reasonable commander" under the like circumstances would have known. The former is a much broader concept of criminal responsibility which has been rejected since the ill-fated decision by the U.S. military commission in the Philippines in the case of Gen. Yamashita.[21]

Shortly after 9/11, the Bush Administration institutionalized a policy of permissible torture in violation of U.S. and international prohibitions, and it was practiced in various international arenas: U.S. military bases at Guantánamo Bay; Bagram, Kandahar, and other locations in Afghanistan; Abu Ghraib and other locations in Iraq; and through proxies in a number of countries, including Egypt, Syria, Pakistan, Romania, and Poland. The Rapporteur for the Council of Europe, Swiss Senator Dick Marty, stated that the "highest state authorities" knew of the secret detention centers run by the CIA in Poland and Romania

---

[21] Lest we forget, it was Gen. Douglas MacArthur who insisted on prosecuting Japanese Maj. Gen. Tomoyuki Yamashita before a U.S. military Commission in the Philippines after WWII ended, using his influence to have him convicted under a strained theory of command responsibility, namely, that "he should have known" (even though he actually did not know) of troops under his command committing war crimes against civilians. *See* A. FRANK REEL, THE CASE OF GENERAL YAMASHITA (1949); RICHARD L. LAEL, THE YAMASHITA PRECEDENT: WAR CRIMES AND COMMAND RESPONSIBILITY (1982). The U.S. Supreme Court affirmed the conviction in *In Re Yamashita*, 327 U.S. 1 (1945), with strong dissent by Justices Murphy and Rutledge, whose intellectual integrity and moral courage has to be applied even 64 years later.

from 2003 to 2005.[22] The latter subterfuge, namely, using the CIA to kidnap non-U.S. nationals for delivery to other governments' secret services for torture, assurances and denials notwithstanding, are nonetheless crimes under any one or more of the sources of law mentioned in Chapter 1 which prohibit torture. On September 6, 2006, George W. Bush confirmed that the CIA was operating a secret detention program outside of the U.S.[23] These cases raise the question of President Bush's command responsibility in ordering the secret detention for purposes of torture, in violation of U.S. law, international law, or both.

In 2003, Secretary Rumsfeld rescinded the memorandum giving blanket authority to use the most severe interrogation techniques that had been previously approved. However, he did not indicate that these techniques violated U.S. or international law. Instead, he stated that all requests for using these techniques must be justified on a case-by-case basis with requests forwarded directly to him.[24]

In July 2007, President Bush signed an Executive Order listing new interrogation techniques for terrorism suspects, yet it cast little light on what the limits of these "enhanced interrogation" techniques were.[25] It is fair to assume that the Bush Administration knew it was in uncharted waters, and the likelihood that subsequent decisions would be considered unlawful induced them to present it in a way that contained defenses such as they were acting reasonably. Most likely the Order was no more than a cover for a future argument of "plausible deniability."[26] Although the Order prohibited torture and cruel, inhuman, or degrading treatment or punishment, it left room for the CIA to continue to violate Common Article 3 of the Geneva Conventions. Violent acts

---

[22]   *See* Elaine Ganley, *Investigator: CIA Ran Secret Prisons*, CHI. TRIB., June 8, 2007. *See also* Tom Hundley, *Remote Polish Airstrip holds clues to secret CIA flights*, CHI. TRIB., Feb. 6, 2007, discussing the flights that arrived and departed from the airstrip from 2003 to 2005.

[23]   *See Bush admits to CIA secret prisons*, BBC NEWS, Sep. 7, 2006.

[24]   Donald Rumsfeld, Memorandum for the General Counsel of the Department of Defense, Subject: Detainee Interrogations, Jan. 15, 2003.

[25]   Exec. Order No. 13400, Interpretation of the Geneva Conventions' Common Article 3 as Applied to a Program of Detention and Interrogation Operated by the Central Intelligence Agency, July 20, 2007.

[26]   *Id.* The Bush Administration said that the prohibitions here did not apply until the Supreme Court ruling in *Hamdan v. Rumsfeld*. Human Rights First's discussion of the order notes:

> In an Executive Order issued last Friday, President Bush laid out legal guidance for the CIA detention and interrogation program, based on his interpretation of standards established by Common Article 3 of the Geneva Conventions, but the order fails to establish clear guidelines concerning prohibited activities and could still permit conduct that would violate Common Article 3. The CIA suspended its program after the Supreme Court ruled in June 2006 that Common Article 3, which prohibits humiliating and degrading treatment, applies to the conflict with al Qaeda. Elisa Massimino, Director of the Washington, D.C. office of Human Rights First, called on the House and the Senate intelligence committees to conduct significant oversight of the program and to explore the legal arguments and techniques now authorized.

> LAW AND SECURITY DIGEST (Human Rights First, Issue No. 157, Jul. 27, 2007).

are prohibited, but only those serious enough to be considered comparable to murder, torture, mutilation, and cruel or inhuman treatment, as defined by the Military Commissions Act.[27] The Act says that cruel and inhuman treatment is: (i) a substantial risk of death; (ii) extreme physical pain; (iii) a burn or physical disfigurement of a serious nature (other than cuts, abrasions, or bruises); or (iv) significant loss or impairment of the function of a bodily member, organ, or mental faculty.[28] It also did not condemn or prohibit "enhanced interrogation" techniques, meaning "the agency can once again hold foreign terror suspects indefinitely, and without charges, in black sites, without notifying their families or local authorities, or offering access to legal counsel."[29] At the end of the Order, it states that the Military Commission Act does not create any rights or benefits to individuals against "the United States, its departments, agencies, or other entities, its officers or employees, or any other person,"[30] in the event that a victim wishes to bring a claim in a U.S. court.

These practices of torture or other cruel and inhuman treatment sanctioned by the Bush Administration are exactly what Article 17 of the Third Geneva Convention prohibits, and what the CAT drafters of Article 1 wanted to avoid. The Bush Administration's legal advisors preposterously claimed that the infliction of severe pain and suffering, as referenced in Article 1 of the CAT, "must be equivalent in intensity to the pain accompanying serious physical injury, such as organ failure, impairment of bodily function, or even death," in order to constitute torture.[31] With respect to psychological techniques, Bybee argued that psychological harm must last "months or even years" to constitute torture.[32] Moreover, as discussed above, government lawyers and the President himself indicated that the Geneva Conventions and customary IHL did not apply to combatants who fought the U.S. when it attacked Afghanistan because the invasion did not technically constitute a war,[33] even though an explicit DOD directive dating back to 1979 requires that the U.S. Armed Forces "comply with the law of war in the conduct of military operations and related activities in

---

27   *Id.*; David Cole, *Bush's Torture Ban is Full of Loopholes*, SALON.COM, July 23, 2007.

28   *See* Cole, *id.*; Exec. Order, *supra* note 25; MCA, *supra* note 2, at §6(c).

29   *See* Jane Mayer, *A Deadly Interrogation*, THE NEW YORKER, Nov. 14, 2005.

30   *See* Cole, *Bush's Torture Ban is Full of Loopholes*, *supra* note 27; Exec. Order, *supra* note 25, at §5.

31   *See* Memorandum from Jay S. Bybee, Assistant Attorney Gen., Office of Legal Counsel, U.S. Dep't of Justice, to Alberto R. Gonzales, Counsel to the President, Standards of Conduct for Interrogation under 18 U.S.C. §§2340–2340A (Aug. 1, 2002) [hereinafter Bybee Memo I], at 172.

32   *Id.*

33   Memorandum from John C. Yoo, Deputy Assistant Attorney Gen., & Robert J. Delahunty, Special Counsel, Office of Legal Counsel, U.S. Dep't of Justice, to William J. Haynes II, Gen. Counsel, Dep't of Defense, Application of Treaties and Laws to al Qaeda and Taliban Detainees (Jan. 9, 2002) [hereinafter Yoo/Delahunty Memo], arguing that Article 2 of the Geneva Conventions applies only to relations between state parties.

armed conflict, however such conflicts are recognized."[34] Consequently, combatants who fought for the Taliban were arbitrarily deemed not to benefit from the Third Geneva Convention Relative to the Treatment of Prisoners of War, in direct contradiction to the CAT.[35] These legal constructions – by competent government lawyers who knew that JAG lawyers and others deemed them in contradiction to IHL and to U.S. law – raise serious questions about legal and ethical responsibility. The Geneva Conventions were designed to prevent the atrocities committed during World War II from happening again. Therefore, the Geneva protections are specifically designed to protect the individual, not to serve state actors, which is why any assertion that combatants or detainees do not deserve Geneva protection is incorrect.[36]

Further, as indicated above, it is clear that government officials at various levels were on notice regarding the effect of the Bush Administration's torture policy, at the very least when an ICRC report reached their desk in February 2004.[37] Condoleezza Rice and her deputy, Steven Hadley, as well as John Bellinger (then respectively Secretary of State, National Security Council Advisor, and DOS Legal Advisor) had an obligation to communicate the information from the ICRC report to the NSC Principals Committee.[38] Whether they did so or not is

---

[34] Department of Defense Directive 5100.77, DOD Law of War Program, para. E(1)(a)(10) (July 10, 1979). The same requirements are also included in the U.S. Army Field Manual 34–52, United States (1992). For a scholarly and expert description of the Geneva Conventions' applicability and the Bush Administration's plain error, see Jordan J. Paust, *Judicial Power to Determine the Status and Rights of Persons Detained Without Trial*, 44 HARV. INT'L L.J. 503 (2003).

[35] *See* Yoo/Delahunty Memo, *supra* note 33; Geneva III, Aug. 12, 1949, 6 U.S.T. 3316, 75 U.N.T.S. 135, at art. 5. Article 5 of the CAT, Dec. 10, 1984, 1465 U.N.T.S. 85, states:
1. Each State Party shall take such measures as may be necessary to establish its jurisdiction over the offences referred to in article 4 in the following cases:
   (a) When the offences are committed in any territory under its jurisdiction or on board a ship or aircraft registered in that State;
   (b) When the alleged offender is a national of that State;
   (c) When the victim is a national of that State if that State considers it appropriate.
2. Each State Party shall likewise take such measures as may be necessary to establish its jurisdiction over such offences in cases where the alleged offender is present in any territory under its jurisdiction and it does not extradite him pursuant to article 8 to any of the States mentioned in paragraph I of this article.
3. This Convention does not exclude any criminal jurisdiction exercised in accordance with internal law.

[36] *See* BARBARA OLSHANSKY, DEMOCRACY DETAINED: SECRET UNCONSTITUTIONAL PRACTICES IN THE U.S. WAR ON TERROR (2007).

[37] International Committee of the Red Cross, *Report of the ICRC on the Treatment by the Coalition Forces of Prisoners of War and Other Protected Persons by the Geneva Convention in Iraq During Arrest, Internment, and Interrogation* (Feb. 2004). *See* Neil A. Lewis, *Red Cross Finds Detainee Abuse in Guantánamo*, N.Y. TIMES, Nov. 30, 2004, A1, finding that the physical and mental coercion of the prisoners at Guantánamo is "tantamount to torture" and the role of physicians was "a flagrant violation of medical ethics".

[38] The Chairman of the Joint Chiefs of Staff is the statutory military advisor to the Council, and the Director of National Intelligence is the intelligence advisor. The Chief of Staff to the

unknown, and if not, whether their failure to do so was deliberate is also an unknown question of fact. Furthermore, the Chairman of the Joint Chiefs of Staff had the responsibility to communicate the information to the other members of the Joint Chiefs, who would in turn have had the obligation to pass it down the chain of command. If such communications did not take place, then those in the upper echelons of the chain of command are responsible. If they did communicate it down the chain of command, then those who had knowledge are responsible under the theory of command responsibility for the actions of their subordinates and for their failure to prevent future violative practices, as well as for their failure to investigate where appropriate to bring military personnel before courts martial.[39] All of these obligations are contained in the UCMJ. Looking the other way or avoiding to see what commanders are supposed to see is as culpable as ordering or committing the violation. This is well established in the military law and practice of this country and in IHL.[40]

The military, all the way through the chain of command, will also have to face legal questions about the Bush Administration's torture policy, but with the difference that under both the laws of armed conflict and the UCMJ they have the duty to refuse to obey an order that is "manifestly unlawful."[41] Their defense could hardly be that the orders they followed were not manifestly unlawful on the basis of the legal opinions of government lawyers. If nothing else, the consistent marginalization of the Judge Advocate General officers from the process of shaping such legal opinions will weigh heavily against those who seek to use the defense of the Bush Administration's civilian lawyers' legal memoranda. Another factor will be the reports of general officers' investigations of Abu Ghraib, Bagram, and Guantánamo, as well as other internal reports and memoranda by military officers, CIA officers and staffers, and FBI agents, some of whom decried or denounced the interrogation practices, while others raised questions about their utility and highlighted their counter-productivity.

Like many JAG and other officers who disapproved of the policy and practices of torture, some senior officials, including then Secretary Powell, likely because of his military background, raised questions about the various legal memoranda and the thrust from the top pushing in the direction of torture.[42] Other government lawyers such as Alberto Mora, General Counsel for the Department of the Navy, and William H. Taft IV, Legal Advisor to the DOS, were among

---

President, Counsel to the President, and the Assistant to the President for Economic Policy are invited to attend any NSC meeting.

[39] *See* Evan Wallach & Maxine Marcus, *Command Responsibility, in* 3 INTERNATIONAL CRIMINAL LAW §4.1 (M. Cherif Bassiouni ed., 3d ed. 2008).

[40] *See supra* note 21.

[41] *See supra* note 20.

[42] *See* Memorandum from Colin L. Powell, Sec'y of State, U.S. Dep't of State to Alberto R. Gonzales, Counsel to the President, Draft Decision Memorandum for the President on the Applicability of the Geneva Conventions to the Conflict in Afghanistan (Jan. 26, 2002).

those who opposed these legal propositions.[43] All these divergent opinions were set aside. Last but not least, a number of former JAG officers, led by Navy JAG Rear Admiral (Ret.) John Hutson, filed an *amicus curiae* brief with the U.S. Supreme Court in *Rasul v. Bush*[44] arguing in opposition to the President's Executive Order establishing Military Commissions to prosecute the Guantánamo detainees outside the framework of the UCMJ and without the benefit of the protections of the Third Geneva Convention.[45] The fact that some in the military, such as Maj. Gen. Antonio Taguba and others, raised questions or objected to the policy and to the practices highlights the failure of others to do the same. This was not a situation where uncertainty was so rampant that no one questioned or opposed what was happening. It was a situation where all too few did the right thing, and all too many did not. Those who failed to carry out their command responsibility should be held accountable, even if only by means of a truth commission or the like. This is necessary in order to avoid repetition of the same conduct in the future. When such failures are reported, condemned, and publicized, they strengthen the resolve of others in the future to question and oppose unlawful conduct.

The Bush Administration sought to maintain plausible deniability by using the technique of compartmentalization in order to shield the President, Vice President, Secretary of Defense, the CIA Director, other senior military officials and military civilians from responsibility.[46] Thus, they erected firewalls between them and specific incidents of torture. More importantly, it was useful to have Executive Orders and orders from other senior officials in the Administration written with enough ambiguity to provide the necessary legal wiggle room should these orders ever come to being questioned. Thus, for example, on September 11, 2001, President Bush signed a secret Presidential Finding authorizing the CIA to create paramilitary teams to "hunt, capture, detain, or kill designated terrorists almost anywhere in the world."[47] Only by keeping that

---

[43]   *See* Memorandum from William H. Taft IV, Legal Advisor, U.S. Dep't of State to Alberto R. Gonzales, Counsel to the President, Comments on Your Paper on the Geneva Convention (Feb. 2, 2002); Memorandum from Alberto J. Mora, Gen. Counsel, Dep't of the Navy, to the Inspector General, Dep't of the Navy, Statement for the Record: Office of General Counsel Involvement in Interrogation issues (Jul. 7, 2004); Statement of Alberto J. Mora to the Senate Committee on Armed Services, Hearing on the Treatment of Detainees in U.S. Custody (June 17, 2008). *See also* Jane Mayer, *The Memo: How an Internal Effort to Ban the Abuse and Torture of Detainees Was Thwarted*, THE NEW YORKER, Feb. 27, 2006.

[44]   Brief for Law Professors et al. as Amici Curiae Supporting Respondents, Rasul. v. Bush, 542 U.S. 466 (2004).

[45]   *Id. See* Military Order of Nov. 13, 2001, Detention, Treatment, and Trial of Certain Non-Citizens in the War Against Terrorism, 66 Fed. Reg. 57,833 (Nov. 16, 2001), app. 3.

[46]   *See* Chapter 3, *The Torture-Enabling Policy*, for a discussion of PHILIP ZIMBARDO, THE LUCIFER EFFECT: UNDERSTANDING HOW GOOD PEOPLE TURN EVIL (2008).

[47]   *Id.*; ACLU, *CIA Finally Acknowledges Existence of Presidential Order on Detention Facilities Abroad*, November 14, 2006. Cheney was known to be actively pushing the CIA to engage in these techniques, including interrogation techniques harkening back to the failed Phoenix program from the Vietnam War, even though, as Mayer reports that a "Pentagon-contract

Executive Order secret could President Bush be shielded from responsibility. However, for insurance, in 2006, the President issued another Executive Order which reaffirmed the obligations of the Geneva Conventions, but said nothing more.[48] Combining the two Orders, one creates high expectations of the CIA, presumably with the knowledge that these expectations could not be fulfilled without engaging in torture and other Grave Breaches of the Geneva Conventions. The second Order is obviously self-serving by restating the obligations to respect the Geneva Conventions, but without giving any guidance of how to do so effectively or avoid engaging in torture – the President should have known this. The two Orders taken together can make a legal argument to absolve the President from responsibility, which unfairly leaves the CIA and its personnel who followed the first Order to carry the weight of the blame.

It should be noted that the official justification for the torture-enabling policy and practices, as mentioned already, is the so-called "war on terrorism" – a term developed and given content by the Bush Administration.[49] This became the backdrop against which domestic and international crimes were committed with impunity.[50] However, international law does not provide any exception to the applicability of the Third Geneva Convention or the CAT, and neither do relevant U.S. laws under the UCMJ and Title 18.[51] Additionally, suppressing terrorism does not constitute war.[52] Thus, the President's "war on terrorism" rationale is not a legal excuse or justification for torture.

Members of the military who participated in enhanced interrogation or torture could be held responsible under the UCMJ and prosecuted via a court martial under the U.S. military justice system.[53] Military law governs both

---

study found that, between 1970 and 1971, ninety-seven percent of the Vietcong targeted by the Phoenix program were of negligible importance." Mayer, *The Memo, supra* note 43. There was no doubt that in light of the Agency's historic mission, structure, and personnel they could not have carried out that function without engaging in torture.

[48]   Exec. Order, *supra* note 25.

[49]   *See* Michael Newton, *Unlawful Belligerency After September 11: History Revisited and Law Revised in* NEW WARS, NEW LAWS? APPLYING THE LAWS OF WAR IN 21ST CENTURY CONFLICTS (David Wippman & Mathew Evangelista eds., 2005); Joseph P. Bialke, *Al-Qaeda & Taliban Unlawful Combatant Detainees, Unlawful Belligerency, and the International Laws of Armed Conflict,* 55 A.F.L. REV. 1 (2004).

[50]   See the various contributions by noted jurists contained in Symposium, *Terrorism on Trial,* 36 CASE W. RES. U. J. INT'L L. 1 (2004).

[51]   *See* Geneva III, *supra* note 35, at Art. 17; CAT, *supra* note 35; Uniform Code of Military Justice, 10 U.S.C. §§801–941 (2000). *See also* John Warner National Defense Authorization Act for Fiscal Year 2007, Pub. L. 109–364.

[52]   *See* Mary Robinson, Speech before the International Bar Association Symposium, *The Rule of Law: Striking a Balance in an Era of Terrorism,* Chicago (Sept. 16, 2006), quoting Hans Corell. *See also* Arunabha Bhoumik, *Democratic Responses to Terrorism: A Comparative Study of the United States, Israel, and India,* 33 DENV. J. INT'L L. & POL'Y 285, 306 (2005), noting that war implies terrorism is a political act, rather than a criminal act.

[53]   10 U.S.C. §801–941. James B. Roan & Cynthia Buxton, *The American Military Justice System in the New Millennium,* 52 A.F.L. REV. 185, 186 (2002).

uniquely military offenses and traditional crimes.[54] Military law is particularly effective because it applies to the armed forces wherever they go. Thus, many of the jurisdictional loopholes available to civilians are not available to members of the military.[55] The UCMJ recognizes the traditional crimes of conspiracy, accessory after the fact, assault and murder.[56] Although the UCMJ does not explicitly recognize the crime of kidnapping, the government could still prosecute a case for conspiracy related to the participation of any military personnel in the abuse of detainees and the destruction of CIA interrogation tapes.[57] Furthermore, military personnel fall under the jurisdiction of the CAT and could be prosecuted by any signatory for any treatment of detainees which amounted to torture, as was the case in Italy,[58] Germany,[59] and the present investigation in Spain.[60]

The War Crimes Act of 1996[61] makes it a federal criminal offense for U.S. military personnel and all U.S. nationals to commit war crimes – which include "grave breaches" of the Geneva Conventions.[62] The Act also prohibits violations of common Article 3 (which provides standards for treatment of persons when a state is involved in non-international conflict), including "murder of all kinds, mutilation, cruel treatment and torture."[63] This prohibition thus applies to all detainees captured as a part of the U.S. "war on terror."

U.S. domestic liability for the forced disappearances of persons, the use of harsh interrogation techniques, and the destruction of CIA tapes may also apply via laws against criminal conspiracies contained in Title 18 U.S. Code. A criminal conspiracy is: "(i) an agreement between at least two parties (ii) to achieve an illegal goal (iii) where the parties possess knowledge of the conspiracy and with actual participation in the conspiracy and (iv) where at least one conspirator committed an overt act in furtherance of the conspiracy."[64]

To successfully prosecute a conspiracy case, the prosecution must establish the conspiracy and the underlying crime. The "extraordinary rendition" program

---

54   *Id.*

55   *Id.* at 190–91.

56   10 U.S.C. §877–934.

57   *Id.*

58   *See* Chapter 4, *The Practice of "Extraordinary Rendition" and the Use of "Black Sites" by the CIA. See also* Rachel Donadio, *Italy Convicts 23 Americans for C.I.A. Renditions*, N.Y. Times, Nov. 4, 2009.

59   Bruce Zagaris, *Germany Charges 13 CIA Operatives in el-Masri Rendition Probe*, 23 Int'l Enforcement L. Reporter 131 (April 2007); *No Justice for El-Masri: Germany Drops Pursuit of CIA Kidnappers*, Spiegel Online, Sep. 24, 2007.

60   *See* Dwyer Arce, *Paper Chase: Spain Judge Garzon Beginning Investigation of Suspected Guantanamo Torture*, Jurist, Jan. 31, 2010.

61   18 U.S.C. §2441.

62   *See* Geneva I, Aug. 12, 1949, 6 U.S.T. 3114, 75 U.N.T.S. 31, at art. 50; Geneva II, Aug. 12, 1949, 6 U.S.T. 3217, 75 U.N.T.S. 85, at art. 51; Geneva III, *supra* note 35, at art. 130; and Geneva IV, Aug. 12, 1949, art. 2, 6 U.S.T. 3516, 75 U.N.T.S. 287, at art. 147.

63   18 U.S.C. §2441 (c)(3).

64   18 U.S.C. §371 (2000).

approved by President Bush and executed by the CIA creates the possibility of charging all involved parties with conspiracy to kidnap. The secret Presidential authorizations to create CIA "black sites," as well as CIA compliance in the kidnapping, detention, and transfer of individuals to foreign countries for interrogation, establish circumstantial proof of the conspiracy to circumvent U.S. kidnapping laws. The major obstacle to proving the underlying crime, however, is the jurisdictional loophole in Title 18 governing kidnapping.[65] If the victims are kidnapped outside of the U.S. and transported to foreign countries, there may be an insufficient connection to U.S. territory and interstate commerce. However, if the conspiracy is committed within the U.S., it would give rise to U.S. jurisdiction if it is deemed criminal under U.S. law.

Another possible theory of criminal responsibility is that the Bush Administration and the CIA engaged in conspiracy to obstruct justice, through denying to a federal judge that the CIA interrogation tapes existed; refusing to hand over the tapes to defendants as potentially exculpatory evidence; and destroying the tapes. Obstruction of justice deals with protecting the integrity of proceedings before the federal judiciary and other government bodies:[66] The Omnibus Provision of §1503 proscribes any activity which interferes with the due administration of justice,[67] and §1503 explicitly prohibits the concealment, alteration, and destruction of subpoenaed documents.[68]

Admissions from the CIA would seem to establish proof of obstruction of justice. While on May 9, 2003, two Assistant U.S. Attorneys denied that any CIA interrogations were recorded when they were asked about it by District Court Judge Leonie Brinkema, CIA admissions prove that not only were the interrogations recorded, but that the tapes were not destroyed until 2005.[69] Either there is no information sharing between U.S. intelligence-gathering organizations and U.S. prosecutors, or the Assistant U.S. Attorneys purposely misled the judge as to the existence of the taped interrogations.

CIA Director Michael Hayden's admission that the tapes of the interrogations of Abu Zubaydah and Abd al-Rahim al-Nashiri were destroyed before Khalid Sheikh Mohammed's trial also provide proof of a conspiracy to obstruct justice. Because government preparation for Mohammed's trial continued for years, and most of the damaging information against Mohammed came from the interrogations of Abu Zubaydah and Abd al-Rahim al-Nashiri, it seems disingenuous for Hayden to claim the tapes were destroyed because they were

---

[65] 18 U.S.C. §1201.

[66] 18 U.S.C. §1501–1520.

[67] *See* Kimberley A. Schaefer & John S. Schowengerdt, *Obstruction of Justice*, 43 Am. Crim. L. Rev. 763 (2006).

[68] 18 U.S.C. §1503 (2000).

[69] *See* Majorie Cohn, *The Torture Tape Cover-up: How High Does It Go?* (Centre for Research on Globalization, Dec. 26, 2007); Mark Mazzetti, *CIA Destroyed Tapes of Interrogations*, N.Y. Times, Dec. 6, 2007.

not relevant to any "judicial inquiries."[70] A more plausible explanation is that the tapes contained evidence of harsh interrogation techniques that the CIA and the Bush Administration did not want released.

Furthermore, a prosecutor is required to turn over to a defendant any exculpatory evidence.[71] All three men in the trial alleged they suffered torture at the hands of the CIA and that they confessed as a result. Certainly those interrogation tapes would have provided exculpatory evidence to the defense. By destroying the tapes before the defense had a chance to view them, the prosecution severely limited available defenses.

As stated earlier, compartmentalization of issues cannot negate responsibility in a conspiracy.[72] To successfully prove conspiracy, the prosecution does not need to demonstrate that every member knew every detail of the conspiracy, but that members of the conspiracy knew "the essential nature of the plan and connections with it."[73] President Bush claimed he "has no recollection" of hearing about the existence or destruction of the CIA tapes prior to a briefing from Hayden.[74] However, Hayden claimed that relevant parties knew the information; for example, both House and Senate intelligence committee leaders were informed of the tapes and the CIA's intention to destroy them.[75] The conspiracy charge should prevail if knowledge or approval of the CIA's intent to destroy evidence could be imputed to members of the Bush Administration outside of the CIA.

Members of the Bush Administration could also be prosecuted for a conspiracy to commit assault.[76] Title 18 prohibits assaults by striking, beating, or wounding; with the use of a dangerous weapon; with the intent to commit murder; or with the intent to commit any felony other than murder.[77] Although the CIA interrogation techniques, as will be shown in graphic detail below, would satisfy the assault requirements, 18 U.S.C. §113 contains a jurisdictional requirement that may prevent prosecution of some party to such "enhanced interrogation" techniques. Any assault prosecuted under Title 18 must occur within U.S. maritime and territorial jurisdiction. Because the CIA often uses interrogation sites located in foreign countries, there may be an insufficient jurisdictional link to prosecute under this theory, at least for acts committed before the PATRIOT Act extended U.S. jurisdiction to U.S. bases abroad and to actions by U.S. citizens abroad.[78] Assault by striking, beating, or wounding

---

[70] Cohn, *The Torture Tape Cover-up, id.*

[71] Brady v. Maryland, 373 U.S. 83 (1963).

[72] Kotteakos v. U.S., 328 U.S. 750 (1946).

[73] Blumenthal v. U.S., 332 U.S. 539, 557 (1947).

[74] *See* Cohn, *Torture Tape Cover Up, supra* note 69.

[75] *See* Pamela Hess, *Hayden Says CIA Videotapes Destroyed*, Associated Press, Dec. 7, 2007.

[76] 18 U.S.C. §113 (2000).

[77] *Id.*

[78] Uniting and Strengthening America by Providing Appropriate Tools Required to Intercept and Obstruct Terrorism (USA PATRIOT) Act of 2001, Pub. L. No. 107–56, §804, 115 Stat. 272,

results in a maximum punishment of six months imprisonment and/or a fine, which is insufficient to bring a member of the military under Title 18.

The use of CIA "black sites" and "enhanced interrogation" techniques also subjects the Bush Administration to potential prosecution for conspiracy to commit torture. Under Title 18, torture is defined as an act committed by a person acting under the color of law specifically intended to inflict severe physical or mental pain or suffering (other than pain or suffering incidental to lawful sanctions) upon another person within his custody or physical control.[79] However, the statute also contains several potential loopholes. First, it requires intent. This higher standard of proof may be difficult to meet. Additionally, the requirement of "severe" pain or suffering allows the possibility to escape liability by arguing that any pain or suffering experienced by a detainee did not rise to the level of "severe." Finally, the Bush Administration could escape liability for any pain experienced by detainees who were handed over to foreign governments for harsh interrogations, because the statute requires that the harm occur while the detainee is in the custody of a U.S. official.[80]

Officials in the Bush Administration and the CIA may also be prosecuted under the Racketeer Influenced and Corrupt Organizations Act (RICO).[81] RICO's purpose is to eliminate organized crime,[82] but the Supreme Court has extended RICO's application to enterprises without profit motive.[83] Under §1962, the prosecution must prove that the defendant: "(i) through the commission of two or more acts constituting a pattern of racketeering activity; (ii) directly or indirectly invested in, maintained an interest in, or participated in, an enterprise; (iii) the activities of which affected interstate or foreign commerce."[84]

The requirement of two predicate acts of "racketeering activity" includes obstruction of justice and obstruction of criminal investigations.[85] As demonstrated, the Bush Administration obstructed justice through the use of illegal interrogation techniques to garner confessions; the suppression of potentially exculpatory evidence; the refusal of Assistant U.S. Attorneys to turn over evidence to a federal judge; and the destruction of CIA tapes. Government entities such as county prosecutor's offices have been found to constitute an enterprise under RICO.[86] Some courts require the enterprise itself affects

---

377 (2001) (codified at 18 U.S.C. §7(9)(A) (2001)); 18 U.S.C. §113 (2000).

[79] 18 U.S.C. §2340 (2000).

[80] 18 U.S.C. §2340 (2000).

[81] 18 U.S.C. §1961–68 (2000).

[82] *Id.*

[83] Nat'l Org. for Women v. Scheidler, 510 U.S. 249, 261 (1994).

[84] 18 U.S.C. §1962 (2000).

[85] 18 U.S.C. §1961(1)(B).

[86] *See* Ross Bagley, Dorian Hurley, & Peter Mancuso, *Racketeer Influenced and Corrupt Organizations,* 44 AM. CRIM. L. REV. 901 (2007); U.S. v. Goot, 894 F.2d 231, 239 (7th Cir. 1990).

interstate commerce[87] while other courts require only that the activities impact interstate commerce by impacting the victim.[88] There is potentially a RICO case against several members of the Bush Administration and the CIA, as well as charges for obstruction of justice under title 18 U.S.C.

5.4. CONSPIRACY TO COMMIT TORTURE

It appears that shortly after the events of 9/11, Vice President Cheney set up what could be called a working group of lawyers, the "war council," chosen to coordinate the "torture-enabling" policy in order to make the U.S. safer from future attacks like those which had occurred. Looking at this from a good faith perspective, it appears like a coordinated effort to make a bureaucracy work better for legitimate purposes. What is different between good administration and criminal conspiracy? At the beginning, we can assume a reasonable good faith belief that an effective security policy was necessary, but where does it end? Because government lawyers are trained as advocates, their mindset is not that of an independent legal advisor who advises on what can and cannot be done under the law. U.S. government lawyers see themselves as the advocates of their clients and look for loopholes and gaps in the law to exploit and sometimes they do not realize that they have gone a bridge too far. Obviously, passing the line between good faith error or even simple negligent error, and intentional conduct is something that is determined by the facts. People who engage in that type of conduct generally do not leave paper traces. They do not record their oral conversations or telephone conversations and they do not record their doubts. Instead, they usually take a very optimistic, positive, and enthusiastic view of what they are advocating, always trying to anchor it down to some presumptively valid legal argument and to some valid interpretations of legal precedents. The advocacy spirit stimulates in government lawyers what is popularly called the "pushing of the envelope," which can easily cross the red lines of the law. That may well be what occurred in the post-9/11 climate. It may have also been stimulated by the rewards of being a good team player. For government officials, particularly political appointees, to stand up against a powerful current emanating from the Vice President and laced with appeals to defend the nation, is not an easy undertaking. Only those with a strong moral compass can do that. In this case, there was a structural relationship between the government lawyers in the Vice President's Office, those in the DOJ, the DOD, and the Office of Legal Counsel of the President whose combination resulted in a policy gone wrong.

There were also meetings of the NSC Principals Committee who review policy and directly advise the President on national security issues. The

---

[87]   U.S. v. Nerone, 563 F.2d 836, 854 (7th Cir. 1977).
[88]   U.S. v. Juvenile Male, 118 F.3d 1344, 1349 (9th Cir. 1997).

Committee's members include the President, Vice President, Secretary of State, Secretary of Defense, the NSC Advisor, the Director of the CIA, and the Attorney General. The meetings were sometimes recorded, and when so, the tapes were held under the highest level of security classification. At other times, there was no recording; only minutes drafted by someone designated by the NSC Advisor who exercised caution in what was recorded in order to protect the Principals from potential legal responsibility. During the Bush Administration, there were several such meetings, whose few declassified minutes indicate that the topic of torture was addressed in one way or another, usually under the rubric of intelligence. What decisions the Principals made was not revealed in the declassified minutes, but what was revealed is that they were apparently all in agreement.

There was no dissenting position ever presented, even though Secretary Powell had publicly and within the DOS, as well as in communications with the CIA, expressed his belief in the applicability of the Geneva Conventions. However, the NSC Principals Committee, of which he was a member, backed the President in declaring that the Geneva Conventions did not apply to the newly established category of "unlawful enemy combatants." A reasonable inference may well be that the Secretary of State, who in other venues and contexts was strongly in support of the applicability of the Geneva Conventions, would not be likely to change his position when the question came before a meeting of the Principals Committee. This means that he either objected or voiced a contrary opinion which was not reflected in the minutes. If that were not the case and he acquiesced to the views of the other Principals, then he too would be accountable for the policy and practices that emerged. The Principals Committee either initiated or approved certain recommendations or measures brought to it by the National Security Council Advisor, then Condoleezza Rice, who subsequently became Secretary of State, based on requests or reports made to the NSC from various government agencies, which in this case would have been the DOJ, the DOD, and the CIA.

The role of Attorney General Ashcroft in the shaping of the torture policy is also in question.[89] The Attorney General is mandated to uphold the Constitution and the laws of the U.S. In fact, all Principals take an oath of office which includes this solemn obligation. All of the above, as well as their legal advisors, such as Yoo, Addington, Bybee, Gonzales, and Haynes,[90] are subject to potential conspiracy charges to commit torture under 18 U.S.C. 19 §371. In order to be found guilty of conspiracy under §371, it would have to be proven that two or

---

[89] The extent of Ashcroft's involvement is uncertain at this point. Although there is evidence that Ashcroft knew of what was happening at the time, such as excessive waterboarding, Jack Goldsmith has stated that Ashcroft was not involved in any decision-making about interrogation techniques, and was in fact kept out of these meetings. JACK GOLDSMITH, THE TERROR PRESIDENCY 24 (2007).

[90] GOLDSMITH, THE TERROR PRESIDENCY, *id.* at 24.

more people conspired to commit any offense against a given law and that one or more persons performed any act to give effect to the object of the conspiracy.[91] The law does not require that each member of the conspiracy commit an act but only that one member commits an overt act in furtherance of the conspiracy. Therefore, one memo by one member of the conspiracy furthering the objective of torture would constitute an overt act sufficient to find the group guilty of conspiracy. What would be left to prove is the specific intent of the co-conspirators, and that too is a question of fact which depends the evidence presented at trial. Proof of guilt is beyond a reasonable doubt, but reasonable grounds to believe that a conspiracy took place are sufficient to initiate an investigation and to initiate prosecution.

Title 18 U.S.C. §2340 defines torture as "an act committed by a person acting under the color of law specifically intended to inflict severe physical or mental pain or suffering upon another person within his custody or physical control."[92] Members of the U.S. government at Guantánamo Detention Center, Bagram Air Base, Abu Ghraib, and elsewhere carried out acts amounting to torture. These acts include, but are not limited to, waterboarding, placing a detainee with fear of insects in a box with an insect he believed was able to cause severe pain, severe beatings, the use of revving a power drill near a naked, hooded, and shackled detainee, and severe sleep deprivation.[93] As soon as a single act of torture is completed, the object of the conspiracy is achieved.

If found guilty of conspiracy to torture under 18 U.S.C. §371, the same actors can also be found guilty of the substantive crime of torture. In the landmark case *Pinkerton v. U.S.*, the Supreme Court held that acts done in furtherance of the conspiracy are attributable to all members of the conspiracy and each member of the conspiracy is responsible for the substantive offense committed by one in furtherance of the conspiracy.[94] In *Pinkerton*, there was no evidence that the defendant had participated directly in the commission of the substantive offense; however, there was ample evidence that the offenses were committed in furtherance of the existing conspiracy.[95] The defendant was convicted for the substantive offenses that he did not physically commit because the conspiracy he engaged in was trying to achieve the substantive acts. He was also convicted of conspiracy as a separate offense.

---

[91] 18 U.S.C. §371 (2000).

[92] 18 U.S.C. §2340.

[93] Special Review of Counterterrorism Detention and Interrogation Activities from September 2001- October 2003 by Office of the Inspector General of the CIA (May 7, 2004); Memorandum from Assistant Attorney General Jay S. Bybee for John Rizzo, General Counsel of the Central Intelligence Agency, memorandum on Interrogation of al Qaeda Operatives (August 1, 2002) [hereinafter Bybee Memo II].

[94] Pinkerton v. United States, 328 U.S. 640, 647 (1946).

[95] *Id*. at 645.

From 2001 through 2003, a legal "war council" consisting of at least Addington, Gonzales, Bybee, Flanigan, Haynes, and Yoo, regularly discussed the war on terror, and more importantly, interrogation techniques that were being used.[96] President Bush did not want any legal constraints from his advisors for his plans for the war on terror.[97] This was made clear through Cheney's legal advisor, Addington, who apparently was present at all or most of these meetings where interrogation was discussed.[98]

The group trusted their legal endeavor to John Yoo, an attorney in the Office of Legal Counsel and able to issue legal opinions extended to the entire Executive Branch.[99] The first act in furtherance of the purported conspiracy was Yoo's memorandum of Dec. 28, 2001 to Haynes advocating that U.S. federal courts would not be able to hear habeas corpus petitions of aliens held at Guantánamo Bay Detention Center.[100] This early memorandum demonstrates the purported conspiracy's intention to keep the detainees in a place where they would not be afforded the protection of legal review.[101] During the next three weeks, Yoo, Bybee, and Gonzales each wrote separate memoranda arguing that the Geneva Conventions did not apply to al-Qaeda or Taliban fighters.[102] The Gonzales memo specifically stated that not applying the Geneva Conventions to detainees would presumably reduce the chance of prosecution for their treatment, and would free the U.S. to treat detainees consistent with the Geneva Conventions "to the extent appropriate and consistent with military necessity" rather than having to adhere to the Conventions.[103] This position was advocated in spite of

---

[96] Lewis "Scooter" Libby was Chief of Staff of Vice President Cheney between 2001 and 2005. He was forced to resign after he was convicted of purjery in connection with his role and that of the Vice President's office in outing CIA agent Valerie Plame, whose husband, Ambassador Joseph Wilson, investigated the phony claims that Iraq purchased enriched uranium from Nigeria, as part of a plan to discredit him. This fabrication of evidence by Cheney's office was designed to reinforce the assumption that Iraq had weapons of mass destruction, thus justifying the U.S. invasion of that country. So far, Libby's name has not appeared in documents relating to the involvement of the the Vice President's "cabal" in the institutionalization of torture through the trickle-down effect described herein. However, the Vice President and his office's role in the falsification of information concerning Iraq is indicative of the pattern evidenced institutionalization of torture by the cabal.

[97] GOLDSMITH, THE TERROR PRESIDENCY, *supra* note 89, at 119.

[98] *Id* at 76–79.

[99] *Id.* at 23.

[100] Memorandum from John C. Yoo, Deputy Assistant Attorney General, to William J. Haynes II, General Counsel for Department of Defense on Possible Habeas Jurisdiction over Aliens Held in Guantanamo Bay, Cuba (Dec. 28, 2001).

[101] *Id.*

[102] Memorandum from John C. Yoo to William J. Haynes II on Application of Treaties and Laws to al Qaeda and Taliban Detainees (Jan. 9, 2002); Memorandum from Jay Bybee, Assistant Attorney General, to Alberto Gonzales and William Haynes on Application of Treaties and Laws to al Qaeda and Taliban Detainees (Jan. 22, 2002); Memorandum from Alberto Gonzales to President George Bush on Decision Re Application of the Geneva Convention on Prisoners of War to the Conflict with al Qaeda and the Taliban (Jan. 25, 2002).

[103] Gonzales Memo, *id.*

the protests by JAG attorneys and the DOS and submitted to President Bush who officially adopted it on February 2, 2002.[104] Whether Gonzales informed the President of the different legal interpretations made known to him is significant in determining whether representations made by Gonzales to the President were in furtherance of a conspiracy, or whether it was only bad legal advice.

Bybee wrote the final in a series of memoranda that laid the necessary legal foundation to cover torture on August 1, 2002. In this memorandum, Bybee concluded that in order to be found guilty of torture under 18 U.S.C. §2340, one would need to have the intent to cause pain as severe as organ failure and long-term mental harm.[105] Furthermore, Bybee provided an analysis of the intent required by the statute that would provide a defense for anyone who could be prosecuted under the statute. He advocated that one must have the specific intent to cause severe pain or suffering and that a good faith belief that one's conduct would not produce severe pain is sufficient to avoid being found guilty.[106] Bybee ended the memorandum by stating that even if one were to be prosecuted for torture, he or she would have a valid affirmative defense of necessity or self-defense.[107] He concluded by asserting that constitutionally the President's powers as Commander-in-Chief cannot be limited by Title 18 U.S.C. §2340.[108] This legal analysis is flawed, as recognized by numerous legal scholars and even by the OLC, who subsequently rescinded the memorandum in 2004.[109]

These memoranda taken together permitted, if not encouraged, torture while couching it in legal terms that had the appearance of legality. It is noteworthy that none of these memoranda addressed the relevant international conventions' intent and purposes. The legislative history of the CAT and Geneva Conventions were apparently not taken into account, nor were the writings of distinguished legal commentators who held differing views than those of Bybee. The fact that these memoranda did not take into account the position of the U.S. delegations who participated in the making of those conventions is particularly telling as to the lack of due diligence by those writing them. It is also telling as to their good faith belief that their memoranda represented what these conventions meant with respect to the definition of torture.

The positions of the Joint Chiefs of Staff, the services' JAGs, and the DOS Legal Advisor appear not to have been in agreement with the legal analysis provided by the OLC. Those who opposed the policy were subsequently kept out of meetings held "to plot legal strategy in the war on terrorism."[110] Those who

---

104   John Yoo, War by Other Means: An Insider's Account of the War on Terror 35 (2006).
105   *See* Bybee Memo I, *supra* note 31.
106   *Id.* at 174–175.
107   *Id.* at 207–212.
108   *Id.* at 214.
109   Goldsmith, The Terror Presidency, *supra* note 89, at 159.
110   Goldsmith, The Terror Presidency, *supra* note 89, at 22.

were excluded from future meetings because they were seen as obstacles that needed to have been overcome in order to advance the policy and practices of torture may be evidence of the deliberativeness of the purported conspiracy.[111]

In April 2002, a working group at the DOD was convened to discuss detainee interrogations in the war on terrorism. This working group accepted the legal analysis that had been provided in Bybee's memo of August 1, 2001, as the authority on which to base their recommendations.[112] Based on the prior memoranda, the group approved category I, II, and III interrogation techniques, although category III which included the harshest techniques was to be used on a case-by-case basis.[113] The working group's report also reiterates the defenses that Bybee had offered as protections in the possibility that charges were brought.[114] Members of the working group who objected to "harsh techniques" or who raised legal objections were shut out of future meetings.[115] It is clear that this group worked together to achieve the goal of providing legal cover for what can be deemed torture.

Methods of torture, including waterboarding, were each approved by the "war council" in several legal memoranda drafted between 2001 and 2003.[116] In an August 2002 memorandum, Bybee went through an analysis for ten requested category III techniques to be used on a detainee and approved each one, including waterboarding.[117] He then reiterated the possible defenses for torture and the unlikelihood that any charges would ever be made. Furthermore, at least Ashcroft and the OLC were aware that their memoranda were being used as authority to waterboard, and that it had been used on Abu Zubaydah 83 times, and on Khaled Sheikh Muhammad 183 times.[118] Bybee reassured the General Counsel for the CIA, John Rizzo, that the CIA was not in violation of the torture statute.[119]

The DOD working group on acceptable interrogation practices relied upon these memoranda as controlling authority.[120] Operators in the field also relied

---

[111]　Goldsmith, The Terror Presidency, *supra* note 89, at 22.

[112]　Department of Defense, *Working Group Report on Detainee Interrogations in the Global War on Terrorism: Assessment of Legal, Historical, Policy, and Operational Considerations* (April 4, 2003).

[113]　*Id.* at 346–347.

[114]　*Id.* at 302.

[115]　Carl Levin, U.S. Senator from Michigan, Senate Armed Services Committee Hearing (June 17, 2008).

[116]　*See* Bybee Memo II, *supra* note 93.

[117]　*Id.*

[118]　Special Review of Counterterrorism Detention and Interrogation Activities from September 2001- October 2003 by Office of the Inspector General of the CIA (May 7, 2004), at 45.

[119]　*See* Bybee Memo II, *supra* note 93. As noted by Jane Mayer, it appears that the Rizzo was "deeply involved in establishing the agency's interrogation detention and policies," a fact which led Senator Ron Wyden to put a hold on Rizzo's confirmation from Acting General Counsel to General Counsel. *See* Mayer, *The Memo, supra* note 43.

[120]　Carl Levin, U.S. Senator from Michigan, Senate Floor Speech on the Amendment to Establish an Independent Commission on Detainee Treatment, Nov. 4, 2005.

on these memoranda when making decisions about interrogations.[121] The CIA reprinted parts of Bybee's memo which approved techniques they were allowed to use in their own reports and materials, demonstrating the extent to which those committing the acts of torture relied on the law given to them by the DOJ.[122] Furthermore, when cases of interrogators who went beyond the scope of memoranda were referred to the DOJ, they were not pursued, sending a clear signal that anything goes.[123] Clearly, the "war council" wanted those conducting interrogations to rely on these memoranda, and ensured that they were acted upon by excluding any contrary opinions. Presumably, President Bush relied on the counsel being given to him by the OLC and those responsible for advising him, such as Gonzales.[124]

Although only one person's overt act is needed to find all involved guilty of conspiracy, here every actor worked in concert with others to achieve the common objective. There are some actors, however, who played a larger role than others. Yoo wrote "opinion after opinion approving every aspect of the administration's aggressive antiterrorism efforts. These opinions gave counter terrorism officials the comfort of knowing that they could not easily be prosecuted later for the approved actions."[125] The memoranda by Yoo, Bybee, Gonzales, and others that came out of the OLC were relied upon in the Executive branch and deemed the controlling authority for interrogations of detainees by those who carried out the practices of "enhanced interrogation" techniques. Both Addington and Gonzales had a responsibility of anticipating problems with the OLC memoranda, but they chose to look the other way when they favored the position of the "war council."[126] Gonzales was also instrumental in drafting the memorandum to President Bush arguing against DOS concerns and stating that the Geneva Conventions need not apply to those held in connection with al-Qaeda and the Taliban.[127] Each of these acts on its own is sufficient to show that an overt act was made by at least one member of the purported conspiracy. Cumulatively, the acts of all concerned when taken jointly, provide probable cause evidence of a purported conspiracy.

If it is established that the "war council" is guilty of conspiracy to commit torture, each member can then be tried under *Pinkerton* for each act of torture committed by interrogators.[128] In *Pinkerton*, the U.S. Supreme Court reasoned that a conspiracy which involves "deliberate plotting to subvert the laws,

---

[121]   GOLDSMITH, THE TERROR PRESIDENCY, *supra* note 89, at 158.

[122]   Special Review of Counterterrorism Detention and Interrogation Activities, *supra* note 118, at 15–23.

[123]   *Id.* at 42.

[124]   Interview by Martha Raddatz, *supra* note 96.

[125]   Special Review of Counterterrorism Detention and Interrogation Activities, *supra* note 118, at 23.

[126]   *Id.* at 170.

[127]   *See* Gonzales Memo, *supra* note 102.

[128]   *Pinkerton*, 328 U.S. 647.

educating and preparing the conspirators for further and habitual criminal practices" needs to be fully punished when finally discovered.[129] Therefore, even though it is not known that a single member of the "war council" was directly involved in the torture of a detainee, the fact that the interrogators relied upon the advice of the council, according to its plan, is sufficient to attribute the acts of torture to the individual members of the "war council" under *Pinkerton*. Each person, therefore, can be charged with conspiracy to commit torture and other substantive crimes.

5.5. THE RESPONSIBILITY OF PRIVATE CONTRACTORS ACTING ON BEHALF OF THE U.S. GOVERNMENT

Private contracting for military services has been used throughout U.S. history, but only recently has it been used to such a wide extent in every U.S. military deployment, with the promise of cost cutting.[130] Almost "no function of government is deemed more quintessentially a 'state' function than the military protection of the state itself."[131] Yet, contractors are being used not only for technology services, but also for long-term operational support.[132] For example, the private contracting firm CACI served alongside the military in Iraq and exercised control over uniformed troops and abused detainees.[133] No matter how

---

[129] *Id.* at 644.

[130] *See* P.W. SINGER, CORPORATE WARRIORS: THE RISE OF THE PRIVATIZED MILITARY INDUSTRY (2003); Laura A. Dickinson, *Public Law Values in a Privatized World*, 31 YALE J. INT'L L. 383, 395 (2006); Laura A. Dickinson, *Government for Hire: Privatizing Foreign Affairs and the Problem of Accountability Under International Law* (University of Connecticut School of Law Working Paper, 2005).

[131] *See* Dickinson, *Public Law Values in a Privatized World, id.* at 383, discussing that some scholars or privatization assume that the military is an area where privatization should not occur, citing Jody Freeman, *Extending Public Law Norms Through Privatization*, 116 HARV. L. REV. 1285, 1295, 1300 (2003). *See also* Clifford J. Rosky, *Force, Inc.: The Privatization of Punishment, Policing, and Military Force in Liberal States*, 36 CONN. L. REV. 879, 882–83 (2004).

[132] *See* Rebecca Rafferty Vernon, *Battlefield Contractors: Facing Tough Issues*, 33 PUB. CONT. L.J. 369, 377 (2004).

[133] Antonio M. Taguba, Major Gen., U.S. Dep't of the Army, *Article 15–6 Investigation of the 800th Military Police Brigade* (2004) [hereinafter Taguba Report], at 26, 38, and 48. *See* Seymour M. Hersh, *The General's Report: How Antonio Taguba, who investigated the Abu Ghraib scandal, became one of its casualties*, THE NEW YORKER, June 25, 2007, discussing how Taguba was forced into early retirement after his report. In addition to CACI, other private contracting firms such as Kellogg, Brown, and Root (earning $1.7 billion annually), assist the military in activities ranging from the military context to humanitarian aid and post-conflict restructuring. Dickinson, *Public Law Values in a Privatized World, supra* note 131, at 393. On July 22, 2004, CACI released a statement saying: "The report by the U.S. Army Inspector General has determined that all interrogators provided by the company satisfied the Army's statement of work criteria," which included its involvement in Abu Ghraib.

artful the contracts issued by the DOD have been, such private contractors are *de facto,* if not *de jure,* agents of the U.S. Government. This means not only that they can be held criminally and civilly responsible for actions which violate U.S. and international law, but also that their responsibility extends to the U.S. government under the agency relationship. Some of these private contractors were specifically contracted to provide "interrogation support and analysis work for the U.S. Army in Iraq" as well as "debriefing of personnel… intelligence report writing/quality control, and screening/interrogation of detainees at established holding areas."[134] Such contractors and the U.S. government are responsible for any crimes committed while they fulfilled these roles.

The use of private contractors in paramilitary operations, even when concluded in artful contractual terms, flies in the face of the International Convention against the Recruitment, Use, Financing and Training of Mercenaries, which prohibits the use of mercenaries whenever private contractors are used in a military, paramilitary, or supportive military capacity.[135] Thus, in and of itself, the use of such civilian contracted personnel in these capacities is a violation of international law.[136] While the U.S. is not a state party to the

---

[134] *See* Andre Verloy & Daniel Politi, *Contracting Intelligence: Department of Interior releases Abu Ghraib Contract* (Center for Public Integrity, July 28, 2004); CACI Int'l Inc. Work Order No. 000071D004. CACI had 31 interrogators in Iraq, of which 35 did not have training in interrogation policies or techniques. *Id.* On July 16, 2004, the Department of the Interior's Inspector General released a report noting that as part of a larger information technology contract, CACI's contract was outside of the original contract scope. *Id.* Agencies should not have been able to get work orders for interrogation or logistics from CACI. *Id.* "Only one out of the 11 orders awarded to CACI was determined to follow the original contract scope." *Id.*

[135] International Convention Against the Recruitment, Use, Financing and Training of Mercenaries, G.A. Res. 44/34, U.N. GAOR, 44th Sess., 72nd plen. mtg., U.N. Doc. A/RES/44/34 (Dec. 4, 1989). *See also* Special Rapporteur on Mercenaries Enrique Ballestros, Report on the Right of Peoples to Self-Determination and its Application to Peoples Under Colonial or Alien Domination or Foreign Occupation: Use of Mercenaries as a Means of Violating Human Rights and Impeding the Exercise of the Right of Peoples to Self-Determination, ECOSOC, U.N. Doc. E/CN.4/2004/15, at §67 (Dec. 24, 2003), discussing the difficulty of distinguishing between mercenary and private military contractors. However, apart from this Convention, there are no other international laws that directly prohibit or restrict the activities of private military contractors. *See* Juan Carlos Zartae, *The Emergency of a New Dog of War: Private International Security Companies, International Law, and the New World Disorder,* 34 STAN. J. INT'L L. 75 (1998); Maj. Todd Milliard, *Overcoming Post-Colonial Mytopia: A Call to Recognize and Regulate Private Military Companies,* 176 MIL. L. REV. 1 (2003); P.W. Singer, *War, Profits, and the Vacuum of Law: Privatized Military Firms and International Law,* 42 COLUM. J. TRANSNAT'L L. 521, 533 (2004); Ellen L. Frye, *Private Military Firms in the New World Order: How Redefining "Mercenary" can tame the "Dogs of War,"* 73 FORDHAM L. REV. 2607 (2005); Deven R. Desai, *Have your Cake and Eat it Too: A Proposal for a Layered Approach to Regulating Private Military Companies,* 39 U.S.F. L. REV. 825 (2005); William C. Peters, *On Laws, Wars, and Mercenaries: The Case for Courts-Martial Jurisdiction Over Civilian Contractor Misconduct in Iraq,* 2006 B.Y.U. L. REV. 367 (2006).

[136] While the Geneva Conventions clearly prohibit torture by the military, their applicability to non-state actors is less clear. *See* Dickinson, *Public Law Values in a Privatized World, supra* note 130, at 152. Also, the application of the CAT to the contractors used by the government for outsourcing torture remains ambiguous. *Id.,* at 398; CAT, *supra* note 35, art. 3. Although,

Convention, it has attempted to circumvent this limitation by claiming that private contractors do not engage in military activities, and therefore are not mercenaries. If that argument was valid, then it would also mean that the U.S. government could not be deemed to have committed a wrongful international act for which it could be liable under the international principles of state responsibility.[137]

There are also limitations under U.S. law for the employment of non-military personnel in military activities, and there are statutory limitations on contracting out to private persons or entities intelligence-related work within the province of the CIA. Nevertheless, private contractors have been engaged in both of these activities in Afghanistan. In March 2010, it was revealed that under an innocuous sounding "information-gathering program" the DOD set up a "network of private contractors in Afghanistan and Pakistan to help track and kill suspected militants."[138] The DOD official, Michael D. Furlong, hired contractors from private security companies that employed former CIA and Special Forces operatives. Furlong is currently under a DOD criminal investigation to discover the extent to which this private spy operation was a rogue operation.[139] This newly discovered information raises the question of whether the Bush Administration was engaging in the practice of torture and assassination by private contractors as part of its overall policy of violating international and U.S. law. Another question raised is whether the fact that DOD lawyers were able to artfully draft contracts which provided plausible deniability to the government and shifted responsibility to the private contractors sufficient to shield the government from civil responsibility and to shield the authors and executors of that policy from criminal responsibility as solicitors or aiders and abettors under Title 18 U.S.C. of the murder and torture of those persons who fell victim to the private contractors acting for the benefit of the U.S. government.

Because private contractors operate on U.S. military bases abroad and alongside the military, it is difficult to maintain that they are not dependent on accompanying personnel within the meaning of the UCMJ and therefore not responsible for war crimes under its provisions. In order to prevent this result,

---

Dickinson goes on to note that alternative legal accountability may exist under private law, such as tort claims. *Id.* at 400. Transparency and democracy can still provide an important check, as well as incorporating disciplinary measures into government contracts and internal institutional accountability. *Id.* at 388.

[137] Responsibility of States for Internationally Wrongful Acts, U.N. Gen. Assembly Resolution, U.N. Doc. G.A. Res. A/56/83 (12 Dec. 2001). *See* JAMES CRAWFORD, THE INTERNATIONAL LAW COMMISSION'S ARTICLES ON STATE RESPONSIBILITY (2002).

[138] Dexter Filkins & Mark Mazzetti, *Contractors Tied to Effort to Track and Kill Militants*, N.Y. TIMES, Marc. 15, 2010. This was first reported by this writer in his capacity as U.N. Independent Expert for Human Rights in Afghanistan. *See* U.N. Econ. & Soc. Council [ECOSOC], Comm. On Human Rights, *Report of the Independent Expert on the Situation of Human Rights in Afghanistan, M. Cherif Bassiouni*, §45, U.N. Doc. E/CN.4/2005/122 (Mar. 11, 2005).

[139] Filkins & Mazzetti, *id.*

the contracts between the DOD and these private enterprises are couched in legal terms that define the latter as independent contractors not subject to the military law. This also means that they are not subject to the command and control structure of the military on a given base, nor are they part of the structure of the DOD.[140] Instead, they operate pursuant to contracts administered by a special office under civilian control and are answerable to the civilian Secretary and Under-Secretary of Defense. Thus, a twist in contract law created a new category of operatives who may engage in military and paramilitary activities, but who are thought to remain outside military command and control and are therefore beyond the reach of the UCMJ.

A further problem with applying responsibility to private contractors under the UCMJ is that before 2007, it did not apply to contractors unless war was declared. However, the 2007 amendment to the UCMJ extended jurisdiction to include times of "declared war or a contingency operation."[141] Therefore, all acts by private contractors subsequent to this amendment are subject to the jurisdiction of the UCMJ.

The legal stratagem used by the Bush Administration to indemnify private contractors from responsibility (and thus to shield themselves from responsibility under the theory of agency) is akin to that of the corporate veil in business law. However, jurisprudence in corporate criminal responsibility has established that the corporate veil cannot be used to conceal conspiracies and crimes.[142] If the appropriate case were to be brought before a conscientious and courageous judge, it would be likely that this corporate veil would be lifted, and those belonging to the offending private contractors could be found subject to the UCMJ's jurisdiction as well as to Title 18 criminal jurisdiction for torture and conspiracy

---

[140] Until the 2007 amendment, UCMJ jurisdiction extended only to civilians who were with or accompanying armed force during a Congressionally declared war, which has only occurred five times in American history. *See* U.S. v. Averette, 19 USCMA 363 (1970), interpreting "war" in the UCMJ to mean declared war by Congress. Also, it covered civilian contractors, but they were rarely held accountable. 10 U.S.C. §802(a)(10). Additionally, "serving with or accompanying an armed force... [must be] not merely incidental to, but directly connected with or dependant upon, the activities of the armed forces or their personnel." U.S. v. Burney, 6 USCMA 776 (1956). *See also* Jordan J. Paust, *Above the Law: Unlawful Executive Authorizations Regarding Detainee Treatment, Secret Renditions, Domestic Spying, and Claims to Unchecked Executive Power*, 2 Utah L. Rev. 345, 398 (2007), at 387, citing War Declared Between Germany and the United States, Pub. L. No. 331–77, 55 Stat. 796 (1941); War Declared Between Japan and the United States, Pub. L. No. 328–77, 55 Stat. 795 (1941); Act of May 13, 1846, ch. XVI, 9 Stat. 9, 9–10; S.J. Res. 24, 55th Cong., 30 Stat. 738 (1898).

[141] John Warner National Defense Authorization Act, *supra* note 51; Jenny Mandel, *Military Justice Code Now Covers Some Contractors*, governmentexecutive.com, Jan. 9, 2007. The change was made by striking the word 'war' and adding 'declared war or a contingency operation.' Peter W. Singer, *The Law Catches Up to Private Militaries, Embeds*, Defense Tech (Jan. 4, 2007).

[142] John Decker, Illinois Criminal Law: A Survey of Crimes and Defenses 189–196, 197–227 (4th ed. 2006), discussing corporate crimes and conspiracy.

to commit torture. One civilian contractor has already been charged and found guilty for an assault on an Afghan detainee who died from his injuries.[143]

Civilian contractors may also face liability under Federal criminal law. A number of federal criminal statutes explicitly cover actions committed outside the territorial boundaries of the U.S., but nevertheless occur within the special or territorial jurisdiction of the U.S., including prohibitions against assault, manslaughter, murder, and torture.[144] The CAT prohibition against torture also applies to acts committed by private contractors outside the territorial jurisdiction of the U.S.[145]

Contractors could face further liability under the War Crimes Act.[146] The Act prohibits U.S. nationals and members of the U.S. Armed Forces from committing war crimes, defined as grave breaches of the Geneva Convention's Article 3.[147] Grave breaches include acts such as murder, torture, cruel or inhumane treatment, rape or taking hostages.

It should also be noted that the DOJ may hold contractors responsible under Title 18 pursuant to the Military Extraterritorial Jurisdiction Act (MEJA), which was adopted in 2000 to close the jurisdictional gap over civilians operating alongside military forces outside the U.S.[148] It applies only to acts which would be considered felonies in the U.S. and does not create any new offenses or punishments.[149] However, MEJA is dependent for its application on the procedural guidelines issued by the DOD in 2005.[150] Under these purposefully complex procedures, it has been impossible for the DOJ to prosecute any civilian contractor irrespective of what the crime may have been.[151] Part of the legal evasion scheme has also been to assign the interrogation of detainees, which includes the use of torture, to contractors operating under an award by another

---

[143] *See* John R. Crook, *Contemporary Practice of the United States*, 100 Am. J. Int'l L. 959 (2006), discussing the conviction of David Passaro, a former CIA contractor in federal court in Raleigh, North Carolina.

[144] Assault, 18 U.S.C. §113; manslaughter, 18 U.S.C. §1112(b); murder, 18 U.S.C. §111(b); and torture, 18 U.S.C. §114. Torture in 18 U.S.C. §114 is defined by 18 U.S.C. §2340.

[145] 18 U.S.C. §2340 and 18 U.S.C. §2340(A).

[146] 18 U.S.C. §2441.

[147] *See* Geneva I, art. 50; Geneva II, art. 51; Geneva III, art. 130; and Geneva IV, art. 147, *supra* note 62.

[148] *See* Military Extraterritorial Jurisdiction Act of 2000, 18 U.S.C. §3261 (2000) [hereinafter MEJA].

[149] *Id.* MEJA gives U.S. courts jurisdiction over crimes that are committed on military installations by U.S. citizens or foreign nationals, including those who are subject to the UCMJ, and those civilians employed by or accompanying the military. 18 U.S.C. §3261(a) (2000).

[150] *See* U.S. Dep't of Def., Instruction 5525.11, Criminal Jurisdiction Over Civilians Employed by or Accompanying the Armed Forces Outside the United States, Certain Service Members, and Former Service Members (Mar. 3, 2005).

[151] Scot J. Paltrow, *Justice Delayed: Budget Crunch Hits U.S. Attorneys' Offices*, Wall St. J., Aug. 31, 2007. Only a U.S. Attorney can prosecute the offense, and must use his own resources to do so.

federal agency other than the DOD. As originally drafted, MEJA and the DOD regulations mentioned above would not apply to such non-DOD contractors. However, in 2004, MEJA was amended to expand jurisdiction to non-DOD federal employees or contractors working in support of DOD missions.[152] It should also be noted that MEJA only applies to crimes committed outside the special maritime and territorial jurisdiction of the U.S.,[153] which, presumably, would make it applicable to such locations as Guantánamo Bay, Afghanistan, Iraq, and anywhere else that interrogations are conducted in a manner that may be deemed torture. However, as noted above, the PATRIOT Act expanded the special maritime and territorial jurisdiction of the U.S. to include the premises of "…any United States government missions or entities in foreign states, including the buildings, part of the buildings, and land appurtenant or ancillary thereto, or used for the purposes of these missions or entities, irrespective of ownership."[154] This means that all the locations mentioned above can be deemed part of the territorial jurisdiction of the U.S., and are therefore no longer outside the territorial jurisdiction of the U.S. for purposes of MEJA's jurisdictional application. Through this jurisdictional gimmick, civilian contractors evade any and all forms of criminal responsibility for their conduct abroad, no matter what crimes they may commit.

The PATRIOT Act may also have an impact on the applicability of Title 18 criminal offenses and the CAT provisions discussed above. However, if an act of torture occurs within the U.S., responsibility may be allocated via federal assault, battery and murder statutes. In addition, a person seeking redress under applicable federal statutory or constitutional tort law could bring a tort claim.[155]

Any abuse of detainees by contractors would also be covered under the Detainee Treatment Act of 2006, which was subsequently amended by the Military Commissions Act of 2006. It provides that:

(1) In general
No individual in the custody or under the physical control of the United States Government, regardless of nationality or physical location, shall be subject to cruel, inhuman, or degrading treatment or punishment.

---

[152]   18 U.S.C. §3261 (2000), *amended by* 18 U.S.C. §3267 (Supp. IV 2004).

[153]   18 U.S.C. §3261 (2000).

[154]   Uniting and Strengthening America by Providing Appropriate Tools Required to Intercept and Obstruct Terrorism (USA PATRIOT) Act of 2001, Pub. L. No. 107–56, §804, 115 Stat. 272, 377 (2001) (codified at 18 U.S.C.A. §7(9)(A) (2001)) (emphasis added). I am grateful to Lt. Col. Michael Newton for sharing his views with me about MEJA. There has only been one prosecution under MEJA, a spouse of a military policeman who stabbed her husband to death was convicted and sentenced to eight years. *See* David Rosenzweig, *Air Force Wife Guilty in Spouse's Fatal Stabbing; A Moreno Valley Woman is Convicted in the 2003 Slaying on a Military Base in Turkey*, L.A. Times, Oct. 16, 2004, at B3.

[155]   *See* Michael John Garcia, CRS Report RL32438, *UN Convention Against Torture (CAT): Overview and Application to Interrogation Techniques* (Congressional Research Service, Library of Congress, Jan. 25, 2006), at 12.

(2) Cruel, inhuman, or degrading treatment or punishment defined
In this subsection, the term "cruel, inhuman, or degrading treatment or punishment" means cruel, unusual, and inhumane treatment or punishment prohibited by the Fifth, Eighth, and Fourteenth Amendments to the Constitution of the United States, as defined in the United States Reservations, Declarations and Understandings to the United Nations Convention Against Torture and Other Forms of Cruel, Inhuman or Degrading Treatment or Punishment done at New York, December 10, 1984.
(3) Compliance
The President shall take action to ensure compliance with this subsection, including through the establishment of administrative rules and procedures.[156]

While it should be clear from the analysis above that the UCMJ may apply to contractors, it has never been applied in this manner, with the exception of one case in 1957, *Reid v. Covert*.[157] However, since the time of *Reid*, there have been changes in the military's reliance on private contractors, and there is an increasing mix between military and civilian criminal justice systems.[158] Nevertheless, impunity for private government employees who tortured prisoners seems ongoing. The DOJ decided not to prosecute over 20 cases that had been referred to it between 2005 and 2006, citing evidentiary problems and difficulty in grasping the legal issues which existed in the DOJ legal opinions that authorized harsh tactics in interrogations.[159]

In September 2007, employees of Blackwater USA (currently known as Xe Services LLC), a private contractor hired to provide armed security forces for the U.S., opened fire in Al Watahba Square in Baghdad, a crowded public area, and killed 17 people.[160] In response to the shooting, the House of Representatives voted overwhelmingly to adopt a bill that brings all U.S. government contractors in the Iraq war zone under U.S. criminal jurisdiction.[161] The law, which passed, did not have retroactive authority over past conduct by contractors, but it required FBI investigation into incidents. In December 2007, the families of 22 Iraqis who were injured and three who were killed in the Al Watahba Square shooting filed a civil lawsuit in federal court against Blackwater and its founder, Erik Prince, alleging Prince, Blackwater, and its affiliated companies violated the

---

[156]   42 U.S.C. §2000dd (2006), amending the Detainee Treatment Act of 2005.

[157]   Reid v. Covert, 354 U.S. 1 (1957). *See also* P.W. Singer, *Frequently Asked Questions on the UCMJ Change and Its Applicability to Private Military Contractors* (Brookings Institution, Jan. 12, 2007).

[158]   *See* U.S. v. Scheffer, 523 U.S. 303 (1998), recognizing this increasing trend of convergence.

[159]   *See* David Johnston, *U.S. Inquiry Falters on Civilians Accused of Abusing Detainees*, N.Y. TIMES, Dec. 19, 2006.

[160]   *See* James Glanz & Alissa Rubin, *Blackwater Shooting 'Murder,' Iraq Says*, N.Y. TIMES, Oct. 8, 2007.

[161]   *See* David M. Herszenhorn, *Bill Applies U.S. Law to Contractors*, N.Y. TIMES, Oct. 5, 2007. In 2003, after the U.S. invasion of Iraq, Paul Bremer issued a decree granting immunity to American military and civilian personnel from criminal prosecution in Iraqi courts, preventing Iraqis from asserting jurisdiction. *Id.*

federal Alien Tort Statute in committing war crimes, and that they should be liable for claims of assault and battery; wrongful death; intentional and negligent infliction of emotional distress; and negligent hiring, training and supervision under state law. The lawsuit sought compensatory damages for death, physical, mental, and economic injuries, as well as punitive damages, and was settled in January 2010.[162] In December 2009, a criminal case against former Blackwater personnel was dismissed in a 90-page opinion by Judge Richard M. Urbina of the U.S. District Court for the Eastern District of Virginia, stating that the "government's mishandling of the case requires dismissal of the indictment against all the defendants."[163] The decision enraged Iraqis, and in attempt to quell political tensions, Vice President Biden announced in Baghdad that the DOJ would appeal the dismissal.[164]

In another case, in September 2009, the D.C. Court of Appeals dismissed a five year old civil suit against two American military contractors, CACI International and L-3 Communications Holdings' Titan unit.[165] Both companies were being sued by Iraqi victims of torture for mistreatment and torture committed at Abu Ghraib; however, the Court dismissed the claim saying that the companies had immunity as government contractors.[166] The opinion went on to say that even if the companies did not have immunity as government contractors, the case would still have been dismissed because the conduct alleged, which included eye gouging, spearing, roping naked prisoners together by their genitals, beatings with an electric stick, sodomy, and urinating on prisoners, was not sufficient to meet the standard of torture.[167]

Although the Federal Tort Claims Act explicitly exempts "contractors with the United States" from the definition of "federal agency,"[168] the Court interpreted the statute to apply to military contractors because contract employees are "under the direct command and exclusive operational control of the military chain of command."[169] The contractors, however, were not under the control of the military, not in the military chain of command, and not subject to military jurisdiction, as the dissenting opinion makes clear.[170] Because the military contractors are private actors, they are subject to civil liability, a point

---

[162]   Abtan, et al. v. Prince et al., Second Am. Compl., No. 1:09CV617-TSE/IDD, 1:09CV1048-TSE/IDD (E.D. Va. 2009); *In re:* Xe Services Alien Tort Litigation, Order dismissing case pursuant to agreed settlement, No. 1:09CV617 (E.D. Va 2010).

[163]   U.S. v. Slough *et al.*, 2009 U.S. Dist. LEXIS 121809 (D.C. Cir. 2009). *See* Charlie Savage, *Charges Against Blackwater Guards Dismissed in Iraq Killings*, N.Y. TIMES, Dec. 31, 2009.

[164]   *See* Ernesto Londoño, *Justice Department to Appeal Dismissal of Blackwater Indictment*, WASH. POST, Jan. 24, 2010.

[165]   *Torture Case Against Iraq Contractors Dismissed*, N.Y. TIMES, Sep. 12, 2009.

[166]   *Id.*

[167]   Haidar Muhsin Saleh, et al., v. Titan Corp. and CACI Internt'l Inc., 580 F.3d 1 (D.D.C. 2009).

[168]   FEDERAL TORT CLAIMS ACT, 28 U.S.C. §§1346(b), 2671–2680.

[169]   *Saleh et al.*, 580 F.3d at 8.

[170]   *Id.* at 15.

which the DOD has stated.[171] Furthermore, neither the Executive branch nor the DOD has defended the contractors' conduct or suggested that it was used for any military purpose which furthers the evidence that the contractors should not be granted immunity as a military extension. By granting immunity, the courts are effectively removing consequences for military contractors who cannot be held accountable under the military or with immunity, under civil law.

The U.S. has the obligation to provide the right to compensation for victims of torture under Art. 14 of the CAT.[172] In utilizing a defense of sovereign immunity to cover the military contractors, the Court is effectively taking away the victims' right to compensation. Furthermore, in meeting the obligation to provide compensation, the U.S. cannot affect the victims' rights to compensation under national law. In this particular case, the plaintiffs had the opportunity to collect compensation under the Army Claims Service for any legitimate claims and therefore the Court stated that plaintiffs were not denied a remedy.[173] The CAT provides, however, that the victims are entitled to redress, which is arguably not just monetary compensation, and furthermore that the victims are still entitled to the right to compensation under national law.[174] In compliance with the CAT, the victims should be entitled to full redress and compensation which does not supersede the victims' rights under U.S. national law. Those rights were removed in granting immunity to the contractors. It is important to note that although in this particular circumstance there may have been an alternative route for monetary compensation, that factor was not considered in the Court's analysis when determining to grant sovereign immunity. This case sets the dangerous precedent of providing contractors with immunity, a precedent which will remain even when other forms of civil remedies and damages may be found not to apply to private contractors.

Recent revelations have shown that private contractors working for the CIA have also engaged in various aspects of "extraordinary rendition." This led CIA Director Leon Panetta to cancel its contracts with Xe Services. It appears from this information that the CIA was disingenuous in claiming lack of knowledge about what private contractors were doing in connection with torture.[175] Xe Services was heavily integrated with CIA operations in Iraq beyond the security detail in its contract, including transportation flights of detainees, raids, and operational decisions pertaining to missions conducted by the CIA.[176] The expanded, and illegal, role of Xe Services affirms the legal vagueness in the law

---

[171]   *Id.*

[172]   CAT, *supra* note 35, at Art. 14.

[173]   *Saleh et al.*, 580 F.3d.

[174]   CAT, *supra* note 35, at art. 14.

[175]   James Risen & Mark Mazzetti, *Blackwater Guards Tied to Secret C.I.A. Raids*, N.Y. Times, Dec. 11, 2009.

[176]   *Id.*

as applicable to private contractors.[177] As Xe Services acted in a governmental capacity, carrying out activities that only government employees may legally perform, it is necessary to determine what law would hold these actors accountable.

5.6. PROSECUTION OF LOW-LEVEL EXECUTORS AS AVOIDANCE AND IMPUNITY FOR SENIOR OFFICIALS

It is not uncommon in situations involving governments or large organizations where there is a top-down effect of a policy in violation of the law, to have low-level executors prosecuted in lieu of senior officials. This technique accomplishes two objectives. The first is to assuage public demand for justice and the second, to provide de facto impunity for the seniors. However, token prosecutions seldom mean appropriate penalties for those found guilty. Token sentences are also the norm. Time and again throughout history this has occurred, and in this situation it has occurred in the U.S.

Many of the two hundred persons estimated to have died in U.S. military custody were never autopsied.[178] This could have been the result of negligence, but presumably the autopsies were skipped to avoid investigations into the deaths and to further proceedings in accordance with the UCMJ if such autopsy reports confirmed the conclusions of the death certificates that indicated death as a result of physical mistreatment. Although the word torture is not specifically used in these death certificates, by inference (sometimes more clearly stated than others), the deaths were attributed to trauma caused by severe beatings and organ failures.[179] Even so, not a single case has been charged under the war crimes provisions of the UCMJ, and not a single case has been investigated, charged, or prosecuted as torture or as a homicide resulting from intentional infliction of serious bodily harm amounting to torture.[180]

Of the many abuses which occurred at Guantánamo, Afghanistan, Iraq, and various "black sites" around the world, those committed at Abu Ghraib have had more investigations and prosecutions than the others, most likely in response to

---

[177] *Id.*

[178] *See* STEVEN H. MILES, OATH BETRAYED: TORTURE MEDICAL COMPLICITY AND THE WAR ON TERROR (2006), at Part II, discussing the failure to make accurate death certificates, death certificates at the time of death, or even death certificates at all, as well as medical personnel involvement in interrogation, homicide, neglect, and silence.

[179] *See* Hina Shamsi, *Command's Responsibility: Detainee Deaths in U.S. Custody in Iraq and Afghanistan* (Human Rights First, Feb. 2006).

[180] *See* Carolyn Patty Blum, Lisa Magarrell, & Marieke Wierda, *Prosecuting Abuses of Detainees in U.S. Counter-terrorism Operations* (International Center for Transitional Justice, Nov. 2009), at 21–23.

the intense international outcry over the publication of the now infamous photos depicting detainees naked and bleeding, hooded and attached to wires, dragged by leashes, and wincing in fear from attack dogs.[181] Soldiers also appeared in these photos, often smiling, laughing, and giving "thumbs up" hand signs. Ultimately, 14 people were held to some form of account through the military justice system. Seven soldiers pleaded guilty for charges including aggravated assault, battery, dereliction of duty, maltreatment of detainees, conspiracy, and commission of indecent acts, with sentences ranging from six months in prison and dishonorable discharge, to eight years in prison.[182] Six others were tried under court martials for charges including aggravated assault, maltreatment of prisoners, conspiracy to maltreat and frighten prisoners, and dereliction of duty. Of these, five were convicted with sentences ranging from reduction in rank to ten years in prison, fines, and dishonorable discharges.[183]

The fifth to stand before a court martial was Lt. Col. Stephen Jordan, the former head of the interrogation center at Abu Ghraib. He was charged with dereliction of duty, lying to investigators, failure to obey lawful orders, and mistreatment of prisoners.[184] Jordan was acquitted of all serious charges, and the one conviction for failure to obey orders was later dismissed on the grounds that Maj. Gen. George Fay, the officer who investigated the Abu Ghraib tortures and

---

[181]   In late April 2004, the television news program *60 Minutes II* first broke the story of abuses at Abu Ghraib, followed shortly thereafter by an investigative piece in *The New Yorker* magazine, relying heavily on the Taguba Report, *supra* note 133. *See* Seymour M. Hersh, *Torture at Abu Ghraib*, THE NEW YORKER, May 10, 2004. *See also* PHILIP GOUREVITCH & ERROL MORRIS, STANDARD OPERATING PROCEDURE (2008), which chronicles the complete story of the abuses at Abu Ghraib, including lengthy interviews with the soldiers who served there.

[182]   *See* Blum, Magarrell & Wierda, *Prosecuting Abuses of Detainees in U.S. Counter-terrorism Operations, supra* note 180, at 21. Those who pleaded guilty include: Specialist Javal Davis, who received a demotion, a sentence of six months in prison, and a discharge for bad conduct; Sgt. Lynndie England, who received a sentence of three years in prison and a dishonorable discharge; Staff Sgt. Ivan Frederick, an NCO, who received a sentence of eight years in prison; Specialist Roman Krol, who received a reduction in rank, a sentence of ten months in prison, and a bad conduct discharge; and Specialist Jeremy Sivits, who received a reduction in rank, a sentence of one year in prison, and a bad conduct discharge.

[183]   *See* Blum, Magarrell & Wierda, *Prosecuting Abuses of Detainees in U.S. Counter-terrorism Operations, supra* note 180, at 22. Those prosecuted include: Specialist Charles Graner, who was sentenced to ten years in federal prison (the longest sentence of anyone prosecuted for abuses at Abu Ghraib) and a dishonorable discharge; Specialist Sabrina Harman, who was sentenced to six months in prison and a bad conduct discharge; Sgt. Michael Smith, who was sentenced to 179 days in prison and a bad conduct discharge; Specialist Megan Ambuhl, who received a reduction in rank and loss of half a month's pay; and Sgt. Santos Cardona, who was sentenced to 90 days of hard labor and a reduction in rank and pay. Sgt. Cardona was transferred to another unit after serving time at Fort Bragg, re-promoted to Sergeant, and was on his way back to Iraq to train Iraqi police officers before news of his return leaked to the media and he was reassigned. *See* Adam Zagorin, *An Abu Ghraib Offender's Return to Iraq is Stopped*, TIME, Nov. 2, 2006.

[184]   *See* Blum, Magarrell & Wierda, *Prosecuting Abuses of Detainees in U.S. Counter-terrorism Operations, supra* note 180, at 22; *Officer to Face Court-Martial on 8 Charges in Abu Ghraib Abuse*, N.Y. TIMES, Jan. 13, 2007, at A9.

who interrogated Jordan, did not have a record of having given him his *Miranda* warnings. Assuming that to be the case, it should not have led to a dismissal of the charges, but merely to the inadmissibility to any confession he may have made. However, the presiding judge dismissed the charges outright, even though the prosecution could have proven the tortures by other means.[185]

All of those who were prosecuted for abuses at Abu Ghraib raised the defense of superior orders, however, no officer was court martialed for command responsibility for any acts that could be deemed torture, including those for which enlisted persons and NCOs have either been disciplined or court martialed. Col. Thomas Pappas, head of the Military Intelligence brigade at Abu Ghraib, was ultimately relieved of his command after receiving an administrative punishment of a fine of $8,000 under Art. 15 of the UCMJ for two instances of dereliction of duty.[186] He also received a General Officer Memorandum of Reprimand, which ultimately ended his military career. However, he served no time in prison for the abuses which occurred under his command. Brig. Gen. Janis Karpinski, Commander at the time of the 800th Military Police Brigade which oversaw Abu Ghraib, was relieved of her command and later demoted to the rank of Colonel, although the demotion was only partially related to the abuses at Abu Ghraib.[187] Karpinski was replaced by Maj. Gen. Geoffrey Miller, the former commander of "Camp X-Ray" at Guantánamo Bay, who was alleged to have brought the torturous "enhanced interrogation" techniques to Abu Ghraib in the first place.[188]

Two others in command in Iraq during the Abu Ghraib abuses not only were never reprimanded, let alone prosecuted or even investigated for their alleged roles, but were eventually promoted. Maj. Gen. Barbara Fast, the former head intelligence official in Iraq, was promoted to command the Army's Intelligence Center at Fort Huachuca in Arizona. Maj. Gen. Walter Wodjakowski, the former deputy commander of U.S. forces in Iraq, later became the head of the Army's Infantry Training School at Fort Benning in Georgia.[189] Lt. Gen. Ricardo Sanchez, who held the top military command post in Iraq at the time of the Abu Ghraib abuses, relinquished his post in June 2004 and went on to command the V Corps in Germany until his retirement from the military in 2006.

A court martial of a non-commissioned officer (NCO) for the killing of Iraqi General Abed Hamed Mowhoush at al-Qaim by means of stuffing him in a sleeping bag and sitting on his chest during interrogation until his death, resulted

---

¹⁸⁵ *See* David Wood, *Counts Dropped in Abu Ghraib Abuse Case*, CHI. TRIB. (Aug. 21, 2007).

¹⁸⁶ *See Abu Ghraib U.S. Colonel Reprimanded*, BBC NEWS, May 12, 2005.

¹⁸⁷ *See* Robert Burns, *Army Demots a One-Star General Accused of Dereliction in Prisoner Abuse Scandal*, ASSOCIATED PRESS, May 6, 2005.

¹⁸⁸ *See* Sewell Chan & Jackie Spinner, *Guantanamo Bay Chief Takes Over After Shameful Jail Abuse*, SYDNEY MORNING HERALD, May 1, 2004.

¹⁸⁹ *See* Blum, Magarrell & Wierda, *Prosecuting Abuses of Detainees in U.S. Counter-terrorism Operations, supra* note 180, at 22.

in a conviction.[190] Although Chief Warrant Officer Lewis Welshofer was found guilty of negligent homicide and negligent dereliction of duty, crimes which carry a modest penalty of up to three years and three months in prison, the NCO faced no jail time, and was restricted to his barracks for 60 days and payment of $6,000 in fines.[191] The charge of negligent homicide is much less severe than the charges he should have received under the UCMJ's articles of war for having killed a prisoner of war in his custody.

Information regarding inquiries and courts martial on the grounds of detainee abuse remains sparse. Even once a case is discovered, further investigation is difficult because none of the branches of the military keep statistics regarding the grounds for courts martial and other forms of disciplinary proceedings. One might argue that the relatively limited number of inquiries, disciplinary proceedings and courts martial, estimated at over 120 cases, was intended to present to the public what is tantamount to yet another fig leaf of plausible deniability by the highest level of civilian and military leadership.[192]

---

[190]   *See* Eric Schmitt, *Army Interrogator is Convicted of Negligent Homicide in 2003 Death of Iraqi General*, N.Y. TIMES, Jan. 23, 2006; Shamsi, *Command's Responsibility*, *supra* note 179, at 6–9. Another military jury convicted a Corporal of kidnapping and conspiring to murder, but acquitted him on murder charges. *See* Allison Hoffman, *Marine Convicted of Conspiracy*, ASSOCIATED PRESS, Jul. 7, 2007. Also, on July 7, 2007, two army soldiers were charged with premeditated murder, but no officers. *See* Robert H. Reid, *Two U.S. Soldiers Charged With Murder in Iraq*, ASSOCIATED PRESS, July 7, 2007.

[191]   *Id.*

[192]   The exact number of investigations and courts martial of military personnel engaged in conduct that can generally be described as torture is unknown, because information is not made public unless the DOD elects to do so. From publicly released information originating with the DOD, there have been no general courts martial of officers for any acts which can be generally described as torture which has been occurring in Iraq, Afghanistan, Guantánamo Bay, and other locations.

One rather telling, if not shocking, reason that research in this area is limited is that the DOD does not maintain any available statistics on disciplinary proceedings and courts martial. While some of the information is available at the level of each branch of services, it is usually classified in accordance with the charge or outcome. Thus, it is possible to know that a certain number of members of a given division of the army of a given core, but it would be almost impossible save for examining the record of each case to connect a case to certain facts. Anyone trying to research the number of investigations, courts martial, and determinations of the two above, will not be able to find that information by references for example to Abu Ghraib or torture. A diligent researcher may find that there have been disciplinary proceedings for conduct "unbecoming an officer" but short of looking at the record, one cannot find whether it is related to mistreating a POW in Iraq. This is the technique employed by military and the DOD in general to avoid being embarrassed by such data. Consequently, any data cited here would describe from media reports and DOD Press Releases or statements, not being indicative of the number of cases or of the facts.

In another case, federal prosecutors sought the death penalty against a former soldier in the Army who was charged with raping a teenage Iraqi girl then shooting her and her entire family inside their home. U.S. v. Steven Green, No. 5:06-CR-19-R (W.D. KY 2009). In March 2006, five U.S. soldiers carried out the gang rape and subsequent killing of a young Iraqi girl and her family at a location near the village of Al-Mahmudiyah, South of Baghdad, in Iraq.

The limited number of investigations and disciplinary proceedings give the public the impression that when abuse is discovered, the civilian and military leadership carry out their legal obligations to investigate and prosecute. However, in none of these cases, except for a handful of disciplinary actions, did the investigations and inquiries go above those immediately involved and upwards into the chain of command. Those held responsible were usually enlisted personnel and NCOs at the bottom of the ladder. There is no known case where an officer was court martialed for dereliction of duty or on the basis of command responsibility. To date, those in the upper levels of the chain of command have been spared the ignominy of investigation and discipline.

Perhaps if the military justice system had been more thorough in the Vietnam era when *United States v. Calley* was decided, the current system of military justice would be more fair and efficient.[193] The 1968 My Lai Massacre of more than 500 innocent civilians resulted only in Lieutenant Calley's prosecution and conviction, which was followed by a Presidential pardon by President Richard Nixon.[194] Calley's immediate superior, Captain Medina, was acquitted; and the regimental commander, Colonel Henderson, received only administrative discipline.[195] Even in Calley's case, the court martial charges were not proffered under the UCMJ's Articles of War.

The law of command responsibility entails that when military commanders in the chain of command issue orders or are aware of the practices of torture, and yet fail to prevent the commission of such crimes, they are personally responsible.[196] The same applies when they discover the crimes and fail to investigate and prosecute those responsible for the deeds – including those in the chain of command if the evidence warrants it.[197] The law of command

---

Steven Green had been discharged from the army for a psychiatric disorder before the charges were brought. As he was not a member of the armed forces, he appeared before a civilian court, the U.S. District Court for the Western District of Kentucky, Paducah Division. On May 7, 2009, the jury found him guilty of rape and murder. On May 21, 2009, Green was spared the death penalty as the jury could not reach a unanimous agreement on the necessary penalty. As a result, he received a life sentence without parole at formal sentencing on September 4, 2009. Concerning the four other soldiers involved in the crimes, three pleaded guilty in court-martial proceedings: Spc. James P. Barker and Sgt. Paul E. Cortez were sentenced to 90 and 100 years respectively, while Pfc. Bryan L. Howard, who had prior knowledge of the plans, was sentenced to 27 months in jail. The fourth, Pfc. Jesse V. Spielman, was convicted by a military jury and sentenced to 110 years. On November 30, 2009, Green filed an appeal with the U.S. Court of Appeals for the Sixth Circuit, challenging the law used to convict him.

[193] U.S. v. Calley, 48 C.M.R. 19 (1973); Calley v. Callaway, 519 F.2d 184 (5th Cir. 1975). *See also* THE MY LAI MASSACRE AND ITS COVER-UP: BEYOND THE REACH OF THE LAW (Joseph Goldstein et al. eds., 1976); Jordan J. Paust, *My Lai and Vietnam: Norms, Myths and Leader Responsibility*, 57 MIL. L. REV. 99 (1972).

[194] *Id.*

[195] Medina v. Resor, 43 CMR 243 (1971). *See also* Paust, *My Lai and Vietnam, supra* note 193.

[196] *See* BASSIOUNI, CRIMES AGAINST HUMANITY, *supra* note 20.

[197] Mark Swanner, a CIA official who interrogated an Iraqi detainee at Abu Ghraib, is believed to have been charged with homicide by a confidential report of the CIA Inspector General. *See*

responsibility also imposes upon commanders the obligation to prevent recurrences of the violations.

The obligation to investigate and prosecute should certainly not be conditioned upon the public's discovery of violations. As seen clearly with regard to Abu Ghraib, few charges were brought against any known violators within the military prior to the horrifying pictures becoming public on American television. In fact, it appears that senior officers who investigated prison conditions in Guantánamo Bay, Afghanistan, and Iraq, such as Maj. Gen. Taguba,[198] all reported in one way or another that torture or something similar was taking place *before* the horrible state of affairs at Abu Ghraib came to light.[199] These reports were mostly classified. The civilian and military commanders who ordered the classifying of these reports therefore had notice of the violations prior to the Abu Ghraib media scandal; because of this, they are themselves responsible, first, for failure to act in the face of these reports, and second, for concealing the reports to prevent legal action in keeping with the requirements of the law.

The command influence, which is believed to have filtered down from the highest echelons of the DOD, not only allowed the practice of torture, but also encouraged it through laxity of command oversight. It permeated the military establishment in the form of disincentives for those officers who would not allow or encourage such illegal practices.[200] Meanwhile, it seems clear that some persons were offered incentives for abandoning criticism of "enhanced

---

Mayer, *A Deadly Interrogation, supra* note 24. It is reported that this information was sent for possible criminal charges to Paul McNulty, the U.S. Attorney for the Eastern District of Virginia – the location of CIA headquarters – but nothing has been acted upon. In October 2005, President Bush nominated McNulty to the position of Deputy Attorney General.

[198] *See* Hersh, *The General's Report, supra* note 133.

[199] *See* Anthony R. Jones & George R. Fay, *Investigation of Intelligence Activities at Abu Ghraib* (Aug. 2004); Inspector Gen., U.S. Dep't of the Army, Detainee Operations Inspection, The Mikolashek Report (July 21, 2004); Taguba Report, *supra* note 83; Donald J. Ryder, Report on Detention and Corrections Operations in Iraq (Nov. 2003); James R. Schlesinger, U.S. Dep't of Defense, Final Report of the Independent Panel to Review DOD Detention Operations 80 (2004). *See generally* MARK DANNER, TORTURE AND TRUTH: AMERICA, ABU GHRAIB, AND THE WAR ON TERROR (2004); SEYMOUR M. HERSH, CHAIN OF COMMAND: THE ROAD FROM 9/11 TO ABU GHRAIB (2004); Diane Marie Amann, *Abu Ghraib*, 153 U. PA. L. REV. 2085 (2005).

[200] As mentioned earlier, Brig. Gen. Jane Karpinski was demoted to Colonel after the Abu Ghraib scandal. Karpinski in several interviews reported that she was targeted to take the fall not only because she was a reserve officer, but also because she was a woman. While it is not possible to make the connection between Karpinski's demotion and its impact on other women in the military, it is nonetheless noteworthy as reported in the Alberto Mora memo that Capt. Jane Dalton, Legal Advisor to the Chairman of the Joint Chiefs of Staff, and Lt. Col. Diane Beaver, apparently failed to take positions opposing torture and/or practices similar to torture. A pattern of command influence and/or intimidation can therefore be seen at different levels. *See* Mora Statement, *supra* note 43; *see also Abu Ghraib Whistleblower Testifies About Government Retaliation Before Congress*, 84 U.S. LAW & SECURITY DIGEST, Feb. 17, 2006.

interrogation" techniques, as in the case of now Maj. Gen. Jacoby, whose report on Afghanistan was made at the time he was Brigadier General.[201] It is believed that his originally drafted report was at least critical of the interrogation techniques conducted there, but that he subsequently amended it. The report was classified and never released, and the author was promoted to Major General and assigned to a post in Alaska.

Some active military personnel, such as Capt. Ian Fishback, demonstrated courage in revealing the existence of torture practices to their superiors. In his case, when his superiors failed to act, he went public with his knowledge and revealed it to Congress.[202] Regrettably, there are too few officers who have done so.

By the standards of command responsibility, either under IHL or under the UCMJ, those in the chain of command up to and including the Secretary of Defense, or, for that matter, the President and the Vice President, may have committed international crimes as well as crimes under the laws of the U.S. Whether they are responsible is a question that may never be answered unless justice establishes it. However, there are certainly enough questions by now that any further action in support of the policy and practices leading to torture cannot be answered by claims of ignorance.

The prosecution of low level persons, mainly enlisted personnel and NCOs, serves only as a way to placate public opinion and for the DOD and Bush Administration senior officials to claim that justice was diligently pursued. As stated above, not a single officer has been court-martialed for torture abuses, and not a single civilian has been charged with a crime relating to torture; and not a single government official who helped shape the policy of permissible torture has been investigated, let alone charged with a crime under U.S. law. Not a single person in the list of senior officials which appears at the beginning of the book has been investigated, let alone prosecuted.

5.7. NUREMBERG: A PRECEDENT FOR THE LEGAL RESPONSIBILITY OF PROFESSIONALS

5.7.1. INTRODUCTION

Violations of the prohibition against torture aided by morally and legally distorted advice in furtherance of national security or other nationalistic aims

---

[201] A United Nations report refers to the Jacoby report. *See Report of the Independent Expert on the Situation of Human Rights in Afghanistan, supra* note 138. Jacoby's promotion to Major General and command assignment in Alaska was not publicized in the same way as other promotions. *See* DOD News: General Officer Announcements, Oct. 29, 2004.

[202] Letter From Ian Fishback, Captain, U.S. Dep't of the Army to Senator John McCain (Sept. 16, 2005), *reprinted in A Matter of Honor,* Wash. Post, Sept. 28, 2005, at A21.

are not new to history. Throughout history, widespread and systematic human rights abuses, including genocide, have almost invariably been founded on rationalizations of national security, the need to defend one's society, and the alleged threat of another group or people.[203]

What makes ordinary people do wrong or evil things is not only because of their personal proclivity to do so; it is also conditioned by the environment they operate in, and, more particularly, the group pressures to which they may be subjected. Thus, it is a combination of dispositional, situational, and systemic factors. Even though criminal responsibility in the U.S. is almost entirely based on the personal factors of the individual actor, the law nonetheless provides some recognition of situational and systemic failures, if for no other purpose than mitigation of punishment. However, these considerations are different in the national criminal law than in situations of mass criminality. The U.S. faced that situation in what is called the Subsequent Proceedings to the Nuremberg Trial after WWII.

In these proceedings, the U.S. assumed the prosecution of 12 major cases involving a number of defendants. Each one of these cases dealt with a systemic phenomenon leading to mass criminality. Two of these cases are relevant to this study. One was regarding judges and lawyers in the Ministry of Justice who subverted the law to achieve the political goals of the Nazi regime's anti-Semitic goals by justifying discriminatory laws against Jews, and who distorted legal processes and procedures to make it all appear as perfectly legal. The other case, also involving a number of defendants, dealt with the doctors and health officials who carried out the policies of unlawful human experimentation. In both cases, the defendants – professionals who took oaths to their respective professions to uphold certain ethical standards – claimed that ethical standards and oaths were not legally binding, and that they were following superior orders. The U.S. as the prosecuting authority took the opposite position, namely that professional oaths and ethical standards of those belonging to such professions as law and medicine are far more than abstract moral platitudes because they are the condition which allows such professionals to have certain legal and other benefits in society; and, that no defense of obedience to orders should apply to such professionals when the order is clearly in violation of their legal and ethical responsibilities.[204]

These two cases were selected by the U.S. to prosecute because of their moral significance. They reveal how power systems (such as a chain of command) exert a direct and pervasive top-down dominance and influence, which creates a multiplier effect that produces mass criminality. Morally it shows how more

---

[203]   *See* SAMANTHA POWER, "A PROBLEM FROM HELL": AMERICA AND THE AGE OF GENOCIDE (2003); and more particularly for the description of the socio-psychological phenomenon of environmental factors impacting collective and individual behavior, PHILIP ZIMBARDO, THE LUCIFER EFFECT: UNDERSTANDING HOW GOOD PEOPLE TURN EVIL (2007).

[204]   For the rejection of that defense *see* KEIJZER, DINSTEIN, GREEN, and MÜLLER-RAPPARD, *supra* note 20.

pernicious this trickle-down effect can be when the agents of this systemic policy are members of professions held in high esteem by society. The credibility of members of legal and medical professions – being well established in society precisely because of their high professional standards and status recognized by law and in public perception – makes their practices likely to be publicly accepted and followed. But the lessons of these post-Nuremberg principles, which the U.S. wanted the world to learn, were lost on the Bush Administration and on those in the legal and medical professions when they violated their ethical codes of professional responsibility.

5.7.2. THE "JUSTICE CASE"

In *United States v. Alstoetter*, which is popularly known as the *Justice Case*, it was clearly established that jurists must uphold their legal obligations, which includes their moral and ethical professional obligations, and must not allow their efforts to serve as a shield for the commission of crimes.[205] The *Justice Case* dealt with senior officials in the German Ministry of Justice who were career judges, prosecutors, and officials who used their legal talents to make sure that the various Nazi laws and regulations were couched in proper legal form and that legal processes and procedures were such that these laws could not be challenged in court. In so doing, they helped to give a valid legal appearance to what was under any other circumstances surely to be considered invalid. The American government lawyers who sought to couch in proper legal terms the resort to torture – either when it was committed directly by U.S. agents, or indirectly, by outsourcing it through "extraordinary rendition"[206] – by giving a semblance of a valid legal status to Guantánamo and other legal limbo categories (like "enemy combatants"), have in some respect acted similarly to those who at that time were in the German Ministry of Justice.

In 1998 the German Ministry of Justice revisited the *Justice Case* and published a three-volume work entitled *In the Name of the German People: Justice and National Socialism*.[207] These volumes emphasize the importance of the rule of law and its connection to democracy, publishing pictures and documents depicting the evolution of the erosion of the rule of law and the corruption of

---

[205]   U.S. v. Alstoetter et. al., 3 T.W.C. 1 (1948) [hereinafter the *Justice Case*]. The *Justice Case* charged 16 defendants with "judicial murder and other atrocities which they committed by destroying law and justice." INGO MULLER, HITLER'S JUSTICE: THE COURTS OF THE THIRD REICH 271 (Deborah Schneider trans., 1991).

[206]   *See* M. CHERIF BASSIOUNI, INTERNATIONAL EXTRADITION: UNITED STATES LAW AND PRACTICE (3d ed. 2007).

[207]   THE FEDERAL MINISTRY OF JUSTICE, IN THE NAME OF THE GERMAN PEOPLE: JUSTICE AND NATIONAL SOCIALISM (Werbedruck Zunkler: Bielefeld 1998); THE FEDERAL MINISTRY OF JUSTICE, IN THE NAME OF THE PEOPLE: ABOUT JUSTICE IN THE COUNTRY OF THE SED (Documents, Research Guide, Catalog) (Anderson Nexo GmbH: Leipzig 1994).

justice. What it reveals is a pattern of behavior whereby government lawyers were in some way co-opted by political processes to achieve political goals of the executive branch. In Nazi Germany, the judges were selected on a political basis, swore a political oath of alliance to the Fuehrer, and considered themselves part of the political system designed to achieve the political goals of the regime. Jurists, whether judges, prosecutors or government attorneys, were expected to carry out official policy. They were not the guardians of the law; whatever oath they may have sworn to uphold the constitution and laws of the country were subordinated to the directions of their political bosses. This was the slippery slope which ultimately led German government jurists to justify the racial laws aimed at Jews and others that the National Socialist Party developed, ironically at Nuremberg, in 1936 and thereafter. Later, politically appointed judges found these laws to be in conformity with whatever was left of the concept of the Constitution and higher laws. Prosecutors enforced these laws, leading first to discrimination; then to the expropriation of property, followed by deportation, reduction of persons into slave labor; and finally to the wholesale physical extermination of persons on the basis of their race or religion. Once the jurists were no longer the guardians of the legality of the law and its lawful processes, there was nothing to stop these and other atrocities, including unlawful human experimentation and torture.[208] The legal profession crumbled under the weight of the Nazi regime's power.

The pattern that was followed by the Nazi regime is in some ways strikingly similar to the pattern followed post-9/11 by the Bush Administration. Though by no means is this analogy intended to equate the two situations, nor to accuse those jurists in the U.S. of criminal activity, because only a thorough and fair investigation can reach this conclusion. The analogy is intended to highlight systematic influences. The pattern which developed in the Bush Administration started with a campaign of fear and intimidation, using the power of the Executive branch to reward those who would advance its agenda and punish those who would not. The pattern also includes a gradualist approach of slowly unraveling legal concepts and disaggregating them as well as compartmentalizing. Using different governmental agencies to develop a legal basis for torture, and then devising mechanisms for its implementation; relying on ambiguities and confusion; all of these tactics tended to produce an overall outcome of a policy promoting torture. Whether this outcome is the result of a conspiracy, or a coincidental concert of action, can only be discovered through a thorough and complete investigation.

The many examples of state-sponsored abuses of power in recent history show that one of the techniques employed is to require different people to do

---

[208] *See* The Nazi Doctors and the Nuremberg Code: Human Right in Human Experimentation (G.J. Annas & M.A. Grodin eds., 1992). *See also* Robert Jay Lifton, The Nazi Doctors: Medical Killing and the Psychology of Genocide (1986).

different things at different times and places, so that each can have the belief that their limited conduct is not related to a greater whole, thus disaggregating parts of the conduct in such a way that each segment, each part, appears lawful without regard to the unlawful entirety. For example, the manufacturers of gas chambers designed to exterminate the Jews and then burn them without a trace could proceed with the belief that their products had a lawful purpose. Those in the railroad who transported prisoners also had no reason to believe they were doing anything unlawful, just as those who installed the gas chambers could have believed that they were for a lawful, utilitarian purpose. It was only when human beings were put into them at places like Auschwitz that the horror became obvious.

The possibility that the pattern could be repeated is precisely the reason why the German Ministry of Justice extensively documented the decline of the rule of law in Nazi Germany on the 50th anniversary of the *Justice Case*. It wanted to remind those entrusted with a public duty that their profession requires them to uphold the constitution and the laws, not only in the formal legal sense, but in respect to an overarching concept of legality, with the aim of providing moral legal counsel.

Similarly, the greatest contribution of the *Justice* and *Nazi Doctors* cases described below is to remind those who are a part of these professions – the legal and medical professions, each of which has an established ethics code and structure for ethical oversight – that they are entrusted with more than legal and professional responsibilities and that they also have a moral obligation that goes to the spirit of legality, and not merely its form. These lessons of the past are not only instructive in the case of the Bush Administration's actions post-9/11, but they should also instruct the legal and medical professions as a foundation for their future professional responsibilities and obligations.

What follows are excerpts of the *Justice Case* judgment, which represent the pronouncements by the judgment – and which, by analogy, can be applicable to American jurists who enabled the policy of torture described in this book. The American judges sitting in Nuremberg in the *Justice Case* held:

> The doctrine that judges are not personally liable for their judicial action is based on the concept of an independent judiciary administering impartial justice. Furthermore, it has never prevented the prosecution of a judge for malfeasance in office. If the evidence cited supra does not demonstrate the utter destruction of judicial independence and impartiality, then we 'never write nor no man ever proved'. The function of Nazi courts was judicial only in a limited sense. They more closely resembled administrative tribunals acting under directives from above in a quasi-judicial manner.

> In operation the Nazi system forced the judges into one of two categories. In the first we find the judges who still retained ideals of judicial independence and who

administered justice with a measure of impartiality and moderation. Judgments which they rendered were act aside by the employment of the nullity plan and the extraordinary objection… The defendants contend that they were unaware of the atrocities committed by Gestapo in concentration camps. This contention is subject to serious question… This Tribunal is not so gullible as to believe these defendants so stupid that they did not know what was going on. One man can keep a secret, two men may, but thousands never…

Under any civilized judicial system [Defendant Oswald Rothaug] could have been impeached and removed from office or convicted of malfeasance in office on account of the scheming malevolence with which he administered injustice…

The evidence conclusively shows that in order to maintain the Ministry of Justice in the good graces of Hitler… defendants who joined in this claim of justification took over the dirty work which the leaders of the State demanded, and employed the Ministry of Justice as a means for exterminating the Jewish and Polish populations, terrorizing the inhabitants of occupied countries, and wiping out political opposition at home. That their program of racial extermination under the guise of law failed to attain the proportions which were reached by the pogroms, deportations, and mass murders by the police, is cold comfort to the survivors of the "judicial" process and constitutes a poor excuse before this Tribunal. The prostitution of a judicial system for the accomplishment of criminal ends involves an element of evil to the State which is not found in frank atrocities which do not sully judicial robes… We are under no misapprehension… We believe that [Defendant Schlegelberger] loathed the evil that he did, but he sold that intellect and that scholarship to Hitler for a mass of political pottage and for the vain hope of personal security.[209]

The movie *Judgment at Nuremberg* popularized these proceedings and presented Spencer Tracy playing the role of the judge who presided over the three-judge panel (all Americans), confronting otherwise distinguished and learned German judges and jurists charged with conspiring and aiding and abetting in the commission of "crimes against humanity."[210] The Iowa judge was bewildered and perplexed as to how it was possible for such distinguished German jurists to sidestep the law and overlook their moral, ethical, and legal obligations in order to serve a repressive regime.[211] Was career advancement so much of an inducement? Was ambition that powerful? Were their consciences that flawed? Was their regime so wicked and vengeful that they dared not oppose its morally and legally wrongful wishes? Was intimidation so pervasive that no one dared to oppose?[212]

---

[209] The *Justice Case, supra* note 205.

[210] JUDGMENT AT NUREMBERG (Metro-Goldwyn-Mayer Inc., 1961).

[211] *Id.*

[212] In the movie *Judgment at Nuremberg* Spencer Tracy's character says while rendering his judgment from the Bench:

   [The Defendant's] record and his fate illuminate the most shattering truth that has emerged from this trial. If he and all of the other defendants had been degraded perverts; if all of the

In *The Justice Case*, the American judges unanimously concluded that:

> Defendants are charged with crimes of such immensity that… [t]he charge, in brief is of that of conscious participation in a nationwide government-organized system of cruelty and injustice, in violation of the laws of war and of humanity, and perpetrated in the name of law by the authority of the Ministry of Justice and through instrumentality of the courts. The dagger of the assassin was concealed beneath the robe of the jurist.[213]

The American military tribunal in the subsequent proceedings considered in the *Justice Case* the proposition that Germans had a traditional history of judicial independence and of separation between the Executive and Judicial branches. Given this history, it was even more damning that lawyers and judges gave in to executive dictates. In the U.S., one therefore must assume that the well-established constitutional doctrine of separation of powers, which distinguishes between the prerogatives of the executive and judicial branches, as well as the history of judicial independence of the U.S., would emphasize the responsibility of those within the American legal system of their legal and ethical responsibilities.

What the German jurists did and what to some extent the Guantánamo trials before the Military Commissions did is reminiscent of the trial of Alice before the King and Queen of the deck of cards. The Queen of Hearts said:

> "Sentence first – verdict afterwards," said the Queen of Hearts.
> "Stuff and nonsense," said Alice loudly.
> "Hold your tongue!" said the Queen.
> "I won't," said Alice.
> "Then off with her head," the Queen shouted at the top of her voice.
> "Who cares for you," said Alice. "You're nothing but a pack of playing cards."[214]

Just as compartmentalization is used as a way of involving a large number of persons in the commission of unlawful conduct without their realization, or as a

---

leaders of the Third Reich had been sadistic monsters, then these events would have no more moral significance than an earthquake or any other natural catastrophe. But this trial has shown that under a national crisis, ordinary, even able and extraordinary men, can delude themselves into the commission of crimes so vast and heinous that they beggar the imagination. How easily it can happen. There are those in our own country too that today speak of the protection of country, of survival. A decision must be made in the life of every nation, at the very moment when the grasp of the enemy is at its throat; then it seems that the only way to survive is to use the means of the enemy, to wrest survival on what is expedient, to look the other way. Only, the answer to that is survival as what? A country isn't a rock; it's not an extension of one's self. It's what it stands for. It's what it stands for when standing for something is the most difficult.

Id. I am indebted to Professor Michael Scharf for this quote.

[213] *See* MULLER, HITLER'S JUSTICE, *supra* note 205.

[214] LEWIS CARROLL, ALICE'S ADVENTURES IN WONDERLAND 128 (1865).

way of giving them a false belief in the benign nature of their acts, governmental abuse of power seeks to make unlawful conduct appear to be banal or trivial.[215] This is accomplished by manipulating public perceptions. This is a different manipulation than enhancing fears, which would tend to justify the violation. Instead, it is a way of portraying things that misrepresents them to the public. The sum total of these techniques of conditioning public opinion, misinforming it, leading it to accept as benign that which is not, also has another purpose: namely to enhance public apathy indifference. That way, there is less resistance or opposition to these abuses of power by states.[216]

5.7.3. THE NAZI DOCTORS' CASE

Standards for the conduct of medical and healthcare professionals in the context of military service were established during the trials of Nazi doctors following World War II in what is now known as the Nuremberg Code.[217] A few years after Nuremberg, the World Medical Association developed and adopted the International Medical Code of Ethics which proscribes doctors' duty to their patients and ethical obligations. A 1975 revision of the Code, known as the Tokyo Declaration, specifically prohibits doctors from participating in, providing knowledge for, or condoning the practice of torture.

As part of the U.S. war on terror, some doctors have been complicit in torture, in contravention of both professional rules and international ethical principles.[218]

---

[215] See HANNAH ARENDT, EICHMANN IN JERUSALEM: A REPORT ON THE BANALITY OF EVIL (1963).

[216] See M. Cherif Bassiouni, *Perspectives on International Criminal Justice*, 50 VA. J. INT'L L. 269 (2010).

[217] United States v. Brandt (The Medical Case), *in* 2 TRIALS OF WAR CRIMINALS BEFORE THE NUREMBERG MILITARY TRIBUNALS UNDER CONTROL COUNCIL LAW NO. 10, 171–297 (1947). *See also* THE NAZI DOCTORS AND THE NUREMBERG CODE, *supra* note 208; LIFTON, THE NAZI DOCTORS, *supra* note 208; Mathew Lippman, *War Crimes Prosecution of Nazi Health Professionals and the Contemporary Protection of Human Rights*, 21 T. MARSHALL L. REV. 11, 50 (1995); Mathew Lippman, *The Nazi Doctors Trial and the International Prohibition on Medical Involvement in Torture*, 15 LOY. L.A. INT'L & COMP. L.J. 395 (1993); George J. Annas & Michael A. Grodin, *Medical Ethics and Human Rights: Legacies of Nuremberg*, 3 HOFSTRA L. & POL'Y SYMP. 111 (1999); M. Cherif Bassiouni et al., *An Appraisal of Human Experimentation in International Law and Practice: The Need for International Regulation of Human Experimentation*, 72 J. CRIM. L. & CRIMINOLOGY 1597 (1981).

[218] *See* Steven Miles, *Medical Ethics and the Interrogation of Guantánamo 063*, 7 AM. J. BIOETHICS 4 (2007), describing the teams of psychologists and psychiatrists who developed interrogation strategies to exploit the detainee's "emotional and physical strengths and weaknesses"; MILES, OATH BETRAYED, *supra* note 178, at 54, discussing the teams of psychologists and psychiatrists who reviewed the medical records of the prisoners to select the approach to interrogation. Additional controversial behavior of the psychologists and psychiatrists was information used to exploit other interrogation techniques, and suggesting rationing cleaning supplies, concealing death certificates, and causes of death. *Id.* at 45, 54, 56. *See also* Steven H. Miles, *Abu Ghraib: Its Legacy for Military Medicine*, 362 LANCET 725, 728 (2004); Andrew Sullivan,

Medical personnel who participate in detainee interrogations violate medical ethics as defined by the American Medical Association, the United Nations, the World Medical Association and the Istanbul Protocol. Despite these explicit obligations to the contrary, medical personnel have engaged in the mistreatment of prisoners.

These ethical, professional, and legal guidelines prohibited doctors and nurses from aiding and abetting in torture. In 1982, the General Assembly adopted the "Principles of Medical Ethics relevant to the role of health personnel, particularly physicians, in the protection of prisoners and detainees against torture and other cruel, inhuman or degrading treatment or punishment."[219] Principle 2 states: "It is a gross contravention of medical ethics, as well as an offence under applicable international instruments, for health personnel, particularly physicians, to engage, actively or passively, in acts which constitute participation in, complicity in, incitement to or attempts to commit torture or other cruel, inhuman or degrading treatment or punishment."[220] In relation to interrogation procedures, Principle 4 states: "It is a contravention of medical ethics for health personnel, particularly physicians: To apply their knowledge and skills in order to assist in the interrogation of prisoners and detainees in a manner that may adversely affect the physical or mental health or condition of such prisoners or detainees and which is not in accordance with the relevant international instruments."[221]

Detainees at Guantánamo participated in organized hunger strikes starting in 2002.[222] These hunger strikes were protests over indefinite detentions, uncertain futures and deplorable living conditions.[223] Military officials responded by force-feeding and forcibly administering intravenous fluids to the hunger strikers, and also by placing the strikers in isolation.[224] The administration of these life-saving treatments was often performed inhumanely. Large tubes were forcibly inserted into a detainee's nose down to their stomach without any anesthesia or sedatives.[225] Declassified notes regarding medical treatment at Guantánamo reveal that military officials would reuse NG tubes among detainees without any sanitation in front of Guantánamo physicians.[226] Sometimes blood and stomach bile from the previous detainee was still visible as the tube was inserted into another detainee.[227] None of the physicians intervened.

How Doctors Got into the Torture Business, TIME, June 23, 2006; Emily A. Keram, *Will Medical Ethics Be a Casualty of the War on Terror?* 34 J. AM. ACAD. PSYCHIATRY 6 (2006); Leonarde S. Rubenstein & Stephen N. Xenakis, *Doctors Without Morals*, N.Y. TIMES, Mar. 1, 2010.

[219] U.N. Doc. A/Res/37/194 (Dec. 18, 1982).

[220] *Id.* Principle 2.

[221] *Id.*

[222] *See* OLSHANSKY, DEMOCRACY DETAINED, *supra* note 31, at 106.

[223] *Id.* at 106–09.

[224] *Id.* at 107–10.

[225] *Id.* at 111.

[226] *Id.*

[227] *Id.*

Often medical procedures, such as the administration of intravenous medication or fluids, were administered by inexperienced medical personnel, resulting in painful, swollen veins from numerous failed attempts at locating appropriate veins.[228]

Medical examinations and interviews of eleven former Guantánamo detainees by Physicians for Human Rights showed that physicians had monitored interrogations and provided medical information to interrogators who participated in torture, and that such physicians made no attempt to stop the abuse.[229] Each of the eleven detainees indicated that they were given injections or medication without their consent, and medical procedures were performed on them against their will.[230] It was also reported that:

> health information was made available routinely to behavioral science consultants and others who were directly responsible for designing and implementing interrogation strategies. Not only did interrogators have access to medical records, but… psychiatrists and psychologists have been part of a strategy that employs extreme stress, combined with behavior-shaping rewards, to extract actionable intelligence from resistant captives.[231]

At least one psychiatrist and one psychologist were part of the Guantánamo Behavioral Science Consultation Team (BSCT). BSCT would prepare psychological profiles for use by interrogators and would sit in on interrogations and provide feedback to interrogators.[232]

The American Medical Association Code of Medical Ethics with respect to interrogations forbids physicians from participating in interrogations because the physician's role is that of a healer, not an interrogator.[233] The Code further prohibits physicians from monitoring interrogations with the intention of

---

228   *Id.*

229   *Broken Laws; Broken Lives: Medical Evidence of Torture by U.S. Personnel and Its Impact* (Physicians for Human Rights, June 2008). *See also Experiments in Torture: Evidence of Human Subject Research and Experimentation in the "Enhanced" Interrogation Program* (Physicians for Human Rights, June 2010).

230   *Id. See also* International Committee of the Red Cross, *Report of the ICRC on the Treatment by the Coalition Forces of Prisoners of War and Other Protected Persons by the Geneva Convention in Iraq During Arrest, Internment, and Interrogation* (Feb. 2004).

231   Donald H.J. Hermann, *Prisoners of War: The Role of Psychologists and Psychologists in Interrogation and Torture* 5 (Sept. 10, 2008) (unpublished paper, University of Rochester Medical Center)(on file with author). *See also* M. Gregg Bloche & Jonathon Marks, *Doctors and Interrogators at Guantánamo Bay*, 353 New Eng. J. Med. 6 (2005).

232   *See* Bloche & Marks, *Doctors and Interrogators at Guantánamo Bay, id.* at 6–8. On July 7, 2010, The Center for Justice and Accountability filed a complaint with the New York Office of the Professions against Dr. John Leso for his role in "enhanced interrogation" techniques at both Guantánamo and Abu Ghraib.

233   *See Opinion 2.068 Physician Participation in Interrogation, in* Code of Medical Ethics (American Medical Association, 2006).

intervening as an interrogator and obligates them to report any interrogations they believe to be coercive.[234]

The World Medical Association Declaration of Tokyo (1975) preamble requires that the "utmost respect for human life is to be maintained."[235] Declaration 1 prohibits a physician from participating in or condoning "torture or other forms of cruel, inhuman or degrading procedures."[236] Declaration 6 prohibits force-feeding prisoners on hunger strikes.[237] This prohibition is rooted in the principle that first a doctor must respect a mentally competent patient's right to refuse treatment. The American Medical Association recently publicly reiterated its support for the Declaration of Tokyo.[238]

The World Medical Association's *Guidelines for Medical Doctors Concerning Torture and Other Cruel, Inhuman or Degrading Treatment or Punishment in Retention and Imprisonment* were specifically designed to limit health care professionals' participation in interrogation.[239] The guidelines provide a broad range of behavior in its concept of torture which it defines as "the deliberate, systematic or wanton infliction of physical suffering by one or more persons acting alone or on the order of any authority, to force another person to yield information, to make a confession, or for any other reason."[240] As demonstrated, the medical personnel at Guantánamo were active participants in the conspiracy to mistreat detainees in conjunction with members of the Bush administration, legal and military communities.

5.8. THE LEGAL PROFESSION'S ETHICAL OBLIGATIONS

The mission of the American Bar Association (ABA) – the largest professional association in the world, with over 400,000 members – is to "serve the public and the profession by promoting justice, professional excellence and respect for the law."[241] While the ABA itself is not responsible for disciplining attorneys for unethical or illegal conduct (this is left to the state bar associations), it acts as a repository for information about disciplinary proceedings, and it produced the ethical guidelines of the legal profession, the American Bar Association Model Rules of Conduct. The ABA views itself as a voice and champion for the rule of law, and as such urged Congress to intervene in the Executive branch's torture

---

[234]   *Id.*

[235]   World Medical Association, *Declaration of Tokyo* (Tokyo: Japan, October 1975).

[236]   *Id.* at Declaration 1.

[237]   *Id.* at Declaration 6.

[238]   Press Release, American Medical Association, *AMA Reiterates Opposition to Feeding Individuals Against their Will*, Mar. 10, 2006.

[239]   *See* Hermann, *Prisoners of War, supra* note 231.

[240]   *Id.*

[241]   *Available online at:* www.abanet.org/about (last visited Feb. 12, 2010).

policy and denial of due process to detainees once reports of detainee abuse became public.[242]

The ABA adopted two different sets of recommendations with regard to the Bush Administration's torture policy. In August 2004, the ABA urged the U.S. government to comply with "…the Constitution and laws of the United States and treaties to which the United States is a party, including the Geneva Conventions of August 12, 1949" and the CAT, to ensure that no U.S. detainee is subjected to torture or other cruel, inhuman or degrading treatment or punishment.[243] The ABA also asked that the U.S. amend 18 U.S.C. §§2340(1) and 2340(A) to prohibit all torture, regardless of the interrogator's underlying motive or purpose.[244] Finally, the ABA recommended that the President and Congress establish a bipartisan commission to investigate the Administration's policy.

In August 2007, the ABA spoke to the President's Executive Order of July 20, 2007, which authorized the CIA's "extraordinary rendition" program. It argued that the Executive Order was inconsistent with U.S. obligations under Article 3 of the Geneva Conventions.[245] In a Recommendation adopted by its House of Delegates, the ABA again urged the U.S. to commit itself to treating all detainees in accordance with the minimum protections afforded by Common Article 3.[246]

Although the ABA expressed disagreement with the Bush Administration's legal analysis regarding torture, it has been hesitant to imply any personal liability on the part of government lawyers. The ABA argued that the 2002 governmental memoranda such as those by Yoo and Gonzales violated the balance of powers by "…attempt[ing] to craft an overall insulation from liability by arguing that the President has the authority to ignore any law or treaty he believes interferes with the President's Article II power as Commander-in-Chief".[247] However, the ABA then significantly weakened its position by stating that it "…do[es] not construe the giving of good faith legal advice to constitute endorsement or authorization of torture."[248]

Certain state bar associations which have adopted a version of the ABA Model Rules of Conduct would have good grounds to investigate the actions of governmental attorneys who promoted the Bush Administration's torture policy. The Rules of Conduct prohibit lawyers from counseling a client to "engage, or assist[ing] a client, in conduct that the lawyer knows is criminal or fraudulent."[249] Also, the model rules discuss the duty lawyers have when representing an

---

[242] See for example the statement by ABA President, William H. Neukom, *It's Time to End Torture* (ABA Newsletter, October 11, 2007).

[243] ABA Report to the House of Delegates, adopted by voice vote August 9, 2004.

[244] *Id.*

[245] *See* ABA Recommendation Adopted by the House of Delegates August 13–14, 2007.

[246] *Id.*

[247] *See* ABA Report, *supra* note 243, at 4.

[248] *Id.*

[249] American Bar Association Model Rules of Professional Conduct (2006), Model Rule 1.2(d). The Comments to Model Rule 1.2 state:

organization to report misconduct of employees or individuals.[250] Being a member of the bar does not indemnify an attorney from the crime of aiding or abetting where the legal advice that is given guides the perpetrator in the commission of a crime. The proscription against aiding a client in a crime includes, but is not limited to, advising a client on how to commit a crime in a way that cloaks the appearance of a crime or in a way that would help evade or mitigate criminal responsibility if the perpetrator is caught.[251] For example, advising a client on how to engage in money laundering, evade taxes,[252] or filing for fraudulent bankruptcy[253] are forbidden.[254]

Further, while many lawyers see their primary obligation as detailing the content of the law applicable to a particular situation, lawyers are also under an

---

> The lawyer is required to avoid assisting the client, for example, by drafting or delivering documents that the lawyer knows are fraudulent or by suggesting how the wrongdoing might be concealed.
>
> Comm. 10 to Model Rule 1.2(d).

[250] Model Rule 1.13 (b), *id.*, states:

> If a lawyer for an organization knows that an officer, employee or other persona associated with the organization is engaged in action, intends to act or refuses to act in a manner related to the representation that is a violation of a legal obligation to the organization, or a violation of law that reasonably might be imputed to the organization, and that is likely to result in substantial injury to the organization, then the lawyer shall proceed as reasonably necessary in the best interest of the organization. Unless the lawyer reasonably believes that it is not necessary in the best interest of the organization to do so, the lawyer shall refer the matter to higher authority in the organization, including, if warranted by the circumstance, to the highest authority that can ac on behalf of the organization as determined by applicable law.

Comment 9 to this rule further specified the duty to government agencies:

> Although in some circumstances, the client may be a specific agency, it may also be a branch of government, such as the executive branch, or the government as a whole. For example, if the action or failure to act involves the head of a bureau, either the department of which the bureau is a part or the relevant branch of government may be the client for purposes of this Rule. Moreover, in a matter involving the conduct of government officials, a government lawyer may have authority under applicable law to question such conduct more extensively than that of a lawyer for a private organization in similar circumstance. Thus, when the client is a governmental organization, a different balance may be appropriate between maintaining confidentiality and assuring that the wrongful act is prevented or rectified for public business is involved.

Government lawyers must "provide a competent and thorough view of the law, particularly when their advice is sought in confidence and when its subject includes, at least in part, contemplated future action that might run afoul of the law." Jose E. Alvarez, *Torturing the Law*, 37 Case W. Res. J. Int'l L. 175, 221 (2006).

[251] *See* U.S. v. Kelly, 888 F.2d 732 (11th Cir. 1989) (aiding, abetting, and counseling possession with intent to distribute cocaine).

[252] *See In re* John H. Haley, 60 F. Supp. 2d 926 (E.D. Ark. 1999).

[253] *See* Oklahoma v. Jim D. Shofner, No. SCBD-4672, 2002 OK 84, Rule 7 Bar Disciplinary Proceedings (Oct. 29, 2002) (conspiracy for fraudulently concealing assets in client's bankruptcy and creating scheme for client to use).

[254] *See also* U.S. v. Abbell, 271 F.3d 1286 (11th Cir. 2001) (federal prosecutor charged under RICO for helping drug cartel launder money). Abbell was subsequently disbarred by the Supreme Court. *See In re* Discipline of Abbell, 541 U.S. 932 (2004).

obligation to give legal *counsel*.[255] A lawyer should engage in "moral dialogue" with clients who they feel are contemplating wrongful or illegal conduct.[256] This moral imperative is thought to apply even in cases where a client does not contemplate criminal action but only contemplates a breach of contract: "Lawyers who give advice about the lawfulness of a breach of contract probably ought to be obligated to at least consider also giving advice that the conduct (1) is or may be morally wrong, (2) may cause unjustifiable harm to specific persons, and even – given a perhaps unusual lawyer and client – (3) such conduct if followed generally might be harmful to the fabric of society."[257] Here we certainly have a case where the harm potentially aided by legal advice – namely, torture – is more serious than the breach of any contract; and where the clients whom appear to be contemplating wrongdoing are special in that their actions can tarnish the reputation of a nation and threaten the security of the nation's military personnel. Hence, it seems clear that government attorneys providing counsel on the "enhanced interrogation" program were obligated to discuss the illegal and immoral aspects of such a program with their clients.

While numerous cases of attorney misconduct have come to trial in both state and federal courts, few of them are reported in a way that identifies the defendants by their professions. Consequently, cases where an attorney is charged with aiding and abetting by giving false or misleading legal advice, or giving legal advice with the intention of evading the law, are seldom reported as such. The most common way these cases can be identified is via denial of the applicability of the attorney-client privilege, which permits the discovery of the unlawful legal advice given.[258] It should also be noted that members of the bar who are willing to give such advice are also likely to commit some participatory act in the criminal scheme and as a result they can be charged with conspiracy or as principals.[259]

Penalties can accrue to attorneys who give unethical advice to their clients irrespective of whether the latter have been convicted for the crime in question.[260] Such penalties available for violations of professional obligations include disbarment, suspension, public or private reprimand, and probation. The D.C. Bar Association, of which Yoo and many other governmental attorneys are members, states in its Comment on Professional Rule 1.3 (Diligence and Zeal)

---

[255]   *See* Stephen Pepper, *Counseling at the Limits of the Law: An Exercise in the Jurisprudence and Ethics of Lawyering*, 104 YALE L.J. 1545 (1995).

[256]   *Id.* at 1563.

[257]   *Id.* at 1563–64.

[258]   *See* U.S. v. Zolin, 491 U.S. 554, 562–63 (1989).

[259]   *See* People v. James Derose, Case No. 99PDJ098 (Color. Aug. 13, 2001) (disciplinary proceedings); *see also* U.S. v. Sattar, 395 F. Supp.2d 66 where a lawyer charged with conspiracy to defraud the U.S. and conspiracy to kill persons in a foreign country was disbarred as a result.

[260]   *See e.g.* Federal Circuit Attorney Discipline Rules, Rules 1, 2; Washington Court Rule, RCW 2.48.180; Colorado Court Rule 20–0–251.20.

that "If the lawyer knows that the client expects assistance that is not in accord with the Rules of Professional Conduct *or other law*, the lawyer must inform the client of the pertinent limitations on the lawyer's conduct" (emphasis added).[261] That is, if an attorney is asked to stretch the interpretation of one law (such as the President's Article 2 power) in violation of a reasonable interpretation of other applicable laws (such as the Geneva Conventions) that lawyer has a duty to inform his client that his obligations to his client are limited by his professional obligations to the rule of law. The government lawyers specifically produced legal advice to allow the senior government officials who wanted to give short shrift to both U.S. and international law to avoid responsibility, seemingly.[262] These clients were primarily: President Bush, Vice President Cheney, Secretary Rumsfeld, Deputy Defense Secretary Paul Wolfowitz, Under-Secretary of Defense Douglas Feith, and Attorney General Ashcroft. Attorneys who failed to make clear the limits provided by a reasonable interpretation of applicable law should be held responsible.

Although an attorney may often be requested to make interpretations of the law for a client, there is a clear difference between matters of professional judgment and clear ethical problems from which a lawyer should avoid. The fundamental challenge in indicting members of the OLC and other departments is determining how far "off the mark" one must be in their legal opinions before they cross the threshold into the territory of criminal responsibility.

An excellent example of an attorney crossing the line between enabling a client to *understand* the limits of the law and attempting to provide a legal shield to enable him or her to *avoid* the law is provided by the 2003 DOJ memo authored by Yoo. In the memo Yoo argued that no domestic or foreign law applies to the treatment of alien unlawful enemy combatants held outside the U.S.[263] Yoo claimed that neither domestic or international law apply to the interrogations conducted abroad, and that if they did apply, their application would violate the President's powers as Commander-in-Chief. Yoo asserted that the CAT is limited to Fifth, Eighth and Fourteenth Amendment protections and that "[c]ustomary international law does not supply any additional standards. Finally, if any of these defenses should fail for any reason, the justification of self-defense would

---

261 DISTRICT OF COLUMBIA RULES OF PROFESSIONAL CONDUCT (revised February 1, 2007), Rule 1.3, at 14.

262 As noted by Barbara Armacost, *Qualified Immunity: Ignorance Excused*, 51 VAND. L. REV. 583 (1998): "While it is sometimes useful to make a distinction between law and policy, there is not neutral legal analysis. Legal reasoning is always in the service of some concrete problem or question, and lawyers choose which arguments to make. Choices about legal arguments, in turn, make some policy choices more or less possible…Lawyers cannot, in my view, claim that they have no responsibility for the policy choices that their arguments make possible… lawyers who make needlessly broad arguments are not immune from blame if others rely on these arguments to justify conduct that pushes the limits of legality."

263 *See* Memorandum from Deputy Ass't Atty General John Yoo to William J. Haynes II, General Counsel of the Dep't of Defense, Memorandum on Military Interrogation of Alien Unlawful combatants Held Outside the United States (Mar. 14, 2003) [hereinafter Yoo Memo].

eliminate any criminal liability for the interrogations." Yoo also noted that 18 U.S.C. §2340 contains a specific intent requirement and a threshold of "severe pain or suffering" or "prolonged mental harm."[264] Yoo's analysis of the torture statute resulted in his finding "that the term [torture] encompasses only extreme acts,"[265] which all but guarantee that prosecution for conduct during "enhanced interrogations" would be nearly impossible.

In his analysis, Yoo determined that the Fifth and Eighth Amendments do not extend to aliens held abroad,[266] asserting that the September 11, 2001 attacks triggered the U.S. right to self-defense and therefore the President's powers as Commander-in-Chief.[267] Yoo then cited law supporting the position that the Fifth Amendment cannot restrict the President's War Powers.[268] Yoo further asserted that the Fifth Amendment does not apply outside of the U.S. to conduct directed towards aliens, citing Supreme Court language which "rejected the claim that aliens are entitled to Fifth Amendment rights outside the sovereign territory of the United States."[269] Yoo denied that "enhanced interrogations" violate the Eighth Amendment, stating the Eighth Amendment applies only to "persons upon whom criminal sanctions have been imposed," and because the "enhanced interrogation" techniques were used against persons who had not yet been punished or sanctioned for a crime, he argued, the Eighth Amendment should not apply. He contended, also, that indefinite detention by the military is "[u]nlike imprisonment pursuant to a criminal sanction."[270] Because the detainees would eventually be released at the end of the conflict, detention "is devoid of all penal character."[271]

Yoo claimed that no criminal statute could infringe upon "the President's complete authority over the conduct of war."[272] Since the U.S. is at war with al-Qaeda, he asserted, federal criminal statutes do not apply to interrogations abroad, as that would infringe on the President's powers as Commander-in-Chief. Focusing on assault, maiming, stalking and torture as prohibited by 18 U.S.C. §2340, Yoo found that the application of any of these federal crimes is precluded during wartime. He also noted some jurisdictional or specific intent requirements that provide loopholes which could prevent the application of Title 18 to persons who carried out "enhanced interrogations." Yoo and the Bush Administration's interpretation of the CAT and the U.S. understandings of it would in essence only permit "the rare case of a Marquis de Sade driven only by

---

264   *Id.*

265   *Id.*

266   *Id.*

267   *Id.*

268   *Id.*; *Military Commissions*, 11 Op. Att'y Gen. 297, 301–02 (1865).

269   *Id.*; U.S. v. Verdugo-Urquidez, 494 U.S. 259, 269 (1990).

270   *See* Yoo Memo, *supra* note 263.

271   *Id.*

272   *Id.*

the desire to inflict only the most severe form of pain would suggest that the U.S. never really adhered to the Torture Convention as it was understood by all."[273] Incredibly, Yoo attempted to assert that Title 18 only prohibits maiming if it involves specific acts inflicted on specific body parts. He asserted that maiming requires not only specific intent to "torture, maim or disfigure," but that it is also limited to "cutting, biting, slitting, cutting out, disabling, or putting" of the "nose, ear, lip, tongue, eye or limb."[274]

Yoo's memo also focused on the CAT and customary international law as it applied to interrogations. He noted that the U.S. ratification of the CAT was not self-executing and lacks an enforcement mechanism, and that it places no obligations on the government. To support this theory that "the President can suspend or terminate any treaty or provision of a treaty,"[275] Yoo cited other legal memoranda sent to the President. In addition, he claimed that customary international law has no binding effect on the U.S., and that if it did apply, the President could override it as his discretion.[276] Finally, Yoo argued that if all other legal defenses fail, necessity and self-defense justify "enhanced interrogations". He cited public policy, national security, and the greater good as support for the justification defense.

None of Yoo's claims demonstrate that "enhanced interrogations" of aliens outside the U.S. are permitted under U.S. or international law. His legal arguments consisted solely of attempts to trigger statutory loopholes while repeatedly claiming that the President has the power to disregard the law in times of war.

It seems clear that Yoo should be investigated for violation of Professional Rule 1.3 of the D.C. Bar. Yoo failed to inform his client of "…the pertinent limitations on the lawyer's conduct," one of those limitations being the obligation an attorney has to a realistic report of the law applicable to any given situation. While cases in which lawyers are disciplined usually require more active involvement in the client's wrongful conduct than the provision of correct advice about the law, one might argue such active steps are not necessary in Yoo's case, because his legal advice was so obviously false.[277] Yoo unreasonably advocated the wholesale dismissal of international standards of treatment for prisoners of war, as well as international and domestic prohibitions against torture. For example, it is now clear that the U.S. cannot avail itself of the excuse that it was using "enhanced interrogation" techniques against persons in a "ticking bomb" situation in order to prevent immediate harm to the public at large. Rather, the U.S. engaged in prolonged detentions and interrogations of persons lasting months or years. Further, other claims of self-defense offered by Yoo are contrary

---

[273]   *See* Jose E. Alvarez, *Torturing the Law,* 37 CASE W. RES. J. INT'L L. 175, 183 (2006).
[274]   *See* Yoo Memo, *supra* note 263.
[275]   *Id.*
[276]   *Id.*
[277]   *See* Pepper, *Counseling at the Limits of the Law, supra* note 255, at 1595.

to any reasonable interpretation of international law. The CAT does not provide a self-defense exception to the prohibition on torture.[278] Yoo's memo was a calculated measure designed to exculpate individuals from liability for past actions and as part of a conspiracy to prevent liability for future acts. This memo should, therefore, be viewed as evidence of a plan to continue to conduct illegal interrogations in such a way as to exploit statutory loopholes and justification defenses so that criminal responsibility is avoided.

In authorizing high-level legal memoranda, government lawyers such as Yoo sought to walk the same narrow path that tax lawyers and tax accountants identify as the difference between tax avoidance and tax evasion – the former being legal, and the latter not.[279] At what point does arguing that the definition of torture should be construed in a way to permit acts that have otherwise been considered torture, or that the laws of armed conflict do not apply to certain combatants, or that the Geneva conventions do not apply to them, constitute legal evasion as opposed to advice of mere legal avoidance? This is a question that goes to the criminal responsibility[280] of those who provided that type of legal advice, but it also applies to their ethical responsibility before the bars to which they have been admitted to practice law.[281]

The ABA's positions on the policy and practices of torture were few and far between during the years of the Bush Administration, during which they were carried out in an open and notorious manner. The ABA, which is the national bar organization, should have been more vocal, consistent, and effective. As a democratic organization, however, it requires membership support for its public positions. That support was lacking during those years as members either

---

[278] *See* Julie Mertus & Lisa Davis; *Guantánamo Bay: The Global Effects of Wrongful Detention, Torture & Unchecked Executive Power*, 10 NYCLR 411, (2007); CAT, *supra* note 30, at art. 19.

[279] *See e.g.* U.S. v. Wilson, 118 F.3d 228 (4th Cir. 1997), finding attorney guilty of tax evasion.

[280] It should be noted that the jurisprudence of the U.S., particularly with respect to white collar crimes, establishes the criminal responsibility of attorneys for conspiracy. It also precludes reliance by clients on patently wrong advice given by attorneys to be used as a shield from criminal responsibility. Attorneys are also responsible and subject to disciplinary sanctions in every state for breach of the canons of ethics. *See generally* DONALD NICOLSON & JULIAN WEBB, PROFESSIONAL LEGAL ETHICS: CRITICAL INVESTIGATIONS (1999); Barry Sullivan, *Professions of Law*, 9 GEO. J. LEGAL ETHICS 1235 (1996); Jim Edwards, *Answering Ashcroft's Challenge: Lawyers for 9–11 Detainees Meet to Consider Coordinated Strategy*, 166 NEW JERSEY L.J. 961 (2001).

[281] As defined *inter alia* in the ABA's *Model Rules of Professional Conduct*: "A lawyer... is a representative of clients, *an officer of the legal system, and a public citizen having special responsibility for the quality of justice.*" MODEL RULES OF PROF'L CONDUCT, pmbl. 1 (2006) (emphasis added). Many have noted the link between legal professionalism and the health of a political system. "The core values of the legal profession are critically important to the maintenance of a democratic society...[which] must constantly be reminded of the values of process, persuasion, consistency and participation, the importance of the rule of law and the acknowledgment of minority rights, and the need to include discordant as well as affirming voices." Barry Sullivan, *The Problem and Possibilities of Professionalism*, 21 DUBLIN U. L.J. 108, 126 (1999).

supported the Bush Administration or the practices, and stood in the way of more effective or forceful action. At best, one can conclude that the ABA covered itself with a fig leaf which is represented by the statements and reports listed above. Otherwise, it remained essentially morally naked. However, if the ABA had only a fig leaf cover, state bar associations lacked even that. For the most part, they did not take positions against torture, most likely with the rationalization that these were issues of national security policy that did not regard the state practice of law. To the best of this writer's knowledge, no state bar association has commenced disciplinary proceedings against any of its members for engaging in legal work aimed at or whose purposes were to justify a practice which they knew or should have known was illegal or unethical. It should also be added that the same criticism of the legal profession extends to the medical profession with respect to the AMA's positions on the policy and practices of torture, and on the participation of members of the medical profession in the practices of torture or in concealing these practices by writing medical reports and death certificates that failed to disclose the commission of torture.[282]

5.9. THOSE WHO ABIDED BY THEIR PROFESSIONAL OBLIGATIONS

Certain lawyers and doctors within and outside the U.S. military have notably upheld their ethical oaths and legal responsibilities despite their involvement in the war on terror. They are a credit to their professions and to their nation; and they should be projected as role models. Military lawyers in the DOD and the DOJ "fought a quiet battle" against the Bush Administration's torture policy and paid a price for it.[283] While at the White House, the former NSC Legal Advisor

---

[282]   *See* Leonard S. Rubenstein & Stephen N. Xenakis, *Doctors Without Morals*, N.Y. TIMES, Feb. 28, 2010.

[283]   *See* Daniel Klaidman et al., *Palace Revolt*, NEWSWEEK, Feb. 6, 2006, at 35. Former Deputy Attorney General James Comey, Jack Goldsmith, former Assistant Attorney General and head of the DOJ's OLC, and Patrick Philbin were ultimately pushed out of their positions by Addington. As explained by Lea Anne McBride, a spokesman for Cheney, "This administration is united in its commitment to protect Americans, defeat terrorism, and grow democracy," meaning that honest and legitimate dissenting views are not permitted. *Id.* at 36. She further added about Addington, "[H]e's committed to the President's agenda," meaning both the Vice President and the President had an agenda on the subject which Addington carried out irrespective of the legality involved, and notwithstanding any contrary legal opinions which were either sidestepped or brushed aside. *Id.* at 37; Tim Golden & Eric Schmitt, *Detainee Policy Sharply Divides Bush Officials*, N.Y. TIMES, Nov. 2, 2005, at A1; David Ignatius, *Cheney's Cheney*, WASH. POST, Jan. 5, 2006, at A19. To distance himself from responsibility for the "torture memos," Goldsmith's book, *The Terror Presidency, supra* note 125, details his disagreements with the DOJ during his nine month stint as legal advisor to Haynes. He describes an Executive branch "go-it-alone" view of power, with the attempt to

John Bellinger (then Legal Adviser to the Secretary of State) took a position against denying the applicability of the Geneva Conventions to the Guantánamo detainees. It seems Goldsmith was also supported by Patrick Philbin, who worked with the Attorney General, although Philbin wrote the original memorandum with Yoo.

Alberto J. Mora, General Counsel of the Navy, was another opponent of the torture policy.[284] Mora's detailed declassified memorandum explained that "enhanced interrogation" techniques skirting the CAT and Geneva legal limitations were advanced by Addington (then Chief of Staff to Vice President Cheney) and his former subordinate Haynes, then General Counsel for the DOD.[285] The memorandum reveals Mora's criticism of Administration policy originated well before the exposure of prisoner abuse in Abu Ghraib. Mora warned his superiors not to circumvent the Geneva Conventions which prohibit "outrages upon personal dignity, in particular humiliating and degrading treatment."[286] He also challenged the legal framework constructed by the Bush Administration to justify expansion of Executive power, describing as "unlawful" and "dangerous" the legal theories used to grant the President the right to authorize abuse.[287]

Bob Woodward described a White House meeting on January 18, 2002 (when the decision was made that the Geneva Conventions did not apply to al-Qaeda or

---

make the Presidency stronger than when they took office. Goldsmith noted that the most important legal policies during the Administration were not made by the OLC, but by a self-appointed 'war council,' which included Gonzales, Addington, Haynes, Bybee, and Yoo. *Id.* These men all apparently shared the belief that the "biggest obstacle to a vigorous response to the 9/11 attacks was the set of domestic and international laws that arose in the 1970s to constrain the President's power in response to the excesses of Watergate and the Vietnam War." *Id.* Goldsmith also described Addington as running the show, and the biggest presence in the room, who discouraged Goldsmith's legal advice when the President had already made the decision that "terrorists do not receive Geneva Convention protections." *Id.* In another incident when Goldsmith attempted to question another Presidential decision, Addington told him, "If you rule that way... the blood of the hundred thousand people who die in the next attack will be on your hands." *Id.* Goldsmith told also of Addington's compartmentalization plan, or "extraordinary concealment," in which NSA lawyers were not even allowed to see what the DOJ was doing. Addington, as well as Yoo, effectively bypassed JAG officers, and instead had persons with little or no legal experience generating legal opinions justifying torture. *Id.*

284   *See* Jane Mayer, *The Hidden Power,* NEW YORKER, July 3, 2006, at 44.

285   *See* Mora Statement, *supra* note 38.

286   *See* Mayer, *The Hidden Power, supra* note 284.

287   *Id.* Mayer notes that "...Top Administration officials have stressed that the interrogation policy was reviewed and sanctioned by government lawyers; last November, President Bush said, "Any activity we conduct is within the law. We do not torture." Mora's statement, however, *supra* note 38, shows that almost from the start of the Bush Administration's "war on terror" the White House, the DOJ, and the DOD, intent upon having greater flexibility, charted a legally questionable course despite sustained objections from some of its own lawyers." *Id. See also* Mayer, *The Memo, supra* note 43, where Mora is quoting as saying "I wonder if they were even familiar with the Nuremberg trials – or with the laws of war, or with the Geneva conventions."

the Taliban) that exemplifies how qualified legal experts such as Mora were bypassed in the Bush Administration's attempt to justify its policies.[288] Woodward reports that Rumsfeld noted that the detainees needed to be kept off the battlefield because they were "bad guy," but that he was not a lawyer and did not know how.[289] Rear Adm. Donald Guter, who was the Navy's chief JAG until June 2002, claimed that he and other JAGs tried unsuccessfully to amend parts of the military-commission plan when they learned of it, days before the Order was formally signed by the President.[290] "We were warning them that we had this long tradition of military justice, and we didn't want to tarnish it. The treatment of detainees was a huge issue. They didn't want to hear it."[291] The concern for military tradition and honor is also reflected by former high-ranking military officials who publicly denounced the policy of the Bush Administration and especially the actions of Cheney. The "enhanced interrogation" techniques have been denounced as compromising the military code of honor, and blame for the torture that took place is placed squarely at the Vice President's door as "moral equivocation about torture at the top of the chain of command" traveled through the ranks and led to the dishonor of the U.S.[292]

At Guantánamo Bay itself, there were many within the ranks of military leadership who, in the early days of its conversion into the notorious detention center, opposed the lawless policies emanating from Washington. Among them was Brig. Gen. Michael Lehnert, who had been tasked to become the new Commander of JTF-160, the detention center at Guantánamo. Lehnert worked

---

[288] *See* BOB WOODWARD, STATE OF DENIAL 86–87 (2006).

[289] *Id* at 276.

[290] *See* Mayer, *The Hidden Power, supra* note 284, at 52.

[291] *Id.*; George Annas notes that the marginalization of the JAG Corps was "planned and vigorously pursued. Even when Congress acted to protect the authority of the JAG Corps" in the Reagan National Defense Authorization Act for Fiscal Year 2005, Pub. L. No. 108–375, §574, 118 Stat. 1811, 1921–22 (2004), Bush in his signing statement wrote:

> Section 574 of the Act… prohibit[s] Department of Defense personnel from interfering with the ability of a military department judge advocate general, and the staff judge advocate to the Commandant of the Marine Corps, to give independent legal advice to the head of a military department of chief of a military service or with the ability of judge advocates assigned to military units to give independent legal advice to unit commanders. *The executive branch shall construe section 574 in a manner consistent with:* (1) the President's constitutional authorities to take care that the laws be faithfully executed, to supervise the unitary executive branch, and as Commander in Chief; (2) the statutory grant to the Secretary of Defense of authority, direction, and control over the Department of Defense… (3) the *exercise of statutory authority by the Attorney General… and the general counsel of the Department of Defense as its chief legal officer… to render legal opinions that bind all civilian and military attorneys within the Department of Defense;* and (4) the exercise of authority under the statutes… by which the heads of the military departments may prescribe the functions of their respective counsels.

> *Id.* (emphasis added). George J. Annas, *Human Rights Outlaws: Nuremberg, Geneva, and the Global War on Terror*, 87 BOSTON U. L. REV. 427,436, n. 43 (April 2007).

[292] Charles C. Krulak & Joseph P. Hoar, *Fear Was No Excuse to Condone Torture*, MIAMI HERALD, Sep. 11, 2009.

tirelessly throughout his tenure at detention center to preserve the law of Geneva and the dignity of the detainees, and before requested the authorization to contact the ICRC from the Pentagon and was denied.[293] The removal of the legal framework that the Geneva Conventions provide left many in JTF-160 perplexed with how to proceed with its hundreds of new detainees. Without clear direction from his superiors, Col. Manuel Supervielle, SOUTHCOM's Staff Judge Advocate took it upon himself to call the ICRC and invite its delegates to visit the detainees – standard operating procedure under the Geneva Conventions – a decision for which he was reprimanded by Washington. "We thought they were POWs. We always did. We were overruled… essentially by the President of the United States."[294]

Years later, acts of honorable resistance from the military continue. Several military prosecutors at Guantánamo have resigned in frustration and disgust with a broken system. One of these prosecutors was Lt. Col. V. Stuart Couch, who had been assigned to the case of Mohammed Ould Salahi, one of the Guantánamo detainees believed to have had a direct relation to 9/11.[295] A veteran pilot, Couch's good friend from the Marines had been a co-pilot of the second plane to hit the World Trade Center. Once Couch discovered the "enhanced interrogation" techniques that had been used on Salahi, he refused to participate any further in the prosecution.[296]

> We cannot compromise our respect for the dignity of every human being. And that goes to somebody that is alleged to have committed heinous crimes against citizens of this country. That doesn't change the immutable characteristic that they're still a human being, and it's a slippery slope that in the name of national security we decide to compromise that. If we compromise that, then al-Qaeda has been able to affect much more of an impact on this country than they have by driving a couple of planes into the World Trade Center or crashing one into the Pentagon. Because they've torn at the very fabric of who we are as Americans.[297]

Another such case is that of Darrel J. Vandeveld, a Lieutenant Colonel in the Army Reserve, and a military lawyer who believed deeply in the cause of the "war on terror". Vandeveld began his assignment at Guantánamo enthusiastically, believing that he was serving his country by prosecuting those responsible for 9/11 and other terrorist attacks upon the U.S. While he had heard the stories of abuse at Guantánamo, he thought they must be the exaggeration and hysteria of those who were probably just terrorist sympathizers.[298] What he found was a

---

[293] GREENBERG, THE LEAST WORST PLACE, *supra* note 2, at 57.

[294] *Id.*, at 50.

[295] *See* Chapter 2, section 2.5, *Case Studies of Interrogation.*

[296] *See* Jesse Bravin, *The Conscience of the Colonel*, WALL ST. J., Mar. 31, 2007.

[297] Interview with David Brancaccio, *Duty vs. Conscience at Gitmo*, PBS Now, Sep. 4, 2009.

[298] Darrel J. Vandeveld, *I Was Slow to Recognize the Stain of Guantanamo*, WASH. POST, Jan. 18, 2009.

system incapable of providing the most basic fundamentals of justice.[299] Eventually, Vandeveld became overwhelmingly distraught over not only the credible claims of torture at the hands of U.S. public agents and military personnel, but by the broken and unfair system of military commissions. Unable to discuss his misgivings with his colleagues for fear of retribution, or with his family or friends because of issues of confidentiality, Vandeveld turned to a Catholic priest, who advised his resignation. After much soul-searching Vandeveld ultimately did tender his resignation, and not only publicly criticized the military commissions in the media and before Congress, but served as a witness for the defense at Guantánamo.[300] In his statement before the House Judiciary Committee, Vandeveld defended his decision:

> I was not always so skeptical about the capacity of military commissions to deliver justice. I entered my job at the Office of Military Commissions as a "true believer." I had heard stories about abuse at Guantánamo, but I brushed them off as hyperbole. When one of the detainees I was prosecuting, a young Afghan named Mohammed Jawad, told the court that he was only 16 at the time of his arrest, and that he had been subject to horrible abuse, I accused him of exaggerating and ridiculed his story as "idiotic." I did not believe that he was a juvenile, and I railed against Jawad's military defense attorney, whom I suspected of being a terrorist sympathizer... I soon discovered a number of disturbing anomalies... I uncovered a confession obtained through torture, two suicide attempts by the accused, abusive interrogations, the withholding of exculpatory evidence from the defense, judicial incompetence, and ugly attempts to cover up the failures of an irretrievably broken system... I simply could not in good conscience continue to work for an ad hoc, hastily-created apparatus – as opposed to the military itself – whose evident resort to expediency and ethical compromise were so contrary to my own and to those the Army has enshrined and preached since I enlisted so many years ago.[301]

Some U.S. military doctors also upheld their professional oaths by signing death certificates evidencing torture as the cause of death when such instances arose in Afghanistan and Iraq.[302] These and other members of the military are the

---

[299]　*Id.* In his resignation letter, Vandeveld wrote, "I am highly concerned, to the point that I believe I can no longer serve as a prosecutor at the Commissions, about the slipshod, uncertain 'procedure' for affording defense counsel discovery. One would have thought that after six years since the Commissions had their fitful start, that a functioning law office would have been set up and procedures and policies not only put into effect, but refined." .

[300]　*Id.* "I made my final appearance before the military commissions at Guantanamo, not as a gung-ho prosecutor, but as a determined witness for the defense. My testimony was a confession of sorts, an acknowledgment of the error of my own ways as well as a candid admission of the shortcomings of the system that I had so enthusiastically supported."

[301]　Testimony of Lt. Col. Darrel Vandeveld Before the Constitution, Civil Rights and Civil Liberties Subcommittee on House Committee on the Judiciary, Hearing on Legal Issues Surrounding the Military Commissions System, Jul. 8, 2009, at 3–5.

[302]　*See* MILES, OATH BETRAYED, *supra* note 181; *see also* Army Surgeon General, Final Report: Assessment of Detainee Medical Operations for OEF, GTMO, and OIF (April 13, 2005);.

unsung heroes of this tragic episode in our American history. Regrettably, many others turned a blind eye to torture, looked the other way, and violated their Hippocratic oaths by going along with the political wishes of the Pentagon's civilian leadership.[303]

5.10. A PRELUDE TO LIMITING CRIMINAL RESPONSIBILITY AFTER THE FACT

After the Supreme Court held in *Rasul v. Bush* that the statutory habeas jurisdiction of federal courts extended to Guantánamo Bay,[304] the Court in *Boumediene v. Bush* held that the section of the Military Commissions Act of 2006 that withdrew jurisdiction from the courts to entertain habeas petitions filed by Guantánamo detainees was an unconstitutional suspension of the writ.[305] *Boumediene* held that detainees were entitled to proceed with habeas challenges under procedures crafted to account for the special circumstances of wartime detention.[306]

Soon after the *Boumediene* decision, the District Court for the District of Columbia heard and denied the habeas petition of Al-Bihani.[307] The case was appealed to the Circuit Court for the District of Columbia as *Al-Bihani v. Obama*.[308] The Court of Appeals affirmed the District Court's decision on January 5, 2010, in which it made surprising findings about international humanitarian law, which supports some of the positions proffered by the Bush Administration lawyers. It stated:

> There is no indication in the AUMF, the Detainee Treatment Act of 2005, Pub. L. No. 109–148, div. A, tit. X, 119 Stat. 2739, 2741–43, or the MCA of 2006 or 2009, that Congress intended the international laws of war to act as extra-textual limiting principles for the President's war powers under the AUMF. The international laws of war as a whole have not been implemented domestically by Congress and are therefore not a source of authority for U.S. courts. *See* Restatement (Third) of Foreign Relations Law of the United States §111(3)–(4) (1987). Even assuming Congress had at some earlier point implemented the laws of war as domestic law through appropriate legislation, Congress had the power to authorize the President in the AUMF and other later statutes to exceed those bounds. *See id.* §115(1)(a). Further weakening their relevance to this case, the international laws of war are not a fixed code. Their dictates and application to actual events are by nature contestable and fluid. *See id.* §102 cmts. b & c (stating there is "no precise formula" to identify a

---

[303] *See* Miles, Oath Betrayed, *supra* note 181.

[304] Rasul v. Bush, 542 U.S. 466, 483–84 (2004).

[305] Boumediene v. Bush, 128 U.S. 2229 (2008); MCA, *supra* note 22.

[306] *Id.* at 2274.

[307] *See* Al-Bihani v. Bush, 588 F. Supp.2d 19 (D.D.C. 2008) (case management order).

[308] Al-Bihani v. Obama, No. 1:05-CV-01312-RJL.

practice as custom and that "[i]t is often difficult to determine when [a custom's] transformation into law has taken place"). Therefore, while the international laws of war are helpful to courts when identifying the general set of war powers to which the AUMF speaks, *see Hamdi*, 542 U.S. at 520, their lack of controlling legal force and firm definition render their use both inapposite and inadvisable when courts seek to determine the limits of the President's war powers.[309]

In his concurring opinion, Judge Brown highlighted the Supreme Court's lack of legal specificity as to IHL:

The Supreme Court in *Boumediene* and *Hamdi* charged this court and others with the unprecedented task of developing rules to review the propriety of military actions during a time of war, relying on common law tools. We are fortunate this case does not require us to demarcate the law's full substantive and procedural dimensions. But as other more difficult cases arise, it is important to ask whether a court-driven process is best suited to protecting both the rights of petitioners and the safety of our nation. The common law process depends on incrementalism and eventual correction, and it is most effective where there are a significant number of cases brought before a large set of courts, which in turn enjoy the luxury of time to work the doctrine supple. None of those factors exist in the Guantánamo context. The number of Guantánamo detainees is limited and the circumstances of their confinement are unique. The petitions they file, as the *Boumediene* Court counseled, are funneled through one federal district court and one appellate court. *See Boumediene*, 128 S. Ct. at 2276. And, in the midst of an ongoing war, time to entertain a process of literal trial and error is not a luxury we have.

While the common law process presents these difficulties, it is important to note that the Supreme Court has not foreclosed Congress from establishing new habeas standards in line with its *Boumediene* opinion. Having been repeatedly rebuffed, *see id.* at 2240 (holding that the DTA's procedures were an inadequate substitute for habeas and that the MCA therefore operated as an unconstitutional suspension of the writ); *Hamdan v. Rumsfeld*, 548 U.S. 557, 576–77 (2006) (holding that the DTA's withdrawal of federal habeas jurisdiction did not apply to petitions pending at the time of the DTA's enactment), Congress may understandably be reluctant to return to this arena to craft appropriate habeas standards as it has done for other habeas contexts in the past. But the circumstances that frustrate the judicial process are the same ones that make this situation particularly ripe for Congress to intervene pursuant to its policy expertise, democratic legitimacy, and oath to uphold and defend the Constitution. These cases present hard questions and hard choices, ones best faced directly. Judicial review, however, is just that: *re*-view, an indirect and necessarily backward looking process. And looking backward may not be enough in this new war. The saying that generals always fight the last war is familiar, but familiarity does not dull the maxim's sober warning. In identifying the shape of the law in response to the challenge of the current war, it is incumbent on the President,

---

[309]   *Id.* at 7.

Congress, and the courts to realize that the saying's principle applies to us as well. Both the rule of law and the nation's safety will benefit from an honest assessment of the new challenges we face, one that will produce an appropriately calibrated response.

Absent such action, much of what our Constitution requires for this context remains unsettled. In this case, I remain mindful that the conflict in which Al-Bihani was captured was only one phase of hostilities between the United States and Islamic extremists. The legal issues presented by our nation's fight with this enemy have been numerous, difficult, and to a large extent novel. What drives these issues is the unconventional nature of our enemy: they are neither soldiers nor mere criminals, claim no national affiliation, and adopt long-term strategies and asymmetric tactics that exploit the rules of open societies without respect or reciprocity.

War is a challenge to law, and the law must adjust. It must recognize that the old wineskins of international law, domestic criminal procedure, or other prior frameworks are ill-suited to the bitter wine of this new warfare. We can no longer afford diffidence. This war has placed us not just at, but already past the leading edge of a new and frightening paradigm, one that demands new rules be written. Falling back on the comfort of prior practices supplies only illusory comfort.[310]

Judge Brown's use of terms such as "Islamic extremists" and the conclusion that the conflict in Afghanistan is only one of the phases of hostility between the U.S. and such "Islamic extremists" portrays his profound ignorance of the nature of the conflict in Afghanistan and how it is being conducted. More telling is the implicit Islamophobia which seeps through. This was not a legal opinion, but a political one that reflected the Bush Administration's distorted view of events, how to deal with them, and more to the point, a distorted view of the law.

What is clear from Judge Brown's interpretation of *Boumediene* and *Hamdi* is that the Supreme Court, by deftly characterizing matters in a way that gives federal district courts the opportunity to identify and apply international humanitarian law on a case-by-case basis. In so doing, the Supreme Court implicitly affirmed the Bush Administration position that international humanitarian law is vague and that it only applies selectively to the U.S., leaving that determination to be made on a case-by-case basis. Save for those U.S. jurists who see things that way, all others will agree that the Geneva Conventions of August 12, 1949 are specific, unambiguous, and applicable to the U.S. without exception. Moreover, provisions of Protocols I and II have risen to the level of customary international law as recognized by various U.S. law sources. Thus, the emphasis on the uncertainties of international humanitarian law applicable to the U.S. is largely a secondary issue to that which is well established in conventional international law. More surprising in this case is the Court of

---

[310]   *Id.* at 26–27.

Appeals positing that because the U.S. did not enact specific legislation to implement the Geneva Conventions of 1949, after 60 years have passed since the U.S. ratification, and nearly 50 years have passed since the incorporation of these norms in the UCMJ, is disingenuous.

5.11. CONCLUSION

As discussed in this chapter, there are three types of responsibility which arise in connection with the policy and practices of torture and other forms of cruel, inhuman, and degrading treatment or punishment; namely, political, ethical, and criminal.

Political responsibility applies essentially to Congress and its failure to carry out Constitutional responsibilities in exercising checks and balances over the abusive practices of the Executive branch of government. At present, there is no indication that Congress is in any way inclined to look at its institutional failure in this respect, no more than it is inclined to examine the ethical responsibility of individual members of Congress – particularly in the leadership and in the intelligence committees who were briefed on "enhanced interrogation" techniques, "black sites" and "extraordinary rendition."

Ethical responsibility arises with respect to lawyers and medical professionals who may have violated their respective professions' ethical codes of conduct. So far, there has been no inquiry by any medical board for the practices of doctors who have either supported torture by means of advising the torturers on how far they could go in inflicting harm upon the victim; in providing medical treatment to victims so that they could withstand additional pain and suffering; by forcefully feeding detainees who have elected to go on hunger strikes, and lastly, to cover up for torture resulting in death by not showing the real cause of death appear in the death certificates.[311] With respect to members of the legal profession, there has also so far been no investigation by any bar association of the authors of the various legal opinions and memoranda which justified "enhanced interrogations," the use of "black sites" and "extraordinary rendition". Only one investigation took place by the DOJ of Bybee and Yoo, discussed above, which resulted in their exoneration from professional misconduct, categorizing their legal memoranda as falling in the category of poor judgment.

Lastly, criminal responsibility, which arises in connection with the development of the policy and the instrumentalization of government bureaucracy as a way of establishing a trickle-down effect, leading to widespread and systematic practices, has yet to lead to any meaningful investigations. This includes those who carried out the practices by inflicting pain and suffering on

---

[311]   *See* Leonard S. Rubenstein & Stephen N. Xenakis, *Doctors Without Morals*, N.Y. TIMES, Mar. 1, 2010.

victims, whether they be civilian or military, and whether the venue may be Guantánamo, U.S. military bases in Afghanistan or Iraq, or "black sites" operated by the CIA. Of the tens of thousands of persons who are believed to have been detained at Guantánamo, U.S. military bases in Afghanistan and Iraq, and in CIA-operated "black sites", and of which over 100 are estimated to have died under torture, none have given rise to even an investigation pursuant to Title 18 U.S.C. There have been a few prosecutions under the UCMJ for non-commissioned officers and enlisted men resulting in minor penalties such as loss of rank and small fines, and limited detentions, such as house arrest or confinement to barracks. Some officers have received a reduction in rank, but none have been court-martialed. No civilian has been prosecuted. No military person or CIA personnel have been charged with battery or with homicide.

Ultimately, there has been no substantive accountability at any level, even when facts would evidence the responsibility of certain individuals in the death or serious injury of victims. The conclusion is that the U.S. has failed to meet the test of political, ethical, and criminal responsibility as demanded by the Constitution and laws of this country. What this wholesale denial of any and all forms of responsibility says about the integrity of the political and legal systems of the U.S. is that politics dominate our system of government, and not the rule of law.

CHAPTER 6

THE OBAMA ADMINISTRATION'S ACTIONS: JANUARY 2009 – APRIL 2010

We reject as false the choice between our safety and our ideals.
Our founding fathers, faced with perils that we can scarcely imagine,
drafted a charter to assure the rule of law and the rights of man,
a charter expanded by the blood of generations. Those ideals still light the world,
and we will not give them up for expedience's sake.

– Barack Obama, Presidential
Inauguration Speech, January 20, 2009

6.1. INTRODUCTION

President Obama's promise, quoted above, has yet to be fulfilled – displaying the wide gap between promises and their realizations. Truth and transparency in governmental policies and practices need to be established in a democracy, and those who are believed to have violated the law should not benefit from impunity. Accountability is at the core of a legal system based on the rule of law. In the U.S., all persons stand equal before the law, and presumably no one is either above it or beyond it. So far, however, no one among those who established the policy of torture has been investigated, let alone prosecuted for violations of international and U.S. law. The full truth has yet to be uncovered, and until then, individual criminal responsibility cannot be established.

During his presidential campaign in 2008, President Barack Obama criticized the Bush Administration's policy in the war on terror, as well as its practices which led to the institutionalization of torture and the indefinite detention of prisoners. On his second day in office, President Obama signed three Executive Orders closing the Guantánamo Bay detention center, ending the CIA's use of secret prisons, and requiring that all interrogations meet the requirements of the Geneva Conventions by following the non-coercive methods of the Army Field Manual.[1] However, the policy rudder of the Obama Administration's ship of

---

[1]   Exec. Order No. 13,491, Ensuring Lawful Interrogations, 74 Fed. Reg. 4893 (Jan. 27, 2009), which created a Special Interagency Task Force on Interrogation and Transfer Policies; Exec. Order No. 13,492, Review and Disposition of Individuals Detained at the Guantánamo Bay

state has not been characterized by linearity. Instead, it has followed a course zigzagging between principles and politics. No sooner had the first Executive Orders been signed that different positions colored by political considerations emerged.[2] Now more than a year later, it is appropriate to assess what the Obama Administration has accomplished in connection with restoring the rule of law, closing Guantánamo and "black sites," eliminating the practices of torture and "extraordinary rendition," and investigating those believed to have committed crimes under U.S. law. This includes conducting an investigation of unlawful torture practices and the potentially unlawful policy and practices described in this study. Truth and transparency in government need to be established in a democracy.

6.2. WHAT WAS DONE AND WHAT HAS YET TO BE DONE

On the matter of the Guantánamo Bay detention center, President Obama set up a timeline of one year from January 22, 2009 for its closure. A Task Force designed to review the status of the detainees and the Guantánamo detention center was established and was to submit a report within six months of the Executive Order. The Task Force, however, requested an extension of time to complete its assessment.[3] As the deadline to close Guantánamo approached, it was clear that it would not be met, and attempts to find alternative detention centers within the U.S. have been met with Congressional opposition. There were several facilities reviewed by the U.S. Bureau of Prisons to find a suitable facility to replace Guantánamo and in December 2009, the Obama Administration announced that detainees would be moving to Thompson, Illinois.[4] Thompson Correctional Center is a maximum security facility located approximately 150 miles west of Chicago and was built in 2001 but has remained practically empty since its completion due to state budget cuts.[5] Widespread support of the plan to use Thompson from local residents and the Illinois government was important

---

Naval Base and Closure of Detention Facilities, 74 Fed. Reg. 4,897 (Jan. 27, 2009); Exec. Order No. 13,493, Review of Detention Policy Operations, 74 Fed. Reg. 4901 (Jan. 27, 2009), which created a Special Interagency Task Force on Detainee Disposition to "identify lawful options for the disposition of individuals captured or apprehended in connection with armed conflicts and counterterrorism operations".

[2]   *See* Jane Mayer, *The Trial: Eric Holder and the Khalid Sheikh Mohammed Trial*, THE NEW YORKER, Feb. 15, 2010; Charlie Savage, *Obama Team is Divided on Anti-Terror Tactics*, N.Y. TIMES, Mar. 28, 2010.

[3]   Ved P. Nanda, *International Law Implications of the United States' "War on Terror,"* 37 DENV. J. INT'L L. POL'Y 513, 517 (2009).

[4]   *See* Andrew Stern, *Guantanamo Detainee Move Not Security Risk*, N.Y. TIMES, Nov. 16, 2009. *See also* Editorial, *Moving Gitmo to America*, N.Y. TIMES Dec. 15, 2009.

[5]   *See* Christi Parsons, *Illinois the next Gitmo?* CHI. TRIB., Nov. 14, 2009.

in the decision.[6] By May 2010, it became clear that the Obama Administration and the Democratic majority in Congress had put the closing of Guantánamo and the acquisition of the Thompson, IL detention facility on the back burner. Once again, principle has given way to politics as the November 2010 election date approaches. This, notwithstanding the fact that President Obama made the closing of Guantánamo his first order of business after being sworn in.

The Graham Amendment, designed to prevent terrorism suspects from being allowed into the territorial U.S. for trial, was introduced before the Senate on November 5, 2009.[7] It seeks to have those detained at Guantánamo tried by military commissions and not by the duly constituted courts of the U.S.[8] The Amendment has thus far been tabled by the Senate and is opposed by the Obama Administration, which sent a statement to the Senate signed by Attorney General Holder and Secretary Gates.[9]

The Obama Administration has defended the Government's right to detain suspected foreign terrorists, although they are no longer classified as "unlawful enemy combatants."[10] In a brief submitted in March 2009 in the District Court of the District of Columbia, the DOJ stated its justification for such continued detention,[11] based on domestic law rather than on Executive power, however questionable that position may be.[12] The Government's brief asserts the right to detain suspected foreign terrorists based on the laws of war and the statutory authority Congress gave to the President in its Authority for the Use of Military Force (AUMF).[13] With a changed style and a departure from the "unlawful enemy combatant" categorization, the position of the Obama Administration has been characterized as a continuation of the Bush Administration position in another form.

In spite of the President's continued support for detention, there have been several progressive steps by the Obama Administration. The term "unlawful enemy combatant" has been dropped from the Administration's lexicon, and the standards for detaining persons have become tighter by changing the language from "merely supported al Qaeda or the Taliban" to "substantially supported al Qaeda or the Taliban."[14] Furthermore, the Obama Administration has also made

---

[6]   See *Moving Gitmo to America*, N.Y. TIMES, Dec. 15, 2009.

[7]   Graham Amendment to H.R. Bill 2487, Nov. 5, 2009.

[8]   See J. Taylor Rushing, *Senate Tables Graham Amendment on Trials for 9/11 Suspects*, THE HILL, Nov. 5, 2009.

[9]   *Id.*

[10]   *Id.*

[11]   See Respondent's Memorandum Regarding the Government's Detention Authority Relative to Detainees Held at Guantanamo Bay, *In Re Guantanamo Bay Detainee Litigation*, Misc. No. 08–442 (D.D.C. 2009).

[12]   Jonathan Tracy, *Detention and Prosecution of Alleged Terrorists and Combatants*, 16 HUM. RTS. BRIEF 51 (2009).

[13]   Nanda, *International Law Implications of the United States' "War on Terror"*, *supra* note 2, at 517–18.

[14]   *Id.* at 519.

it clear that this policy is to apply only to those held at Guantánamo while also trying to resolve the situation of their continued detention.[15]

Attorney General Eric Holder has for the most part pursued a principled position with respect to moving Guantánamo prosecutions from military commissions to civilian criminal trials, with all that comports of applying Constitutional rights. For political reasons, some in Congress oppose this principled position, and the Obama White House has been receptive to these political considerations. In November 2009, he announced plans to try Khaled Sheikh Mohammed and four other alleged masterminds behind 9/11 in the Federal District Court for the Southern District of New York. This plan brought mixed reactions from citizens and victims of the attacks, and after strong lobbying by the political right, the plan was eventually tabled.[16] Trying the detainees in federal court is seen as an important achievement for those who would like to see the military commissions abandoned entirely, however, Holder also announced that five other detainees would be tried by military commissions.[17] These commissions were re-endorsed as a viable option for legal recourse in a Preliminary Report published in July 2009 by the Obama Administration.[18] There is concern that the military commissions are an *ad hoc* system that has yet to be proven.[19] As they stand, they have failed to live up to elementary constitutional rights and standards, making those who deserve punishment as if each of them was a "martyr as victims of an unjust system," and leaving those who are innocent without the chance to receive a fair trial.[20]

The difficulties, however, arising out of what to do with persons who have been tortured at Guantánamo and elsewhere are self-evident. If they are to be tried by U.S. Courts, their confessions would be held inadmissible and they would be set free, even if there is evidence that they did participate in or support terrorist activities directed against the United States. Holder has convened panels of experts which have identified the existence of sufficient evidence untainted by torture to be used in such prosecutions, and apparently these panels of experts have also concluded that the evidence available would be sufficient to convict. As of February 2010, however, the course of transferring persons from military commissions to civilian criminal trials has been challenged by some in the White House, including Chief of Staff Rahm Emmanuel, who is urging a direction that

---

[15]   *Id.*

[16]   Charlie Savage, *Accused 9/11 Mastermind to Face Civilian Trial in N.Y.*, N.Y. TIMES, Nov. 13, 2009.

[17]   *Id.*

[18]   *See Detention Policy Task Force, Memorandum to the Attorney General and Secretary of Defense, Preliminary Report*, July 20, 2009.

[19]   *See* Gabor Rona, *Military Commissions, The Gold Rule and the Law of War*, 31 NAT'L SECURITY L. REP. 2 (Jul-Oct 2009).

[20]   *Id.* at 6.

is guided by political considerations.[21] It is regrettable that these issues have become mired in politics without any regard for the higher principles of upholding the Constitution and the laws of the U.S. Moreover, these political considerations ignore the harmful consequences of these approaches to the moral standing of the U.S. at the international level, and more specifically throughout the Muslim world, which has become a breeding ground for extremists who feel justified in their actions against the U.S. in response to its policies and practices of the past decade.

It should be noted that the opposition to civilian criminal trials on principled grounds should be distinguished from issues arising with the trial of Khaled Sheikh Mohammed and others in the Federal District Court's facility in Foley Square in New York City. The choice of an appropriate venue has nothing to do with the principle of prosecuting offenders before the Constitution's Article 3 Courts those persons who committed crimes in the U.S. The continued push to have these prosecutions conducted before military commissions because of the damaging effects of the use of torture to which these accused persons have been subjected, ignores the merits of upholding the rule of law in U.S. courts. Similar prosecutions occurred in the Moussaoui and Reid cases, as well as others who have been prosecuted before federal district courts.[22] These cases are no different than the bombing of the Oklahoma federal building in 1995, which was also a terrorism case.[23]

The venue of such prosecutions should of course take into account security considerations, but that is a far cry from claiming that the Constitution and laws of the U.S. should be suspended with respect to certain prosecutions in order to cover up the torture practices inflicted upon the defendants to be tried. Even assuming that for security reasons such prosecutions should be conducted before military commissions, there is nothing in the Constitution or laws of the U.S. that justifies the reduction of the rights of the defense in such cases. Such military commissions which would apply the Constitution could well be established to carry out that task because of the exceptional circumstances involving certain security considerations, but it would be contrary to the Constitution and to this country's rule of law principles to curtail the rights of the defense only as a way to cover up for the torture to which the prospective defendants were subjected in the past. Evidence of guilt can be found outside the statements obtained under torture. Whether a trial is before a federal court or before a military commission,

---

21   *See* Mayer, *The Trial*, *supra* note 2; Jodi Kantor & Charlie Savage, *After 9/11 Trial Plan, Holder Hones Political Ear*, N.Y. TIMES, Feb. 14, 2010; Peter Baker, *The Limits of Rahmism*, N.Y. TIMES MAGAZINE, Mar. 8, 2010.

22   United States v. Zacarias Moussaoui (4th Cir., Jan. 4, 2009); *see also* Bill Mears, *Terrorist Zacarias Moussaoui's Appeal of Life Sentence Denied*, CNN.COM, Jan. 4, 2010; United States v. Richard C. Reid, 214 F.Supp.2d 84 (D.Mass. Jul. 26, 2002).

23   United States v. Timothy McVeigh, 153 F.3d 1166 (10th Cir. 1998).

or whether it is held in Foley Square or Guantánamo are not the central issues. Fairness and impartiality are the central issues.

Another disappointment in the Obama Administration has been its consistent positions in matters involving litigation brought by former Guantánamo detainees to defend the legitimacy and legality of previous practices, involving cruel, inhuman and degrading treatment, as well as torture. In the various cases referred to in this book, the DOJ of the Obama Administration has consistently opposed civil actions brought by former Guantánamo detainees in their pursuit of legal remedies under U.S. law. It is not clear why Holder, who from the beginning of his tenure as Attorney General expressed principled positions opposing the policy and practices of torture conducted under the Bush Administration, has allowed this DOJ policy of defending the perpetrators of these violations. In that respect, the DOJ's positions are simply a continuation of the positions taken by the Department under the Bush Administration's two Attorneys General, Ashcroft and Gonzales.

In keeping with the Obama Administration's efforts to oppose liability cases arising out of the practices described in this book, as well as to contain litigation, Attorney General Holder opposed the petitions of 105 former Guantánamo detainees who had been released into the custody of a foreign country.[24] As a result, the U.S. has managed to convince other countries to continue the detention some of the former Guantánamo detainees, much as it used foreign countries as surrogate for torture in the "extraordinary rendition" program discussed earlier in Chapter 4. Judge Thomas F. Hogan of the District Court for the District of Columbia denied these 105 habeas petitions on the grounds that the questions raised are moot, even though the memorandum opinion admits that "their petition raises one of the many questions left unanswered by the U.S. Supreme Court in *Boumediene v. Bush* – what happens to a Guantánamo detainee's claim once he is transferred or released?"[25]

Moreover, the DOJ's professional conduct investigation of Bybee and Yoo exonerated them from professional misconduct, thus precluding bar associations' ethics committees to consider the discipline of these two lawyers.[26] It was concluded that the two lawyers in question had acted in violation of professional conduct standards, and that upon review by a longstanding DOJ prosecutor, the determination was reduced from professional misconduct to merely "poor judgment".[27] The reviewer, David Margolies is probably the DOJ's best expert on organized crime, but he has no expertise in IHL, or for that matter of international law generally. To any outside observer this would appear

---

[24] In Re Petitioners Seeking Habeas Corpus Relief in Relation to Prior Detentions at Guantanamo (Misc. No. 08–0444 (TFH)) (D.D.C. Apr. 2010).

[25] *Id.*

[26] *See* Michael Isikoff & Daniel Klaidman, *Justice Official Clears Bush Lawyers in Torture Memo Probe*, NEWSWEEK, Jan. 29, 2010.

[27] *Id.*

incongruous – even politically motivated – and would be no more logical than to have the senior expert on anti-trust law express a reviewing opinion on legal subjects of which he or she would have scant expertise. The consequences of this position will make it difficult for any bar association ethics investigation to reach a contrary position, and will also be a serious impediment to any civil action brought by victims against these two lawyers. Moreover, it precludes any impeachment proceedings against Bybee, who currently serves as a federal appeals judge.

In response to calls for investigation and eventual prosecutions in torture cases, in August 2009 Holder appointed a special prosecutor to investigate those actions by the CIA that went beyond the policy approved by the Bush Administration.[28] This position, reflected in memoranda issued by the DOJ and the CIA, provides however, a tacit acceptance of the policy that was reflected in various Bush Administration memoranda discussed herein. By implication, this approach could be deemed to affirm their validity. The investigation ordered by Holder is also limited to those actions taken by CIA operatives and does not include military participation in these actions.

Notwithstanding the appointment of a Special Prosecutor to conduct investigations into CIA practices such as extraordinary rendition and the use of "black sites", President Obama in a speech before the Agency in April 2009 made it clear that no one in the CIA will be subject to prosecution, thus in effect undermining the whole exercise of the investigation. This is probably what led Jay Bybee, now a federal appeals court judge whose memos as DOJ's Legal Counsel started the process of institutionalizing torture, to state before the House Judiciary Committee on May 26, 2010 that the CIA never sought approval of some of the practices they engaged in, such as dousing detainees with cold water to keep them awake, or forcing detainees to wear diapers or to soil themselves. To the amazement of many, he claimed that those techniques were never authorized, according to a transcript released by the Committee. That Bybee would absolve himself by shifting responsibility to the CIA is astounding, but he was probably reassured by President Obama's statements that no prosecutions of CIA operatives would ensue. Like other members of the "cabal", as the Cheney team was informally referred to, their strategy is to claim good faith and deflect responsibility by indicating that what happened was due to a series of misinterpretations and misunderstandings.

On the positive side, President Obama has delivered on his promise to end torture in the U.S., rejecting the "enhanced interrogation" techniques developed by the Bush Administration.[29] In an Executive Order issued January 27, 2009, President Obama reinstated the Geneva Conventions' Common Article 3 and

---

[28]   *See* Carrie Johnson, *Prosecutor to Probe CIA Investigations*, WASH. POST, Aug. 24, 2009.

[29]   Nanda, *International Law Implications of the United States' "War on Terror"*, *supra* note 2, at 524.

revoked all Executive Directives, Orders, and Regulations issued from 9/11 to the end of the Bush Administration which are inconsistent with this new Order.[30] Detainees are to be treated in accordance with the CAT, and all relevant laws and treaties of the U.S.[31]

President Obama also abolished secret prisons, opened Guantánamo for inspection by the ICRC, and established a task force to review all interrogation methods, including those in the Army Field Manual.[32] Notwithstanding these positive developments, the President has allowed the CIA to continue the practice of "extraordinary rendition," provided that the receiving countries give assurances that such surrendered persons are not to be tortured.[33] This was the Bush Administration's official position, even though there was evidence that the countries providing these assurances did not live up to them. The problem, then and now, is the credibility and reliability of these assurances and the fact that "extraordinary rendition" may violate the laws of the states where such persons are seized. Moreover, these forms of rendition outside of a formal legal process violate elementary standards of international due process of law.[34] The Obama Administration has also failed to place limitations on the U.S. use of surrogates in Afghanistan. In this practice, anti-terrorism paramilitary forces trained and funded by the U.S. use torture against Afghans and others in secret locations in Afghanistan.

The positive steps taken by the Administration, however, are outweighed by President Obama's continued support for indefinite detention of some foreign detainees, discussed earlier in Chapter 3 – a position which led former Bush Administration officials to state that the President's position is fundamentally the same of that of the Bush Administration.[35] While that assertion has been challenged by the Obama Administration, some perplexity remains.[36]

Furthermore, while President Obama has ended the use of torture in the U.S., he has failed to investigate those in the Bush Administration who established the policy and practices of torture and those who carried them out. In a speech in April 2009, President Obama stated that "[w]e have been through a dark and painful chapter in our history. But at a time of great challenges and disturbing disunity, nothing will be gained by spending our time and energy laying blame

---

[30]   Exec. Order No. 13,491, Ensuring Lawful Interrogations, *supra* note 1.

[31]   *See* Nanda, *International Law Implications of the United States' "War on Terror"*, *supra* note 2, at 523.

[32]   *Id.*

[33]   *See* Leila Sadat, *A Presumption of Guilt:The Unlawful Enemy Combatant and the U.S. War on Terror*, 37 Denv. J. Int'l L. Pol'y 539, 552 (2009).

[34]   *See* M. Cherif Bassiouni, International Extradition: United States Law and Practice 332 (5th ed. 2007), at 332 on unlawful seizures of persons.

[35]   *See* Jane Mayer, *The Trial: Eric Holder and the Battle Over Khaled Sheikh Mohammed*, The New Yorker, Feb. 15, 2010.

[36]   *See* Tracy, *Detention and Prosecution of Alleged Terrorists and Combatants*, *supra* note 11.

for the past."[37] This statement is inconsistent with another statement President Obama made during an address on the anniversary of the CAT in which he stated "[T]he United States must never engage in torture, and must stand against torture wherever it takes place."[38] The international and national obligations to prevent torture include investigation and eventual prosecution. So far, the Obama Administration has failed to carry out these obligations.

President Obama has taken many positive steps to restore the U.S. to a country that is governed by the rule of law. He swiftly ended the use of torture in the U.S. and against anyone in American custody and has made an effort to close Guantánamo detention center. In spite of these significant changes, the Obama Administration has failed to end the indefinite detention policy instituted by the Bush Administration, choosing instead to call it by a different name. This is inconsistent with the goal of returning the U.S. to a country governed by the rule of law.

There is also the question of how damaging to the reputation of the U.S. such trials before U.S. Courts would be. Moreover, the disclosure of the torture would require prosecution of U.S. personnel engaged in such tortures. These disclosures, and eventual prosecutions, would have a demoralizing effect on the CIA, and they would also hinder their intelligence gathering capabilities. The downside of previous practices would, therefore, have a multiplier effect that would be deleterious measures to intelligence and foreign policy interests of the U.S.

There are also domestic political consequences. Defenders of the Bush Administration anti-terrorism policies led by former Vice President Cheney argue that these policies kept America safe, and that regression from these policies would expose America to renewed danger. The Obama Administration is, therefore, placed in the position of having to prove wrong this argument, and that is an impossible task because no one can logically prove a negative.[39] The proponents of the first argument have placed themselves in a political position that would force their opponents, for domestic political purposes, to go slow on dismantling prior policies. This may explain why the Obama Administration has been soft on official criminal investigations that would possibly lead to prosecutions. These political positions have so far influenced the course of events. However the Obama Administration has failed to address the issue of principle through its failure to open official investigations into the torture policies and practices. The American people are entitled to know the truth. And those who

---

[37]   Press Release, The White House, *Statement of The President on the Release of OLC Memos*, Apr. 16, 2009.

[38]   Press Release, The White House, *Statement by President Barack Obama on United Nations International Day in Support of Torture Victims*, June 26, 2009.

[39]   The approach of Cheney and others is reminiscent of an absurd psychology example of elephants hiding in cherry trees. Since no one has ever seen an elephant in a cherry tree, it must mean that their hiding place works. By analogy, because no acts of terrorism like 9/11 have occurred since, it must mean that the gathering of intelligence through torture works.

have violated its laws deserve to be investigated, and if probable cause exists, prosecutions should ensue. That is what a government of laws is about. This is also the best way by which to re-establish American credibility in the world, particularly at a time when the spread of terrorism worldwide needs to be vigorously addressed by lawful means and by international cooperation. Success in this difficult endeavor is best ensured by seeking the moral high road.

6.3. CONCLUSION

The process which started with President Obama's Executive Orders in January 2009 to close Guantánamo is still ongoing. Members of Congress are still opposed to having some of the detainees there be tried in Federal Courts with the same due process guarantees available to any other defendant, and they are also opposed to releasing a number of detainees who have not been charged and who are not likely to be charged, since they are not known to have committed any crime against the U.S. Those who are expected to be tried are still the subject of much legal and political debate about whether they should be tried in federal court or whether they should be tried in a federal court elsewhere such as in Illinois in the Thompson prison facility which the DOJ seeks to acquire. There is also uncertainty about whether the military commissions will continue and for how long, and how many cases they may be actually seized of. The debate centers on four or five persons who were involved in the 9/11 attacks, more particularly because they have been so blatantly and consistently tortured, that any trial under any rule of law that excludes well-documented evidence of torture may prove to be a difficult undertaking. However, considering that there may also be sources of evidence obtained independently, it could be argued that their prosecution either before federal courts or before military commissions using the rules of procedure and evidence of the UCMJ would result in their conviction.

In addition to the uncertainty of prosecution of senior policymakers in the Bush Administration, and senior executors at the levels of military commanders, there is also uncertainty with respect to the discovery of truth through a senate or joint congressional committee, or through an independent commission. Political and institutional considerations have arisen and have apparently restrained President Obama. On the political side, there is the fear of antagonizing Republican members of Congress and the Republican base. At the institutional level it is the concern with what such inquiries would do to tarnish the reputation of the military who have, for the most part, opposed the policy and rejected the practices, but who have also weakened in the face of pressures by civilian political appointees, as well as the pressures of some of the military commanders who have used command influence to support or allow torture.

More problematic are the continued practices of extrajudicial executions in Afghanistan and Pakistan as well as in other areas through practices of drones and targeted assassinations.[40] The practice of torture in Afghanistan continues, and particularly at the hand of Afghan surrogates in the anti-terrorism Special Forces.

Last but not least, it is difficult to understand why the DOJ continues to consistently take positions similar to those of the Bush Administration and in defense thereof in various judicial proceedings. One would think that of all the actions, the Obama Administration would refrain from is the continued defense of the Bush Administration's policy and practices in the context of judicial proceedings, whether of a civil or criminal nature. However, as the saying goes in the legal profession, the jury is still out on the Obama Administration's promise of restoring the rule of law.

---

[40] *See* Robert Mackey, *Drone Strikes are Legal, U.S. Official Says*, N.Y. TIMES, Mar. 26, 2010, referring to Harold Hongjuh Koh, DOS Legal Adviser.

APPENDIX 5: STATUS OF CASES BEFORE THE MILITARY COMMISSIONS, JULY 2010

Detainees to be possibly transferred to and tried before Federal Court, or to be tried before the Military Commissions

All have been charged with the following crimes: conspiracy to commit terrorism, attacking civilians and civilian objects, causing serious bodily injury, murder in violation of the laws of war, hijacking, terrorism and providing material support for terrorism.

Khalid Sheikh Mohammed
Walid Muhammad Salih Mubarek Bin 'Attash
Ramzi Binalshibh
Ali Abdul Aziz Ali
Mustafa Ahmed Adam al Hawsawi

Ahmed Khalfan Ghailani (transferred from Guantánamo to the Federal District Court of the Southern District of New York on June 9, 2009)

Detainees on trial before the Military Commissions:

Omar Ahmed Khadr, charged with attempted murder and providing material support for terrorism

Detainees sworn before the Military Commissions:

Abdul Ghani, charged with conspiracy, attempted murder in violation of the laws of war, and providing material support for terrorism
Obaidullah, charged with conspiracy to commit terrorism and murder, and providing material support for terrorism
Faiz Mohammed Ahmed Al Kandari, charged with conspiracy to commit terrorism and providing material support for terrorism
Jabran Said Bin Al Qahtani, charged with conspiracy to commit terrorism and providing material support for terrorism
Ghassan Abdullah al Sharbi, charged with conspiracy to commit terrorism and providing material support for terrorism
Sufyian Barhoumi, charged with conspiracy to commit terrorism and providing material support for terrorism

Noor Uthman Mohamed, charged with conspiracy to commit terrorism and providing material support to terrorism

Detainees who have been referred to Military Commissions:

Ahmed Mohammed Ahmed Haza al Darbi, charged with conspiracy to commit terrorism and providing material support for terrorism
Tarek Mahmoud El Sawah, charged with conspiracy and providing material support for terrorism
Mohammed Kamin, charged with providing material support for terrorism

Detainees who have been tried and convicted before the Military Commissions:

Salim Ahmed Hamdan, convicted of providing material support for terrorism. Released from Guantánamo in November 2008 with one month to be served in Yemen, and released in January 2009.
David M. Hicks, convicted of providing material support for terrorism, and plea bargained to serve the remainder of his sentence in Australia. He was released in December 2008.
Ali Hamza Ahmad Suliman al Bahlul, convicted of conspiracy to commit murder, providing material support for terrorism, and destruction of property. Sentenced to life in prison.
Ibrahim Ahmed Mahmoud al Qosi, charged with providing material support for terrorism, pleaded guilty on July 7, 2010

Charges Withdrawn, but remain in detention:

Mohammed Al-Qahtani
Abd al-Rahim al-Nashiri

Charges withdrawn and released:

Binyam Mohamed
Mohammed Jawad
Mohammed Hashim
Fouad Mahmoud Hasan Al Rabia

CHAPTER 7

CONCLUDING ASSESSMENT

The policy and practices described in this book developed within a relatively short period of time after the September 11, 2001 attack on the U.S. It was the first time that the country had been attacked since Pearl Harbor in 1941. The blow was struck by a shadowy network of individuals of little military, economic, or political significance in comparison to the U.S. The U.S. learned from this experience that being a powerful nation is no guarantee against vulnerability from terror-violence attacks by small groups who have none of the characteristics of states. Americans wondered how the mightiest power in the world could be vulnerable to such an apparently unsophisticated group of people as the followers of Osama bin Laden – the bearded, turbaned, ascetic leader of al-Qaeda living in the mountainous border region between Afghanistan and Pakistan, who has eluded capture since September 11, 2001.

The Bush Administration proceeded to use post-9/11 national sentiment to marshal support for a variety of new political and military initiatives, including two practices known as "enhanced interrogation" techniques, "extraordinary rendition," and the use of "black sites." These practices were supported by policies that eventually lent justification to the use of torture as a way of gaining intelligence that would make the U.S. less vulnerable to attack, although no one assessed the usefulness of these practices. Even if one, arguendo, accepts the utilitarian approach professed by the Bush Administration, it is impossible to argue that actionable intelligence can be obtained after years of detention.

Alongside the post-9/11 expressions of anger, which generated some popular demand for revenge, the Bush Administration enhanced the public perception of fear, which was used to expand Presidential powers and turn public attention away from the security failures that preceded the attack. Anger, humiliation, and fear became the U.S. government's counsels, and they were not wise counsels.

The resort to vengeful responses led by Vice President Cheney carried the nation to what he called "the dark side" in order to terrorize those who wanted to terrorize us.[1] What Cheney and others in the Bush Administration ignored is

---

[1]   *See* Rep. John Conyers, Jr., Chairman of the U.S. House of Representatives Committee on the Judiciary, *Reining in the Imperial Presidency: Lessons and Recommendations Relating to the Presidency of George W. Bush* (January 2009):

    A few days after the 9/11 attacks [on 16 September 2001], Vice President Dick Cheney appeared on [NBC's] *Meet the Press*, where he was interviewed by Tim Russert. One part of

that the moral dimension of this nation's character is not founded upon the "dark side" of human nature, but on its commitment to the rule of law and justice and on its compliance with the commonly shared values of morality embraced by the people of the U.S. Ultimately many among the American people came to reject the Bush Administration's tactics, and to repudiate its policies and practices, although regrettably, not all Americans shared in this belief of a higher order of morality. For the latter, security comes first at whatever cost, and they are willing to act outside what they derogatorily considered to be legal niceties. In so doing, they ignored the fact that great nations hold fast to morality and to the rule of law, if for no other reason than to distinguish themselves from nations endowed only with might. The lessons of history were lost on them, and they had no concern for the consequences that may befall our nation.

The vulnerability of the U.S. to attack by terrorist groups is an inevitable consequence of being a free and open society. To reduce that vulnerability necessarily means a change in the habits of an open society. Anyone traveling by air knows that. However, as Americans, we accept risks in order to preserve freedom, openness, and due process over absolute security. As Benjamin Franklin stated so eloquently in 1775 as part of his notes for a proposition at the Pennsylvania Assembly: "Those who would give up essential liberty to purchase a little temporary safety, deserve neither liberty nor safety."[2]

In 1978 I was involved in probably the first governmental initiative to assess terrorism threats to the U.S. It was concluded then that there were so many targets of high vulnerability in this country that it would be literally impossible to defend them all and keep any semblance of being a free and open society. This is still true today, but much progress has been made to enhance public safety and to prevent terrorists from attacking the U.S., as well as its interests and citizens abroad. This was accomplished within the boundaries of the law.

---

the interview went as follows: "We also have to work, though, sort of the dark side, if you will. We've got to spend time in the shadows in the intelligence world. A lot of what needs to be done here will have to be done quietly, without any discussion, using sources and methods that are available to our intelligence agencies, if we're going to be successful. That's the world these folks operate in, and so it's going to be vital for us to use any means at our disposal, basically, to achieve our objective." For years, it was not clear what the "dark side" consisted of, what was meant by the "shadows of the intelligence world," and what were the "sources and methods" that the Vice President considered to be "available to our intelligence agencies" that were among the "any means at our disposal." Over time, however, at least some of the facts have emerged. The [Bush] Administration engaged in a series of unilateral actions at the direction of the President through his subordinates in connection with detention, interrogation, and intelligence collection that were characterized by the assertion of unreviewable executive power and the rejection of congressional and judicial limitations on this power.

Id. at 75–76.

2   Benjamin Franklin, *Pennsylvania Assembly: Reply to the Governor, Nov. 11, 1755, in* 6 THE PAPERS OF BENJAMIN FRANKLIN 242 (Leonard W. Labaree ed., 1963). This quote is inscribed on the pedestal of the Statue of Liberty.

After September 11, 2001, the Bush Administration turned against the moral ideal expressed by John Adams wrote in 1780 that the U.S. be "an empire of laws, and not of men."[3] After 2001, torture, "secret evidence" in trials, judicially uncontrolled surveillance of communication, intrusive legislation limiting the right of privacy and expanded presidential powers – free from legislative and judicial controls – became part of the American system. The very practices which for decades we pointed to as hallmarks of what President Reagan called "evil empires," became part of our own practices but fortunately, not for too long a time. We are still a democracy and the rule of law prevails, its quirks notwithstanding.

At the height of the Bush Administration's influence in 2002 and 2003, strong emotions spurred by ideologically-based assumptions and an eagerness to expand Executive powers left no room for reasonable discourse on policy, particularly one that involved legal considerations. Specifically, enemies captured in Afghanistan were purposely denied privileged combatant status under the Geneva Conventions, and non-combatant civilians as well as protected civilians were not treated as such. The faulty argument advanced was that in a time of war, legal niceties can be displaced. However, it is precisely at these times that the rule of law is most needed, as is respect for IHL and other international legal obligations.

Parallel to developments in the Afghanistan theater of operation, the U.S. security apparatus at home embarked on both a domestic and worldwide program to obtain information from those indiscriminately identified as "terrorists."[4] The terrorist label was applied to a wide range of individuals and organizations irrespective of the legitimacy of their goals, and the actual means the group might employ to advance its views. A wide net was cast to catch all sorts of fish, in all sorts of waters, irrespective of how likely it was that those captured would provide actionable intelligence, and regardless of what had to be done to extract that information. The official policy was to obtain results within as short a period of time as possible, because the dangers perceived did not allow the luxury of acting differently. In short, for the Bush Administration, the ends justified the means, and that is contrary to a government of laws where the means are subject to the due process of law.

"Enhanced interrogation" techniques were seen as the best way to achieve the desired results. As reported in a number of studies cited throughout this book, including Barton Gellman's *Angler: The Cheney Vice Presidency* (2008), Jane Mayer's *The Dark Side* (2008), and Philippe Sands' *Torture Team* (2008), the Bush Administration sent the message that government lawyers as well as intelligence

---

[3]   John Adams, *Novanglus Papers, No. 7*, 4 THE WORKS OF JOHN ADAMS (Charles Francis Adams ed., 1851), at 106.

[4]   For a critique of the Bush Administration's anti-Muslim policies after 9/11, see LOUISE CAINKAR, HOMELAND INSECURITY (2009).

and military specialists should seek ways to get results. As former CIA Director George Tenet said in his self-serving autobiography, *At the Center of the Storm*, "In situations like this, you don't call in the tough guys; you call in the lawyers."[5] And so it was that Cheney called in the lawyers who did his bidding, outside of established constitutional and legal frameworks in order to achieve goals of national security by unlawful means.

It is important to ask whether the unlawful policy and illegal practices of institutionalized torture could have been grounded in good faith. Even if the Bush Administration's policy on torture had been benign in its genesis, something happened as "enhanced interrogation" techniques, "extraordinary rendition," and the use of "black sites" evolved. Perhaps over-zealous or less-than-conscientious government lawyers found ways to stretch the law more and more until it broke; or perhaps they simply disregarded the law by working around it. Whether they were acting in good faith is something that only a full and transparent investigation can reveal. The limited Obama Administration DOJ reviews of Yoo and Bybee, and of the CIA interrogation tape cover-up are simply not enough to address the scope and magnitude of the policy and practices. If evidence is adduced that crimes have been committed, then they must be prosecuted, as our laws require.

Nothing herein is intended to attribute criminal responsibility to anyone mentioned. What this and other studies reveal is that there are sufficient grounds to believe that violations of U.S. and international law have been committed, and that alone should support the appointment of a special prosecutor to investigate what transpired.

In the course of the evolution of this policy and its practices, the circle of its advocates widened to include government lawyers from the White House, the DOD, the DOJ, and the CIA. Their legal efforts had the effect of subverting or overturning legal positions and practices on interrogations that were well established to protect prisoners of war and civilians. Short shrift was made of legal distinctions of all types. To say the least, they sought to avoid international and U.S. law, and that avoidance soon turned into evasion of the law – a distinction which, if nothing else, may constitute a crime and a violation of professional ethics.

In time, the original DOJ position on torture was reversed, and other legal positions were changed by that same Administration. The practices were also changed at Abu Ghraib and Guantánamo, but by then, a number of years had passed and the secret policy on torture had become public knowledge. The U.S. was discredited worldwide, losing the moral high ground that it had occupied since World War II as well as the world's sympathy, which it had obtained after 9/11.

---

[5]   George Tenet, At the Center of the Storm: My Years at the CIA (2007), at 241.

To paraphrase Winston Churchill: The U.S. will almost always end up doing the right thing, but only after exhausting all other alternatives. President Obama has reversed course and seems committed to doing the right thing. On only his second day in office, President Obama signed three Executive Orders closing the Guantánamo Bay detention center, ending the CIA's use of secret prisons, and requiring that all interrogations meet the requirements of the Geneva Conventions by following the non-coercive methods of the Army Field Manual. In April 2009, however, President Obama expressed reluctance to prosecute those responsible for implementing the unlawful policy and illegal practices of torture when he stated that "We have been through a dark and painful chapter in our history. But at a time of great challenges and disturbing disunity, nothing will be gained by spending our time and energy laying blame for the past."[6] In the same speech, President Obama re-affirmed his dedication to righting the course of the U.S. and commitment to being a nation of laws. These orders are important steps toward re-establishing the rule of law and the U.S. reputation as a nation of laws. However, one more step is required, namely, the prosecution of those who are criminally responsible.

As existing problems are addressed, researchers must turn their attentions to past problems by recording how the torture policy developed. As a nation, we must document how the Constitution and laws of this country could be so easily subverted; why Congress failed to exercise its Constitutional duty of "checks and balance"; why the Judiciary, and particularly the Supreme Court, shied away from the traditional role of guaranteeing "due process of law"; why the bar associations were silent; and why was there no indignation in the reaction of Americans. Last but not least, we must determine who the villains were and who the heroes were. More importantly those who have committed crimes (including the leaders who have initiated the policy and the lawyers who have also breached public trust in distorting that law) must be investigated and if evidence exists, they must be prosecuted. Congress must also establish a mechanism that will prevent the recurrence of similar abuses of power by the executive branch of government.

Ultimately, how can we understand the torture policy and practices which took place during the Bush Administration? Apart from morality and legality, the decisions which were made and actions which took place defy common sense, good judgment, and sound intelligence practices. How could so many errors have been made by so many people, for so long, and not have been detected by anyone up the chain of command? If they had been detected, why did no one dare to act? Two hypotheses are that there was either some superior political moving force that pushed in the direction of these continued practices, or that those who engaged in it were truly evil and malevolent persons. What is more likely is that it was simply the product of bureaucratic compartmentalization,

---

[6]   Press Release, *Statement of The President on the Release of OLC Memos*, Apr. 16, 2009.

with each bureaucracy fearing to appear ineffective or to be embarrassed. In other words, as military intelligence, the CIA, private contractors, and others continued their separate interrogations and mistreatments, without communicating their results to one another and perhaps without analysis by superior officers, each bureaucracy continued along their separate paths, fearing that another agency or group involved might discover something that they missed. This embarrassment factor continued after discoveries that persons in question were either not active terrorists nor had any significant intelligence. Fear of embarrassment may explain why some of the detainees mentioned in this book were kept imprisoned and mistreated for several years, even when everything indicated that many of these individuals had little or no potential threat to the security of the U.S. The bureaucratization and embarrassment factor, coupled with command influence from the top and the political pressure to obtain results combined to produce these utterly nonsensical and counterproductive intelligence practices.

This assessment may be overly generous, however, in light of the declaration by Col. Lawrence B. Wilkerson, who served as Chief of Staff to Secretary of State Colin Powell, made in the U.S. District Court for the District of Columbia on behalf of a former Guantánamo detainee who was wrongfully arrested and detained, and who filed civil litigation against Bush, Rumsfeld, and others. In the declaration, he states:

> 9. a. With respect to the assertions by Mr. Hamad that he was wrongfully seized and detained, it became apparent to me as early as August 2002, and probably earlier to other State Department personnel who were focused on these issues, that many of the prisoners detained at Guantánamo had been taken into custody without regard to whether they were truly enemy combatants, or in fact whether many of them were enemies at all. I soon realized from my conversations with military colleagues as well as foreign service officers in the field that many of the detainees were, in fact, victims of incompetent battlefield vetting. There was no meaningful way to determine whether they were terrorists, Taliban, or simply innocent civilians picked up on a very confused battlefield or in the territory of another state such as Pakistan. The vetting problem, in my opinion, was directly related to the initial decision not to send sufficient regular army troops at the outset of the war in Afghanistan, and instead, to rely on the forces of the Northern Alliance and the extremely few U.S. Special Operations Forces (SOF) who did not have the necessary training or personnel to deal with battlefield detention questions or even the inclination to want to deal with the issue.
>
> b. A related problem with the initial detention was that predominantly U.S. forces were not the ones who were taking the prisoners in the first place. Instead, we relied upon Afghans, such as General Dostum's forces, and upon Pakistanis, to hand over prisoners whom they had apprehended, or who had been turned over to them for bounties, sometimes as much as $5,000 per head. Such practices meant that the likelihood was high that some of the Guantánamo detainees had been turned in to

U.S. forces in order to settle local scores, for tribal reasons, or just as a method of making money. I recall conversations with serving military officers at the time, who told me that many detainees were turned over for the wrong reasons, particularly for bounties and other incentives.

c. In fact, by late August 2002, I found that of the initial 742 detainees that had arrived at Guantánamo, the majority of them had never seen a U.S. soldier in the process of their initial detention and their captivity had not been subjected to any meaningful review. A separate but related problem was that often absolutely no evidence relating to the detainee was turned over, so there was no real method of knowing why the prisoner had been detained in the first place. Secretary Powell was also trying to bring pressure to bear regarding a number of specific detentions because children as young as 12 and 13 and elderly as old as 92 or 93 had been shipped to Guantánamo. By that time, I also understood that the deliberate choice to send detainees to Guantánamo was an attempt to place them outside the jurisdiction of the U.S. legal system.

d. It was clear to me that, as I learned about how the majority of the Guantánamo prisoners had been detained, the initial group of 742 detainees had not been detained under the processes I was used to as a military officer. It was also becoming more and more clear that many of the men were innocent, or at a minimum their guilt was impossible to determine let alone prove in any court of law, civilian or military. If there were any evidence, the chain protecting it had been completely ignored.

10. While Mr. Hamad was brought to Guantánamo after August 2002, I have no reason to believe that any more thorough process was used to determine whether his seizure or transfer to Guantánamo was justified. Moreover, Mr. Hamad was at Guantánamo when, during Secretary Powell's morning updates, he often expressed that he was particularly troubled by the lack of a plan regarding final disposition for the detainees, especially if the idea was to keep them in indefinite detention, without trial, forever. During the morning briefings, Ambassador-at-Large for War Crimes, Pierre Prosper, who was a primary person working on negotiating transfers, would discuss the difficulty he encountered in dealing with the Department of Defense, and specifically Secretary of Defense Rumsfeld, who just refused to let detainees go.

11. I came to understand that there were several different reasons for the refusal to release detainees in Guantánamo, even those who were likely innocent. These reasons continued to the time of my departure from the Department of State in 2005.

a. At least part of the problem was that it was politically impossible to release them. The concern expressed was that if they were released to another country, even an ally such as the United Kingdom, the leadership of the Defense Department would be left without any plausible explanation to the American people, whether the released detainee was subsequently found to be innocent by the receiving country, or whether the detainee was truly a terrorist and, upon release were it to then occur, would return to the war against the U.S. Another concern was that the detention efforts at Guantánamo would be revealed as the incredibly confused operation that they were. Such results were not acceptable to the Administration and would have been severely detrimental to the leadership at DOD.

b. Another part of the political dilemma originated in the Office of Vice President Richard B. Cheney, whose position could be summed up as "the end justifies the means", and who had absolutely no concern that the vast majority of Guantánamo detainees were innocent, or that there was a lack of any useable evidence for the great majority of them. If hundreds of innocent individuals had to suffer in order to detain a handful of hardcore terrorists, so be it. That seemed to be the philosophy that ruled in the Vice President's Office.

c. I discussed the issue of the Guantánamo detainees with Secretary Powell. From these discussions, I learned that it was his view that it was not just Vice President Cheney and Secretary Rumsfeld, but also President Bush who was involved in all of the Guantánamo decision making. My own view is that it was easy for Vice President Cheney to run circles around President Bush bureaucratically because Cheney had the network within the government to do so. Moreover, by exploiting what Secretary Powell called the President's "cowboy instincts," Vice President Cheney could more often than not gain the President's acquiescence.

d. For the Vice President, Secretary Rumsfeld and others, the primary issue was to gain more intelligence as quickly as possible, both on Al Qaeda and its current and future plans and operations but increasingly also, in 2002–2003, on contacts between Al Qaeda and Saddam Hussein's intelligence and secret police forces in Iraq. Their view was that innocent people languishing in Guantánamo for years was justified by the broader war on terror and the capture of the small number of terrorists who were responsible for the September 11 attacks, or other acts of terrorism. Moreover, their detention was deemed acceptable if it led to a more complete and satisfactory intelligence picture with regard to Iraq, thus justifying the Administration's plans for war with that country.

12. The attitude described above affected the treatment of prisoners such as Mr. Hamad.

…

b. As a related matter, my investigation into the Abu Ghraib detentions revealed that some 50–60% of those imprisoned in Abu Ghraib were probably innocent. They were swept up in combat operations and gotten off the battlefield by imprisoning them – an understandable tactic by military forces operating with too few assets to accomplish the mission, always the case in Iraq. No real records existed of evidence or facts that incriminated them, just as had happened at Guantánamo Bay.

…

d. I personally did not know that we had been torturing captives in Iraq, Afghanistan, and elsewhere until I did the research for Secretary Powell on the Abu Ghraib issue. I had known that there had been limited renditions in specific isolated instances in the past, largely as a result of the War on Drugs. I had no idea that the Administration had turned renditions into a counterterrorist policy and apparently conducted hundreds of them. If standard practice was followed, in order for the organized renditions to occur, there would have to be, at minimum, a Presidential finding that would order the Director of Central Intelligence (DC1) to carry them out. Others, such as the aircraft pilots involved in moving those rendered, would of course be in the know. Other high officials within the Administration may have known general information about suspected Al Qaeda terrorists being treated differently but may not have known the specifics.

13. I have made a personal choice to come forward and discuss the abuses that occurred because knowledge that I served in an Administration that tortured and abused those it detained at the facilities at Guantánamo Bay and elsewhere and indefinitely detained the innocent for political reasons has marked a low point in my professional career and I wish to make the record clear on what occurred. I am also extremely concerned that the Armed Forces of the United States, where I spent 31 years of my professional life, were deeply involved in these tragic mistakes.[7]

The concept of counter-productiveness must be emphasized because each one of those persons who was tortured, mistreated, or unlawfully detained for years, is likely to become an enemy of the U.S. Each such person is also likely to have a circle of relatives and friends who, in accordance to the cultures of many Asian, Arab, and African societies, require vengeance as a matter of honor. Thus, the circle of those who are likely to become enemies of the U.S. expands, adding to the threats posed to national security.

Furthermore, there are 1.4 billion Muslims in the world, many of whom are in the West and feel emotionally affected by these practices which are used exclusively against their own co-religionists. Thus, the circle of enemies and revenge seekers widens. They feel legitimized in attacking the U.S., U.S. citizens, and U.S. interests in the same indiscriminate manner as they feel their co-religionists, co-nationals, tribal or family members, have been indiscriminately harmed and humiliated by U.S. agents.

Of course, no one can ascertain how far and how wide this predictable social phenomena ranges. However, if for every detainee at Guantánamo, and for that matter, Abu Ghraib, Bagram, and CIA "black sites," there are a potential one hundred persons who are willing to risk their lives to avenge the indignities committed by the U.S. against people with whom they identify. This nation is made more unsafe than before. These practices have engendered thousands of persons who are likely to become a threat to national security. By any common sense, sound reasoning, good judgment, and good intelligence practice, the policy and practices of torture as described in this book, could not have been a better way of recruiting potential terrorists against the U.S. and the West.

It is my hope that this book, along with others on the same topic, will serve to remind Americans of the risks arising out of abuse of powers, and as a record for establishing the responsibility of the decision-makers and those who executed their policy. It is the contention of this book that such persons are not above the law, and that the American system of justice, as well as the international criminal justice system, demands that those who were involved in the decision-making, planning, and execution of the policy and practices of torture be investigated, and if the evidence warrants, be tried fairly and with the full legal rights offered

---

[7]   Declaration of Colonel Lawrence B. Wilkerson (Ret.), March 24, 2010, in Adel Hassan Hamad v. George W. Bush, Donald Rumsfeld, Jay Hood and Brice Gyurisko, CV 05–1009JDB (D.D.C. 2010), at 4–12.

by the Constitution – even though they denied such rights to others. Those who are members of the bar should also be investigated for violations of professional ethics as embodied in the various codes of conduct for lawyers. Congress should establish a national non-partisan commission to produce a legislative record of all aspects of this policy and its practices – in short, a truth commission. No one should be above the law, politics notwithstanding. When this happens, the U.S. will have fully restored itself to a nation operating under the rule of law, and it will once again regain the status of a great nation as opposed to being only a mighty one. That is the difference between a respected nation and a feared nation.

*　*
*

If you see a wrong you must right it,
with your hand if you can,
or, with your words,
or in your heart, but that is the weakest of faith.
Prophet Mohammed

*　*
*

If you want peace, work for justice.
Pope Paul VI

*　*
*

The world rests on three pillars: On Truth, on Justice, and on Peace.
Rabban Simeon Ben Gamaleil

If Justice is realized, truth is vindicated, and peace results.
Talmudic Commentary

TABLE OF AUTHORITIES

A.   BOOKS

AMERICAN BAR ASSOCIATION MODEL RULES OF PROFESSIONAL CONDUCT (2006)

THE NAZI DOCTORS AND THE NUREMBERG CODE: HUMAN RIGHT IN HUMAN EXPERIMENTATION (G.J. Annas & M.A. Grodin eds., 1992)

HANNAH ARENDT, EICHMANN IN JERUSALEM: A REPORT ON THE BANALITY OF EVIL (1963)

JOSÉ LUIS DE LA CUESTA ARZAMENDI, EL DELITO DE TORTURA (1990)

M. CHERIF BASSIOUNI, CRIMES AGAINST HUMANITY: HISTORICAL EVOLUTION AND CONTEMPORARY PRACTICE (2010)

M. CHERIF BASSIOUNI, INTERNATIONAL EXTRADITION: UNITED STATES LAW AND PRACTICE (5th ed. 2007)

THE LAW OF DISSENT AND RIOTS (M. Cherif Bassiouni ed., 1971)

M. CHERIF BASSIOUNI, 1–3 THE LEGISLATIVE HISTORY OF THE INTERNATIONAL CRIMINAL COURT: INTRODUCTION, ANALYSIS, AND INTEGRATED TEXT (2005)

A MANUAL ON INTERNATIONAL HUMANITARIAN LAW AND ARMS CONTROL AGREEMENTS (M. Cherif Bassiouni ed., 2000)

INTERNATIONAL CRIMINAL LAW: A GUIDE TO U.S. PRACTICE AND PROCEDURE (M. Cherif Bassiouni & Ved P. Nanda eds., 1987)

INTERNATIONAL RULES: APPROACHES FROM INTERNATIONAL LAW AND INTERNATIONAL RELATIONS (Robert J. Beck et al. eds., 1996)

HOWARD BELL, BUSH, THE DETAINEES, AND THE CONSTITUTION: THE BATTLE OVER PRESIDENTIAL POWER IN THE WAR ON TERROR (2007)

J. HERMAN BURGERS & HANS DANELIUS, THE UNITED NATIONS CONVENTION AGAINST TORTURE (1988)

LOUISE CAINKAR, HOMELAND INSECURITY (2009)

JIMMY CARTER, OUR ENDANGERED VALUES: AMERICA'S MORAL CRISIS (2005)

MARJORIE COHN, COWBOY REPUBLIC: SIX WAYS THE BUSH GANG HAS DEFIED THE LAW (2007)

DAVID COLE, ENEMY ALIENS: DOUBLE STANDARDS AND CONSTITUTIONAL FREEDOMS IN THE WAR ON TERRORISM (2003)

JANE CORBIN, AL-QAEDA: IN SEARCH OF THE TERROR NETWORK THAT THREATENS THE WORLD (2003)

JAMES CRAWFORD, THE INTERNATIONAL LAW COMMISSION'S ARTICLES ON STATE RESPONSIBILITY (2002)

MARK DANNER, TORTURE AND TRUTH: AMERICA, ABU GHRAIB, AND THE WAR ON TERROR (2004)

JOHN DECKER, ILLINOIS CRIMINAL LAW: A SURVEY OF CRIMES AND DEFENSES (4th ed. 2006)

ALAN DERSHOWITZ, WHY TERRORISM WORKS (2002)

YORAM DINSTEIN, THE DEFENSE OF "OBEDIENCE TO SUPERIOR ORDERS" IN INTERNATIONAL LAW (1965)

DISTRICT OF COLUMBIA RULES OF PROFESSIONAL CONDUCT (rev. February 1, 2007)

TYLER DRUMHELLER, ON THE BRINK: AN INSIDER'S ACCOUNT OF HOW THE WHITE HOUSE COMPROMISED AMERICAN INTELLIGENCE (2006)

POEMS FROM GUANTÁNAMO: THE DETAINEES SPEAK (Marc Falkoff ed. 2007)

DOUGLAS FEITH, WAR AND DECISION: INSIDE THE PENTAGON AT THE DAWN OF THE WAR ON TERRORISM (2009)

THOMAS M. FRANCKE, THE POWER OF LEGITIMACY AMONG NATIONS (1990)

THE ANNOTATED ALICE: THE DEFINITIVE EDITION (Martin Gardner ed., 2000)

BARTON GELLMAN, ANGLER: THE CHENEY VICE PRESIDENCY (2008)

JACK GOLDSMITH, THE LIMITS OF INTERNATIONAL LAW (2005)

JACK GOLDSMITH, THE TERROR PRESIDENCY: LAW AND JUDGMENT INSIDE THE BUSH PRESIDENCY (2007)

THE MY LAI MASSACRE AND ITS COVER-UP: BEYOND THE REACH OF THE LAW (Joseph Goldstein et al. eds., 1976)

PHILIP GOUREVITCH & ERROL MORRIS, STANDARD OPERATING PROCEDURE (2008)

LESLIE C. GREEN, SUPERIOR ORDERS IN NATIONAL AND INTERNATIONAL LAW (1976)

KAREN J. GREENBERG, THE LEAST WORST PLACE: GUANTANAMO'S FIRST 100 DAYS (2009)

THE TORTURE DEBATE IN AMERICA (Karen J. Greenberg ed., 2006)

THE ENEMY COMBATANT PAPERS: AMERICAN JUSTICE, THE COURTS, AND THE WAR ON TERROR (Karen J. Greenberg & Joshua Dratel eds., 2008)

THE TORTURE PAPERS: THE ROAD TO ABU GHRAIB (Karen J. Greenburg & Joshua L. Dratel eds., 2005)

OREN GROSS & FIONNUALA NI AOLAIN, LAW IN TIMES OF CRISIS: EMERGENCY POWERS IN THEORY AND PRACTICE (2006)

DAVID HARVEY, THE NEW IMPERIALISM (2003)

PRISCILLA HAYNER, UNSPEAKABLE TRUTHS: CONFRONTING STATE TERROR AND ATROCITY (2002)

JEAN-MARIE HENCKAERTS & LOUISE DOSWALD-BECK, 1, 2 CUSTOMARY INTERNATIONAL HUMANITARIAN LAW (2005)

LOUIS HENKIN, HOW NATIONS BEHAVE: LAW AND FOREIGN POLICY (2d ed. 1979)

SEYMOUR M. HERSH, CHAIN OF COMMAND: THE ROAD FROM 9/11 TO ABU GHRAIB (2004)

THOMAS HOBBES, ON THE CITIZEN 30 (Richard Tuck & Michael Silverthorne eds., 1998)

MICHAEL IGNATIEFF, AMERICAN EXCEPTIONALISM AND HUMAN RIGHTS (2006)

CHALMERS JOHNSON, THE SORROWS OF EMPIRE: MILITARISM, SECRECY, AND THE END OF THE REPUBLIC (2004)

FRITS KALSHOVEN, BELLIGERENT REPRISALS (2005)

NICO KEIJZER, MILITARY OBEDIENCE (1978)

RICHARD L. LAEL, THE YAMASHITA PRECEDENT: WAR CRIMES AND COMMAND RESPONSIBILITY (1982)

John H. Langbein, Torture and the Law of Proof (1977)

Robert Jay Lifton, The Nazi Doctors: Medical Killing and the Psychology of Genocide (1986)

Joseph Margulies, Guantánamo and the Abuse of Presidential Power (2006)

Jane Mayer, The Dark Side: The Inside Story of How the War on Terror Turned Into a War on American Ideals (2008)

David McCullough, John Adams (2001)

Theodor Meron, The Humanization of International Law (2006)

Steven H. Miles, Oath Betrayed: Torture Medical Complicity and the War on Terror (2006)

Stanley Milgram, Obedience to Authority: An Experimental View (1974)

Gail H. Miller, Defining Torture (2005)

2 The International Criminal Tribunal for Rwanda (Virginia Morris & Michael Scharf eds., 1998)

Ingo Muller, Hitler's Justice: The Courts of the Third Reich (Deborah Schneider trans., 1991)

Ekkehart Müller-Rappard, L'Order Superieur Militaire et la Responsibilite du Subordinne (1965)

John F. Murphy, The United States and the Rule of Law in International Affairs (2004)

Donald Nicolson & Julian Webb, Professional Legal Ethics: Critical Investigations (1999)

Martin Niemoller, Of Guilt and Hope (1947)

Manfred Nowak & Elizabeth McArthur, The United Nations Convention against Torture: A Commentary (2008)

Mary Ellen O'Connell, The Power and Purpose of International Law (2009)

Barbara Olshansky, Democracy Detained: Secret Unconstitutional Practices in the U.S. War on Terror (2007)

Mark J. Osiel, The End of Reciprocity: Terror, Torture, and the Law of War (2009)

Jordan J. Paust, Beyond the Law: The Bush Administration's Unlawful Responses in the "War" on Terror (2007)

Samantha Power, "A Problem from Hell": America and the Age of Genocide (2003)

Lila Rajiva, The Language of Empire: Abu Ghraib and the American Media (2005)

A. Frank Reel, The Case of General Yamashita (1949)

Restatement Third of the Foreign Relations Law of the United States (1987)

James Risen, State of War: The Secret History of the CIA and the Bush Administration (2006)

Lawrence P. Rockwood, Walking Away from Nuremberg (2007)

Fred Rosen, Contract Warriors: How Mercenaries Changed History and the War on Terrorism (2005)

Karl Rove, Courage and Consequence: My Life as a Conservative in the Fight (2010)

Leila Nadya Sadat, Forging a Convention for Crimes Against Humanity (forthcoming, 2010)

Philippe Sands, Lawless World (2005)

Philippe Sands, Torture Team: Rumsfeld's Memo and the Betrayal of American Values (2008)

George Santayana, The Life of Reason (1905)

Erik Saar & Viveca Novak, Inside the Wire: A Military Intelligence Soldier's Eyewitness Account of Life at Guantánamo (2005)

William A. Schabas, Genocide in International Law (2000)

Michael P. Scharf & Paul R. Williams, Shaping Foreign Policy in Times of Crisis: The Role of International Law and the State Department Legal Advisor (2010)

Michelle Shephard, Guantanamo's Child: The Untold Story of Omar Khadr (2008)

Ronald J. Sievert, Defense, Liberty, and the Constitution (2005)

P.W. Singer, Corporate Warriors: The Rise of the Privatized Military Industry (2003)

Ervin Stam, The Roots of Evil: The Origins of Genocide and of Group Violence (1989)

Henry J. Steiner & Philip Alston, International Human Rights in Context (2007)

Ron Suskind, The One Percent Doctrine: Deep Inside America's Pursuit of its Enemies Since 9/11 (2006)

Educing Information, Interrogation: Science and Art – Foundations for the Future (Russell Swenson & Robert Fein eds., National Defense Intelligence College, 2006)

George Tenet, At the Center of the Storm: My Years at the CIA (2007)

Henry David Thoreau, Civil Disobedience (1849)

U.S. Dep't of Army, Operational Law Handbook (2003)

James Waller, Becoming Evil: How Ordinary People Commit Genocide and Mass Killing (2002)

David Weissbrodt & Connie de la Varga, International Human Rights Law: An Introduction (2007)

New Wars, New Laws? Applying the Law of War in 21st Century Conflicts (David Wippman & Matthew Evangelista eds. 2005)

Bob Woodward, State of Denial (2006)

John Yoo, Crisis and Command: A History of Executive Power from George Washington to George W. Bush (2010)

John Yoo, The Powers of War and Peace: The Constitution and Foreign Affairs After 9/11 (2006)

John Yoo, War by Other Means: An Insider's Account of the War on Terror (2006)

Philip Zimbardo, The Lucifer Effect: Understanding How Good People Turn Evil (2008)

B.   JOURNAL ARTICLES

The Prevention and Suppression of Torture, 48 Revue Internationale de Droit Pénal (1977)

Abraham Abramovsky, *A Critical Evaluation of the American Transfer of Penal Sanctions Policy*, 61 Wis. L. Rev. 25 (1980)

John Adams, *Novanglus Papers, No. 7*, 4 The Works of John Adams (Charles Francis Adams ed., 1851)

George H. Aldrich, *Prospects for United States Ratification of Additional Protocol I to the 1949 Geneva Conventions*, 85 Am. J. Int'l L. 1 (1991)

Jose E. Alvarez, *Torturing the Law*, 37 Case W. Res. J. Int'l L. 175 (2006)

Diane Marie Amann, *Abu Ghraib*, 153 U. Pa. L. Rev. 2085 (2005)

Kai Ambos, *Prosecuting Guantánamo in Europe: Can and Shall the Masterminds of the "Torture Memos" be Held Criminally Responsible on the Basis of Universal Jurisdiction?*, 42 Case W. Res. J. Int'l L. 405 (2009)

George J. Annas, *Human Rights Outlaws: Nuremberg, Geneva, and the Global War on Terror*, 87 Boston U. L. Rev. 427 (2007)

George J. Annas & Michael A. Grodin, *Medical Ethics and Human Rights: Legacies of Nuremberg*, 3 Hofstra L. & Pol'y Symp. 111 (1999)

Barbara Armacost, *Qualified Immunity: Ignorance Excused*, 51 Vand. L. Rev. 583 (1998)

Dwyer Arce, *Paper Chase: Spain Judge Garzon Beginning Investigation of Suspected Guantanamo Torture*, Jurist, Jan. 31, 2010

Ross Bagley, Dorian Hurley, & Peter Mancuso, *Racketeer Influenced and Corrupt Organizations*, 44 Am. Crim. L. Rev. 901 (2007)

John Q. Barrett, *The Nuremberg Roles of Justice Robert Jackson*, 512 Wash. U. Globe S. Rev. 511 (2007)

M. Cherif Bassiouni et al., *An Appraisal of Human Experimentation in International Law and Practice: The Need for International Regulation of Human Experimentation*, 72 J. Crim. L. & Criminology 1597 (1981)

M. Cherif Bassiouni, *An Appraisal of Torture in International Law and Practice: The Need for an International Convention for the Prevention and Suppression of Torture, in* 48 Revue Internationale de Droit Pénal 23 (1977)

M. Cherif Bassiouni, *Crimes Against Humanity: The Case for a Specialized Convention*, 9 Wash U. Global Stud. L. Rev. (forthcoming 2010)

M. Cherif Bassiouni, *Great Nations and Torture, in* The Torture Debate in America 256 (Karen J. Greenberg ed., 2006)

M. Cherif Bassiouni, *The History of Universal Jurisdiction and Its Place in International Law, in* Universal Jurisdiction: National Courts and the Prosecution of Serious Crimes Under International Law (Stephen Macedo, ed. 2004)

M. Cherif Bassiouni, *Legal Status of U.S. Forces in Iraq from 2003–2008*, 11 Chicago J. Int'l L. (forthcoming 2010)

M. Cherif Bassiouni, *The New Wars the Crisis of Compliance with the Law of Armed Conflict by Non-State Actors*, 98 J. Crim. L. & Criminology 712 (2008)

M. Cherif Bassiouni, *The Normative Framework of International Humanitarian Law: Overlaps, Gaps, and Ambiguities*, 8 Transnat'l L. & Contemp. Probs. 199 (1998)

M. Cherif Bassiouni, *Perspectives on International Criminal Justice*, 50 Va. J. Int'l L. 269 (2010)

M. Cherif Bassiouni, *Perspectives on the Transfer of Prisoners Between the United States and Mexico and the United States and Canada*, 11 Vand. J. Transnat'l L. 249 (1978)

M. Cherif Bassiouni, *Universal Jurisdiction for International Crimes: Historical Perspectives and Contemporary Practice*, 42 Va. J. Int'l L. 81 (2001)

Steven W. Becker, *"Mirror, Mirror on the Wall…": Assessing the Aftermath of September 11th*, 37 Val. U. L. Rev. 563 (2003)

Emmanuel Kijo Bentil, Note, *United States v. Verdugo-Urquidez: The U.S. Supreme Court's Effort to Halt the Trade in Illegal Drugs*, 15 N.C. J. Int'l L. & Com. Reg. 511 (1990)

Arunabha Bhoumik, *Democratic Responses to Terrorism: A Comparative Study of the United States, Israel, and India*, 33 Denv. J. Int'l L. & Pol'y 285, 306 (2005)

Joseph P. Bialke, *Al-Qaeda & Taliban Unlawful Combatant Detainees, Unlawful Belligerency, and the International Laws of Armed Conflict*, 55 A.F.L. Rev. 1 (2004)

Christopher L. Blakesley & Dan E. Stigall, *The Myopia of U.S. v. Martinelli: Extraterritorial Jurisdiction in the 21st Century*, 39 Geo. Wash. Int'l L. Rev. 1 (2007)

M. Gregg Bloche & Jonathon Marks, *Doctors and Interrogators at Guantánamo Bay*, 353 New Eng. J. Med. 6 (2005)

Carolyn Patty Blum, Lisa Magarrell, & Marieke Wierda, *Prosecuting Abuses of Detainees in U.S. Counter-terrorism Operations* (International Center for Transitional Justice, Nov. 2009)

Curtis A. Bradley, *The* Charming Betsy *Canon and Separation of Powers: Rethinking the Interpretive Role of International Law*, 86 Geo. L.J. 479 (1998)

Curtis A. Bradley, *The Military Commissions Act, Habeas Corpus, and the Geneva Conventions*, 101 Am. J. Int'l L. 322 (April 2007)

Curtis Bradley & Jack Goldsmith, *Customary International Law as Federal Common Law: A Critique of the Modern Position*, 110 Harv. L.R. 815 (1997)

Bruce Bryan, Note, *The Constitutional Rights of Nonresident Aliens Prosecuted in the United States*, 3 Fordham Int'l L.J. 221 (1980)

Allen Buchanan, *Democracy and the Commitment to International Law*, 34 Ga. J. Int'l & Comp. L. 305 (2006)

Jeffrey Butts & Ojmarrh Mitchell, *Brick by Brick: Dismantling the Border Between Juvenile and Adult Justice*, 2 Boundary Changes in Criminal Justice Organizations 167 (U.S. DOJ, National Institute of Justice, 2000)

Mary Cheh, *Should Lawyers Participate in Rigged Systems? – The Case of the Military Commissions*, 1 J. Nat'l Sec. L & Pol'y 375 (2005)

Kathleen Clark, *Ethical Issues Raised by the OLC Torture Memorandum*, 1 J. Nat'l Sec. L. & Pol'y 455 (2005)

Majorie Cohn, *The Torture Tape Cover-up: How High Does It Go?* (Centre for Research on Globalization, Dec. 26, 2007)

Committee Against Torture, *Consideration of Reports Submitted by State Parties under Article 19 of the Convention, Conclusions and Recommendations of the Committee against Torture: United States of America*, CAT/C/USA/CO2 (May 18, 2006)

Council of Europe Parliamentary Assembly, Committee on Legal Affairs and Human Rights, *Alleged Secret Detentions in Council of Europe Member States*, AS/Jur (2006), Jan. 22, 2006

John R. Crook, *Contemporary Practice of the United States*, 100 Am. J. Int'l L. 959 (2006)

John R. Crook, *Contemporary Practice of the United States Relating to International Law* 101 Am. J. Int'l L. 487 (2007)

Mark P. Denbeaux, *Death in Camp Delta* (Seton Hall Law Center for Policy and Research, Dec. 2009)

Mark P. Denbeaux, *June 10th Suicides at Guantanamo: Government Words and Deeds Compared* (Seton Hall Law Center for Policy and Research, Aug. 21, 2006)

Mark Denbeaux & Joshua Denbeaux, *The Guantanamo Detainees: A Profile of 517 Detainees through Analysis of Department of Defense Data* (Seton Hall University School of Law, 2006)

Mark Denbeaux & Joshua Denbeaux, *No-Hearing Hearings, CSRT: The Modern Habeas Corpus?* 3 (Seton Hall Public Law Research Center, Dec. 13, 2006)

Daniel Derby, *The International Prohibition of Torture, in* 1 International Criminal Law: Sources, Subjects, and Contents 621 (M. Cherif Bassiouni ed., 3d ed. 2008)

Deven R. Desai, *Have your Cake and Eat it Too: A Proposal for a Layered Approach to Regulating Private Military Companies*, 39 U.S.F. L. Rev. 825 (2005)

Christian M. DeVos, *Mind the Gap: Purpose, Pain, and the Difference between Torture and Inhuman Treatment*, 14 Hum. Rts. Brief 4 (Winter 2007)

Laura A. Dickinson, *Government for Hire: Privatizing Foreign Affairs and the Problem of Accountability Under International Law* (University of Connecticut School of Law Working Paper, 2005)

Laura A. Dickinson, *Public Law Values in a Privatized World*, 31 Yale J. Int'l L. 383 (2006)

Jim Edwards, *Answering Ashcroft's Challenge: Lawyers for 9–11 Detainees Meet to Consider Coordinated Strategy*, 166 New Jersey L.J. 961 (2001)

European Parliament, *Report on the Alleged use of European Countries by the CIA for the Transportation and Illegal Detention of Prisoners*, 2006/2200(INI), Temporary Committee on the alleged use of European countries by the CIA for the transportation and illegal detention of prisoners, Rapporteur: Giovanni Claudio Fava (Jan. 26, 2007)

European Parliamentary Assembly, Report from the Commission on Legal Affairs & Human Rights, *Lawfulness of Detentions by the United States in Guantánamo Bay*, Doc. No. 10497 (2005)

Marc Falkoff, *This is To Whom it May Concern: A Guantánamo Narrative*, 1 DePaul J. Social Justice 153 (2008)

Benjamin Franklin, *Pennsylvania Assembly: Reply to the Governor, Nov. 11, 1755, in* 6 The Papers of Benjamin Franklin 242 (Leonard W. Labaree ed., 1963)

Jody Freeman, *Extending Public Law Norms Through Privatization*, 116 Harv. L. Rev. 1285 (2003)

Ellen L. Frye, *Private Military Firms in the New World Order: How Redefining "Mercenary" can tame the "Dogs of War,"* 73 Fordham L. Rev. 2607 (2005)

Michael John Garcia, *The War Crimes Act: Current Issues* (Congressional Research Service, RL33662, U.S. Library of Congress, Jan. 22, 2009)

Michael John Garcia, *UN Convention Against Torture (CAT): Overview and Application to Interrogation Techniques* (Congressional Research Service RL32438, Library of Congress, Jan. 25, 2006)

David E. Graham, *The Dual U.S. Standard for the Treatment and Interrogation of Detainees: Unlawful and Workable*, 48 WASHBURN L.J. 325 (2009)

Stuart Grassin, *Psychiatric Effects of Solitary Confinement*, 22 WASH UNIV. J. L. POL'Y 325 (2006)

Karen J. Greenberg, *Guantánamo Is Not Prison: 11 Ways to Report on Gitmo without Upsetting the Pentagon* (Center on Law and Security, Mar. 9, 2007)

Amos Guiora, *Anticipatory Self-Defence and International Law – A Re-evaluation*, 13 J. CONFLICT & SECURITY L. 3 (2008)

Amos Guiora, *What Makes a Targeted Attack Legal or Illegal: The Experience of a Former IDF Advisor*, FOREIGN POLICY, Jul. 13, 2009

George C. Harris, *The Rule of Law and the War on Terror: The Professional Responsibilities of Executive Branch Lawyers in the Wake of 9/11*, 1 J. NAT'L SEC. L. & POL'Y 409 (2005)

Kenneth J. Harris & Robert Kushen, *Surrender of Fugitives to the War Crimes Tribunals for Yugoslavia and Rwanda: Squaring International Legal Obligations with the U.S. Constitution*, 7 CRIM. L.F. 563 (1996)

Oona A. Hathaway & Ariel N. Lavinbuk, *Rationalism and Revisionisms in International Law*, 119 HARV. L. REV. 1404 (2006)

Donald H.J. Hermann, *Prisoners of War: The Role of Psychologists and Psychologists in Interrogation and Torture* 5 (Sept. 10, 2008) (unpublished paper, University of Rochester Medical Center)

Kristine A. Huskey, *Standards and Procedures for Classifying "Enemy Combatants": Congress, What Have You Done?. 43* REX. INT'L L.J. 41 (2007)

International Committee of the Red Cross, *Developments in U.S. Policy and Legislation Towards Detainees: The ICRC Position* (International Committee of the Red Cross, Oct. 19, 2006)

International Committee for the Red Cross, *ICRC Report on the Treatment of Fourteen "High Value Detainees" in CIA Custody*, Feb. 14, 2007

International Committee of the Red Cross, *Report of the ICRC on the Treatment by the Coalition Forces of Prisoners of War and Other Protected Persons by the Geneva Convention in Iraq During Arrest, Internment, and Interrogation* (Feb. 2004)

Aaron R. Jackson, *The White House Counsel Torture Memo: The Final Product of a Flawed System*, 42 CAL. W. L. REV. 149 (2005)

Emily A. Keram, *Will Medical Ethics Be a Casualty of the War on Terror?* 34 J. AM. ACAD. PSYCHIATRY 6 (2006)

Seth F. Kreimer, *"Torture Lite," "Full Bodied" Torture, and the Insulation of Legal Conscience*, 1 J. NAT'L SECURITY L. & POL'Y 187 (2005)

Mathew Lippman, *The Nazi Doctors Trial and the International Prohibition on Medical Involvement in Torture*, 15 LOY. L.A. INT'L & COMP. L.J. 395 (1993)

Mathew Lippman, *War Crimes Prosecution of Nazi Health Professionals and the Contemporary Protection of Human Rights*, 21 T. MARSHALL L. REV. 11 (1995)

David Luban, *Liberalism, Torture, and the Ticking Bomb*, 91 Va. L. Rev. 1425 (2005)

General Douglas MacArthur, *Duty, Honor, Country*, Thayer Award Acceptance Address, West Point, NY (May 12, 1962)

Peter Marguiles, *Foreword: Risk, Deliberation and Professional Responsibility*, 1 J. Nat'l Sec. L & Pol'y 357 (2005)

David A. Martin, *Judicial Review and the Military Commissions Act: On Striking the Right Balance*, 101 Am. J. Int'l L. 344 (2007)

David A. Martin, *Offshore Detainees and the Role of Courts After Rasul v. Bush: The Underappreciated Virtue of Deferential Review*, 2 B.C. Third World L.J. 125 (2005)

Jamie Mayerfield, *Playing by Our Own Rules: How U.S. Marginalization of International Human Rights Law Led to Torture*, 20 Harv. Hum. Rts. J. 89 (2007)

Theodor Meron, *The Humanization of Humanitarian Law*, 94 Am. J. Int'l L. 239 (2000)

Theodor Meron, *International Criminalization of Internal Atrocities*, 1995 Am. J. Int'l L. 89 (1995)

Julie Mertus & Lisa Davis; *Guantánamo Bay: The Global Effects of Wrongful Detention, Torture & Unchecked Executive Power*, 10 NYCLR 411 (2007)

Steven H. Miles, *Abu Ghraib: Its Legacy for Military Medicine*, 362 Lancet 725 (2004)

Steven H. Miles, *Medical Ethics and the Interrogation of Guantánamo 063*, 7 Am. J. Bioethics 4 (2007)

Todd Milliard, *Overcoming Post-Colonial Mytopia: A Call to Recognize and Regulate Private Military Companies*, 176 Mil. L. Rev. 1 (2003)

Winston Nagan & Lucie Atkins, *The International Law of Torture: From Universal Proscription to Effective Application and Enforcement*, 14 Harv. Hum. Rts. J. 87 (2001)

Ved P. Nanda, *International Law Implications of the United States' "War on Terror,"* 37 Denv. J. Int'l L. Pol'y 513 (2009)

William H. Neukom, *It's Time to End Torture* (ABA Newsletter, October 11, 2007)

Michael Newton, *Unlawful Belligerency After September 11: History Revisited and Law Revised in* New Wars, New Laws? Applying the Laws of War in 21st Century Conflicts (David Wippman & Mathew Evangelista eds., 2005)

Manfred Nowak, *What Practices Constitute Torture: U.S. and U.N. Standards*, 28 Hum. Rts. Q. 809 (2006)

Mynda G. Ohman, *Integrating Title 18 War Crimes into Title 10: A Proposal to Amend the Uniform Code of Military Justice*, Air Force L. Rev. 49 (Winter 2005)

Mark J. Osiel, *The Banality of Good: Aligning Incentives Against Mass Atrocity*, 105 Colum. L. Rev. 1751 (Oct. 2005)

Erin Louise Palmer, *Reinterpreting Torture: Presidential Signing Statements and the Circumvention of U.S. and International Law*, 14 Hum. Rts. Brief 21 (Fall 2006)

William H. Parks, *Command Responsibility for War Crimes*, 62 Mil. L. Rev. 1 (1973)

Jordan J. Paust, *Above the Law: Unlawful Executive Authorizations Regarding Detainee Treatment, Secret Renditions, Domestic Spying, and Claims to Unchecked Executive Power*, 2 Utah L. Rev. 345 (2007)

Jordan J. Paust, *Civil Liability of Bush, Cheney, et al. for Torture, Cruel, Inhuman, and Degrading Treatment and Forced Disappearance*, 42 Case W. Res. J. Int'l L. 359 (2009)

Jordan J. Paust, *Constitutional Limitations on Extraterritorial Federal Power: Persons, Property, Due Process and the Seizure of Evidence Abroad, in* M. CHERIF BASSIOUNI & VED P. NANDA, INTERNATIONAL CRIMINAL LAW: A GUIDE TO U.S. PRACTICE AND PROCEDURE 449 (1987)

Jordan J. Paust, *Customary International Law and Human Rights Treates* are *Law of the United States*, 20 MICH. J. INT'L L. 301 (1999)

Jordan J. Paust, *Executive Plans and Authorizations to Violate International Law*, 43 COLUM. J. TRANSNAT'L L. 811 (2005)

Jordan J. Paust, *Judicial Power to Determine the Status and Rights of Persons Detained Without Trial*, 44 HARV. INT'L L.J. 503 (2003)

Jordan J. Paust, *My Lai and Vietnam: Norms, Myths and Leader Responsibility*, 57 MIL. L. REV. 99 (1972)

Jordan J. Paust, *Prosecuting the President and his Entourage*, 14 ILSA J. INT'L & COMP. L. 539 (2007)

Jordan J. Paust, *The Second Bybee Memo: A Smoking Gun*, THE JURIST (April 22, 2009)

Jordan J. Paust, *The Unconstitutional Detention of Prisoners by the United States, Under the Exchange of Prisoners Treaties, in* INTERNATIONAL ASPECTS OF CRIMINAL LAW 204 (Richard B. Lillich ed., 1981)

Jordan J. Paust, *War and Enemy Status After 9/11: Attacks on the Laws of War*, 28 YALE J. INT'L L. 325 (2003)

Stephen Pepper, *Counseling at the Limits of the Law: An Exercise in the Jurisprudence and Ethics of Lawyering*, 104 YALE L.J. 1545 (1995)

William C. Peters, *On Laws, Wars, and Mercenaries: The Case for Courts-Martial Jurisdiction Over Civilian Contractor Misconduct in Iraq*, 2006 B.Y.U. L. REV. 367 (2006)

Broken Laws, Broken Lives: Medical Evidence of Torture by U.S. Personnel and Its Impact (Physicians for Human Rights, June 2008)

Experiments in Torture: Evidence of Human Subject Research and Experimentation in the "Enhanced" Interrogation Program (Physicians for Human Rights, June 2010)

Eric A. Posner, *Do States Have a Moral Obligation to Obey International Law?*, 55 STAN. L. REV. 1901 (2003)

Richard A. Posner, *Torture, Terrorism, and Interrogation, in* TORTURE: A COLLECTION 291 (Sanford Levinson ed., 2004)

A. John Radsan, *The Collision between Common Article Three and the Central Intelligence Agency*, 56 CATH. UNIV. L. REV. 959 (2007)

Michael D. Ramsey, *Toward a Rule of Law in Foreign Affairs*, 106 COLUM. L. REV. 1450 (2006)

Gabor Rona, *Military Commissions, The Gold Rule and the Law of War*, 31 NAT'L SECURITY L. REP. 2 (Jul-Oct 2009)

James B. Roan & Cynthia Buxton, *The American Military Justice System in the New Millennium*, 52 A.F.L. REV. 185 (2002)

Clifford J. Rosky, *Force, Inc.: The Privatization of Punishment, Policing, and Military Force in Liberal States*, 36 CONN. L. REV. 879 (2004)

Leila Nadya Sadat, *Extraordinary Rendition, Torture and Other Nightmares from the War on Terror*, 75 GEO. WASH. L. REV. 1200 (2007)

Leila Nadya Sadat, *Ghost Prisoners and Black Sites: Extraordinary Rendition Under International Law*, 37 Case W. Res. J. Int'l L. 309 (2006)

Leila Sadat, *A Presumption of Guilt: The Unlawful Enemy Combatant and the U.S. War on Terror*, 37 Denv. J. Int'l L. Pol'y 539 (2009)

Stephen A. Saltzburg, *The Reach of the Bill of Rights Beyond the Terra Firma of the United States*, 20 Va. J. Int'l L. 741 (1980)

Yves Sandoz, *Penal Aspects of International Humanitarian Law, in* 1 International Criminal Law 293 (M. Cherif Bassiouni ed., 3d ed. 2008)

Margaret L. Satterthwaite, *Rendered Meaningless: Extraordinary Rendition and the Rule of Law*, 75 Geo. Wash. L. Rev. 1333 (2007)

Kimberley A. Schaefer & John S. Schowengerdt, *Obstruction of Justice*, 43 Am. Crim. L. Rev. 763 (2006)

David Scheffer, *Introductory Note to Military Commissions Act of 2006*, 45 ILM 1241 (2006)

Elizabeth Sepper, *The Ties that Bind: How the Constitution Limits the CIA's Actions in the War on Terror*, 81 N.Y.U. L. Rev. 1805 (2007)

Hina Shamsi, *Command's Responsibility: Detainee Deaths in U.S. Custody in Iraq and Afghanistan* (Human Rights First, Feb. 2006)

P.W. Singer, *Frequently Asked Questions on the UCMJ Change and Its Applicability to Private Military Contractors* (Brookings Institution, Jan. 12, 2007)

P.W. Singer, *War, Profits, and the Vacuum of Law: Privatized Military Firms and International Law*, 42 Colum. J. Transnat'l L. 521 (2004)

Peter W. Singer, *The Law Catches Up to Private Militaries, Embeds*, Defense Tech (Jan. 4, 2007)

Paul B. Stephan, *Constitutional Limits on International Rendition of Criminal Suspects*, 20 Va. J. Int'l L. 777 (1980)

Barry Sullivan, *The Problem and Possibilities of Professionalism*, 21 Dublin U. L.J. 108, 126 (1999)

Barry Sullivan, *Professions of Law*, 9 Geo. J. Legal Ethics 1235 (1996)

Stacy Sullivan, *Confessions of a Former Guantanamo Prosecutor* (Human Rights Watch, Oct. 28, 2008)

Stacy Sullivan, *The Forgotten Kid of Guantanamo* (Human Rights Watch, May 27, 2008)

Symposium, *Terrorism on Trial*, 36 Case W. Res. U. J. Int'l L. 1 (2004)

Jonathan Tracy, *Detention and Prosecution of Alleged Terrorists and Combatants*, 16 Hum. Rts. Brief 51 (2009)

U.N. Comm. Against Torture, *Consideration of Reports Submitted by State Parties Under Article 19 of the Convention, Second Periodic Reports of States Parties Due in 1999*, U.N. Doc. CAT/C/48/Add.3 (June 29, 2005)

U.N. High Commissioner for Human Rights, *Human Rights, Terrorism and Counter-terrorism* (Fact Sheet No. 32, July 2008)

U.N. High Commissioner for Human Rights, *Manual on Effective Investigation and Documentation of Torture and Other Cruel, Inhuman or Degrading Treatment or Punishment* (August 9, 1999)

Christine Van den Wyngaert, *War Crimes, Genocide and Crimes Against Humanity – Are States Taking National Prosecutions Seriously?, in* 3 International Criminal Law 235 (M. Cherif Bassiouni ed., 3d ed. 2008)

Andre Verloy & Daniel Politi, *Contracting Intelligence: Department of Interior releases Abu Ghraib Contract* (Center for Public Integrity, July 28, 2004)

Rebecca Rafferty Vernon, *Battlefield Contractors: Facing Tough Issues*, 33 Pub. Cont. L.J. 369 (2004)

Stephen I. Vladeck, *Reflecting on Boumediene: The Substance of Habeas and the Futility of Exhaustion*, 30 ABA Comm. on Law and Nat'l Sec. Law Report 1 (2008)

Evan Wallach, *Drop by Drop: Forgetting the History of Water Torture in U.S. Courts*, 45 Colum. J. Transnat'l L. 468 (2007)

Evan J. Wallach, *The Logical Nexus Between the Decision to Deny Application of the Third Geneva Convention to the Taliban and al Qaeda and the Mistreatment of Prisoners in Abu Ghraib*, 36 Case W. Res. J. Int'l L. 541 (2004)

Evan Wallach & Maxine Marcus, *Command Responsibility*, in 3 International Criminal Law (M. Cherif Bassiouni ed., 3d ed. 2008)

David Weissbrodt & Amy Bergquist, *Extraordinary Rendition and the Torture Convention*, 46 Va. J. Int'l L. 585 (2006)

David Weissbrodt & Amy Bergquist, *Extraordinary Rendition: A Human Rights Analysis*, 19 Harv. Hum. Rts. J. 123 (2006)

Bradley Wendel, *The Torture Memos and the Demands of Legality*, 12 Legal Ethics 107 (2009)

Eric Wiebelhaus-Brahm, *Truth Commissions*, in 1 The Pursuit of International Criminal Justice: A World Study on Conflicts, Victimization, and Post-Conflict Justice (M. Cherif Bassiouni ed., 2010)

David Wippman, *Introduction: Do New Wars Call for New Laws? in* New Wars, New Laws? Applying the Law of War in 21st Century Conflicts 11 (David Wippman & Matthew Evangelista eds. 2005)

World Medical Association, *Declaration of Tokyo* (Tokyo: Japan, October 1975)

Bruce Zagaris, *Australian David Hicks Pleads Guilty After U.S. Threatens Military Defense Counsel*, 23 Int'l Enforcement L. Reporter 185 (May 2007)

Bruce Zagaris, *Germany Charges 13 CIA Operatives in el-Masri Rendition Probe*, 23 Int'l Enforcement L. Reporter 131 (April 2007)

Mark S. Zaid, *The U.S. War Crimes Act of 1996*, in 3 International Criminal Law 407 (M. Cherif Bassiouni ed., 3d ed. 2008)

Juan Carlos Zartae, *The Emergency of a New Dog of War: Private International Security Companies, International Law, and the New World Disorder*, 34 Stan. J. Int'l L. 75 (1998)

C.   NEWSPAPERS, PERIODICALS, AND PRESS RELEASES

Spencer Ackerman, *Key Player in 'Enhanced' Interrogations Still at CIA*, Wash. Independent, April 23, 2009

ACLU, Press Release, *CIA Finally Acknowledges Existence of Presidential Order on Detention Facilities Abroad*, Nov. 14, 2006

ACLU, Press Release, *CIA Provides Further Details on Secret Interrogation Memos*, Jan. 10, 2007

ACLU, Press Release, *Guantánamo Prisoner Successfully Challenges Unlawful Detention*, Apr. 9, 2009

ACLU, Press Release, *Innocent Victim of CIA Extraordinary Rendition Program Takes Case to International Tribunal*, Apr. 9, 2008

ACLU, Press Release, *Judge Orders Release of Guantánamo Detainee Mohammed Jawad*, July 30, 2009

ACLU Press Release, *Supreme Court Declines Case of Innocent CIA Kidnapping Victim Khaled El-Masri*, Oct. 9, 2007

American Medical Association, Press Release, *AMA Reiterates Opposition to Feeding Individuals Against their Will*, Mar. 10, 2006

Ian Austen, *Canada Suspected U.S. Plan for Muslim*, CHI. TRIB., Aug. 10, 2007

Ian Austen, *Canadian General Acknowledges Risk to Afghan Detainees*, N.Y. TIMES, Dec. 9, 2009

Jo Becker, *The War on Teen Terror*, SALON.COM, June 24, 2008

Richard Benedetto, *Bush Defends Interrogation Tactics: 'We do not torture'*, USA TODAY, Nov. 11, 2005

Dan Bilefsky, *European Inquiry says C.I.A. Flew 1,000 Flights in Secret*, N.Y. TIMES, Apr. 27, 2006

Jesse Bravin, *The Conscience of the Colonel*, WALL ST. J., Mar. 31, 2007

John F. Burns, *Britain Pledges Inquiry into Torture*, N.Y. TIMES, Jul. 6, 2010

Robert Burns, *Army Demots a One-Star General Accused of Dereliction in Prisoner Abuse Scandal*, ASSOCIATED PRESS, May 6, 2005

Bush Admits to CIA Secret Prisons, BBC NEWS, Sep. 7, 2006

Doreen Caravajal, *Groups Tie Rumsfeld to Torture in Complaint*, N.Y. TIMES, Oct. 27, 2007

Sewell Chan & Jackie Spinner, *Guantanamo Bay Chief Takes Over After Shameful Jail Abuse*, SYDNEY MORNING HERALD, May 1, 2004

Marjorie Cohn, *First They Came for the Lawyers*, AFTERDOWNINGSTREET.ORG, Jan. 15, 2007

David Cole, *Bush's Torture Ban is Full of Loopholes*, SALON.COM, July 23, 2007

John Crewdson, *Italy: CIA Email Ties Agents to Abduction*, CHI. TRIB., Jan. 20, 2006

John Crewdson & Alessandra Maggiorani, *Italians Press for Extradition of CIA Agents*, CHI. TRIB., Nov. 11, 2005

Mark Danner, *U.S. Torture: Voices from the Black Sites*, N.Y. REVIEW OF BOOKS, Apr. 9, 2009

Bill Dedman, *Can '20th Hijacker' Ever Stand Trial? Aggressive Interrogation at Guantanamo May Prevent his Prosecution*, MSNBC.COM, Oct. 26, 2006

Alan Dershowitz, *Is There a Torturous Road to Justice?*, L.A. TIMES, Nov. 8, 2001

Karen DeYoung, *CIA Director Panetta Says Agency is No Longer Operating Secret Prisons*, WASH. POST, Apr. 9, 2009

Elizabeth Dickinson, *Chuckie Taylor Sentenced to 97 Years*, FOREIGN POLICY, Jan. 9, 2009

Rachel Donadio, *Italy Convicts 23 Americans for C.I.A. Renditions*, N.Y. TIMES, Nov. 4, 2009

Editorial, *A Bagram Reckoning*, N.Y. TIMES, Jan. 18, 2010

Editorial, *Gitmo, Justice – and justice,* CHI. TRIB., May 14, 2007

Editorial, *Moving Gitmo to America,* N.Y. TIMES, Dec. 15, 2009

Steven Edwards, *U.S. Looks for Way to Return Khadr,* NATIONAL POST (Canada), Mar. 8, 2010

Dan Eggen & Walter Pincus, *FBI, CIA Debate Significance of Terror Suspect,* WASH. POST, Dec. 18, 2007

Dexter Filkins & Mark Mazzetti, *Contractors Tied to Effort to Track and Kill Militants,* N.Y. TIMES, Mar. 15, 2010

Peter Finn, *Justice Task Force Recommends about 50 Guantanamo Detainees to be Held Indefinitely,* WASH. POST, Jan. 22, 2010

Brigadier General Patrick Finnegan, *Letter to the Editor,* THE NEW YORKER, May 3, 2010

Cpt. Ian Fishback, U.S. Dep't of the Army to Senator John McCain (Sept. 16, 2005), *reprinted in A Matter of Honor,* WASH. POST, Sept. 28, 2005, at A21.

Erich Follath et al., *America's Shame: Torture in the Name of Freedom,* SPIEGEL, Feb. 20, 2006

Elaine Ganley, *Investigator: CIA Ran Secret Prisons,* CHI. TRIB., June 8, 2007

William Glaberson, *Supreme Court to Hear Guantánamo Detainees' Case,* N.Y. TIMES, June 29, 2007

James Glanz & Alissa Rubin, *Blackwater Shooting 'Murder,' Iraq Says,* N.Y. TIMES, Oct. 8, 2007

Tim Golden & Eric Schmitt, *Detainee Policy Sharply Divides Bush Officials,* N.Y. TIMES, Nov. 2, 2005

Amy Goldstein, *Justices Against Refuse Guantánamo Bay Cases,* WASH. POST, May 1, 2007

Gonzales: U.S. Has Little Control over Foreign Prisoner Torture, ASSOCIATED PRESS, Mar. 7, 2005

Glenn Greenwald, *The Suppressed Fact: Deaths by U.S. Torture,* SALON.COM, Jun. 30, 2009

Stephen Grey, *CIA Prisoners "Tortured" in Arab Jails,* BBC NEWS, Feb. 8, 2005

John Heilprin, *Pentagon Disavows Law Firm Boycott Call,* CHI. TRIB., Jan. 14, 2007

John Hendren, *CIA May Have Held 100 'Ghost' Prisoners,* L.A. TIMES, Sept. 10 (2004)

Seymour M. Hersh, *Annals of National Security: The General's Report,* THE NEW YORKER, Jun. 25, 2007

Seymour M. Hersh, *The General's Report: How Antonio Taguba, who investigated the Abu Ghraib Scandal, Became One of its Casualties,* THE NEW YORKER, June 25, 2007

Seymour M. Hersh, *Torture at Abu Ghraib,* THE NEW YORKER, May 10, 2004

David M. Herszenhorn, *Bill Applies U.S. Law to Contractors,* N.Y. TIMES, Oct. 5, 2007

David M. Herszenhorn, *Bill Curbing Terror Interrogators is Sent to Bush, Who Has Vowed to Veto It,* N.Y. TIMES, Feb. 14, 2008

Pamela Hess, *Hayden Says CIA Videotapes Destroyed,* ASSOCIATED PRESS, Dec. 7, 2007

Hicks 'Silenced' Before Election, THE AGE (Australia), Apr. 5, 2007

Christopher Hitchens, *Believe Me, It's Torture,* VANITY FAIR (August 2008)

Allison Hoffman, *Marine Convicted of Conspiracy,* ASSOCIATED PRESS, Jul. 7, 2007

Scott Horton, *The Guantanamo "Suicides": A Camp Delta Sergeant Blows the Whistle,* HARPER'S (February 2010)

Scott Horton, *The Plea Bargain of David Hicks,* HARPER'S (April 2007)

Scott Horton, *State of Exception: Bush's War on the Rule of Law*, HARPER'S MAGAZINE (July 2007)

Scott Horton, *Which Came First, Memo or Torture?*, L.A. TIMES, Apr. 21, 2008

Human Rights Watch, *Releasing Jawad: A Boy's Life at Guantanamo* (Jan. 11, 2010)

Human Rights Watch, *Still at Risk: Developments Regarding Diplomatic Assurances Since April 2004* (2005)

Human Rights Watch, *U.S.: Stop Unfair Trial of Guantánamo Youth* (Feb. 1, 2008)

Tom Hundley, *Remote Polish Airstrip holds clues to secret CIA flights*, CHI. TRIB., Feb. 6, 2007

Inside the Interrogation of Detainee 063, TIME, June 12, 2005

David Ignatius, *Cheney's Cheney*, WASH. POST, Jan. 5, 2006

Michael Isikoff, *Ali Soufan Breaks his Silence*, NEWSWEEK, May 4, 2009

Michael Isikoff & Mark Hosenball, *Will Holder Probe on CIA Detainee Abuse Fall Flat?*, NEWSWEEK, Aug. 24, 2009

Michael Isikoff & Daniel Klaidman, *Justice Official Clears Bush Lawyers in Torture Memo Probe*, NEWSWEEK, Jan. 29, 2010

Italy Seeks Arrests in Kidnapping Case, N.Y. TIMES, Dec. 24, 2005

Greg Jaffe & David Cloud, *Officials in Iraq Knew Last Fall Of Prison Abuse – Red Cross Report Was Seen by U.S. Military Leaders Two Months Before Inquiry*, WALL ST. J., May 19, 2004

Douglas Jehl, *Report Warned C.I.A. on Tactics in Interrogation*, N.Y. TIMES, Nov. 9, 2005

Douglas Jehl, *The Struggle for Iraq: Military Contradictions*, N.Y. TIMES, May 14, 2004

Carrie Johnson, *Holder Hires Prosecutor to Look into Alleged CIA Interrogation Abuses*, WASH. POST, Aug. 25, 2009

Carrie Johnson, *Prosecutor to Probe CIA Investigations*, WASH. POST, Aug. 24, 2009

David Johnston, *U.S. Inquiry Falters on Civilians Accused of Abusing Detainees*, N.Y. TIMES, Dec. 19, 2006

David Johnston & Scott Shane, *Debate Erupts on Techniques used by C.I.A.*, N.Y. TIMES, Oct. 5, 2007

Jodi Kantor & Charlie Savage, *After 9/11 Trial Plan, Holder Hones Political Ear*, N.Y. TIMES, Feb. 14, 2010

Daniel Klaidman et al., *Palace Revolt*, NEWSWEEK, Feb. 6, 2006

Charles C. Krulak & Joseph P. Hoar, *Fear Was No Excuse to Condone Torture*, MIAMI HERALD, Sep. 11, 2009

Charles Krauthammer, *The Truth About Torture*, THE WEEKLY STANDARD, Dec. 5, 2005

Mark Landler, *German Court Challenges C.I.A. over Abduction*, N.Y. TIMES, Feb. 1, 2007

Jason Leopold, *Blistering Indictment Leveled Against Obama Over His Handling of Bush-Era War Crimes*, TRUTHOUT.ORG, Dec. 12, 2009

Neil A. Lewis, *Red Cross Finds Detainee Abuse in Guantánamo: U.S. Rejects Accusations*, N.Y. TIMES, Nov. 30, 2004

Eric Lichtblau & Scott Shane, *Justice Department Report Finds John Yoo and Jay Bybee Not Guilty of Misconduct*, N.Y. TIMES, Feb. 19, 2010

Adam Liptak, *Supreme Court Refuses Ruling on Chinese Uighurs Held at Guantánamo*, N.Y. TIMES, Mar. 2, 2010

Dahlia Lithwick, *Why is the Obama Administration Clinging to an Indefensible State-Secrets Doctrine?*, SLATE, Feb. 10, 2010

Dahlia Lithwick, *Presidential Signing Statement are more than just Executive Branch Lunacy,* SLATE.COM, Jan 30, 2006

Ernesto Londoño, *Justice Department to Appeal Dismissal of Blackwater Indictment,* WASH. POST, Jan. 24, 2010

Robert Mackey, *Drone Strikes are Legal, U.S. Official Says,* N.Y. TIMES, Mar. 26, 2010

Jenny Mandel, *Military Justice Code Now Covers Some Contractors,* GOVERNMENTEXECUTIVE.COM, Jan. 9, 2007

Joseph Marguiles, *Abu Zubaydah's Suffering,* L.A. TIMES, Apr. 30, 2009

Jane Mayer, *The Black Sites: A Rare Look Inside the CIA's Secret Interrogation Program,* THE NEW YORKER, Aug. 13, 2007

Jane Mayer, *A Deadly Interrogation,* THE NEW YORKER, Nov. 14, 2005

Jane Mayer, *The Hidden Power,* NEW YORKER, July 3, 2006

Jane Mayer, *The Memo: How an Internal Effort to Ban the Abuse and Torture of Detainees Was Thwarted,* NEW YORKER, Feb. 27, 2006

Jane Mayer, *Outsourcing Torture: The Secret History of America's "Extraordinary Rendition" Program,* THE NEW YORKER (Feb. 8, 2005)

Jane Mayer, *The Trial: Eric Holder and the Khalid Sheikh Mohammed Trial,* THE NEW YORKER, Feb. 15, 2010

Mark Mazzetti, *Bush Officials Linked to Debate on Interrogation Methods for Detainees,* N.Y. TIMES, Sep. 24, 2008

Mark Mazzetti, *CIA Destroyed Tapes of Interrogations,* N.Y. TIMES, Dec. 6, 2007

Mark Mazzetti, *Letters Give C.I.A. Tactics a Legal Rationale,* N.Y. TIMES, Apr. 27, 2008

Bill Mears, *Terrorist Zacarias Moussaoui's Appeal of Life Sentence Denied,* CNN.COM, Jan. 4, 2010

Souad Mekhennet & Craig Smith, *German Spy Agency Admits Mishandling Abduction Case,* N.Y. TIMES, June 2, 2006

Michael Melia, *Father of Pakistani Alleges U.S. Torture,* WASH. POST, Apr. 16, 2007

Randall Mikkelsen, *CIA Says Shuttering Detention Black Sites,* REUTERS, Apr. 9, 2009

Steven Miles, *Interview for Democracy Now, Oath Betrayed: Torture, Medical Complicity, and the War on Terror,* DEMOCRACY NOW, June 30, 2006

David Morgan, *White House under pressure over Guantánamo ruling,* REUTERS, June 5, 2007

No Justice for El-Masri: Germany Drops Pursuit of CIA Kidnappers, SPIEGEL ONLINE, Sep. 24, 2007

Richard Norton-Taylor, *Binyam Mohamed Torture Evidence Must be Revealed, Judges Rule,* GUARDIAN, Feb. 10, 2010

Richard Norton-Taylor, *Top Bush Aides Pushed for Guantanamo Torture,* THE GUARDIAN, Apr. 19, 2008

Officer to Face Court-Martial on 8 Charges in Abu Ghraib Abuse, N.Y. TIMES, Jan. 13, 2007

Scot J. Paltrow, *Justice Delayed: Budget Crunch Hits U.S. Attorneys' Offices,* WALL ST. J., Aug. 31, 2007

Christi Parsons, *Illinois the next Gitmo?* CHI. TRIB., Nov. 14, 2009

Priti Patel, *A Wider Torture Loophole?,* L.A. TIMES, Aug. 18, 2006

Public Remains Divided Over Use of Torture (Pew Research Center for the People & the Press, Apr. 23, 2009)

Physician Participation in Interrogation, in CODE OF MEDICAL ETHICS (American Medical Association, 2006)

Walter Pincus, *U.S. Has Detained 2,500 Juveniles as Enemy Combatants*, WASH. POST, May 15, 2008

PM Faces Internal Pressure Over Hicks Trial, SYDNEY MORNING HERALD, Aug. 3, 2005

Samantha Power, *Boltonism*, NEW YORKER, Mar. 21, 2005

Dana Priest, *CIA Holds Terror Suspects in Secret Prisons*, WASH. POST, Nov. 2, 2005

Robert H. Reid, *More Photos Emerge of Abuse*, CHI. TRIB., Feb. 16, 2006

Robert H. Reid, *Two U.S. Soldiers Charged With Murder in Iraq*, ASSOCIATED PRESS, July 7, 2007

Warren Richey, *Obama Endorses Military Commissions for Guantánamo Detainees*, CHRISTIAN SCIENCE MONITOR, Oct. 29, 2009

James Risen & Mark Mazzetti, *Blackwater Guards Tied to Secret C.I.A. Raids*, N.Y. TIMES, Dec. 11, 2009

Mary Robinson, Speech before the International Bar Association Symposium, *The Rule of Law: Striking a Balance in an Era of Terrorism*, Chicago, Sept. 16, 2006

Carol Rosenberg, *New Court Can Silence Captives Who Tell Secrets*, MIAMI HERALD, Feb. 4, 2008

Carol Rosenberg, *Obama Appoints New Chief for War Court at Guantanamo*, MIAMI HERALD, Mar. 25, 2010

David Rosenzweig, *Air Force Wife Guilty in Spouse's Fatal Stabbing; A Moreno Valley Woman is Convicted in the 2003 Slaying on a Military Base in Turkey*, L.A. TIMES, Oct. 16, 2004

James Rowley, *CIA Prisons to be Evaluated in One-Year Review by Senate Panel*, BLOOMBERG, Mar. 5, 2009

Leonard S. Rubenstein & Stephen N. Xenakis, *Doctors Without Morals*, N.Y. TIMES, Mar. 1, 2010

Alissa J. Rubin & Sangar Rahimi, *Bagram Detainees Named by U.S.*, N.Y. TIMES, Jan. 17, 2010

J. Taylor Rushing, *Senate Tables Graham Amendment on Trials for 9/11 Suspects*, THE HILL, Nov. 5, 2009

Sayed Salahuddin, *Afghan was Taken to Guantanamo Aged 12: Rights Group*, REUTERS, May 27, 2009

Charlie Savage, *Accused 9/11 Mastermind to Face Civilian Trial in N.Y.*, N.Y. TIMES, Nov. 13, 2009

Charlie Savage, *Bush Could Bypass New Torture Ban*, BOSTON GLOBE, Jan. 4, 2006

Charlie Savage, *Charges Against Blackwater Guards Dismissed in Iraq Killings*, N.Y. TIMES, Dec. 31, 2009

Charlie Savage, *Obama Team is Divided on Anti-Terror Tactics*, N.Y. TIMES, Mar. 28, 2010

Charlie Savage, *Senator Proposes Deal on Handling of Detainees*, N.Y. TIMES, Mar. 3, 2010

Charlie Savage & James Risen, *Federal Judges Finds N.S.A. Wiretaps Were Illegal*, N.Y. TIMES, Mar. 31, 2010

David Savage, *Bush Administration Memos on Presidential Powers Stun Legal Experts*, L.A. TIMES, Mar. 4, 2009

Eric Schmitt, *Army Interrogator is Convicted of Negligent Homicide in 2003 Death of Iraqi General*, N.Y. TIMES, Jan. 23, 2006

Eric Schmitt, *House Defies Bush and Backs McCain on Detainee Torture*, N.Y. TIMES, Dec. 15, 2005

John Schwartz, *Attacks on Detainee Lawyers Split Conservatives*, N.Y. TIMES, Mar. 9, 2010

Andrew O. Selsky, *Judges at Guantánamo Throw out Two Cases*, CHI. TRIB., June 5, 2007

Richard Serrano, *Teenage Militant Case at Tribunal*, L.A. TIMES, Apr. 28, 2010

Scott Shane, *U.S. Approves Targeted Killing of American Cleric*, N.Y. TIMES, Apr. 6, 2010

Scott Shane, David Johnston & James Risen, *Secret U.S. Endorsement of Severe Interrogations*, N.Y. TIMES, Oct. 4, 2007

Thom Shanker & David E. Sander, *New to Pentagon, Gates Argued for Closing Guantánamo Prison*, N.Y. TIMES, Mar. 23, 2007

Marlise Simons, *Spanish Court Weighs Inquiry on Torture for 6 Bush-Era Officials*, N.Y. TIMES, Mar. 29, 2009

R. Jeffrey Smith, *Memo Gave Intelligence Bigger Role, Increased Pressure Sought on Prisoners*, WASH. POST, May 21, 2004

R. Jeffrey Smith, *War Crimes Act Changes Would Reduce Threat of Prosecution*, WASH. POST, Aug. 9, 2006

R. Jeffrey Smith, *Worried CIA Officers Buy Legal Insurance*, WASH POST, Sept. 11, 2006

Ali Soufan, *My Tortured Decision*, N.Y. TIMES, Apr. 22, 2009

Andrew Stern, *Guantanamo Detainee Move Not Security Risk*, N.Y. TIMES, Nov. 16, 2009

Andrew Sullivan, *How Doctors Got into the Torture Business*, TIME, June 23, 2006

Andrew Sullivan, *How the Nazis Defended "Enhanced Interrogation"*, THE ATLANTIC (June 2007)

Torture Case Against Iraq Contractors Dismissed, N.Y. TIMES, Sep. 12, 2009

Transcript, President Bush's Speech on Terrorism, N.Y. TIMES, Sep. 6, 2006

Don Van Natta et al., *Germany Weighs if it Played Role in Seizure by U.S.*, N.Y. TIMES, June 2, 2006

Joby Warrick & Dan Eggen, *Hill Briefed on Waterboarding in 2002: In Meetings, Spy Panels' Chiefs Did Not Protest, Officials Say*, WASH. POST, Dec. 9, 2007

Josh White, *Australian's Guilty Plea is First at Guantánamo*, WASH. POST, Mar. 27, 2007

David Wood, *Counts Dropped in Abu Ghraib Abuse Case*, CHI. TRIB. (Aug. 21, 2007)

Bob Woodward, *Detainee Tortured Says U.S. Official: Trial Overseer Cites 'Abusive Methods' Against 9/11 Suspect*, WASH. POST, Jan. 19, 2010

Andy Worthington, *Guantánamo Trials: Where Are The Terrorists?* THE HUFFINGTON POST, Feb. 8, 2008

Darrel J. Vandeveld, *I Was Slow to Recognize the Stain of Guantanamo*, WASH. POST, Jan. 18, 2009

Adam Zagorin, *An Abu Ghraib Offender's Return to Iraq is Stopped*, TIME, Nov. 2, 2006

D.   U.S. GOVERNMENT DOCUMENTS

U.S. Dep't of the Army, The Law of Land Warfare, Field Manual No. 27–10 (Jul. 18, 1956)

U.S. Dep't of Defense Directive 5100.77, DOD Law of War Program, para. E(1)(a)(10) (July 10, 1979)

U.S. Dep't of the Army, Field Manual 34–52, Intelligence Interrogation (Sept. 28, 1992)

Military Order of Nov. 13, 2001, Detention, Treatment, and Trial of Certain Non-Citizens in the War Against Terrorism, 66 Fed. Reg. 57,833 (Nov. 16, 2001)

Memorandum from John C. Yoo, Deputy Assistant Attorney General, to William J. Haynes II, General Counsel for Department of Defense on Possible Habeas Jurisdiction over Aliens Held in Guantanamo Bay, Cuba (Dec. 28, 2001)

Memorandum from John C. Yoo, Deputy Assistant Attorney Gen., & Robert J. Delahunty, Special Counsel, Office of Legal Counsel, U.S. Dep't of Justice, to William J. Haynes II, Gen. Counsel, Dep't of Defense, Application of Treaties and Laws to al Qaeda and Taliban Detainees (Jan. 9, 2002)

Memorandum from William H. Taft IV, Legal Advisor, Dep't of State to John Yoo, Office of Legal Counsel, Dep't of Justice, *Your Draft Memorandum of January 9* (Jan. 11, 2002).

Memorandum from Donald Rumsfeld, Secretary of Def., Dep't of Def., to Chairman of the Joint Chiefs of Staff, Status of Taliban and Al Qaeda (Jan. 19, 2002)

Memorandum from Jay S. Bybee, Assistant Attorney Gen., Office of Legal Counsel, U.S. Dep't of Justice, Alberto R. Gonzales, Counsel to the President, and William J. Haynes II, Gen. Counsel, Dep't of Def., on Application of Treaties and Laws to al Qaeda and Taliban Detainees (Jan. 22, 2002)

Memorandum from Alberto Gonzales, White House Counsel, to President George Bush on Decision Re Application of the Geneva Convention on Prisoners of War to the Conflict with al Qaeda and the Taliban (Jan. 25, 2002)

Memorandum from Colin L. Powell, Sec'y of State, U.S. Dep't of State to Alberto R. Gonzales, Counsel to the President, Draft Decision Memorandum for the President on the Applicability of the Geneva Conventions to the Conflict in Afghanistan (Jan. 26, 2002)

Letter from John Ashcroft, Attorney Gen., U.S. Dep't of Justice, to President George W. Bush (Feb. 1, 2002)

Memorandum from William H. Taft IV, Legal Advisor, U.S. Dep't of State to Alberto R. Gonzales, Counsel to the President, Comments on Your Paper on the Geneva Convention (Feb. 2, 2002)

Memorandum from George W. Bush, President, to the Vice President, Secretary of State, Secretary of Defense, the Attorney General, Chief of Staff to the President, Director of Central Intelligence, Assistant to the President for National Security Affairs, and Chairman of the Joint Chiefs of Staff, RE: Humane Treatment of Taliban and al Qaeda Detainees (Feb. 7, 2002)

Memorandum from Jay S. Bybee, Assistant Attorney Gen., Office of Legal Counsel, U.S. Dep't of Justice, to Alberto Gonzales, White House Counsel, Status of Taliban Forces Under the Fourth Geneva Convention (Feb. 7, 2002)

Memorandum from Jay S. Bybee, Assistant Attorney Gen., Office of Legal Counsel, U.S. Dep't of Justice, to William J. Haynes II, Potential Legal Constraints Applicable to Interrogations of Persons Captured by US Forces in Afghanistan (Feb. 26, 2002)

Memorandum from Jay S. Bybee, Assistant Attorney Gen., Office of Legal Counsel, U.S. Dep't of Justice, to William J. Haynes II, Re: The President's Power as Commander in Chief to Transfer Captured Terrorists to the Control and Custody of Foreign Nations (Mar. 13, 2002)

U.S. Dep't of Def., Military Commission Order No. 1: Procedures for Trials by Military Commissions of Certain Non-United States Citizens in the War Against Terrorism (Mar. 21, 2002)

Memorandum from Jay S. Bybee, Assistant Attorney Gen., Office of Legal Counsel, U.S. Dep't of Justice, to Alberto R. Gonzales, Counsel to the President, Standards of Conduct for Interrogation under 18 U.S.C. §§2340–2340A (Aug. 1, 2002)

Memorandum from Jay S. Bybee Assistant Attorney Gen., Office of Legal Counsel, U.S. Dep't of Justice, to John Rizzo, General Counsel, Central Intelligence Agency, on Interrogation of al Qaeda Operatives (Aug. 1, 2002)

Lt. Col. Jerald Phifer, Memorandum for Commander, JTF-170, *Request for Approval of Counter-resistance Strategies* (Oct. 11, 2002)

Memorandum from U.S. Army Commander General James T. Hill to the Joint Chiefs of Staff, Re: Counter-Resistance Techniques (Oct. 25, 2002)

Memorandum from William J. Haynes, II, Gen. Counsel, U.S. Dep't of Def. to Donald Rumsfeld, Sec'y of Def., U.S. Dep't of Def., Counter-resistance Techniques (Nov. 27, 2002)

Donald Rumsfeld, Memorandum for the General Counsel of the Department of Defense, Subject: Detainee Interrogations (Jan. 15, 2003)

Memorandum from William J. Haynes II, Gen. Counsel, U.S. Dep't of Def. to Mary L. Walker, Gen. Counsel, Dep't of the Air Force, Working Group to Assess Interrogation Issues (Jan. 17, 2003)

Memorandum for General Counsel of the Dep't of the Air Force, Subject: Draft Report and Recommendations of the Working Group to Access Legal, Policy and Operational Issues Related to Interrogation of Detainees Held by the U.S. Armed Forces in the War on Terrorism (March 3, 2003)

Memorandum from John Yoo, Deputy Ass't Atty General, Dep't of Justice, to William J. Haynes II, General Counsel of the Dep't of Defense, Memorandum on Military Interrogation of Alien Unlawful combatants Held Outside the United States (Mar. 14, 2003)

Memorandum from Deputy Assistant Attorney General John Yoo to William J. Hayes II, General Counsel of the Dep't of Defense, Re: Military Interrogation of Alien Unlawful combatants Held Outside the United States, Mar. 14, 2003

Dep't of Defense, *Working Group Report on Detainee Interrogations in the Global War on Terrorism: Assessment of Legal, Historical, Policy, and Operational Considerations* (Apr. 4, 2003)

Memorandum from Donald Rumsfeld, Secretary of Defense, to James T. Hill, Commander of the U.S. Southern Command, Counter-Resistance Techniques in the War on Terrorism (Apr. 16, 2003)

Maj. Gen. Geoffrey D. Miller, *Assessment of DOD Counter-terrorism Interrogation and Detention Operations in Iraq* (Sept. 2003)

Office of the Inspector General, Central Intelligence Agency, Special Review of Counterterrorism Detention and Interrogation Activities from September 2001-October 2003 (May 7, 2004)

Antonio M. Taguba, Major Gen., U.S. Dep't of the Army, *Article 15–6 Investigation of the 800ᵗʰ Military Police Brigade* (2004)

Memorandum from Alberto J. Mora, Gen. Counsel, Dep't of the Navy, to the Inspector General, Dep't of the Navy, Statement for the Record: Office of General Counsel Involvement in Interrogation Issues (Jul. 7, 2004)

Inspector Gen., U.S. Dep't of the Army, Detainee Operations Inspection, The Mikolashek Report (Jul. 21, 2004)

Anthony R. Jones & George R. Fay, *Investigation of Intelligence Activities at Abu Ghraib* (Aug. 2004)

Department of Defense, Article 15–6 Investigation of CJSOTF-AP and 5th SF Group Detention Operations (Abu Ghraib) by BG Richard P. Formica, Investigating Officer (Nov. 8, 2004)

James R. Schlesinger, U.S. Dep't of Defense, Final Report of the Independent Panel to Review DOD Detention Operations 80 (2004)

Memorandum from Daniel Levin, Acting Assistant Attorney Gen., Office of Legal Counsel, U.S. Dep't of Justice, to James B. Comey, Deputy Attorney Gen., Office of Legal Counsel, U.S. Dep't of Justice, Regarding Legal Standards Applicable Under 18 U.S.C. §§2340–2340A (Dec. 30, 2004)

U.S. Dep't of Def., Instruction 5525.11, Criminal Jurisdiction Over Civilians Employed by or Accompanying the Armed Forces Outside the United States, Certain Service Members, and Former Service Members (Mar. 3, 2005)

U.S. Dep't of the Army, Surgeon General, Final Report: Assessment of Detainee Medical Operations for OEF, GTMO, and OIF (April 13, 2005)

Memorandum for John Rizzo, Senior Deputy General Counsel, C.I.A., Application of 18 U.S.C. §§2340 to Certain Techniques That May Be Used in the Interrogation of a High Value al-Qaeda Detainee (May 10, 2005)

Memorandum for John Rizzo, Senior Deputy General Counsel, C.I.A., Application of United States Obligations Under Article 16 of the Convention Against Torture to Certain Techniques that May Be Used in the Interrogation of High Value al-Qaeda Detainees (May 30, 2005)

Carl Levin, U.S. Senator from Michigan, Senate Floor Speech on the Amendment to Establish an Independent Commission on Detainee Treatment (Nov. 4, 2005)

Press Release, The White House, *President Discusses Creation of Military Commissions to Try Suspected Terrorists*, Sept. 6, 2006

Dept. of Defense, Office for the Administration Review of the Detention of Enemy Combatants at U.S. Naval Base Guantánamo Bay, Cuba, Summary of Evidence for Combatant Status Review Tribunal for Khalid Shaykh Muhammad (Feb. 8, 2007)

Press Release, Dep't of Defense, *Seasoned Judge to Tapped to Head Detainee Trials*, Feb. 20, 2007

Verbatim Transcript of Combatant Status Review Tribunal Hearing for Khalid Shaykh Muhammad, ISN #10024 (March 10, 2007)

Exec. Order No. 13400, Interpretation of the Geneva Conventions' Common Article 3 as Applied to a Program of Detention and Interrogation Operated by the Central Intelligence Agency, July 20, 2007

Office of the Inspector General, *A Review of the FBI's Involvement in and Observations of Detainee Interrogations in Guantanamo Bay, Afghanistan, and Iraq* (May 2008)

Statement of Alberto J. Mora to the Senate Committee on Armed Services, Hearing on the Treatment of Detainees in U.S. Custody (June 17, 2008)

Exec. Order No. 13400, Interpretation of the Geneva Conventions' Common Article 3 as Applied to a Program of Detention and Interrogation Operated by the Central Intelligence Agency, July 20, 2007

Report of the Committee on Armed Services, U.S. Senate, *Inquiry into the Treatment of Detainees in U.S. Custody* (Nov. 20, 2008)

Rep. John Conyers, Jr., Chairman of the U.S. House of Representatives Committee on the Judiciary, *Reining in the Imperial Presidency: Lessons and Recommendations Relating to the Presidency of George W. Bush* (January 2009)

Exec. Order No. 13,491, Ensuring Lawful Interrogations, 74 Fed. Reg. 4893 (Jan. 27, 2009)

Exec. Order No. 13,492, Review and Disposition of Individuals Detained at the Guantánamo Bay Naval Base and Closure of Detention Facilities, 74 Fed. Reg. 4,897 (Jan. 27, 2009)

Exec. Order No. 13,493, Review of Detention Policy Operations, 74 Fed. Reg. 4901 (Jan. 27, 2009)

Press Release, The White House, *Statement of The President on the Release of OLC Memos*, Apr. 16, 2009

Press Release, The White House, *Statement by President Barack Obama on United Nations International Day in Support of Torture Victims*, June 26, 2009

Memorandum for the Attorney General, Memorandum of Decision Regarding the Objections to the Findings of Professional Misconduct in the Office of Professional Responsibility's Report of Investigation Into the Office of Legal Counsel's Memoranda Concerning Issues Relating to the CIA's Use of "Enhanced Interrogation Techniques" on Suspected Terrorists (Jan. 5, 2010)

Press Release, Attorney General, U.S. Dep't. of Justice, *U.S. Transfers Three Guantanamo Bay Detainees to Albania*, Feb. 24, 2010

E. U.S. CASES

Abtan, et al. v. Prince et al., Second Am. Compl., No. 1:09CV617-TSE/IDD, 1:09CV1048-TSE/IDD (E.D. Va. 2009)

Al-Bihani v. Bush, 588 F. Supp.2d 19 (D.D.C. 2008)

Al-Bihani v. Obama, No. 1:05-CV-01312-RJL

Al-Marri v. Wright, 487 F.3d 160 (4th Cir. 2007)

Al-Najjar v. Ashcroft, 257 F.3d 1262 (11th Cir. 2001)

Anderson v. Creighton, 483 U.S. 635, 639 (1987)

Ashcraft v. State of Tennessee, 327 U.S. 274 (1946)

Berlin Democratic Club v. Rumsfeld, 410 F. Supp. 144 (D.D.C. 1976)

Blumenthal v. U.S., 332 U.S. 539, 557 (1947)

Boumediene v. Bush, 128 S. Ct. 2229 (2008)

Boumediene v. Bush, 127 S. Ct. 1478, 1479, *cert. denied* (2007)

Brady v. Maryland, 373 U.S. 83 (1963)

Bridge v. Phoenix Bond & Indem. Co., 553 U.S. (2008), 128 S. Ct. 2131, 2135 n.1 (2008)

Brown v. Mississippi, 297 U.S. 298 (1936)

Brulay v. United States, 383 F.2d 345, 348 (9th Cir.), *cert. denied*, 389 U.S. 986 (1967)

Butera v. District of Columbia, 235 F.3d 637, 652 (D.C. Cir. 2001)

Calley v. Callaway, 519 F.2d 184 (5th Cir. 1975)

Chambers v. Florida, 309 U.S. 227 (*1940*)

El-Masri v. United States, 479 F.3d 296, 313 (4th Cir. 2007)

Escobedo v. United States, 623 F.2d 1098 (5th Cir. 1980)

Frisbie v. Collins, 342 U.S. 519 (1952)

Graham v. Florida, 560 U.S. (2010)

Griswold v. Connecticut, 381 U.S. 479 (1965)

Hamdan v. Gates, 552 U.S. 994 (2007)

Hamdan v. Rumsfeld No. 04–5393 (D.C. Cir., July 15, 2005)

Hamdan v. Rumsfeld, 126 U.S. 2749, 2762–69 (2006)

Hamdi v. Rumsfeld, 542 U.S. 507, 533 (2004)

Hamdi v. Rumsfeld, 124 U.S. 2633 (2004)

In Ex parte Orozco, 201 F. 106, 111–12 (W.D. Tex. 1912)

In re Discipline of Abbell, 541 U.S. 932 (2004)

In re John H. Haley, 60 F. Supp. 2d 926 (E.D. Ark. 1999)

In re Kaine, 55 U.S. (14 How.) 103 (1852)

In re Metzger, 17 F. Cas. 232 (S.D.N.Y. 1847) (No. 9,511)

In Re Petitioners Seeking Habeas Corpus Relief in Relation to Prior Detentions at Guantanamo (Misc. No. 08–0444 (TFH)) (D.D.C. Apr. 2010)

Johnson v. Eisentrager, 339 U.S. 763 (1950)

Jones v. United States, 137 U.S. 202, 212 (1890)

Kennedy v. Louisiana, 554 U.S. (2008)

Ker v. Illinois, 11 9 U.S. 436 (1886)

Khadr v. Bush, 587 F.Supp.2d 225 (D.D.C. 2008)

Kiyemba v. Obama, 555 F.3d 1022 (D.C. Cir. 2009)

Kotteakos v. U.S., 328 U.S. 750 (1946)

Lin v. United States, No. 08–5078, slip op. at 8–9 (D.C. Cir. April 7, 2009)

Little v. Barreme, 6 U.S. 170 (1804)

Mapp v. Ohio, 367 U.S. 643 (1961)

Medina v. Resor, 43 CMR 243 (1971)

Mohamed et al. v. Jeppesen Dataplan, Inc., 579 F.3d 943 (9th Cir. 2009)

Murray v. Schooner Charming Betsy, 6 U.S. 64, 118 (1804)

Nat'l Org. for Women v. Scheidler, 510 U.S. 249, 261 (1994)

Ntakirutimana v. Reno, 184 F.3d 419, 428, 430 (5th Cir. 1999)

Oetjen v. Cent. Leather Co., 246 U.S. 297, 302 (1918)

Pinkerton v. United States, 328 U.S. 640, 647 (1946)

Price v. Socialist People's Libyan Arab Jamahiriya, 294 F.3d 82, 92–93 (D.C. Cir. 2002)

Rasul v. Bush, 542 U.S. 466 (2004)

Reid v. Covert, 354 U.S. 1 (1957)

Rochin v. California, 342 U.S. 165 (72 S.Ct. 205, 96 L.Ed. 183) (1952)

Roper v. Simmons 543 U.S. 551 (2005)

Rosado v. Civiletti, 621 F.2d 1179 (2d Cir. 1980)

Sackie v. Ashcroft, 270 F. Supp. 2d 596 (E.D. Pa. 2003)

Saleh, et al., v. Titan Corp. and CACI Internt'l Inc., 580 F.3d 1 (D.D.C. 2009)

Silverthorne Lumber Co. v. United States, 251 U.S. 385 (1920)

Sosa v. Alvarez-Machain, 542 U.S. 692 (2004)

Stonehill v. United States, 405 F.2d 738, 743 (9th Cir.), *cert. denied*, 395 U.S. 960 (1969)

Trop v. Dulles, *356 U.S. 86* (1958)

United States Ex Rel. Lujan v. Gengler, 550 F.2d 62 (2d Cir. 1975)

United States v. Abbell, 271 F.3d 1286 (11th Cir. 2001)

United States v. Alstoetter et. al., 3 T.W.C. 1 (1948)

United States v. Alvarez-Machain, 504 U.S. 655 (1992)

United States v. Averette, 19 USCMA 363 (1970)

United States v. Burney, 6 USCMA 776 (1956)

United States v. Calley, 48 C.M.R. 19 (1973)

United States v. Charles Emmanuel, F.Supp.2d (S.D. Fla. 2008)

United States v. Fernandez-Morris, 99 F. Supp. 2d 1358 (S.D. Fla. 1999)

United States v. Goot, 894 F.2d 231, 239 (7th Cir. 1990)

United States v. Juvenile Male, 118 F.3d 1344, 1349 (9th Cir. 1997)

United States v. Kelly, 888 F.2d 732 (11th Cir. 1989)

United States v. Lee, 106 U.S. 196, 220 (1882)

United States v. McVeigh, 153 F.3d 1166 (10th Cir. 1998)

United States v. Moussaoui (4th Cir., Jan. 4, 2009)

United States v. Nerone, 563 F.2d 836, 854 (7th Cir. 1977)

United States v. Reid, 214 F.Supp.2d 84 (D.Mass. Jul. 26, 2002)

United States v. Scheffer, 523 U.S. 303 (1998)

United States v. Slough *et al.*, 2009 U.S. Dist. LEXIS 121809 (D.C. Cir. 2009)

United States v. Toscanino, 500 F.2d 267 (2d Cir. 1974)

United States v. Verdugo-Urquidez, 494 U.S. 259 (1990)

United States v. Williams, 617 F.2d 1063, 1099 (5th Cir. 1980)

United States v. Wilson, 118 F.3d 228 (4th Cir. 1997)

United States v. Zolin, 491 U.S. 554, 562–63 (1989)

Vermilya-Brown Co. v. Connell, 335 U.S. 377 (1948)

Wang v. Ashcroft, 320 F.3d 130 (3d Cir. 2003)

Weeks v. United States, 232 U.S. 383 (1914)

Weems v. United States, 217 U.S. 349 (1910)

Wilson v. Girard, 354 U.S. 524 (1957)

Yamashita v. Styer, 327 U.S. 1 (1946)

F.   NON-U.S. CASES

Aksoy v. Turkey, Case No. 21987/93, Judgment of the ECHR (Dec. 18, 1996)

Case of Lori Berenson Mejia v. Peru, 2004 Inter-Am. Ct. H.R. (ser. C) No. 119 (Nov. 25, 2004)

Case of Plan de Sánchez Massacre, Case 11.763, Inter-Am. C.H.R., Report No. 31/99, I/A (2004)

Ireland v. United Kingdom, 25 Eur. Ct. H.R. (ser. A) (1978)

Mehmet Eran v Turkey, Case No. 32347/02, Judgment of the ECHR (October 2008)

Military and Paramilitary Activities (Nicar. v. U.S.), 1986 I.C.J. 14 (June 27)

Prosecutor v. Brdjanin, Case No. IT-99–36-T, Decision on the Defense Objection to Intercept Evidence (Mar. 1, 2004),

Prosecutor v. Furundzija, Case No. IT-95–17/1, Judgment, paras. 144, 154 ff (Dec. 10, 1998)

Prosecutor v. Nikolic, Case No. IT-94–2-PT, Decision on Defense Motion Challenging the Exercise of Jurisdiction by the Tribunal, (Oct. 9, 2002).

Prosecutor v. Krnojelac, Judgment, ICTY Trial Chamber, Case No. IT-97–25-T (Mar. 15, 2002)

Prosecutor v. Limaj et al., Judgment, ICTY Trial Chamber, Case No. IT-03–66-T (Nov. 30, 2005)

Prosecutor v. Kvocka et al., Judgment, ICTY Trial Chamber, Case No. IT-98–30/1-T (Nov. 2, 2001)

Prosecutor v. Naletilic and Martinovic, Judgment, ICTY Appeals Chamber, Case No. IT-98–34-A (May 3, 2006)

Ribitsch v. Austria, Case No. 42/1994/489/571, Judgment of the ECHR (Dec. 4, 1995)

Tomasi v. France, Case No. 12850/87, Judgment of the ECHR (Aug 27, 1992)

(For additional cases of interest, see THE ENEMY COMBATANT PAPERS: AMERICAN JUSTICE, THE COURTS, AND THE WAR ON TERROR (Karen J. Greenberg & Joshua Dratel eds., 2008))